D1131310

GEORGE WHITEFIELD

America's Spiritual Founding Father

Thomas S. Kidd

Yale

UNIVERSITY

PRESS

New Haven & London

Published with assistance from the Annie Burr Lewis Fund.
Published with assistance from the Mary Cady Tew Memorial Fund.

Yale University Press books may be purchased in quantity for educational, business,
or promotional use. For information, please e-mail sales.press@yale.edu (U.S. office) or
sales@yaleup.co.uk (U.K. office).
Set in Electra type by IDS Infotech Ltd., Chandigarh, India.
Printed in the United States of America.

Library of Congress Cataloging-in-Publication Data
Kidd, Thomas S.
George Whitefield : America's spiritual founding father / Thomas S. Kidd.
pages   cm
Includes bibliographical references and index.
ISBN 978-0-300-18162-3 (hardback)
1. Whitefield, George, 1714–1770.   2. Evangelists—Great Britain—Biography.
3. Evangelists—United States–Biography.   4. United States—Church history.
I. Title.
BX9225.W4K48 2014
269'.2092–dc23
[B]
2014012873

A catalogue record for this book is available from the British Library.

This paper meets the requirements of ANSI/NISO Z39.48–1992 (Permanence of
Paper).
10 9 8 7 6 5 4 3 2

CONTENTS

INTRODUCTION

On October 12, 1740, in the fading light of a cool autumn evening, the twenty-five-year-old evangelist George Whitefield ascended a platform on Boston Common. Before him stood twenty thousand people. If the crowd estimates were reasonably accurate, this was the largest assembly ever gathered in the history of the American colonies. (Boston's entire population was only seventeen thousand in 1740.) Whitefield had already seen crowds this massive—even larger—in the great city of London, but the teeming New England throngs, gathered in the region's small fishing villages and provincial towns, amazed him.

Sometimes the pressing people frightened him, too. There were volcanic outbursts of emotion. He regularly had to cut his preaching short, unable to be heard over the cacophony of weeping and screeching. At the Common, Whitefield implored the people to put their faith in Jesus Christ, the kind of sincere faith their Puritan forefathers had embraced. It did not matter whether their parents were Christians. It did not matter whether they prayed and attended church and read their Bibles. Whitefield wanted to know whether they had experienced the "new birth" of conversion.

Concluding the sermon, his countenance falling, he told them that it was time for him to go; other audiences needed his gospel preaching, too. "Numbers, great numbers, melted into tears, when I talked of leaving them," Whitefield wrote. He had begun to forge a special bond with the American colonists. "Boston people are dear to my soul," he confessed.[1]

Reports about this wondrous boy preacher began to appear in the colonies' newspapers in 1739. By 1740 he had become the most famous man in America. (In 1740 George Washington was eight years old, John Adams was four, Thomas Jefferson was not even born. Benjamin Franklin's fame as a printer, which did not extend much beyond Philadelphia, was enhanced considerably by becoming Whitefield's publisher.) Whitefield was probably the most famous man in Britain, too, or at least the most famous aside from King George II. From his humble beginnings in Gloucester, England, no one would have guessed that Whitefield's celebrity would reach so far, so high, or so soon.

Three hundred years after his birth, George Whitefield is not entirely forgotten, but his fame now is far dimmer than it was on that fall evening in Boston. Today, Whitefield's renown is surpassed by that of his friends, including Ben Franklin and Jonathan Edwards, the great pastor-theologian of Northampton, Massachusetts. Most U.S. history survey courses and textbooks still mention Whitefield, thanks to two major academic biographies, Harry Stout's *The Divine Dramatist: George Whitefield and the Rise of Modern Evangelicalism* (1991) and Frank Lambert's *"Pedlar in Divinity": George Whitefield and the Transatlantic Revivals* (1994). These biographies, as well as a surge of recent studies of the Great Awakening, have established Whitefield as a fixture in the standard story of American history for the foreseeable future. Still, we know too little about him.

I do not come to this new biography of the great evangelist with a historical axe to grind. All the major Whitefield biographies, from confessional Christian approaches such as Luke Tyerman's *The Life of the Rev. George Whitefield* (2 vols., 1877) and Arnold Dallimore's *George Whitefield: The Life and Times of the Great Evangelist of the Eighteenth-Century Revival* (2 vols., 1970, 1980), to Stout's, Lambert's, and Jerome Mahaffey's more recent books, make essential contributions upon which I gratefully build. Readers familiar with my work know that I am both a university-based historian and an evangelical Christian, so perhaps I can help bridge the academic and Christian perspectives on Whitefield that have clashed in recent decades. (More on this clash later.)

I admire the work of Tyerman and Dallimore, especially because they were not professional historians, but ministers. They painstakingly pieced together comprehensive biographies through archival research, consulting original sources and manuscripts whenever possible. Dallimore, a small-town pastor in Ontario, worked for thirty years on his biography, facing poverty and complaints from his parishioners that he was wasting time. Dallimore ultimately resigned his pastorate in 1973 so he could devote himself full-time to the biography's second volume. Tyerman and Dallimore appear constantly in scholars' footnotes because they remain the two most detailed treatments of Whitefield's own life and ministry.[2]

Of course, Tyerman and Dallimore did not provide the kind of context for Whitefield's life that one would expect from academic historians. Stout,

Lambert, Mahaffey, and others have helped us interpret Whitefield within the framework of eighteenth-century Anglo-American culture. Lambert examined Whitefield in light of the "consumer revolution" of the eighteenth century. As a "pedlar in divinity," Whitefield mastered the use of publicity, newspapers, and inexpensive print to promote his preaching tours and the gospel he expounded. Stout, on a related theme, presented Whitefield as "Anglo-America's first religious celebrity, the symbol for a dawning modern age." Even though Whitefield denounced the theater after his conversion, his background as an actor, and familiarity with England's theater culture, prepared him for a fabulously successful preaching career.[3]

In two recent books on Whitefield, the communications scholar Jerome Mahaffey has expanded on earlier proposals by Stout and the historian Alan Heimert by considering how Whitefield became an "Accidental Revolutionary," the man most responsible for priming America for its Revolution. Whitefield was the "central figure" in the process by which disparate colonists became Americans, prone to think in zealous, adversarial terms about religion, rights, and liberties. Whitefield's Awakening may not have caused the Revolution, Mahaffey argued, but it had a profound conditioning influence on Americans as the Revolution approached. Heimert memorably argued that whether "the enlightened sage of Monticello [Jefferson] knew it or not, he had inherited the mantle of George Whitefield."[4]

Whitefield and commerce, Whitefield and religious celebrity, Whitefield and the Revolution: all these arguments have considerable merit, even if I have doubts about certain aspects of them. The main problem with these approaches, however, is that they do not really focus on Whitefield's primary significance or on the way he viewed himself. The argument of this biography is straightforward: George Whitefield was the key figure in the first generation of Anglo-American evangelical Christianity. Whitefield and legions of other evangelical pastors and laypeople helped establish a new interdenominational religious movement in the eighteenth century, one committed to the gospel of conversion, the new birth, the work of the Holy Spirit, and the preaching of revival across Europe and America. Until now, we have not had a scholarly biography of Whitefield that places him fully in the dynamic, fractious milieu of the early evangelical movement. That is what I seek to do here.

Writing biographies, and writing religious biographies in particular, presents significant challenges. The temptation to write hagiography—the biography of a pristine saint—is ever present. In placing Whitefield within the new evangelical world, I am not offering an unsullied picture of a sanctified man, nor is my primary aim to edify readers spiritually. Yet historians today know that none of us is fully objective—personal perspectives matter. So let me admit it up front: I have a high regard for Whitefield. I identify personally with the religious movement he helped start. Yet I hope that I have also been fair to his critics and transparent about his obvious failings as a man and minister. Included in these failings were his besetting inability to maintain peace with evangelical colleagues, his appalling behavior in relationships with women, including his wife, and his advocacy of slavery and personal ownership of slaves.

In his 1747 autobiography, Whitefield addressed the difficulties of the genre. "In the accounts of good men which I have read," he said, "I have observed that the writers of them have been partial. They have given us the bright, but not the dark side of their character. This, I think, proceeded from a kind of pious fraud, lest mentioning persons' faults should encourage others in sin. It cannot, I am sure, proceed from the wisdom which cometh from above." Although he might not appreciate how I have highlighted some less attractive aspects of his life, Whitefield and I are in full agreement about the danger of fashioning "pious frauds" of historical memory. This seems to be a special temptation for modern American evangelicals, one to which I hope I have not fallen prey.[5]

A couple of notes on my method of writing: I have silently modernized the spelling and punctuation of many quotations, although I occasionally leave them in their original renderings in order to give some flavor of the time. I have added the chapter and verse in brackets for many scripture references that Whitefield used in his journals and other writings. Without these, readers might miss some of the quotations as coming from the Bible. The references should help readers see how much the Bible framed Whitefield's rhetoric; he not only spoke about the King James Bible, but also spoke its very language.

On dates: when Britain replaced the Julian calendar with the Gregorian, Parliament rectified the discrepancy between the two by decreeing that the day following September 2, 1752, would jump to September 14, 1752. Before that date, I use "Old Style" dates, and after, "New Style." Unless one accounts for this, there are some puzzling date references, such as when Whitefield refers to his birthday as December 27 instead of December 16, which he began to do after the switch to New Style.[6]

"The Circumstance of My Being Born in an Inn": George Whitefield and Eighteenth-Century England

Two inns in December, one in Bethlehem of Judea, and the other in Gloucester, England. These were the humble birthplaces of Jesus and, seventeen centuries later, one of his most celebrated disciples, George Whitefield. Whitefield himself made this connection to Jesus in the original edition (it was excised in later ones) of his *Journals,* one of the best-selling publications of the eighteenth century in England and America. (*A Short Account of God's Dealings with the Reverend Mr. George Whitefield,* which covered his early life and conversion in college, was first published in 1740, a couple years after the initial publication of his early travel journals.) "The circumstance of my being born in an inn," he wrote, "has been often of service to me in exciting my endeavours to . . . follow the example of my dear Saviour, who was born in a manger belonging to an inn."[1]

The Gloucester of Whitefield's birth was a plain town, neither cosmopolitan nor rustic. It lay about a hundred miles west of London, England's vast metropolis. In spite of the ravages of the Great Plague and Great Fire of the 1660s, London's population still stood at about 500,000, making it one of the world's largest cities. Around 1660, the population of Gloucester was just under 5,000, making it one of the thirty largest provincial towns in England. An early nineteenth-century town booster, George Counsel, lamented that "it has been much the fashion with tourists to describe Gloucester as a dull heavy, place," yet even he—an Englishman enamored of the history of kings—claimed that from 1687 (a visit by James II) to 1788 (a visit by George III), "no interesting event" had occurred there. From the perspective of religious history, Counsel's statement is laughable.[2]

Gloucester's economy was inextricably connected with Bristol, about thirty-five miles to the southwest. The Whitefield family was likewise deeply linked with that city. At the beginning of the eighteenth century, Bristol's population was more than 20,000. It was England's second-largest seaport. The thriving town teemed with sailors, merchants, and customs officers. At a mile-long quay, dockworkers loaded and unloaded cargo from across the Atlantic world. Countinghouses, churches, sugar refineries, taverns, and coffeehouses ringed the town's wharfs and the river Avon. One of Bristol's merchants was Thomas Whitefield, George's father, who worked in the imported wine business, a long-time staple of Bristol trade. Later he would open Gloucester's Bell Inn. Whitefield's oldest brother, Andrew, also worked in Bristol, and George visited him there as a teenager. Bristol was a critical commercial hub for Britain and America, and Whitefield would regularly preach in and pass through the town during his career.[3]

Whitefield was born in a time of profound political and religious transition for England. Nearly two centuries earlier, in 1534, King Henry VIII had broken with the Roman Catholic Church and formed the Church of England, setting in motion a persistent conflict over faith, politics, and Britain's monarchy. By the end of Queen Elizabeth I's long reign (1559–1603), the English people had become firmly Protestant, but clashes over the denominational allegiance of the monarch persisted. Beginning in 1642, feuding between Parliamentarians (many of them Puritans) and Royalists (many of them moderate Anglicans) precipitated the English Civil War, leading King Charles I to flee London for his safety.

Gloucester played a key role in the war. The town was a Parliamentarian stronghold in the generally Royalist southwestern region of England. In August 1643, the king's army laid siege to the town, hoping to stage a campaign against London from Gloucester. Charles ordered a siege rather than an assault because of concern over the potential for high casualties. Gloucester's small garrison entrenched itself behind the town's ancient Roman-era walls, earthworks, and moat while the Royalist army—some thirteen thousand strong—began a fierce bombardment. The shelling continued through the warm nights of August, when cannonballs, according to one diarist, seemed to fly "through the air like a star shooting."[4]

Gloucester's defenders had come perilously close to running out of supplies and ammunition, with only three barrels of gunpowder left, when town leaders called for a day of prayer and fasting (for noncombatants) on September 5. As watchmen peered over the Roman wall that day, they beheld a surprising sight: the Royalist army began burning its siege huts and retreating from the city. The king's men had received word that a Parliamentarian army of fourteen thousand was approaching from the east, having been raised in London to relieve beleaguered Gloucester. On September 8, the Parliamentarian army entered Gloucester, to the jubilation of its suffering residents. The Parliamentarians ultimately defeated King Charles I, leading to his arrest and public beheading in London in 1649. Following the siege, Gloucester rebuilt the damaged south gate of the city and placed an inscription upon it: "A city assailed by man, but saved by God." King Charles II (Charles I's son) reclaimed the English throne in 1660, and he remembered well Gloucester's resistance during the war. He ordered the city's walls to be torn down in 1662.[5]

Even after the restoration of the monarchy, the question of the king's faith still stirred fear and resentment. Charles II converted to Catholicism on his deathbed in 1685. His brother and successor, James II, had embraced Catholicism earlier in life. Could Protestantism survive if England's king was Catholic? Many English Protestants thought not; they pointed to the cruel fate of the French Protestants, who had just suffered a horrific crackdown under the forces of Louis XIV following the revocation of the Edict of Nantes in 1685, the same year James II came to the English throne. Catholics were bent on utter domination, militant Protestants believed, and could never be trusted with political power in a Protestant nation. Moreover, James II kept unnervingly close connections with the French government. He repeatedly tried to free Catholics from various disadvantages imposed on them by English law. An anonymous pamphlet spoke for many, in anti-Catholic themes that George Whitefield would later echo, when it described Catholicism as the most "destructive religion in the world; as not deeming any people worthy to live upon the earth, but the slaves of papal jurisdiction."[6]

When James's wife bore him a son in 1688, the prospect of a Catholic succession seemed more certain than ever. It was time to act. So Protestant leaders forced James II from the throne in late 1688 in what Protestants called the Glorious Revolution. He was replaced by his Protestant daughter Mary—who apparently had no reservations about booting out her father—and her Dutch Calvinist husband, William of Orange. The couple were actually first cousins, both of them grandchildren of Charles I. James II was England's last Catholic king. William and Mary's coronation left no doubt that their Protestantism was of preeminent importance: for the first time, a copy of the Authorized Version of the Bible (King James's 1611 translation) was included in the royal procession to Westminster Abbey. The new king and queen had to swear, also for the first time, to rule according to the "Protestant reformed religion established by law."[7]

William and Mary's assumption of the throne would have settled the matter of the monarch's religion, except that they were childless. When William died in 1702 (Mary had died of smallpox in 1694), the crown passed to Mary's younger sister, Anne. Anne suffered through eighteen pregnancies in her life, thirteen resulting in miscarriages or stillborn children. Compounding her tragedies, four of her five children who survived childbirth then died in infancy. Even her son William, who lived to age eleven, died in 1700. This development incited panic among monarchy watchers, for all of Anne's closest relatives—and candidates to succeed her—were Catholics. But Parliament passed the Act of Settlement in 1701, which stipulated that anyone who "should profess the popish religion" or who married a Catholic could not become England's king or queen. This law remains in effect in Britain today.[8]

When Anne died in August 1714, five months before George Whitefield's birth, the crown of England passed over more than fifty of her closer Catholic relatives to Georg Ludwig (anglicized to George Louis) of Hanover, part of the Holy Roman Empire (present-day Germany), a fifty-four-year old nobleman who spoke almost no English. That linguistic deficiency did not matter, for George I was a Protestant (a Lutheran, to be precise). Most Protestants in England and the colonies celebrated the accession of George I as heralding permanent Protestant control of the monarchy. A Dissenting (non-Anglican) minister in London proclaimed, "The hand of Providence hath touched the Revolution over again." Even during the week of Whitefield's birth, the *London Daily Courant* reported on the celebrations honoring the new king in New York City, which were accompanied by fireworks, toasts to the king's health, and many "huzzas and great acclamations of joy." The colonists wanted George I to know that he had no better friends than the devoted Protestants of America.[9]

George Whitefield's future celebrity in places like New York City and Boston seemed highly improbable when his mother Elizabeth gave birth at the Bell Inn on December 16. He was the youngest of seven children. Nine days later, on Christmas Day, baby George was baptized at his family's twelfth-century parish church, St. Mary de Crypt, which stood just a hundred yards down the street from their inn. He was baptized according to the tradition of the Anglican Church (and almost all other Protestants at the time), which sprinkled infants with water soon after birth. For more than a hundred years, the small Baptist movement in England had been insisting that baptism was not for infants—to them, only the baptism of adults by immersion accurately reflected the inner transformation of a believer saved by God's grace. Whitefield's parents had no such qualms. Baptizing their baby placed him under the protective canopy of the Anglican Church and, they hoped, set him on the path of salvation.

At Whitefield's baptism, the rector at St. Mary de Crypt, according to the liturgy of the Book of Common Prayer and the language of the Gospel of John, prayed that God would "give thy Holy Spirit to this infant, that he may be born again." Many Anglicans believed that baptism was directly connected to this new birth, which would normally follow baptism as part of a believer's maturing devotion to God. Whitefield would remain an Anglican, yet he would come to sharply distinguish the wrenching experience of the new birth from infant baptism. The new birth, to Whitefield, was a discernible, sometimes torturous experience of renouncing sin and turning to God for forgiveness in Christ. People weren't born again because they were baptized, or because they were Anglicans, or because they were British. They had to surrender their lives personally to Christ. If they didn't, they remained subject to God's wrath and in danger of going to hell. Preaching the new birth would become the center of Whitefield's gospel ministry and the defining cause of his life.[10]

At the outset of the baptismal liturgy, the rector intoned, "Dearly beloved, for as much as all men are conceived and born in sin . . . I beseech you to call upon God." Ask God, he urged, to show the infant mercy and to make him part of the divine kingdom. Here the pastor identified the fundamental problem with humanity, even with the seemingly innocent baby before him: all people were tainted with sin—original sin, the sin of Adam—which separated them from their Creator.[11]

Whitefield soon came to recognize the truth about his own sinful nature. In the best-selling account of his life, written for devotional and evangelistic purposes, Whitefield opened the narrative (following his December birth in an inn) by describing the darkness of his heart, in language directly repeating the rector's prayer: "I can remember such early stirrings of corruption in my heart, as abundantly convinces me that I was conceived and born in sin; that in me dwelleth no good thing by nature, and that if God had not freely prevented me by his grace, I must have been for ever banished from his divine presence."[12]

The doctrine of original sin—the notion that all are corrupted by, and even guilty because of, Adam's sin—was coming under criticism by 1714, but the rector's prayer and Whitefield's wholehearted acceptance of the principle remind us that Whitefield grew up in a world largely convinced of the depravity of man and the brokenness of creation. These grim realities entered the world upon Adam and Eve's fall from grace in the Garden of Eden. The idea of original sin was a hallmark of Reformation thought. John Calvin, the French theologian and pastor of the Protestant movement in Geneva, Switzerland, wrote in his *Institutes of the Christian Religion*, "Original sin is a hereditary corruption and perversity of our nature . . . All are tangled up in original sin and stained with its spots." Even children were fatally tainted with this sinful nature, Calvin wrote, so that their moral character could "only be displeasing and hateful to God."[13]

To modern sensibilities, this talk of a perverse nature of humankind—even of children—and of God hating us for it, may seem extreme. But Anglo-Americans in Whitefield's world widely accepted Calvin's views, even if more liberal theologians had begun to question his tenets. The Thirty-Nine Articles of Religion of the Anglican Church (1563), a codification of English Protestant theology, defended the principle of inherent depravity. Original sin, said the ninth article, "is the fault and corruption of the nature of every man . . . therefore in every person born into this world, it deserveth God's wrath and damnation." Recalling the misdeeds of one's childhood became a standard feature of evangelical autobiography. Belief in depravity was not just theoretical speculation by male theologians, either. If anything, evangelical women seemed to take a darker view of their sinful natures than did men.[14]

Whitefield's English people did not just believe in sin because of statements like the Thirty-Nine Articles. They saw evidence for the brokenness of creation all around them. War, disease, fire, and crime ravaged their world. Just a year before Whitefield's birth, the Treaty of Utrecht had ended the War of the Spanish Succession, the latest in a long line of conflicts over religion, monarchies, and the European balance of power. The Battle of Malplaquet (1709), pitting allied British and Dutch forces against the French, was the bloodiest battle in eighteenth-century Europe, in which 120,000 troops suffered 30,000 casualties, resulting in a pyrrhic victory for the British. A devout British officer walked the battlefield afterward and found that his horse could not move without treading upon the bodies heaped across the bloody ground. "God makes the nations a scourge to each other to work his holy ends," the soldier mused, "by sweeping sinners off the face of the earth."[15]

Most Britons needed no convincing about the world's pervasive iniquity. Whitefield, though, saw his sin manifested not in titanic battles or nefarious crimes, but in his mundane life as a child in Gloucester. Other than what is recorded in Whitefield's *Journals*, we do not have much information about his early childhood, but since he grew up in an inn, without a father in his house between the ages of two and eight (his father died in 1716), we might imagine . that Whitefield had some exposure to the temptations of the flesh. He surely amplified his sinfulness for literary and theological effect, writing bluntly, "I was froward from my mother's womb." "Froward" is a term from the King James Bible meaning "wandering" or "perverse." Its first appearance in the Bible refers to the sins of youth: "They are a very froward generation, children in whom is no faith" (Deuteronomy 32:20). That such words flowed easily from Whitefield's pen reflects his deep saturation in the rhetoric of the King James Bible, which a century earlier had become the standard Bible of the English-speaking world. Whitefield's preaching perpetuated the fame of that Bible, and its application to individual lives, in Britain and America.[16]

Whitefield was haunted by memories of his "early acts of uncleanness." Even from boyhood, he wrote, he was "addicted" to "lying, filthy talking, and foolish jesting." With deeper regret, he recalled regularly stealing from his widowed mother. His father died of unknown causes at the age of thirty-five. Death apparently came quickly: Thomas composed his will on December 23 (only a week after George's second birthday) and passed away on the 26th. Undoubtedly, Whitefield helped his mother make ends meet, both before and after her troubled second marriage, but in his journal he chose to emphasize his audacious thefts of her money. He used the pilfered cash, he recalled, to satisfy his "sensual appetite" by buying fruits, tarts, and other treats.[17]

Whitefield might have had Saint Augustine in mind when he recalled this childhood thievery, which echoed Augustine's spiritual autobiography. In one of the most famous passages of his *Confessions*, Augustine stole a neighbor's pears, not for a lack of food, but only to enjoy "the theft and the sin itself." Whitefield believed, with Augustine, that in childhood his sinful nature had begun to manifest itself in such spiteful acts. To Whitefield, stealing from his mother confirmed his Calvinist convictions about innate depravity. "If I trace myself from my cradle to my manhood," he wrote, "I can see nothing in me but a fitness to be damned." But this episode had the effect of presenting him in a more accessible light to readers. How many remembered their own senseless acts of disrespect toward their parents? Whitefield was no exalted saint; he was a wretch who had cheated his widowed mother when given the chance. His sin was as bad as any of those who converted under his preaching; he needed God's grace as much as they did.[18]

Whitefield's journal also mimicked Augustine's autobiography in the way that Whitefield inserted biblical phrases and tropes at every turn of the narrative. Sometimes Whitefield compared himself to biblical characters, including Christ (as with his birth in an inn). Some readers (then and now) have found these associations with Christ at least slightly disconcerting, but the deep biblicism of the journal reflected the culture of eighteenth-century Anglo-America, the literature of the longer Christian tradition, and Whitefield's own mindset. From Augustine to John Bunyan, great Christian writers had narrated their life experiences through stories of the Bible. To them, the Bible's themes—fall and redemption, struggling with sin, and finding liberation from its captivity—were replayed in one's own autobiography. The patterns of biblical history echoed through the centuries in the lives of individual believers.

When Whitefield was almost eight, his mother, Elizabeth, married an iron-monger named Capel Longden. It seemed like a good decision at first, since Longden came from a solid family background and was a church member at St. Mary de Crypt. But the union was a disaster. Whitefield called it "an unhappy match." Longden took over the Bell Inn and ran it into the ground; Whitefield's older brother Richard wrested control of the inn from Longden in 1729. Elizabeth left Longden six years after their marriage. As a college student, Whitefield worried about how to take care of his aging mother, who, he wrote, had "been greatly reduced by marrying a second husband." Longden died in 1738.[19]

Since Whitefield's father died when he was two, and his stepfather was an absent ne'er-do-well, what effect did this lack of a father have on Whitefield? He cast it in a redemptive light in his autobiography: "God overruled it for good . . . and made an uncommon impression upon my own heart." The effects of childhood trauma, such as the lack of a father figure, are unpredictable. In Whitefield's case, it seems to have fostered a determination to make something of himself in spite of his difficult circumstances. As he grew into adulthood, that resolve flowered into a sense of divine destiny, one that would lead him to associate his birth in an inn with his Lord's. His difficult childhood bred an early sense of independence too, along with a willingness to work hard to provide for himself and his mother, his thefts from her notwithstanding.[20]

His mother, similarly, was determined not to let the family's misfortunes ruin Whitefield's opportunities for advancement. The key to those opportunities was education. When he was twelve, Whitefield enrolled at the school run by St. Mary de Crypt. He had had some earlier formal schooling, but this was the educational experience he first described at length. For all Whitefield's talk of his wayward youth, it is worth remembering that in addition to attending church, he studied at the church's school as well, and his thoughts had already begun to turn toward his becoming a serious Christian and a minister. He saved money to buy Bishop Thomas Ken's *Manual of Prayers for the Scholars Belonging to Winchester College*, a popular devotional book that was, Whitefield wrote, "of great benefit to my soul." This book fostered Whitefield's emerging devotion to God. Designed primarily for Ken's Anglican boys' school, it advised students (again in the language of the King James) to "remember now thy Creator in the days of thy youth" and to "fly youthful lusts" (Ecclesiastes 12:1; 2

Timothy 2:22). Bishop Ken offered the kind of program for piety and prayer that Whitefield was starting to crave, a regimen that did not shy away from mentioning temptations and experiences common to adolescent boys. Ken's morning prayer, one that Whitefield may have uttered many times, read:

> Glory be to thee, Lord God Almighty; glory be to thee, for renewing thy mercies to me every morning . . .
>
> Lord, forgive whatever thou hast seen amiss in me this night; [*Here if you are conscious to yourself of any sin committed in the night, confess it.*] O Father of mercies, wash me thoroughly from my wickedness . . .

Whitefield, like many children, found his teenage years particularly challenging, fighting the temptations brought on by surging hormones and the new vistas opening to him in Gloucester.[21]

It was not all strict piety at St. Mary de Crypt's school. Whitefield's teachers noticed that he had talent in rhetoric and public performance—how could they not? They chose him to give special speeches before annual meetings of the school's corporation. But Whitefield's passion was for plays and acting. For centuries, Puritans—Calvinists who promoted further reformation in the Anglican Church—and other conservative Protestants had railed against impious plays. One 1583 pamphlet asked, "Do [plays] not maintain bawdry, insinuate foolery, and renew the remembrance of heathen idolatry? Do they not induce whoredom and uncleanness?" To be fair, many Puritans supported wholesome plays (some even admired Shakespeare), but many believed, as Whitefield would also, that plays cultivated temptations to sin and inculcated degenerate values.[22]

In repudiating the theater, Whitefield may have been drawing on Augustine's experiences again. The saint attended plays in Carthage, but came to regret those experiences as fleshly indulgences. "Stage plays also captivated me," Augustine wrote in the *Confessions*, "with their sights full of the images of my own miseries: fuel for my own fire." He regarded it as "wretched madness" to enjoy viewing plays about the suffering and misery of others. Doing so was evidence not of compassion, but of sin. Attending plays unleashed "huge tides of loathsome lusts in which [compassion] is changed and altered past recognition, being diverted and corrupted from its celestial purity by its own will." Whitefield did not explicitly refer to Augustine in his thoughts on theater, but his educational background and occasional comments about the saint in other writings suggest that he was familiar enough with Augustine to appropriate themes from the *Confessions* and other writings. Like the Bible, the works of great Christian writers such as Augustine framed Whitefield's mental world.[23]

Whitefield's schoolmaster had no qualms about the stage. Indeed, he himself wrote plays for the students. Whitefield so loved acting that he would skip school just to focus on preparing for the plays. The memory of these school plays became bitter, not least because the master adopted the common practice in the English theater of having boys, including Whitefield, dress as girls to play the female characters. "The remembrance of this has often covered me with confusion of face," Whitefield wrote. "Confusion of face" was another evocative phrase from the King James Bible (see Daniel 9:7–8); it is usually translated as "shame" in modern English editions. While Whitefield was deeply influenced by his Anglican schooling, this was a point on which he criticized his upbringing. "This way of training up youth," he caustically noted, "has a natural tendency to debauch the mind, to raise ill passions, and to stuff the memory with things contrary to the Gospel of Jesus Christ, as light to darkness, heaven to hell."[24]

It was also common to have women play male roles in the English theater. Such theatrical reversals became less common in the late eighteenth century, when the switching of genders onstage was more likely to elicit moral revulsion. Nevertheless, people were already complaining in the early eighteenth century not only about gender confusion in the theater, but also about the more widespread habit of men wearing "female" clothes and of women adopting manly fashions. One pamphlet published when Whitefield was in his early twenties cited Deuteronomy 22 to the effect that "the promiscuous use of apparel" was an "abomination unto the Lord thy God." Men who wore women's styles of clothes or wore their hair in feminine fashions, the author averred, "deface manhood, and ridiculously depart from the dignity of the sex."[25]

So it was not theater per se, but its frivolity, gender-bending casts, and profane content that bothered Christian critics. In the decades following the restoration of Charles II, certain plays did have shockingly ribald content. One of the most popular at the time of Whitefield's schooling, George Farquhar's raunchy play *The Recruiting Officer* (1706), was full of jokes about bastardy, polygamy, and the like. This kind of play was not just reserved for adults: as an eleven-year-old in 1727, the future English acting celebrity David Garrick put on *The Recruiting Officer* with friends at school. The play was a hit throughout the empire; it was the first production ever held at the Dock Street Theatre in Charleston, South Carolina, in 1736, only a few years before Whitefield would indict the people of that town for their obsession with worldly entertainments.[26]

Frivolity and profanity aside, the theater taught Whitefield a great deal about how to perform in public. He resented the unwholesome aspects of his education, but praised his tutor for teaching students "to speak and write correctly."

And indeed, Whitefield could speak correctly. David Garrick reportedly said later that Whitefield could "make men weep or tremble by his varied utterances of the word 'Mesopotamia.'"[27]

Yet Whitefield grew restless at school. Really enjoying only playacting, he saw no point in studying Latin and other topics suited only to boys who could reasonably hope to attend Oxford or Cambridge. Because of his family circumstances, Whitefield did not think he was one of those boys. So he began assisting his mother at the Bell Inn; as he described it, "I put on my blue apron and my [candle] snuffers, washed mops, cleaned rooms, and, in one word, became a professed and common drawer for nigh a year and a half."[28]

He served drinks, cleaned rooms, and pondered his future. He winced as he watched his former classmates walking past the inn and going to St. Mary's school. He wondered about a career. He didn't want to become an innkeeper. He wondered about God. Did God have some particular calling for him? Mulling over the prospect of preaching, he sketched a few rudimentary sermons and stayed up late reading the Bible. He reflected on own his standing before God, but found that he was "very unwilling to look into [his] heart." As Whitefield moved into adulthood, he entered a season of spiritual crisis.[29]

Whitefield's contemplation of the priesthood reflected his growing spiritual commitment, but also represented interest in social advancement. He had several Anglican parsons in his family background: an ancestor named William Whitefield attended Magdalen College at Oxford in the 1570s and became the vicar of Mayfield, southeast of London, in 1605. George's great-uncle Samuel Whitefield graduated from Hart Hall (later Hertford College), Oxford, in 1671, and served as rector of Rockhampton (between Gloucester and Bristol) for almost forty-five years. For an ambitious, spiritually sensitive boy with Whitefield's aptitude for speaking, the ministry was a serious vocational possibility. But his mother could envision no way to pay for him to attend college, and Anglican ordination required a college education. A friend would sometimes ask Whitefield, while he was tending the bar, why he did not go to Oxford. "I wish I could," Whitefield replied.[30]

Whitefield's prospects for college did not brighten when his brother Richard began running the Bell Inn. Whitefield disliked Richard's wife. He began feuding with her and would refuse to speak to her for weeks on end. He believed that God was prompting him to leave the inn; in the words of Isaiah 12, he said, God was calling him "from drawing wine for drunkards, to draw water out of the wells of salvation for the refreshment of his spiritual Israel." He quit the inn and went to visit his older brother Andrew in Bristol.[31]

Whitefield tarried in Bristol for two critical months. He was adrift professionally, but his spiritual journey moved forward. In Bristol, he wrote, "God was pleased to give me great foretastes of His love." He began to experience "unspeakable raptures," especially in one episode at St. John's Church in Bristol, when he was "carried out" beyond himself. This was a common testimony of evangelical converts, the feeling of having one's soul or spirit seemingly leave the body to commune with God and savor his grace and love.[32]

St. John's—which still stands in Bristol—is a remarkable medieval church built right into the city wall in the late 1300s. Its interior is striking, with a single aisle running between two rows of wooden pews. The sanctuary is narrow but the ceiling is high, conveying feelings of both reverence and intimacy. It was there that the "unspeakable raptures" filled Whitefield's mind and heart, probably during a special communion service, since he wrote how he "felt great hungerings and thirstings [for] the blessed Sacrament." At the Lord's Supper, the minister would have given the bread and wine to the kneeling Whitefield, saying in the words enjoined by the Book of Common Prayer, "The Body of our Lord Jesus Christ, which was given for thee . . . The Blood of our Lord Jesus Christ, which was shed for thee." Whitefield was coming to realize that Christ did indeed suffer *for him,* and he found the notion overwhelming. He wrote to his mother and assured her that he would never serve patrons at the inn again.[33]

Whitefield keyed his personal awakening to his reading habits. In the days of his visit to Bristol, he was poring over Thomas à Kempis's *The Imitation of Christ,* to his "great delight." *The Imitation of Christ (De Imitatione Christi)* was the most popular devotional book of the period, appearing in a remarkable 444 Latin and vernacular editions during the seventeenth century. The author was a Catholic monk in fifteenth-century Holland, but in spite of its medieval Catholic origins, the *Imitation* became a favorite of many Anglo-American evangelicals, including Whitefield's soon-to-be colleague John Wesley. Wesley later prayed that God would write "the rules of self-denial and love laid down by Thomas à Kempis" in his followers' hearts.[34]

No doubt Whitefield read all of the *Imitation,* but given the context of the reference, we can be sure that Whitefield especially valued Thomas à Kempis's reflections on communion, the topic of the fourth and final section of the *Imitation.* There he spoke of the Lord's Supper as offering "foretastes" of immortality: "To be invited to eat of thy most blessed body, and admitted to partake of the lively figures of thy divine blood; the commemorations of thy death, and sure pledges of salvation! Lord! what am I, that I should thus be suffered to approach thee?" This intimate, tangible access to the divine Savior staggered both Thomas à Kempis and Whitefield.[35]

Given Whitefield's emerging emphasis on the new birth and God-initiated conversion, one might think that he would have balked at some of Thomas à Kempis's theology, such as his notion that conversion entailed an individual's decision to repudiate sin and embrace full devotion to Christ. But Whitefield was not averse to a kind of spiritual bricolage in his reading habits. He loved Thomas à Kempis's depiction of the Christian disciplines, so he did not register disagreement with the author when he encouraged readers to convert themselves to Christ, even as Christ converted them to him. Clarifying the exact process of conversion in response to a late-medieval Catholic interlocutor was not a pressing matter. Whitefield later engaged in debates about conversion with Protestant rivals when controversy over religious revivals began to erupt in the early 1740s.[36]

With Whitefield's reading of Thomas à Kempis and his new experiences of God, he was unwittingly entering an emerging world of intense Protestant spirituality. In Europe, Britain, and colonial America, many pietistic Protestants were rediscovering a "religion of the heart," as opposed to religion defined by doctrinal or liturgical conformity. Of course, religion of the heart was a biblical theme ("The sacrifices of God are a broken spirit: a broken and a contrite heart, O God, thou wilt not despise," the psalmist wrote). But across Europe and America in this period—beginning as early as the 1670s in Germany, with a notable British-American surge in the 1730s—young men and women sought an authentic relationship to God that went beyond religious duties and formality. This desire helps explain similarities in the spiritual journeys of Whitefield, John and Charles Wesley, and other nascent leaders of the evangelical movement, whose quest for heart knowledge of God had commenced before they met one another.[37]

Whitefield had not yet experienced conversion, and his spiritual elation in Bristol was not to last. He returned to Gloucester and relapsed into sluggishness. He moved in with his mother, sleeping on a pallet on the ground in her tiny home. He had "nothing to do." The devil used his listlessness to lure him back into old habits and old friendships. "Much of my time I spent in reading plays," he wrote, "and in sauntering from place to place." The sense of God's presence wore off, replaced by surging temptations.[38]

Soon Whitefield fell, as he recalled, into "abominable secret sin, the dismal effects of which I have felt, and groaned under ever since." He did not say what this sin was, but we can be virtually certain that it was masturbation. Indeed, in an unpublished diary held today at the British Library in London, Whitefield noted that in the spring of 1736 he began excerpting the popular book *Onania;*

or, the Heinous Sin of Self-Pollution, intending to publish a tract-length version of it. (Onan was a man who "spilled [his seed] on the ground" in Genesis 38.) On April 24, Whitefield wrote that he was "greatly assisted in extracting Onania," adding, "I hope God will enable me to finish it to his honour as a proof of [my] repentance." This leaves little doubt as to the nature of the secret sin. Although Whitefield never published the extract, John Wesley did publish a similar one on the "sin of Onan" in the 1760s.[39]

Whitefield's veiled admission of this private indiscretion was undoubtedly designed to enhance his rapport with readers who endured similar struggles. But critics seized upon the tantalizing reference to the "abominable secret sin" and relentlessly speculated about its meaning. One anti-Whitefield tract, *The Expounder Expounded,* even included the reference in its subtitle, promising that the secret transgression would be "particularly illustrated and explained" within. "Perhaps no passage that ever dropped from the pen of a sacred writer," the pamphleteer whispered, "hath afforded so much speculation to the public, as the abominable secret sin . . . When a man is become of so much importance to the world, as the reverend gentleman, whose writings I am expounding, people will be for remarking the most trivial occurrences of his life, and particularly a practice for which he has expressed so ungovernable an affection." The pamphlet, which examined all possible meanings of the secret sin, settled on masturbation as the most likely diagnosis. A 1749 satirical print of sailors rioting in London similarly featured both *Onania* and Whitefield's memoirs being cast out of a brothel and into a bonfire. Whitefield had the dubious distinction of becoming one of the first people in world history whose personal life became a topic of rampant conjecture in the mass media.[40]

God was faithful to Whitefield, even though the young seeker was, in his own estimation, "continually doing despite to the Spirit of Grace." Again Whitefield turned to scripture to understand his life's narrative, this time to Ezekiel, chapter 16: "He saw me with pity and compassion, when lying in my blood. He passed by me; He said unto me, *Live.*" God began speaking to and through Whitefield regarding his pastoral calling. One morning while (notably) reading a play to his sister, he said to her, "God intends something for me which we know not of . . . God will provide for me some way or other that we cannot apprehend." These words don't seem that remarkable now, but to Whitefield, they seemed touched with prophecy. "How I came to say these words I know not," he wrote. "God afterwards showed me they came from him."[41]

God disclosed his plan to Whitefield through a former schoolmate who was attending Oxford. The student was working as servitor at Oxford's Pembroke College (Oxford was and is a federation of semi-independent colleges), a position that allowed him to cover his expenses. Whitefield and his mother were apparently not aware that this arrangement was a possibility, even though many students worked as servitors at Oxford colleges. In Whitefield's telling, when his mother heard of the student's employment, it struck her immediately as the means of George's college education. "This will do for my son," she announced. (Elizabeth had obviously been wondering how she would get the teenager off his pallet and moving toward viable employment.)[42]

"Will you go to Oxford, George?" she asked. "With all my heart," he answered. Whitefield had found his ticket into the ministry. Although he did not realize it at the time, this was also the circumstance that would lead to his introduction to John and Charles Wesley, his conversion, and, eventually, his meteoric rise to fame.[43]

"THE DAY STAR AROSE IN MY HEART": WHITEFIELD'S CONVERSION

George Whitefield was a wreck. He shuffled through the halls of Oxford's Pembroke College wearing "dirty shoes," ratty wool gloves, and a patched scholar's gown. Other students gawked at him and whispered; some mocked and pelted him with dirt. But his earthly tormentors did not particularly concern him. Instead, Whitefield was convinced that the devil was assaulting him, just as God had given the devil permission to torment Job in ancient times. Day and night Whitefield writhed on the floor of his room, praying and commanding the devil to leave his body, in the name of Jesus. He cringed as he entered the darkened stairwells of Pembroke, thinking that at any turn he might meet his evil adversary face-to-face. He hardly slept. He often fasted. When he occasionally ate, he intentionally chose the "worst sort of food."[1]

In Whitefield's world, conversion to faith in Christ was no polite, simple affair. You did not just walk an aisle and ask Jesus to come into your heart. It was a titanic spiritual struggle—the defining struggle of one's life—to find out whether God or the devil would ultimately command your soul's allegiance. Not that the devil had as much power as God: the dark enemy was infinitely weaker than the eternal Father. But for a lost, blinded sinner like Whitefield, the devil was the heart's default option. God had to rescue you from the enemy's clutches. God had to change your desires; he had to make you want to be rescued.

So Whitefield waited. As he recalled, "Every day God made me willing to renew the combat." During Lent, he fasted even more assiduously than before, eating nothing but "coarse bread" and drinking only unsweetened sage tea. He became emaciated and extremely ill. He insisted upon going out on frosty mornings without his wool gloves. One of his hands began to turn black.[2]

This may all seem a bit extreme, and some today might question Whitefield's mental health. But to this Oxford student, the months-long ordeal represented a path to redemption. For years he had carried the burden of his unforgiven sin and the separation it created between him and God. His bodily sickness was an outward manifestation of deep interior dislocation. But the Holy Spirit began ministering to him in his illness, purifying his soul and preparing him to fully identify with his Lord and Savior.

One day during the penitential season of Lent, Whitefield found himself beset by a physical thirst he could not slake. He wrote: "It was suggested to me," presumably by the Holy Spirit, "that when Jesus Christ cried out, 'I thirst,' his sufferings were near at an end." Whitefield seized upon this prompting, flung himself on his bed, and began bellowing, "I thirst, I thirst!"[3]

Now came Whitefield's deliverance. The clouds of oppression began to lift: "The spirit of mourning was taken from me, and I knew what it was truly to rejoice in God my Savior." The ordeal was over: "After a long night of desertion and temptation, the Star, which I had seen at a distance before, began to appear again." Whitefield knew that, for him, this was the moment to which 2 Peter 1:19 referred: "the Day Star arose in my heart," he wrote. The Spirit took "possession" of his soul. The experience that Whitefield would soon herald to untold thousands had happened to him. He was born again.[4]

Before his spiritual transformation, once Whitefield and his mother realized that he might gain admission to Oxford as a servitor, they immediately began making preparations for his matriculation. First he went back to the classical school at St. Mary de Crypt. But returning to school placed him in bad company again, and he began to consort with "a set of debauched, abandoned, atheistical youths." "Atheism," to Whitefield and most eighteenth-century writers, did not mean literal unbelief in God, but acting as if God did not exist. Continually sinning with no guilt was a form of atheism. For a time, egged on by his schoolmates, Whitefield lived this way. He repeated the tantalizing reference to his "secret sin." Justifying his behavior, he asked, "Why [has] God had given me passions, and not permitted me to gratify them?" His "secret and darling sin" became more urgent with his rising sexual awareness as a teenager. But he indulged in other occasional indiscretions, too, such as being "overtaken in liquor." Clearly, however, drunkenness was a negligible misdeed compared with his secret transgression: he recalled being truly drunk only two or three times in his life.[5]

Reading wholesome books constrained Whitefield's temptations, as did attending church, which he did twice a day. He diligently read the assigned classics as well as the Greek New Testament. Whitefield has deservedly become known for his emphasis on religious experience, but he, like most of his pastoral colleagues in the Great Awakening, was a thoroughly educated man, the product of Latin- and Greek-based schooling in Gloucester and at Oxford. He possessed much more classical learning than typical evangelical pastors do today. This is not to say that Whitefield was an outstanding intellectual figure of his time, just that he typified the classically educated Oxford- and Cambridge-trained clergy of the mid-eighteenth century. He never countenanced anti-intellectualism; he just did not believe that the mind alone could carry a person to a saving faith.

Whitefield eagerly read texts on practical piety. One particularly meaningful book for him during this period was the French Protestant pastor Charles Drelincourt's *The Christian's Defense against the Fears of Death*, a popular devotional that was translated into English as early as the 1670s. Given Whitefield's personal struggles, he may have taken particular note of Drelincourt's warnings about the wrath of God against dying sinners, who "know there is a sentence of eternal death pronounced against them in the court of the King of Kings, and that from this sentence there is no appeal nor escape." Drelincourt invited readers to envision a damned person languishing in the exquisite miseries of hell, "devoured with worms, burning in hot flames, who is broken and tortured continually, in[to] whose wounds kindled brimstone is poured without intermission, with boiling lead and burning pitch . . . All this will give us but a light, and an imperfect image of hell torments." This was horrifying imagery, but to Whitefield and other English people, hell and judgment seemed utterly real and dreadful.[6]

With these troubling thoughts churning in his mind, Whitefield dreamt one night that he was going to meet God on Mount Sinai, "but was afraid to meet him." (Although Christian authorities debated the supernatural significance of dreams, or the lack thereof, few in evangelical circles doubted that one should pay attention to the messages they conveyed.) Sinai, as Whitefield's readers would have known, was the place where God gave Moses the law. The dream was not difficult to interpret: as Drelincourt's book had suggested, Whitefield—like all sinners—was proceeding, inexorably, toward death and judgment. If he had to meet God with the burden of guilt he carried, he would not be found righteous. He told an unnamed "gentlewoman," possibly a spiritual confidant at church, about the dream, and she said, "George, this is a call from God." A call to the ministry, perhaps, but more fundamentally, a call to salvation.[7]

The dream of God on Mount Sinai drove Whitefield to moral effort. He relentlessly pursued his penitential quest; he began "receiving the Sacrament monthly, fasting frequently, attending constantly on public worship, and praying often more than twice a day in private." But moral effort did little more than keep him from falling to temptation. It did not resolve his fundamental crisis.[8]

While running an errand for his mother one night, Whitefield received a spiritual impression—an inexplicable belief or conviction that, to him, had divine sanction—that he would soon become a preacher. His mother, who may have cared more about Whitefield maximizing his talents than cultivating his piety, mocked the impression when he told her about it. Whitefield attributed her reaction to the devil. Even after his spiritual struggle was resolved, he tended to see demonic forces behind opposition to his efforts.[9]

The time came for Whitefield to go up to Oxford. The university town lay about fifty miles to the east, between Gloucester and London. Even though a majority of Oxford students were studying for the ministry, they had a frivolous reputation (see figure 2.1). They had to apply themselves in order to stay in school, but wealthy students made plenty of time for fun and socializing. The top social rank of students was formed by gentlemen commoners. These were the Oxford men whom lower-class students like Whitefield served. One of Whitefield's contemporaries was a gentleman commoner named Erasmus Phillips, who combined his schooling with genteel recreations: horse races, cockfights, fox hunts, and fishing. Phillips' experience was not unusual. One ditty from the era lampooned the Oxford student's less than rigorous schedule:

I rise about nine, get to breakfast by ten,
Blow a tune on my flute and perhaps make a pen,
Read a play till eleven or cock my lac'd hat,
Then step to my neighbour's till dinner to chat.
From the coffee house then I to tennis away,
And at five I post back to my College to pray . . .
When in punch or good claret my sorrows I drown,
And toss off a bowl 'To the best in the town.'
At one in the morning I call what's to pay,
Then home to my college I stagger away,
Thus I tope all the night as I trifle all day.[10]

The other most famous student from Pembroke during Whitefield's era was Samuel Johnson, the English author immortalized in James Boswell's biography of him. Johnson, who was in the middle rank of "commoners," was not always the most diligent student. Students could be fined for skipping class at

Pembroke, and when a particularly dull professor fined Johnson, he tartly retorted, "Sir, you have sconced me twopence for a lecture not worth a penny."[11]

On the other hand, Johnson (like Whitefield) found his Oxford years to be a time of spiritual maturation, mediated in part by the reading of works such as William Law's *A Serious Call to a Devout and Holy Life*, a text that would hold great meaning for Whitefield too. Johnson recalled that, having become a sort of amateur skeptic as a teenager, he expected to find Law's "a dull book . . . and perhaps to laugh at it." Instead, he found the book quite challenging, and it helped renew his interest in true Christianity. One also gets a flavor for the classical education at Pembroke from Boswell's *Life of Johnson*. "He told me," Boswell wrote, "what he read solidly at Oxford was Greek; not the Grecian historians, but Homer and Euripides, and now and then a little Epigram; that the study of which he was the most fond was Metaphysics." Still, Johnson's time at Pembroke was full of pranks and escapades. One colleague recalled that Johnson was "loved by all about him, was a gay and frolicksome fellow, and passed there the happiest part of his life."[12]

Whitefield, by then nearly eighteen, did not go up to Oxford to frolic. He had had enough of that already, and the servitor's life did not offer much space for high jinks. Tending bar at the Bell Inn had prepared him well for the rigors of serving Oxford gentlemen commoners, as he noted: "By my diligent and ready attendance, I ingratiated myself into the gentlemen's favour." Soon a number of the wealthy students chose him as their servitor. He would clean their clothes, mop their rooms, and serve drinks at their parties. In an unpublished diary from 1735, Whitefield jotted down his daily duties: "fetch coal," "fetch oatmeal," and the like. The elite students did not include him in their circle of friends; indeed, he later became an object of their derision. It was a lonely time for Whitefield, as freshman year is for many college students. He recalled, "I went to Oxford without a friend; I had not a servant; I had not any one to introduce me; but God, by his Holy Spirit, was pleased to raise me up to preach for his great name's sake."[13]

Of course, even among the servitors there were opportunities for rowdiness, but Whitefield sustained his zeal for holy living. His servitor friends badgered him to "join in their excess of riot," but he refused. Repeatedly rebuffed, they reckoned he was a prude and left him alone "as a singular odd fellow."[14]

Oxford authorities were concerned about the riotous living of some undergraduates, but worried also about the extreme piety of students like Whitefield. Oxford (along with Cambridge) was a profoundly conservative institution, an arm of the established Church of England, and a pillar of religious stability against rabble-rousers of all kinds. The future archbishop of Canterbury (and future adversary of Whitefield) Thomas Secker gave a well-regarded address at

Oxford in the summer after Whitefield arrived, in which he extolled the kind of tempered moral education offered at Oxford. The best educator, Secker argued, would squelch all disruptive tendencies among the students. Even spiritual pursuits of "well-meant fervor he will prudently moderate, when they give religion a gloomy appearance, or add to it a needless burden." Secker also appreciated the threat of foolish exploits at Oxford, for he recommended an even stricter repression of "the opposite extreme of libertinism and profaneness." Whitefield gravitated toward the spiritual extremes of what many Anglican officials nervously regarded as "well-meant fervor."[15]

Continuing to plumb the depths of spiritual discipline, Whitefield finally decided to repudiate plays and the theater. One day while fasting, Whitefield grabbed a copy of a play in order to read a funny passage to a classmate. Then "God struck my heart," he wrote, "with such power, that I was obliged to lay it down again; and, blessed be his name, I have not read any such book since." For years, Whitefield had whipsawed between enjoying the theater and embracing an ascetic life of piety. Now he was committed: he would no longer read plays. Of course, a flair for the theatrical would never leave him; it was too wired into his talents and vibrant personality. But Whitefield now deplored the plays' bawdy content.[16]

Godly books helped fill the gap left by abandoning plays. One of the most important of these books, as for Samuel Johnson, was Law's *A Serious Call.* Though Whitefield had been familiar with the book while living in Gloucester, he had no money to buy a copy until coming to Oxford. "God worked powerfully" on his soul through *A Serious Call,* Whitefield wrote. Law offered the kind of rigorous, hourly piety that Whitefield was looking for. "He therefore is the devout man, who lives no longer to his own will . . ., but to the sole will of God, who considers God in everything . . ., who makes all the parts of his common life, parts of piety, by doing everything in the name of God," Law wrote. Law particularly warned against those who were pious at church but who spent the rest of their lives in "idleness and folly," including play going. *A Serious Call* spoke to Whitefield's daily struggles and helped him envision an integrated life of holiness.[17]

A Serious Call became one of the most popular devotional books of the eighteenth century. John Wesley would publish an abridged edition, calling the book "a treatise which will hardly be excelled, if it be equaled, in the English tongue, either for beauty of expression, or for justness and depth of thought." (Although its fame has receded in recent decades, *A Serious Call* was still listed in 25 *Books Every Christian Should Read* [2011], a guide to spiritual classics published by the evangelical ministry Renovaré.)[18]

Inspired by Law, Whitefield began a thrice-daily regimen of praying and psalm singing, and also renewed his regular participation in communion. It was through his attendance at communion services that he first encountered the Methodists. This group of students had sprung up around John and Charles Wesley. They were committed to a life of serious spiritual discipline. John Wesley had graduated from Oxford and received ordination as an Anglican minister in 1728. But like Whitefield, who was eleven years younger, Wesley craved more than just education and a respected clerical position; he wanted to find real spiritual depth and commitment to God. Also like Whitefield, Wesley struggled to renounce fleshly temptations and entertainments. With Oxford friends in the mid-1720s, Wesley frequented coffeehouses and taverns, attended horse races, and played billiards. He even read plays and went to the theater. But as Wesley became dissatisfied with his mediocre faith, he began pursuing higher levels of holiness.[19]

In 1730, Wesley read Law's *A Serious Call*, which helped him see "the exceeding height, and breadth, and depth of the law of God." Law's book precipitated a new phase of his spiritual quest. "The light flowed in so mightily upon my soul that everything appeared in a new view," Wesley wrote. One critic of the Methodists, Josiah Tucker, who graduated from Oxford in 1736, claimed that the Methodists saw Law "as their schoolmaster to bring them to Christ."[20]

In retrospect, one can see in Whitefield and the Wesleys' use of Law more evidence of spiritual bricolage, especially in the early days of the evangelical movement. Whereas Thomas à Kempis had spoken of the individual deciding to convert himself, Law hardly spoke of conversion or the new birth at all. Law focused rigorously on Christian disciplines but did not emphasize the need for a preceding work of grace. Charles Wesley, for one, realized this problem after his own conversion, noting that because of Law, he had sought sanctification before he had the spiritual power to achieve it. Charles concluded that he needed justification by faith before sanctification, a distinction that Whitefield would come to affirm as well. But for the Wesleys and Whitefield, the craving for a holy life also helped precipitate conversion, since they despaired at how little strength they found to discipline themselves without an infusion of God's transforming power.[21]

Whitefield arrived at Oxford at a transitional moment for the little group (or, more accurately, groups, at several Oxford colleges) that critics called Methodists, also known as the "Holy Club," or "Bible-Moths." They had begun to attract attention for their ascetic practices, including fasting on Wednesdays and Fridays, getting up extremely early (especially for college students) for devotions, and dressing and eating as frugally as possible. They recorded their daily quest for holiness in carefully kept diaries. One antagonist ridiculed them for fastidiously monitoring such minutiae as "how many slices of bread and butter they ate."[22]

The diary of a Methodist student named Benjamin Ingham gives a feel for the strict piety the group pursued. On March 1, 1734, Ingham recorded rising at four in the morning, noting that he "dressed, meditated," and prayed. At five he meditated for another hour. (Methodist meditation gave deep attention to God's holy and loving attributes, against which one's own imperfections would become clearer.) Then Ingham read a commentary on the New Testament for an hour, attended a prayer service, and prayed privately for fifteen minutes. At ten a.m. he witnessed a commencement service at which William IV, the prince of Orange, was awarded a doctor of civil law degree. At two fifteen he met with Charles Wesley, who worked with him on keeping an "exacter diary." Ingham broke his fast at three. At five he attended another prayer service, and at five thirty he wrote in his diary for a half an hour. He and his friends read Law's *A Serious Call* at seven and discussed it for a couple hours. The day's last entry recorded more meditation at nine forty-five. The next morning, a Saturday, he arose at four and began his disciplines again.[23]

When one of the Methodists' earliest adherents died, rumors spread that fanatical rounds of fasting had killed him. John Wesley, who had preaching duties in and around Oxford, delivered a "landmark sermon," as the editor of Wesley's papers put it, at St. Mary's Church two months after Whitefield's matriculation. The sermon, "The Circumcision of the Heart," explained that the Methodists' rigorous commitment to holiness modeled on expectations set out in scripture. They sought "that habitual disposition of soul which in the sacred writings is termed holiness; . . . being cleansed from sin," and "being so 'renewed in the spirit of our mind,' as to be 'perfect as our Father in heaven is perfect.'" True holiness was available through the Holy Spirit. To the Methodists, there was a level of commitment to God far above the nominal Christianity of everyday English culture.[24]

This was music to Whitefield's ears. Here were the "spiritual friends" he had been seeking. He watched them from a distance, a bit intimidated by these older, radically committed scholars. A "ridiculing crowd" would sometimes assemble to watch the zealous students as they entered St. Mary's to celebrate communion.[25]

When Whitefield came to Oxford, Charles Wesley had taken a more hands-on role in training initiates in Methodist ways. Charles was the eighteenth child born to Samuel and Susanna Wesley. He was more reticent than his more famous brother, more given to counseling, writing, and composing hymns. During his life, he composed some nine thousand songs and sacred poems. But he was also an effective preacher: one of his sermons, "Awake Thou That Sleepest," became the best-selling publication by either of the Wesley brothers during their careers.[26]

Finally, Whitefield introduced himself to Charles, who quickly sized Whitefield up as a promising protégé and invited him to breakfast. It was a memorable meal, and "one of the most profitable visits I ever made in my life," Whitefield recalled. The Methodists delighted in sharing edifying books with new recruits, and Charles urged several upon Whitefield. He began tutoring Whitefield in what one scholar has called "spiritual literacy," which for the Methodists included the disciplines of reading the Bible and other godly books, keeping a diary, and writing edifying letters. The most important book Charles suggested to Whitefield was Henry Scougal's *The Life of God in the Soul of Man* (1677).[27]

For Whitefield, reading *The Life of God in the Soul of Man* represented another key breakthrough. The book fundamentally challenged Whitefield's spiritual motivations. "Though I had fasted, watched and prayed, and received the Sacrament so long, yet I never knew what true religion was, till God sent me that excellent treatise by the hands of my never to be forgotten friend," he remembered. Religious duties were meaningless, Whitefield realized, in the absence of vital communion with God. Scougal identified legalistic ritual as one of the most common false forms of religion, in which all the focus was on "the outward man, in a constant course of external duties, and a model of performances." Other false forms focused too much on correct doctrine or on emotional experiences. For Scougal, real Christianity was something more spiritually profound; it was a "union of the soul with God, a real participation in the Divine Nature, the very image of God drawn upon the soul, or in the Apostle's phrase, it is Christ formed within us." By following sources such as Thomas à Kempis and Law, Whitefield had previously seen Christianity primarily as the repression of sin and the cultivation of devotion. He had not really known what Scougal called the "Divine Life."[28]

Whitefield said that this distinction shook him. Upon reading Scougal, he recalled, a "ray of divine light was instantaneously darted in upon my soul, and from that moment, but not until then, did I know that I must be a new creature." As Scougal wrote, acts of obedience to God, for the true Christian, were the "natural employments of the new born soul."[29]

Later in life, Whitefield credited Scougal with showing him that good works could contribute absolutely nothing to his salvation. For all his prayers, church attendance, and fasting, he "knew no more that I was to be born again in God, born a new creature in Christ Jesus, than if I was never born at all." Reading

Scougal devastated his religious pretensions: he recoiled at first and thought of burning the book or throwing it away, but he could not get it off his mind. Whitefield finally stood, literally with Scougal's book in hand, and prayed out loud: "Lord, if I am not a Christian, if I am not a real one, God, for Jesus Christ's sake, show me what Christianity is, that I may not be damned at last." Aside from the Bible, Scougal was the most important book in introducing Whitefield to God-initiated conversion as the beginning of the Christian life.[30]

He began writing home, sending copies of Scougal and telling friends and relatives about the new birth. The letters got a "cold reception." His correspondents wrote back and suggested that he was "going beside" himself. They implied that perhaps he was losing his mind; some "counted [his] life madness." Disappointed with this reaction, Whitefield pursued deeper friendships with his new spiritual comrades. He sought more guidance from Charles, who (in spite of his new reservations about external practices) instructed him to practice spiritual disciplines with the same intensity as fellow Methodists such as Benjamin Ingham. He engaged in acts of charity, visiting prisoners, the sick, and the poor and reading godly books with them. In one of his earliest surviving letters, Whitefield told a Gloucester friend in 1734 that "early rising in the morning, public and private prayer, [and] a due temperance in all things" would help him achieve "true heavenly-mindedness." Whitefield also began to feel the sting of other students' scorn, which he received as he took communion with the Methodists. "I was set up as a mark for all the polite students that knew me to shoot at," he wrote.[31]

Sometime around Whitefield's twentieth birthday, he entered the last phase of his conversion travail. We should remember that Whitefield first related his conversion in print in 1740, at the height of the period of religious revival we conventionally call the Great Awakening. The itinerant penned the account for public consumption in order to present himself as an example of what penitents might expect to happen in conversion. He intended A *Short Account of God's Dealings with the Reverend Mr. George Whitefield* to communicate his personality and spiritual journey, which could only help draw more people to his meetings. Whitefield later deleted a number of the more extreme references in this narrative, such as his attempts to make Satan depart from him in the "Name of Jesus."

Should we take Whitefield's conversion testimony literally if he felt free to revise and edit it years later? There seems no reason to doubt its overall trajectory. Logic might suggest too that the earlier version—less cautious and more detailed—was more reflective of what he experienced in those intense months

at Oxford. Whatever the case, it is important to remember that Whitefield fashioned the conversion account, like all his published journals, for an audience.

For years, going back to his time in Gloucester and Bristol, Whitefield had
sought to resolve the grinding tension between his fleshly desires and devotion
to God. Now he felt that he was on the edge of a final spiritual discovery. He
was becoming an adult, he was charting his own path, and he had found
like-minded friends at college who encouraged his spiritual zeal. Not surprisingly, the devil sought to derail his quest for divine resolution. "God was pleased
to permit Satan to sift me like wheat," Whitefield concluded (Luke 22:31).
He became, for some months, seriously ill. When kneeling to pray, he was
often overcome with sweaty "heavings." He felt like a man "locked up in iron
armour."[32]

The bodily effects of the devil's assaults on Whitefield—sickness, rigidity,
and nausea—could have been interpreted by some in his era as symptoms of
demonic possession. It is not clear exactly how Whitefield understood the
devil's role in this phase of his conversion. Protestants undergoing the throes of
conversion sometimes recalled experiencing extreme satanic temptations to
sin. It was less common among Protestants, however, for the contest to become
so focused on the penitent's physical state or for the prospective convert to pray
for the devil to leave his body, as Whitefield did. Unlike Catholics, Protestants
did not employ official exorcists, but any person could use prayer, fasting, or
other means of devotion to combat the devil.[33]

Among Whitefield's tools of resistance against temptation were spiritual
books. Adding another literary item to his spiritual bricolage, he turned to the
writings of Juan de Castaniza, a Spanish Benedictine monk of the sixteenth
century. Whitefield's world was heavily anti-Catholic, and his preaching would
become explicitly hostile toward Catholicism in the mid-1740s, but that did not
eliminate regard for the classic works of Catholic authors such as Castaniza and
Thomas à Kempis. Castaniza's *The Spiritual Combat* was translated into
English in the 1650s. He prescribed methods for seeking "Christian Perfection,"
methods rooted in "the true knowledge of God's goodness and greatness, and of
our own baseness, misery, and nothingness . . . the hatred of our selves, and the
love of God."[34]

This was the spiritual state at which Whitefield wished to arrive. But he
found himself (prompted by suggestions from the devil, he believed) taking
Castaniza too far, "into a state of quietism." For example, whereas Castaniza
advised believers to "talk but little," Whitefield pushed it to the limit: "Satan
said I must not talk at all." Castaniza advised silent meditation, so Whitefield

resolved never to pray out loud again. He was whipsawing spiritually, looking for an end to his ordeal, but instead finding only dead ends and overwrought extremes.[35]

Not surprisingly, Whitefield's turmoil took a toll on his schoolwork. He was supposed to make regular oral presentations to his tutor, but soon he skipped one meeting, and then at the next he told his tutor that he "could not make a theme." The tutor fined him for both episodes, but kindly inquired why Whitefield was not doing his work. Whitefield "burst into tears" and told the teacher that he meant no offense, but he simply could not perform his scholarly duties. The tutor worried that Whitefield was going mad.[36]

A concerned classmate reminded Whitefield that the scriptures required Christians to be subject to those in authority over them. Whitefield responded, "Yes, but I had a new revelation." Contemporaries called this kind of talk anti-nomianism or "enthusiasm." A new revelation? To polite Oxford folks, that sounded like something Quakers or other spiritual radicals might say. It was a dangerous path.[37]

Whitefield briefly tried isolating himself from his Methodist friends, since he was impressed with the Gospel of Mark's account of Christ's temptation in the wilderness, thinking that perhaps this was the next step in his arduous journey. Instead of meeting with his fellow students, he went out into the forested Christ Church Walk, praying under the trees, sometimes kneeling, sometimes pros-trate. He began missing scheduled meetings and neglecting the Methodists' program of spiritual disciplines, including church services. But soon he realized that this solitariness was another diabolical deception. He skipped a breakfast meeting with Charles Wesley, who tracked him down and told him that he should start meeting with his older brother John. He did so, and John's advice helped deliver him, as Whitefield saw it, from the "wiles of Satan."[38]

Whitefield's temptations were not strictly spiritual. He continued to confess to falling "into sensuality." But by prayer, godly reading, and church atten-dance—especially at communion services—he found ways to escape from his sin. Nothing, he wrote to a Gloucester friend in early 1735, "so much be-dwarfs us in religion . . . as starving our souls by keeping away from the heavenly banquet" of the Lord's Supper.[39]

He also caught a glimpse of his vocational calling in ministering to the poor at the Oxford town jail. A poor woman whose husband was confined there confessed to Whitefield that she had considered suicide, but his ministry had helped dissuade her. He met with her and her husband at the jail, and both of them came to realize how profoundly they needed God's help. From his time in the "wilderness" and his pastoral work with the distraught couple, Whitefield concluded, "Satan for some weeks had been biting my heel, [but] God was pleased to show me that I should soon bruise his head" (Genesis 3:15). Perhaps, he thought, he could emerge from his inner tumult and begin influencing others for Christ, as the Wesleys were doing.[40]

Indeed, the time had come for Whitefield to emerge from darkness. It was the late-winter season of Lent in 1735. Methodist students "strictly" observed Lent's forty days of penance. Intense fasting left Whitefield emaciated and weak; he could barely climb the stairs at Pembroke. His tutor sent for a doctor, but Whitefield thought his fasting had had its desired result: "Though I had been imprudent, and lost much of my flesh, yet I had nevertheless increased in the Spirit."[41]

Whitefield's Lenten illness wracked him for seven weeks. Confirming some physical details of his travail, he noted in his unpublished diary that he lay "abed ill" all morning on April 3, and felt "great pressures in stomach" on the 4th. Surely, he thought, the Holy Spirit was using the sickness to purge him of his evil inclinations. He wrote down all the sins that he could identify, both sins of the heart and of actions, and confessed them to God. He pored over his Greek New Testament late into the night.[42]

Finally, the end arrived. His original version of the conversion associated it with Christ's thirst on the cross, but he deleted that bold comparison in later versions, which related his entire new-birth experience in less provocative terms: "After having undergone innumerable buffetings of Satan, and many months' inexpressible trials by night and day under the spirit of bondage, God was pleased at length to remove the heavy load [and] to enable me to lay hold on his dear Son by a living faith." Even in the revised edition, this was a moment of intense emotion, when his "joys were like a spring tide, and, as it were, overflowed the banks." As he strolled through the university, he happily sang psalms to himself, his heart filled with the joy of forgiveness.[43]

The experience left him weak, and Whitefield's doctor ordered him to go to Gloucester to regain his strength. Cities like Oxford were widely regarded as unwholesome; a "change of air" would ostensibly help cure one's ailments. Whitefield sought out John Wesley, asking whether he thought it was God's will for him to go home. Wesley said yes. So although it was not exactly a country retreat (in his terse reply to Whitefield, Wesley jotted "Gloucester air worse"), Whitefield made his way back to Gloucester.[44]

Upon arrival, old Gloucester friends hassled him about his newfound spiritual mission. Why was Whitefield always talking about Jesus and going to church, they asked? Whitefield looked for new like-minded friends and continued ministering to the poor in Gloucester and Bristol, which he also visited again. He had gotten into some debt at Oxford during his illness, but now he found that God provided for him through unexpected channels. His brother (probably Andrew) returned from a sea journey and gave him some money. Even without speaking to him about his financial situation, other people offered financial help. Whitefield became increasingly convinced of the literal meaning of the "promise which I always pleaded," he noted in his journal, "Seek first the kingdom of God and his righteousness, and all these things shall be added unto you" (Matthew 6:33).[45]

As he grew in his faith, the Bible became his chief source of guidance. He would not only pray kneeling, but also read the Bible kneeling. Kneeling helped him maintain a properly submissive attitude as he studied. As he read the Word and prayed, the Holy Spirit ministered "knowledge of divine things" to him. He compared his reception of divine insight to the priests of ancient Israel consulting the Urim and Thummim, sacred objects used for divination. God now led him "even in the minutest circumstances," Whitefield wrote. He began to sketch sermon outlines as an outlet for his new insights.[46]

He continued to read devotional books, too, especially books written by English Puritans that would become standards in the emerging evangelical movement. Two of these were Richard Baxter's *A Call to the Unconverted* (1658) and Joseph Alleine's *An Alarm to Unconverted Sinners* (1672). It is notable that even after Whitefield experienced conversion, he often read tracts like these, which were directed toward the "unconverted." They spoke to his need for security in Christ, but also to his growing fascination with conversion itself. Calling people to divine transformation would become the center of his gospel ministry.[47]

Baxter's *Call to the Unconverted* helped Whitefield articulate exactly what conversion entailed. Conversion was, Baxter wrote, "another kind of work, than most are aware of." It was not the performance of religious duties. Conversion turned a person into a new kind of being, one with a God-ward inclination in his or her soul. The converted person, Baxter wrote, has "a new Understanding, a new Will, and Resolution, new Sorrows, and Desires, and Love, and Delight; new Thoughts, new Speech, new Company (if possible) and a new Conversation." This change was just what Whitefield had been looking for.[48]

Alleine's *Alarm to Unconverted Sinners* emphasized the sinner's desperate state before God before conversion and insisted that conversion was entirely a work of God's free grace. God found "nothing in a man to turn his heart, but to turn his stomach," he warned. Alleine demanded that sinners—as well as converted Christians—take seriously the gravity of their sin: "Look back on thy self . . . reflect upon thy swinish nature, thy filthy swill, thy once beloved mire . . . Open thy sepulchre . . . Art thou struck almost dead with the hellish damp? Behold thy putrid soul, thy loathsome members. O stench unsufferable, if thou dost but sense thy own putrefaction!" Seeing the offense of one's sin was a sign of conversion. People who thought their own sin was not so bad were still lost. Comprehending the seriousness of sin also helped the converted understand that the mercy of God alone, not any religious effort, moved him to bestow "converting grace" on sinners. Moreover, Alleine asserted, God made an effective offer of salvation only to the elect, those whom he had chosen for redemption. This understanding of free grace would, in time, precipitate a rift between Whitefield and the Wesleys.[49]

In the meantime, Whitefield leaned heavily on John Wesley for guidance. In the absence of a biological father, Whitefield called Wesley his "spiritual father in Christ." He asked him myriad questions on topics including the healthiest diet, the best place to recuperate, theological dilemmas, and family struggles. In a lengthy letter from July 1735, Whitefield asked Wesley about a Dissenting friend who wished to join the Anglican Communion. Was Dissenting baptism legitimate, or did his friend need to be rebaptized before joining the Anglican Church? Whitefield also asked, wearily, what he should do about his mother and her no-account husband. They had not been "cohabitating" for years, yet his stepfather refused to give his mother adequate financial assistance. He inquired whether she could "on any terms can justify living separate from her husband"? (Wesley's response does not survive.) Covering the gamut of spiritual topics, Whitefield even asked Wesley whether he should insist on having group prayer over a meal when eating with less devoted friends. One wonders whether Wesley grew weary of answering so many questions—he had many correspondents, after all.[50]

During Whitefield's time of recuperation in Gloucester, the Anglican bishop there approached Whitefield about receiving holy orders, first as a deacon and then as a priest. Wrestling with his worthiness to become a minister, he worried about Paul's warning in his first letter to Timothy against ordaining "novices, lest being puffed up with pride he fall into the condemnation of the devil." God assured Whitefield that he was truly calling him, however, by giving him a revelatory dream about a meeting with the bishop (one to which he had yet to be summoned). He dreamed that the bishop gave him gold coins during their conversation. Sure enough, it was not long before the bishop asked for an appointment with Whitefield. The bishop told him that although he had intended never to ordain anyone under the age of twenty-three, the minimum age recommended by the church, he had decided to make an exception in

Whitefield's case. (Whitefield was twenty-one.) Then the bishop gave Whitefield a gift of five guineas to buy a book. As the coins clinked in his hand, Whitefield remembered the dream, and his "heart was filled with a sense of God's love."[51]

He would later come under fierce criticism for accepting dreams as divine validation of his vocation. Whitefield excised references to his revelatory dreams from later editions of the autobiography. But Whitefield, like many early Methodist itinerants, had focused on the role of dreams only in his conversion and ordination, not in his public ministry. As the historian Phyllis Mack has shown, this reflected a difference between male and female Methodist piety: while male leaders' records of dreams typically stopped after they began preaching, nocturnal visions remained central to female Methodists' piety. The prominent late eighteenth-century Methodist Sarah Boyce asked God to help her understand particular questions about faith and practice through dreams; her contemporary Hester Roe Rogers even fasted to facilitate the formation of intense dreams.[52]

The fulfillment of Whitefield's dream convinced him to seek Anglican orders. The only question was where he would begin his ministerial work. Oxford friends implored him to return there to lead the Methodist cohort. As we shall see, the Wesleys had already left Oxford to serve as missionaries in the new colony of Georgia, and the Methodists' work in Oxford was in disarray. Then Whitefield received an offer from one of the Methodists' benefactors, Sir John Philips of Picton Castle, Pembrokeshire (in southwestern Wales), a member of Parliament. If Whitefield would work at Oxford, Philips would provide him £30 a year. Whitefield was persuaded, and in March 1736 he returned to Oxford, where he began to study for the oral examination required to complete his bachelor's degree, and also for his ordination.[53]

At Oxford, Whitefield continued to bask in the delights of his newly converted state. In an unpublished diary running from March to June, most entries spoke of the Holy Spirit's presence. Over and over, he wrote that he was "full of the Holy Ghost" or felt "joy in the Holy Ghost" for hours on end. On May 6, he exulted that he experienced "joy in the Holy Ghost Grace Grace Free Grace." The Holy Spirit was an emotionally and mentally tangible presence to him. Whitefield often spoke to private meetings of friends, noting that the Holy Spirit assisted him in knowing what to say. On one occasion, the Spirit enabled him "to apply all the promises made to the Apostles to us." On another, he (the Spirit) "suggested" to him "things just applicable to what we were discoursing," and he even "put words into my mouth," Whitefield noted. He concluded that one of the Spirit's ministries to believers was "to point out appropriate particular texts to [their] particular circumstances."[54]

This emphasis on the Holy Spirit would be a consistent theme in Whitefield's career, although he would in time back away from claims for his immediate guidance. As I argued in my book *The Great Awakening*, many eighteenth-century evangelicals focused heavily on the work of the Spirit. Outpourings of the Spirit generated revivals, but the Spirit also regenerated sinners, giving them new life in Christ. Moreover, the Spirit comforted and guided individual believers, offering them the assurance and joy of salvation, and strength through trials.[55]

The most common definition of evangelicalism, one crafted by the historian David Bebbington, suggests that four primary characteristics mark evangelicals: conversionism (an emphasis on the need for a life-transforming encounter with God), activism (the conviction that the gospel demands action), biblicism (the idea that the Bible is the unique source of God's truth), and crucicentrism (the theological primacy of Jesus's death on the cross for sinners). While this definition, known as the "Bebbington quadrilateral," accurately reflects four distinctive emphases of evangelical faith, it does not account for the enormous weight that evangelicals such as Whitefield put on the Holy Spirit's ministry. Along with conversion, the experience of the Holy Spirit's presence and power was what struck Whitefield and other evangelicals as the most novel aspect of their newborn lives.[56]

Life in the Spirit hardly negated the life of the mind for the new convert. Whitefield passed his Oxford examination in May, writing in his diary that he was enabled to recall "the true Greek text: Horace—Sallust offhand, fluently," and "to translate an English book into Latin immediately." Yet during the exams he was terribly nervous. Struggling to speak, he trembled violently, even during practice sessions. He would exhibit similar anxieties during public performances, including sermons, for much of his early career.[57]

Two weeks later Whitefield returned to Gloucester. Travel hampered his physical recovery, but he was still much better off than when he had returned to Gloucester for his convalescence. Leaving Oxford, he reflected on how far he had come since serving drinks and cleaning rooms at the Bell Inn: "How short a time it was since I was a common drawer in a publick house—had to be forcibly pulled out from thence to divine grace. I should have been the most abandoned wretch living." Now he would become the "head of the Methodists" at Oxford.[58]

His ordination was scheduled for June 20, 1736, at Gloucester Cathedral (see figure 2.2). After preaching and praying, the bishop asked Whitefield whether he believed he was "truly called according to the will of our Lord Jesus Christ, and the due order of this realm, to the ministry of the church?" Having answered this and every other question as honestly as he could, Whitefield knelt at the altar. The bishop laid his hands on Whitefield's head and charged him: "Take thou authority to execute the office of a Deacon in the Church of God committed unto thee; in the name of the Father, and of the Son, and of the Holy Ghost." The jubilant Whitefield wrote to a friend, "When the Bishop laid his hand upon me, I gave myself up to be a martyr for him, who hung upon the cross for me."[59]

The next morning, while praying, Whitefield asked God what to do next. Of course he would be returning to Oxford to lead the Methodists, but he also had some sermons he had been working on privately. Should he begin to deliver those immediately, he wondered? As he was praying, the words "Speak out, Paul" surged into his mind. "Immediately my heart was enlarged," he wrote. "God spake to me by his Spirit, and I was no longer dumb." Yes, it was time. Now he would begin to preach.[60]

"God is Preparing Me for Something Extraordinary": Whitefield the Methodist Missionary

A capacity crowd pressed into pews at Gloucester's St. Mary de Crypt church on June 27, 1736. They had come to hear George Whitefield preach publicly for the first time. His mother, Elizabeth, forsaken by her husband but loved by her son, sat beaming in the front row. Many friends and acquaintances were there, happy for the Gloucester boy who had made them proud by graduating from Oxford. This was the church where Whitefield had received baptism and first communion; here he had attended the St. Mary's Church school and first tested his talents in public speaking.[1]

If the crowd was expecting a polite, appreciative sermon, it did not get one. Whitefield wrote that his preaching kindled a "fire" in the audience, and that he was "enabled to speak with some degree of gospel authority." Some discomfited audience members jeered at him for coming on so strong, but most seemed awed (or "struck," as Whitefield put it). Afterward, some complained to the bishop—the man who had just ordained Whitefield—that the boy's preaching had driven fifteen overwrought people "mad." Whitefield was not concerned, though. He was delighted. "Glory! Glory! Glory!" he wrote.[2]

The title of Whitefield's first sermon, "The Necessity and Benefits of Religious Society," does not sound very exciting. Whitefield's sermons, when read today, seem doctrinally conventional, but not brilliant, certainly not as brilliant as sermons of his contemporary Jonathan Edwards. It requires imagination to envision how Whitefield turned his sermons into emotional masterpieces. Some of the explanation for their powerful effects lay in Whitefield's talent for public speaking. But he also noted how he leaned on his training in rhetoric, both in school and in speaking to prisoners during his time at Oxford. (He had spoken regularly in private meetings too in the months leading up to his debut.) These experiences made him "accustomed to public speaking" and kept him from being "daunted over much." Whitefield may have struggled with nervousness before preaching, but once in the pulpit, he dazzled.[3]

That first public sermon reflected his Methodist experiences at Oxford. Escaping the dangers of lukewarm religion, Whitefield insisted, required surrounding oneself with like-minded believers. They could bolster a Christian's faith as he in turn bolstered theirs. He lauded the benefits of belonging to such a group: "It [is] an invaluable privilege to have a company of fellow soldiers continually about us, animating and exhorting each other to stand our ground, to keep our ranks, and manfully to follow the Captain of our Salvation, though it be through a sea of blood." To Whitefield, Christianity was not for the faint of heart: it was for the manly and the martial.[4]

Still, Whitefield believed that even religious societies could mask hypocrisy. He warned the congregation of God's coming judgment, in which all would be revealed. "Think not that it will be sufficient for you to plead at the last day, 'Lord, have we not assembled ourselves together in thy Name, and enlivened each other, by singing psalms, and hymns, and spiritual songs?' For verily, I say unto you notwithstanding this, our blessed Lord will bid you depart from him; nay, that you shall receive a greater damnation, if, in the midst of these great pretensions, you are found to be workers of iniquity," he cautioned. Even the Methodists' intense disciplines could not hide an unregenerate heart in the end. Hypocrisy would show itself eventually, usually in the indulgence of secret sins. Only the true believer would maintain consistent public and private holiness.[5]

Some in Whitefield's Gloucester audience must have found his vision of the devout Christian life unsettling. He had no patience for the obligatory routine of church attendance. Instead, he called people to discipline and accountability, summoning them to enter the "narrow passage of a sound conversion," which was the "one way now to heaven." This was a life reordered around Christ and the fellowship of true believers. To some, it was an exhilarating prospect. Others considered Whitefield's message puritanical and picky.[6]

His conversion, ordination, and impending graduation from Oxford boosted Whitefield's confidence. It also helped him find his pastoral voice. Shortly after preaching his first sermon, he wrote to a Gloucester friend and urged her to bear up under earthly difficulties with thoughts of heaven's glories. Meditate on the time, he recommended, when "we shall see the blessed Jesus, whom our souls have so eagerly thirsted after in this life, surrounded with glory, and attended with myriads of his holy angels, who will rejoice at our safe arrival to their happy mansions." Certainty of heaven made Whitefield's proclamation of the new birth more urgent. Whitefield became a religious celebrity without peer, but we shouldn't forget that theological conviction underlay his gospel preaching and the promotion of his ministry.[7]

Shortly after giving his sermon at Gloucester, Whitefield returned to Oxford, fortified by the salary from Sir John Philips, to continue building the Methodist movement there. He found "few friends" left at Oxford, the Wesleys having departed for Georgia. Hostility to the Methodists lingered; their names "stunk" to fellow students. Nevertheless, Whitefield remained optimistic. Soon after coming back to the university, he formally received his bachelor's degree.[8]

Whitefield planned also to pursue an MA. This was the usual path for ministers. The Oxford MA was not rigorous, mostly involving unmonitored requirements to attend lectures. Candidates also had to present formal addresses (ostensibly) of their own composition, but students often found themselves giving these recitations to empty rooms, which explains why many called the MA speeches "wall lectures." Some students plagiarized previous orations.[9]

Whitefield found he had plenty of other things to do as he worked on his MA. He not only was the key Methodist leader at Oxford, but also soon received a call from a friend, Thomas Broughton, to preach for a couple months at the chapel of the Tower of London, where Broughton was an assistant minister. In early August, Whitefield rode to the great metropolis by stagecoach. Even relatively cosmopolitan Oxford had not prepared the boy preacher for the sights of England's behemoth city, where hundreds of thousands of residents lived in conditions ranging from opulence to squalor.[10]

On his way to the tower, Whitefield traveled on the north bank of the Thames, passing London Bridge on his right. This bridge had existed in various forms since the time of Christ, in ancient Roman Britain. By the 1730s, the bridge had become overcrowded and bulging with so many buildings that it looked more like a city street than a normal bridge. English rulers had traditionally placed the heads of traitors on pikes on the bridge, the most famous such head belonging to the Scottish rebel William Wallace, who was decapitated, drawn, and quartered in 1305.

The Tower of London was a royal palace and fortress on the Thames, dating back to the eleventh century and the rule of William the Conqueror. The starkly beautiful St. John's Chapel, where Whitefield was to preach, occupied the second floor of the White Tower, the oldest part of the compound, and featured white stone pillars and Norman arches (see figure 3.1).

Whitefield rambled through the city's streets in his clerical gown and cassock, gawking at the shops and theaters, knowing that when he was younger, the attractions of London would have proved irresistible. "Not many years ago," he wrote, "I would have given much money, would my circumstances have permitted, to have [gone] up and seen a play." But now he was surrounded by evangelical friends, including his patron, John Philips, and he found countless opportunities for ministry.[11]

One of these opportunities—one fitting the Methodists' emphasis on reaching the destitute—was to preach at London's Ludgate Prison every Tuesday. This prison, also on the Thames's north bank, normally housed respectable citizens convicted of less serious crimes, including excessive debt. (Newgate Prison was used for felons.) But a critic in 1725 called Ludgate the "worst of prisons," contending that it was wracked with corruption and extortionist practices that kept its residents mired in insolvency.[12]

Whitefield's fame as a preacher began to spread in London. The Tower Chapel was thronged with people when he spoke on Sundays. Methodists eagerly came to hear him, and he began to attract younger followers who were, he wrote, "under serious impressions, to hear me discourse about the new birth." But after two months, Broughton returned, and Whitefield returned to Oxford. These were happy times for Whitefield, who wrote that he had a "delightful life" at the university as his prominence grew.[13]

While in London, Whitefield received a letter from John Wesley, who was in the Georgia colony, with Charles, to establish a Methodist mission. "Does your heart burn within you," Wesley asked, "to turn many others to righteousness? Behold, the whole land, thousands of thousands, are before you! . . . Who will bring them up in the nurture and admonition of the Lord, till they are meet to be preachers of righteousness? Here are adults from the farthest parts of Europe and Asia, and the inmost kingdoms of Africa. Add to these the known and unknown natives of this vast continent, and you will indeed have a great multitude which no man can number." This plea jarred Whitefield. He was just getting comfortable with his preaching duties in London and Oxford. But Wesley's letter made him think that perhaps there was an even higher level of commitment to Christ—the kind of commitment required of a missionary— that he had not yet reached.[14]

Georgia was, to the Methodists, like a new New World. Founded in 1732, it was the last addition to the thirteen mainland American colonies that would rebel against the British four decades later. Georgia's trustees believed that the colony could achieve several desirable ends at once. It would serve, the charter said, as a buffer against the aggression of Spanish and Indian "savages," as an outlet for resettling "poor subjects" from the masses of London, as a market for British refined goods, and as a model Christian society at a time when some of the other colonies seemed to have lost their original, pious character. The Georgia founders hoped to attract Christian settlers from across Europe, and accordingly, they guaranteed "liberty of conscience" and "free exercise of their religion" to all Christians except Catholics. The prospect of imperial war between Catholic and Protestant powers always loomed, so Catholics were unwelcome in the frontier colony.[15]

An early booster visited tiny Savannah, Georgia, and proclaimed that the place had "the pleasantest climate in the world, for it's neither too warm in the summer, nor too cold in the winter; they have certainly the finest water in the world, and the land is extraordinarily good." It is not known whether this visitor actually stayed through an oppressive Savannah summer, but the piece was written to promote the colony, which the author called the "Land of Canaan." When the Wesleys came to Savannah, it remained a village of frame houses and huts cut out of the surrounding pine forests, perched on a cliff over-looking the Savannah River (see figure 3.2). The town's modest homes rarely lasted long, since termites wreaked havoc on their wooden foundations. Settlers discovered that all manner of wildlife, from toads to rattlesnakes, easily entered their shacks.[16]

The trustees envisioned Georgia as a holy experiment. This aspiration partly explains their decision to ban slavery from the colony. James Oglethorpe, the chief organizer, was no radical abolitionist, but he and other trustees thought that if Georgia was to become a model of Christian virtue, they would have to exclude chattel slavery. Anglo-Americans widely believed that while slave plantations—especially the sugar plantations of the Caribbean—were great engines of agricultural profit, they fostered corruption and laziness among whites. Slaves destabilized colonies in times of military emergency. The importation of slaves did not comport with the Georgia trustees' mercantile and imperial goals, or with their intention to employ poor Englishmen as laborers.[17]

Georgia trustees, including Oglethorpe and the Oxford pastor and scholar John Burton, began recruiting John Wesley in August 1735. "Surely," Oglethorpe wrote to Wesley, "there are more persons capable of doing the offices required by the Church in England than there are capable of undergoing all that is necessary for propagating the gospel in new countries." For the Methodists, the prospect of reaching higher levels of devotion to the gospel was always tantalizing.[18]

Wesley, however, had not yet experienced Whitefield's clarity about salvation. Having agreed to go to Georgia, Wesley frankly explained to John Burton that his "chief motive" in taking on the mission was "the hope of saving [his] own soul." The emerging evangelical movement would emphasize good works and Christian activism, but not as means of salvation. Wesley here revealed that in 1735, he still conflated sanctification (the process of becoming more holy) with redemption.[19]

In Wesley's romantic image, Georgia seemed like an oasis of innocence where he could start fresh with an unadulterated gospel. He was particularly intrigued by the prospect of preaching to the "heathens," who had no pseudo-Christian philosophy to corrupt their minds, as Englishmen did. He could leave behind the frustrations of ministering to lukewarm cultural Christians. In the New World, Wesley anticipated learning from the childlike faith of Native American converts and discovering "the purity of that faith which was once delivered to the saints" (Jude 3). He envisioned Georgia as a spiritual Eden.[20]

The Wesley brothers landed at Savannah in February 1736. They joined hundreds of new settlers, including a number of Moravians. These German Pietist Christians had recently begun a missionary campaign of unprecedented scope, establishing stations across the Atlantic world. Contacts between early Methodists and Moravians added an international quality to the evangelical movement. One of the key Moravian leaders, August Spangenberg, visited Wesley and, in a legendary exchange, pressed the young Englishman about his spiritual state. "Does the spirit of God bear witness with your spirit, that you are a child of God?" Spangenberg inquired. Wesley wrote, "I was surprised, and knew not what to answer." Spangenberg asked, "Do you know Jesus Christ?" Wesley paused and said, "I know he is the Saviour of the world." "True," replied Spangenberg, "but do you know he has saved you?" Wesley answered meekly, "I hope he has died to save me." The conversation shook Wesley, making him realize his uncertain state before God.[21]

A series of tawdry episodes soon shattered Wesley's hopes for the mission. Charles, whom Oglethorpe employed as a personal secretary, encountered scandalous claims by a Mrs. Hawkins and a Mrs. Welch that they had become intimately involved with Oglethorpe. What Charles did not realize was that the women were apparently telling Oglethorpe the same things about him! (John would face similar charges, and the unstable Mrs. Hawkins once assaulted John with a pair of scissors and a pistol, threatening to shoot him in the head.) Whatever the truth of Mrs. Hawkins and Mrs. Welch's intrigues, Charles and Oglethorpe's relationship grew quite strained.[22]

Charles found Georgia strange and forbidding. The settlers constantly worried about attacks from the Spanish or Native Americans. Even daily tasks entailed exotic dangers. In the summer, Charles recorded that he bathed in the

Savannah River before sunrise because the water was cooler but also because "the alligators were not stirring so soon." Hating his tedious secretarial work, Charles started to think that he had made a terrible mistake in coming to Georgia. He became physically ill and ultimately decided to leave the colony, departing for England in July 1736.[23]

John stayed on in Charles's absence, but he likewise found his Georgia ministry derailed by personal conflicts. The bitterest controversy surrounded his relationship with Sophy Hopkey, a seventeen-year-old he met in March 1736. The thirty-two-year-old Wesley became smitten with the spiritually sensitive teenager. He had initially thought that coming to America would solve his previous sexual struggles, but upon meeting Sophy, his craving for intimacy came raging back. They engaged in months of emotionally charged courting, one day resolving to break off the relationship, the next engaging in reckless behavior. At one point they spent several nights together on a deserted island, but Wesley congratulated himself that they did not engage in any sexual indiscretions, although he did admit (in his private diary) to some hugging and kissing.[24]

Wesley brought up the topic of marriage with her, but never got around to proposing directly. At some of his Methodist colleagues' behest, he drew lots to seek God's guidance on marrying her. (This was also a common practice of the Moravians.) John picked a slip of paper that told him, "Think of it no more." But Wesley could not bring himself to end the relationship.[25]

Growing frustrated with Wesley's indecisiveness, Sophy began a rapid courtship with another man, William Williamson. In March 1737, Sophy informed Wesley that she was marrying Williamson, whom Wesley considered "not remarkable for handsomeness, neither for genteelness, neither for wit or knowledge or sense, and least of all, for religion." Wesley's low view notwithstanding, Sophy wished for him to publish the banns, the parish announcement of the couple's intent to wed. Wesley understandably balked, and the couple absconded for South Carolina, where they were married. Wesley spitefully resolved to deny Sophy communion for her actions, which precipitated an ugly series of legal and ecclesiastical charges between Sophy's new husband and Wesley. Wesley was accused of defaming Sophy's character and of denying her communion without reasonable cause, and he faced a possible fine of £1,000.[26]

By the end of 1737, Savannah was in turmoil over the sordid affair. Although the colonial magistrates forbade him to leave the colony, Wesley became convinced that he had no hope of a fair hearing from the indignant Georgians, so he fled. After sunset on December 2, as the tide began to go out, Wesley said that he "shook off the dust of my feet and left Georgia." He had been there less than two years. One of the Georgia trustees, the Earl of Egmont, wrote that the board was happy to see him resign, "he appearing to us to be a very odd mixture of a man, an enthusiast and at the same time a hypocrite, wholly distasteful to the greater part of the inhabitants."[27]

Whitefield had obviously not anticipated Wesley's spectacular debacle as he considered the invitation to come to Georgia, which Wesley made while his romance with Sophy was waxing. Whitefield continued ministering in Oxford, and he also supplied the pulpit in a relatively isolated parish in Dummer, south-west of London. "Thoughts of going to Georgia still crowded continually in," Whitefield wrote. He received another letter from Wesley, reminding him that in Georgia, the harvest was great, but the laborers few. "What if thou art the man, Mr. Whitefield?" Wesley asked pointedly.[28]

Charles Wesley, having arrived back in England, contacted Whitefield to tell him that he was recruiting more ministers for the colony. (Whitefield did not realize, or Charles did not yet know, that Charles was not going back.) Things began to fall into place: his friend Charles Kinchin, for whom Whitefield was substituting at Dummer, received an appointment at Oxford, where he could oversee the Methodists' ministry. The parish at Dummer likewise got a permanent replacement, so he was not needed there any longer. No obvious barriers stood between him and Georgia.[29]

In late December 1736, Whitefield wrote to Charles and said he would go to America, declaring, "I throw myself blindfold into the hands of my Heavenly Father, to conduct me where he pleases." Whitefield perceived Charles's dissatisfaction with Georgia, and began chiding him. Why, he asked, did Charles agree to be James Oglethorpe's secretary instead of working as a missionary? "Did the bishop ordain us, my dear friend, to write bonds, receipts, etc., or to preach the gospel?" He suggested that Charles did not trust God enough to supply his material needs as a missionary. But then he backed off. "I go too far," he wrote. "You know I was always heady and self-willed."[30] This was an aggressive tone for Whitefield to take with Charles, and it hinted at his coming break with the Wesleys. Charles's irresolution, as well as John's troubles in Georgia, eroded Whitefield's veneration of them as spiritual fathers just as Whitefield was beginning to realize what a powerful ministry he could have on his own.

The young minister now entered a peculiar phase of his early career. He had decided to go to Georgia, but his departure was delayed for the better part of 1737. In the intervening months, Whitefield "began to grow a little popular," as he put it in his journals. His celebrity began to ascend just as he was about to leave the country. In fact, his imminent departure seemed to generate more widespread fascination with his preaching. Whitefield started to understand the value of a farewell tour.[31]

He preached for some weeks in Gloucester, but he began to see truly spectacular results during weeks of ministry in Bristol. People from a variety of denominations — Quakers, Baptists, and Presbyterians in addition to Anglicans — pressed in to hear him, and some were turned away for lack of seating. "The Word, through the mighty power of God, was sharper than a two-edged sword," he wrote, quoting Hebrews 4:12. His teaching on the new birth and justification by faith "made its way like lightning into the hearers' consciences." Attendees crowded around him during breaks to ask advice about their spiritual state. Some offered him salaries if he would stay in Bristol instead of going to Georgia, but he would not be deterred.[32]

In March, Whitefield made his way to London to meet with James Oglethorpe and the Georgia trustees. Oglethorpe had been a member of Parliament since 1722, and was known as an outspoken, ambitious, and generous man. He repeatedly traveled between Georgia and London to raise support for the colony, and in 1737 he focused on convincing Parliament to provide military support for the colony to defend itself against possible Spanish aggression. The Spanish in Florida were none too pleased with the new English colony to their north, and they were mulling an attack.[33]

The well-connected Oglethorpe introduced Whitefield to a number of Anglican luminaries, including the archbishop of Canterbury (the highest-ranking cleric of the Church of England) and the bishop of London. But Whitefield had to wait on Oglethorpe to finish his business in England before they could depart. While waiting, he took a temporary pastoral position in Stonehouse, south of Gloucester. Although Whitefield would never settle into a permanent parish ministry, he loved the people in this country village. Crowds overflowed as he spoke at the church and parsonage, and his own soul was refreshed in ways reminiscent of his conversion ordeal. He "found uncommon manifestations granted" from God. At many waking moments, Jesus visited him in spirit: "Could the trees of a certain wood near Stone-House speak, they would tell what sweet communion I and some more dear souls enjoyed with the ever blessed God there." Sometimes he felt as if his soul "would go out of the body." At other times he was so overcome with emotion that he would throw himself on the ground. He offered his "soul as a blank in [God's] hands, to write on it what he pleased."[34]

On one memorable night, the villagers were alarmed as the sky grew unaccountably bright. Many of his parishioners were frightened, and Whitefield was determined to "stir them up to prepare for the coming of the Son of Man." He and one of his friends, a "poor but pious countryman," went out into the fields, "exulting in our God, and longing for that time, when Jesus should be revealed from heaven in a flame of fire!" He thought it was the happiest night of his life.³⁵

Still, Whitefield was becoming ever more restless for Oglethorpe's departure, and it did not appear imminent. In May, Whitefield returned to Bristol, where his celebrity began to crest. He preached five times a week, and crowds packed the churches well beyond normal capacity to get a glimpse of him. "People hung upon the rails of the organ-loft, climbed upon the [roof] of the church, and made the church itself so hot with their breath, that the steam would fall from the pillars like drops of rain," he wrote. Whitefield had to push his way through the masses to get to the pulpit.³⁶ Whitefield stayed for about a month in Bristol, and reported that when he bade farewell in June 1737, many wept bitterly and promised to follow him to Gloucester. So he left Bristol at three in the morning, hoping to avoid a protracted, emotional good-bye. After brief stays in Gloucester and Oxford, he went again to London. There his Methodist supporters encouraged him to begin publishing his sermons, including what would become one of his signature exhortations, "The Nature and Necessity of Our New Birth in Christ Jesus."

As his fame grew, so did the consternation of some church officials, who had begun to grumble about Whitefield's views on conversion.³⁷ Whitefield countered the "aspersions of enemies" in the printed preface to the sermon, in which he said he wished that his "reverend brethren, the ministers of the Church of England . . . would more frequently entertain their people with discourses of this nature, than they commonly do: And that they would not, out of a servile fear of displeasing some particular persons, fail to declare the whole will of God . . . nor suffer their people to rest satisfied with the shell and shadow of religion." This critical statement irritated a number of clergymen, and two banned him from preaching in their churches when he refused to retract it.³⁸

By the time he preached "The Nature and Necessity of Our New Birth," Whitefield saw conversion as an individual, deeply felt experience. This understanding of conversion was not new to him—he had learned it from works such as Joseph Alleine's *Alarm to Unconverted Sinners*, and from his Methodist colleagues. (Whitefield would have argued that he found the doctrine in the Bible, especially in the Gospel of John, chapter 3, when Jesus told the Pharisee Nicodemus that "except a man be born again, he cannot see the kingdom of God.") Seventeenth-century Puritan and Pietist spirituality also emphasized the individual's discernible moment of conversion. Alleine implored readers to ask themselves, "When was the time, where was the place, or what was the means by which this thorough change of the new birth was wro't in [your] soul?"³⁹

Although the doctrine of the new birth was not new, Whitefield was the most important popularizer of the concept in Anglo-American history, at least until Billy Graham's revivals of the twentieth century. In "The Nature and Necessity of Our New Birth" (preached originally in Bristol), Whitefield displayed the focused attention on conversion that would mark his career. He called the new birth "one of the most fundamental doctrines of our holy religion" and "the very hinge on which the salvation of each of us turns." Despite the importance of being born again, Whitefield insisted that the experience was not "experimentally understood by the generality" of nominal Christians. A renovation of the heart was required for people to become fit for heaven. Religious duties— attending church, praying, and fasting—were important and could help put a person in the path of grace. But to Whitefield, observing churchly rituals had nothing to do with securing the new birth, which required a miraculous infusion of faith, effected by the Holy Spirit. Nothing short of a soul-transforming conversion would save people.[40]

The volume containing "The Nature and Necessity of Our New Birth" began to spread Whitefield's fame in print, running through three editions by 1738. Whitefield said that the sermon "began the awakening at London, Bristol, Gloucester, and Gloucestershire." By "awakening," Whitefield meant spiritual excitement and inquisitiveness, especially among those who had not experienced conversion. Supporters subsidized *The Nature and Necessity of Our New Birth* so that people could buy and distribute the published sermon in bulk ("two guineas per hundred to those who give them away," it advertised).[41]

Published sermons were important to Whitefield's fame, but nothing matched newspapers for generating interest in his ministry. News of Whitefield's preaching began to appear as early as April 1737, when the London papers the *Weekly Miscellany* and *Common Sense or The Englishman's Journal* reported that someone had donated £50 to Whitefield to help build a church in Frederica, Georgia. Then in July, supporters paid to advertise *The Nature and Necessity of Our New Birth* in the *Daily Gazetteer*.[42]

Whitefield, Wesley, and Edwards's evangelicalism rode on new capabilities in media and transportation. Evangelicalism was truly a "movement": it was a movement of ideas and people, but also a movement of methods and technologies, ones that were changing broader Anglo-American culture and the British Empire. Whitefield traversed the Atlantic on ships that were faster and more dependable, and (except during wartime) that made more trips, than ever before. American and Caribbean colonial ports saw ship traffic double between 1700 and 1750. In addition, Wesley and Whitefield itinerated on rapidly improving road networks within Britain. Their letters and publications traveled in coaches and ships along these same expanding routes. As we scramble today to understand the changes wrought by digital media and commerce, we may better understand the mood of the eighteenth century's own "age of speed."[43]

The key figure in the new media promotion of Whitefield was a Methodist convert named William Seward. Seward's professional background was in finance, stocks, and publicity. He played a major role in the South Sea Bubble debacle of 1721, a speculative scheme that resulted in one of the first great stock crashes in modern economic history. After becoming an evangelical believer, Seward set about promoting Whitefield with the same sort of entrepreneurial energy, but for a more godly cause. Paid newspaper pieces focused on Whitefield's charity sermons, but gave colorful information about Whitefield's personality and the unprecedented excitement he generated. They also made sure to note that the rising star meant to "go voluntarily to preach the gospel in Georgia."[44]

When Whitefield first saw one of his sermons described in the newspaper, he said that the notice "chagrined" him. He even asked the printer not to run any more stories about his preaching. The printer answered that he was "paid for doing it, and that he would not lose two shillings for anybody." Whether the news of the payment came as a surprise to Whitefield, we do not know, but it did not take long for Whitefield to accept the tactic of paid publicity. It attracted more hearers, and more hearers meant exposure for the gospel. In October, he wrote sheepishly in a letter that he supposed a Gloucester friend had "heard of my mighty deeds, so called, by reading the news-papers."[45]

At long last, in December 1737, it came time for Whitefield to leave. Oglethorpe was still not ready, but a detachment of his soldiers was going, so Whitefield began saying his final good-byes. Everyone knew that there was no guarantee of returning safe from any transatlantic voyage, so his parting was bittersweet. Whitefield's Oxford follower John Scote, for one, seemed nearly undone by the experience, writing that he felt the "utmost perplexity" and "inexpressible uneasiness" upon the minister's departure. He conceded, however, that had Whitefield's ministry not touched him so deeply, he "could not have been so tenderly so sensibly affected with losing you." He accepted that Whitefield had had to move on to London, but what, Scote wondered, would he do when the evangelist left for Georgia?[46]

This kind of intense devotion to Whitefield was becoming common, and it brought out mockers. *Read's Weekly Journal or British Gazetteer* reported with a touch of cynicism that when Whitefield preached for the last time at St. Helen's Church, hundreds of people had to stand outside, "only to have the happiness of touching his garment." (This was a reference to Matthew 14:36, in which crowds of the sick "besought [Jesus] that they might only touch the hem of his garment: and as many as touched were made perfectly whole.") Whitefield recalled the moment less skeptically, of course. As he bade farewell at "great St. Helen's"—a capacious twelfth-century church where William Shakespeare once worshipped—people moaned and wept openly. It took him a half an hour to get out the door after his sermon. On New Year's Eve, Whitefield sailed to Gravesend, the port town on the south bank of the Thames where the river begins to open into the North Sea. After visiting Whitefield to send him off, Charles Wesley admiringly wrote to John Wesley that "God has poured out his Spirit" upon Whitefield and his Methodist colleagues. Finally, on January 6, 1738, Whitefield boarded the *Whitaker*, bound for America.[47]

Whitefield's closest companion on the voyage to Georgia was James Habersham. Habersham, a London merchant a year younger than Whitefield, had experienced conversion under Whitefield's preaching, and Whitefield had recruited Habersham as a schoolmaster for the Georgia mission. They studied Latin and sang psalms together, and Whitefield prayed that he might be "made an instrument of breeding [Habersham] up for God."[48]

Sailing ships like the man-of-war *Whitaker* were heavily dependent on weather conditions, and adverse winds forced the boat to remain on the English coast. Within a few days, Whitefield wrote that the "winds and storms are blustering about our ears and teaching us lessons of obedience as fast as they can." The ship docked at Deal for several weeks. Whitefield took the opportunity to preach in town, which kindled a "holy flame" of revival there. Overflowing crowds thronged the churches, and in one instance people stood on the roof of the church, peering in the upper windows to see Whitefield preaching.[49]

Coincidentally, John Wesley's ship, returning from Georgia, arrived at Deal just before Whitefield's departure. Wesley knew that Whitefield and Habersham were in the port, yet he did not go to visit them. Wesley was undoubtedly feeling embarrassed about the circumstances of his leaving Georgia. He apparently resorted again to casting lots to inquire whether he should visit Whitefield. The lot he drew said no. So Wesley left a letter for Whitefield and headed back to London. Whitefield politely responded to Wesley, but later, when they publicly split over theological differences, Whitefield threw the incident in Wesley's face, writing in 1741, "The morning I sailed from Deal for Gibraltar, you arrived from Georgia.—Instead of giving me an opportunity to converse with you, tho' the ship was not far off the shore; you drew a lot, and immediately set forwards to London."[50]

In London, Wesley met the Moravian minister Peter Böhler, who (like Spangenberg in Georgia) questioned whether, in the midst of all his spiritual disciplines, John had actually come to know Jesus as his savior. Böhler similarly challenged Charles Wesley, and both brothers became convinced that they had not undergone conversion, with its accompanying assurance of salvation and forgiveness of sins. Within days of one another in May 1738, Charles and John experienced their breakthroughs. Charles wrote of his: "I now found myself at peace with God and rejoiced in the hope of loving Christ." John famously wrote that at a fellowship meeting on Aldersgate Street, while one of the leaders was reading Martin Luther's preface to Romans, "I felt my heart strangely warmed. I felt that I did trust in Christ, Christ alone for salvation."[51]

On February 2, 1738, Whitefield and the *Whitaker* finally sailed from Deal. Whitefield, unsurprisingly, took spiritual charge of the passengers, especially the soldiers on board. He held regular sermons and prayer services. As they rocked along in the rough seas of the Bay of Biscay, the captain ordered that makeshift pews be set up on deck for services. This was no cruise liner, and the landlubbers on board—including Whitefield—struggled with seasickness. Whitefield did not coddle the passengers or crew, devoting one afternoon's sermon to "the eternity of hell torments," preaching with the cries of seagulls in the background. Temperatures probably hovered in the forties (°F), sometimes even a bit lower.[52]

After two weeks, the *Whitaker* arrived at Gibraltar, the two-and-a-half-square-mile peninsula just off the southern tip of Spain. The town had come under British control in 1704, but had experienced centuries of Catholic Spanish and Moorish influence before that. An eighth-century Moorish castle and fort loomed over the rocky landscape. Whitefield was impressed by the imposing tower, writing that he could "scarce avoid crying out, 'Who is so great a God as our God?'"[53]

The preacher found the sights of the diverse port fascinating yet troubling. A 1725 census put the population of Gibraltar at eleven hundred, the majority Catholic Genoese and Spaniards, and the minority Jews and Britons. Whitefield preached in town and drew crowds that he estimated at a thousand. (Whitefield's crowd estimates could be a bit inflated, however.) He was surprised by this enthusiastic response, and concluded, "Christ has a flock, though but a little flock, in all places."[54] Whitefield repeatedly visited the "Romish chapel," probably the sixteenth-century Cathedral of St. Mary the Crowned. He had little direct experience with Roman Catholics, although he had been reared in the anti-Catholic milieu of English Protestantism. In the cathedral, he saw "relics of a vast deal of pageantry, and several images of the Virgin Mary, dressed up, not like a poor Galilean, but in her silks and [Moorish] damasks." He wondered why the Catholics "should thus depart from the simplicity of Christ, and go a whoring after their own inventions?"[55]

He also visited Gibraltar's synagogue, Sha'ar HaShamayim, which had opened in 1724. A rabbi welcomed him warmly, saying that he appreciated a sermon Whitefield had delivered in town against vices such as swearing. The rabbi gave Whitefield a seat of honor, but Whitefield confessed that during the service he was praying (in words from 2 Corinthians 3:14–16 and Romans 11:23–26) that "the veil might be taken from their hearts" and that the "blessed time might come when his chosen people should again be engrafted into their own olive-tree, and all Israel be saved." Whitefield, like many English Protestants, believed that Jews were suffering from spiritual blindness, having failed to recognize Jesus as their Messiah. But he also believed that in the last days Jews would be converted en masse to Christianity.[56]

Back in London, Whitefield's ally the bookseller and printer James Hutton had already begun to capitalize on the itinerant's popularity by selling his sermons and "metzotinto" (mezzotint) prints of his likeness. Whitefield began supplying Hutton with journal accounts of his travels and spiritual experiences, sending a copy of his journal and a packet of letters to England during the stop-over at Gibraltar. Whitefield intended eventually to make these journals public, but Thomas Cooper, a rival publisher who "clandestinely and treacherously" had gotten an early draft, printed the first version in August 1738, without Hutton's authorization. Hutton denounced Cooper for publishing the "surreptitious copy." Hutton soon made his own version available (which went through at least three editions by year's end), and apparently paid Cooper to destroy his original copy of the journal. Regardless of this controversial start, the journals would become the most important publications for Whitefield and his booming ministry. Much more than a recitation of autobiographical facts, each edition of the journals entertained readers with colorful details of his travels. Spiritually, they identified his own struggles with his readers' and gave them a model for a faithful (though hardly trouble-free) Christian life. The journals preached the gospel as much as his sermons did.[57]

In early March, the *Whitaker* left Gibraltar, and Whitefield soon fell ill with seasickness. He prayed that the malady would do him some spiritual good and "purge" his body. On board ship, and on two other vessels accompanying the *Whitaker*, Whitefield worked to reform the crass habits of soldiers and other passengers. He traded godly tomes for "bad books" and playing cards, which he promptly pitched overboard. He received requests to marry engaged couples, and Whitefield generally complied, regardless of the couple's spiritual seriousness.

But in one wedding, the groom behaved badly, snickering out loud as Whitefield read the liturgy. Whitefield slammed shut his Book of Common Prayer and glared at the man, who was probably drunk. The groom, worried that his boorish behavior had cost him and his betrothed their chance to be married at sea, began to cry. Whitefield grudgingly finished the ceremony, gave them a Bible, and told them to live in holiness together.[58]

Despite the trials of sea travel, the "beauty of the great deep" charmed the twenty-three-year-old. He saw a "shark about the length of a man" trailing the ship, and "a large grampus [probably a killer whale] rolling and spouting." The captain caught and butchered a porpoise. It had a "head much like a pig" and was about six feet long, Whitefield wrote. The passengers dined on its liver. These were the kinds of details one would have expected from popular travel journals of the period. The appeal of Whitefield's account was not exclusively religious.[59]

It is remarkable that Whitefield did not die on any of his trips across the Atlantic. Sickness and other dangers were ever present, and several passengers perished on the *Whitaker*'s voyage. Whitefield himself caught a fever in late April that nearly killed him. There was not much one could do for sick passengers—and they often did better if they received no care at all. Medical care was still based on the ancient assumption that illnesses represented imbalances of bodily "humors." In a typical treatment, the ship's doctor subjected the ailing Whitefield to bloodlettings three times, and blistering and vomiting once each. Whitefield saw the malady as a battle for his body and soul, in which he "had many violent conflicts with the powers of darkness . . . but Jesus Christ prayed for [him]." He came to the "last extremity" and felt that "Satan as it were had dominion" over him, but at the last moment God restored him. Taking the near-death experience as a sign, he reflected that "God is preparing me for something extraordinary."[60]

Whitefield's journals presented his many illnesses in a way that made him more accessible to audiences, many of whom struggled with similar maladies. Unlike John Wesley, Whitefield spent relatively little time exploring new treatments for illnesses or methods of preventative care. Wesley urgently recommended healthy habits and exercise to followers, insisting that their lives were at stake if they would not regularly engage in outdoor physical activity. He also prescribed a range of herbal remedies, including radish juice, garlic, and marigolds; onions and honey to cure baldness; and apples to keep insanity at bay. His *Primitive Physic* went through twenty-three editions during Wesley's career.[61]

Whitefield did not actively promote such treatments, viewing bodily ailments as providential tests or even as infernal assaults (as seen in his sense that Satan had nearly defeated him during his shipboard fever). God could always redeem disease, however, and even turn it into a catalyst for conversion, as he did for Whitefield at Oxford. After his new birth, ever-present sickness helped Whitefield keep a loose grip on the things of the world. As he presented it, illness was an agent of sanctification, for his followers as well as him. The devout kept the faith in the face of sickness. Doing so was a sign of a heart fully committed to God.[62]

Two months after sailing from Gibraltar, the *Whitaker* sighted land and the mouth of the Savannah River. Whitefield found Georgia's coast congenial. "America is not so horrid a place as it is represented," he wrote to a friend in England. The weather was not bad, he wrote. In another account, however, he confessed that the heat of the summer was nearly intolerable, "sometimes burning me almost through my shoes." He busied himself with ministerial duties, visiting house to house, catechizing, preaching, and reading liturgies from the Book of Common Prayer.[63]

Soon after arriving, Whitefield visited the ailing Creek Indian leader Tomochichi. He was known to Whitefield and other associates of the Georgia trustees, since Tomochichi had accompanied Oglethorpe on a promotional trip to England from 1734 to 1736. He even met with King George II and presented him with eagle feathers as a "sign of everlasting peace." The Creek chief repeatedly called for a closer alliance with English authorities and appealed for them to educate Creek youths in Christianity.[64]

Whitefield found Tomochichi in fragile health (he died the next year), and he depended on translators to speak with him. He pressed the leader about his eternal destination, should he die. Tomochichi said he believed he would go to heaven, but Whitefield was dubious. "How can a drunkard enter there?" Whitefield wrote. He told Tomochichi's nephew, their translator, "not to get drunk," and said that because he understood English, he would be held accountable for following the gospel of Christ. The nephew "would be punished the more, if he did not live better." The man indicated that he believed in heaven, but not hell. Whitefield observed "how natural it is to all mankind to believe there is a place of happiness," but "how averse they are to believe in a place of torment, because they wish it may not be so."[65]

Hell was on Whitefield's mind in those days. He had already preached a sermon on the topic in Gibraltar, and he delivered it again in Savannah. A Savannah parishioner had recently denied that the torments of hell were eternal, Whitefield discovered. It was a position that Whitefield regarded as "Antichristian." Certain Anglicans, including Archbishop John Tillotson

(1630–1694), had suggested the possibility of the annihilation of sinners in hell, rather than their perpetual agony. Whitefield would controversially highlight his disagreement with Tillotson on this point in 1740, citing it as one of the reasons he thought Tillotson "knew no more about true Christianity than Mahomet."[66]

Evangelicals believed in an eternal hell just as much as they believed in an eternal heaven. Pressed by new latitudinarian challenges to the traditional understanding of God's eternal wrath, preachers like Whitefield and Jonathan Edwards addressed the doctrines of judgment and hell more frequently and explicitly than some of their Reformed (Calvinist) predecessors. Edwards did so most famously in his revival sermon "Sinners in the Hands of an Angry God." To Edwards, God's mercy did not negate his justice. He thought it "unreasonable and unscriptural" to suggest that God was so gracious that he could not "bear that penal justice should be executed." God perfectly balanced judgment and grace, Edwards insisted.[67]

In spite of Edwards's running battle against Tillotson and other latitudinarians, his congregants knew that eternal damnation was only an occasional topic in his much larger theological corpus. Similarly, Whitefield's preaching did not inordinately focus on hell, but a belief in eternal torment undergirded his evangelistic preaching. Superb orator though he was, Whitefield thought that preachers needed "no great art of rhetoric to persuade any understanding person to avoid and abhor those sins, which without repentance will certainly plunge him into this eternal gulf." He admittedly found the topic of hell torments "melancholy," but—especially because Tillotson and others had undermined the doctrine—he felt compelled to warn people about the wrath of God and their path of escape through Christ.[68]

In the meantime, Whitefield began making plans to open an orphanage. The Georgia trustees had instructed Charles Wesley to look into this prospect, and orphanages fit easily into the Methodists' charitable vision. The Oxford Methodists were familiar with a large orphanage built by August Hermann Francke, a German Pietist pastor in Halle. (Whitefield, who had begun reading Francke's *Pietas Hallensis* [1705] in early 1736, commented that he hoped to imitate Francke in his own ministry.) He also visited Ebenezer, a Salzburg Lutheran settlement about twenty-five miles up the river, which had an orphanage housing seventeen children. The Salzburgers loved "Herr Whitefield's" preaching, especially his focus on justification by faith alone. They were also impressed that he did not speak from a written outline, but "from the abundance of the heart." Likewise impressed with the Lutherans' orphanage, Whitefield thought this was just the sort of project that Savannah needed. "What I have most at heart," he wrote, "is the building of an orphan-house, which I trust will be effected at my return to England."[69]

Anglo-American and Continental evangelicals made benevolent endeavors central to their work. These included mission societies, charity schools, and orphanages. But unlike more liberal humanitarians, who increasingly saw charity and service as the heart of Christian devotion, evangelicals maintained a conflicted view of good works. Works could not save, and the lost needed much more than a warm meal and a roof over their heads. Whitefield mused on this in his sermon "The Great Duty of Charity Recommended": "Our enemies say we deny all moral actions; but, blessed be God, they speak against us without cause . . . we highly value them; but we say, that faith in Christ, love of God, being born again, are of infinite more worth." However, he cautioned that "you cannot be true Christians without having charity to your fellow creatures." Benevolent works were among the fruits of true conversion, so making a Halle-style orphanage was an attractive project.[70]

Whitefield concluded in August that it was time to leave. Even before arriving in Savannah, the restless Whitefield had thoughts of recrossing the Atlantic. He knew that he needed to be ordained an Anglican priest, which would require a return to England. There were no bishops to ordain him in America. His decision to stay only three months caused some irritation among the Georgia trustees. One of them, Lord Egmont, spoke more than he knew when he said that the decision showed that Whitefield had a "roving temper."[71]

Whitefield gave his farewell sermon to Savannah before an overflow crowd. Supporters brought him gifts of food and drink—"wine, ale, cake, coffee, tea, and other things proper for my passage," he wrote. Making his way up the coast to Charleston, South Carolina, Whitefield found that city more established and sophisticated than Savannah. He met Charleston's Anglican commissary, Alexander Garden, a man he called "a good soldier of Jesus Christ," even though they would soon clash. Finally, he boarded the *Mary*, bound for England (the ship ended up going by way of Ireland, because of terrible delays and a resulting lack of supplies).[72]

Although he would spend relatively little time there, the Savannah orphanage became the center of Whitefield's philanthropic ministry. Evangelism was always the focus of his preaching, but he closely linked conversion with a life of holiness and benevolence. The Savannah orphanage provided a ready application for converts: having learned to trust Christ, they should act on their faith. One way to do this was by supporting the indigent children of Georgia. Fund-raising for Georgia also helped blunt some of the fierce criticism leveled against Whitefield. Who could argue with a man raising money for orphans? Whitefield wrote that Savannah, "the place I intended to hide myself in, became . . . a means of increasing that popularity which was already begun." He insisted that this happy conjunction of popularity and benevolence "was absolutely unforeseen, and as absolutely undesigned."[73]

As Whitefield sailed for England, he stood at the threshold of the kind of widespread celebrity only hinted at by his debut sermon two years earlier. Whitefield did not know the magnitude of what was coming, yet it was clear that Savannah would never become his permanent base. As he sailed east into the Atlantic, he wrote to his Savannah followers, reminding them of "that one thing needful [Luke 10:42], of that new birth in Christ Jesus, that ineffable change which must pass upon our hearts before we can see God." And to a friend in England, he wrote, "The seed of the glorious gospel has taken root in the American ground, and, I hope, will grow up into a great tree."[74]

4

"The Fiery Trial of Popularity": George Whitefield, Field Preacher

Whitefield's English friends prayed for him while he was in Georgia. At the Aldersgate meeting—the place where John Wesley's heart had been "strangely warmed" a month earlier—participants read out loud from the first installment of Whitefield's journal at a crowded service in June 1738. In August, the wildly popular journal of his journey to Savannah was printed. Finally, in December, newspapers published the stirring report: Whitefield was returning to England.[1]

But for the itinerant, this Atlantic crossing was nearly deadly. Unfavorable winds interminably slowed the voyage from Charleston. By November, supplies were running dangerously low, and passengers faced acute dehydration. The captain cut daily rations to a pint of water, a bit of salty beef, and flour cake. Whitefield suspected that the devil was delaying the ship, seeking to prevent his further ministry in England.[2] Withered and listless, he shivered on his bed, wrapped in a buffalo-skin blanket. The desperate captain diverted the ship to the west coast of Ireland, where they finally landed in mid-November. Whitefield believed that God had a purpose in putting him through the ordeal, humbling him in preparation for the "fiery trial of popularity."[3]

Rejuvenated by water, food, and rest, Whitefield traveled across Ireland, from Kilrush to Dublin, to gain passage to England. He found the poverty in Ireland appalling, with many peasants living in squalid thatch huts. But even more appalling to Whitefield was, as he perceived it, the people's ignorant "Romish profession." The Bible, which Whitefield called the "key of knowledge," had been translated into Irish in the seventeenth century, but the Catholic hierarchy frowned upon the vernacular edition, and it hardly penetrated Irish culture. Thus, to Whitefield, the Irish lacked the essential tool for religious reformation.[4]

Whitefield crossed the Irish Sea, landed in England, and arrived in London in early December 1738. Delighted to be back among Methodist friends, he concluded that the Lord had "greatly watered the seed sown" by his earlier ministry in the metropolis. The night of his arrival, he attended a "truly Christian society in Fetter Lane." In doing so, Whitefield entered into a meaningful, though temporary, alliance with the Moravians.[5]

The Moravians made a powerful imprint on Anglo-American evangelicals in the 1730s, not least because they helped precipitate John and Charles Wesley's conversions. Led by Peter Böhler, Moravians began meeting for prayer and spiritual accountability with Methodists at Fetter Lane in May 1738. The Moravians' role reminds us that eighteenth-century Anglo-American revivalism had broader, Continental roots. In 1722, Pietists from Moravia, seeking religious freedom, had migrated to the estate of Count Nikolaus Ludwig von Zinzendorf in Upper Lusatia, an area of Saxony, near Dresden. The community, called Herrnhut, experienced a quasi-Pentecostal awakening in 1727, which mobilized Moravian missionaries to seek out like-minded believers across Europe and in the American colonies. The Moravians combined fervent piety, intense missionary zeal, and an interdenominational sensibility, all of which matched Whitefield's convictions. London was the hub for the Moravians' international network, and they readily identified with the Methodist movement there.[6]

In April 1738, Böhler began working with James Hutton (Whitefield's publisher), speaking at a fellowship led by Hutton. (This in spite of the fact that Böhler knew almost no English.) As Böhler recalled, "The movement among the English grew and grew. They invited me here and there [and] asked me again and again to tell them something of the Savior." Soon he was addressing meetings of hundreds, with friends translating his combined German and Latin addresses into English. On May 1, the Methodists and Moravians formed a new society committed to prayer and mutual confession of sin. Böhler soon departed to continue his missionary work in America. Hutton then led the fellowship, which rented a room on Fetter Lane once it outgrew his print shop. The Wesley brothers attended frequently. By fall, the society had begun holding "love-feasts," gatherings with simple meals, singing, and testimonies of spiritual experiences.[7]

The week after his return to London, Whitefield turned twenty-four years old. He was entering a frenzied season of ministry. The excitement of his pre-Georgia preaching had weathered his absence. The London-based Methodists, along with the Moravians and larger crowds of admirers, composed a volatile mass eager for revival. Whitefield saw the unfolding awakening as a work of the Holy Spirit. He continued writing of a "feeling possession of the Holy Spirit," a divine presence residing in his body and bringing guidance, comfort, and courage. The "Holy Spirit makes me do things," he wrote. He was certain that the Holy Spirit had moved powerfully not just in the gospels or the book of Acts, but that he was "the common privilege and portion of all believers in all ages."[8]

Within days of the itinerant's return, overflowing crowds pressed into London churches, and scores made professions of new faith in Christ. Whitefield viewed these scenes through biblical lenses. His preaching was blessed, he wrote, "with great demonstration of the Spirit, and with power," echoing the Apostle Paul's words to the church of Corinth in 1 Corinthians 2:4. Some who had been converted a year earlier under Whitefield had become influential laypeople or ministers themselves, partly through the training supplied by his "dear friends and fellow-labourers, John and Charles Wesley." God was pouring out the Holy Spirit on London, Whitefield concluded, mindful of Old Testament promises such as Isaiah 44:3, "I will pour my spirit upon thy seed, and my blessing upon thine offspring," and Joel 2:28, "It shall come to pass afterward, that I will pour out my spirit upon all flesh."[9]

God was also pouring out the Spirit at Fetter Lane. On Christmas Eve 1738, Whitefield stayed at Fetter Lane until four in the morning, "in prayer, psalms, and thanksgiving, with many truly Christian brethren"; he added, "God gave me a great spirit of supplication [prayer]. Adored be his free grace in Christ Jesus." He did not go to bed, but instead visited another society early on Christmas morning, preaching in a sultry room packed with hundreds of people. That day he preached again three more times.[10]

On the night of New Year's Day 1739, the Methodists and Moravians had a wondrous love-feast at Fetter Lane that reached unprecedented fervor. John Wesley recorded: "The power of God came mightily upon us, insomuch that many cried out for exceeding joy, and many fell to the ground." The assembly "broke out with one voice, 'We praise thee, O God; we acknowledge thee to be the Lord.'" God sustained Whitefield as he stayed up all night again. "It was a Pentecost season indeed," he recalled. "Often have we been filled as with new wine," with people crying out "Will God, indeed, dwell with men upon the earth! [2 Chronicles 6:18] How dreadful is this place! This is no other than the house of God, and the gate of heaven! [Genesis 28:17]."[11]

The Methodists found both ancient and modern sources for this revivalistic zeal. The book of Acts is filled with scenes similar to what the Methodists were experiencing. Moreover, the Wesleys and Whitefield had heard of other recent accounts of revival. The most immediate sources were their Moravian contacts, who had seen similar awakenings on the Continent, particularly during the 1727 revival at Herrnhut. John Wesley visited Herrnhut in mid-1738, where they assured him that the abiding "indwelling of the Holy Ghost" and "full assurance of faith" were available to believers today.[12]

Wesley had also read Jonathan Edwards's account of the remarkable revival of 1734–35 in Northampton, Massachusetts, which was published in two London editions in the late 1730s by two prominent English evangelicals, John Guyse and the hymn writer Isaac Watts. Edwards's account, which established his international fame—and which continues to be the most influential revival narrative in modern Christian history—recorded how almost everyone in the frontier town developed a "deep concern about their eternal salvation."[13]

A number of émigré French Protestants in London, especially a group called the "French Prophets," had also begun to explore the kinds of spiritual experiences described in Acts. Charles Wesley had recently met an Englishman, Isaac Hollis, who had been influenced by the French Prophets. Wesley was once staying the night at Hollis's home, where he received an unpleasant introduction to Hollis's charismatic proclivities. While they were preparing to retire for the night—as was typical when hosting guests in a small house, Wesley and his host were occupying the same bed—Hollis "fell into violent agitations," Wesley wrote, "and gobbled like a turkey-cock." Hollis was speaking in tongues. Wesley thought Hollis was suffering from demonic possession. The Methodist faced down the infernal force by quoting Jesus in the Gospel of Mark, who had rebuked a disease-causing demon by saying, "Thou dumb and deaf spirit, I charge thee, come out of him, and enter no more." Hollis soon recovered from his fit of inspiration. Then the two awkwardly proceeded to bed, with Wesley "not half liking [his] bedfellow."[14]

The new evangelical movement was emerging simultaneously across America, Wales, Scotland, England, and the Continent. So striking was this simultaneity that many Christians saw the hand of God's providence behind the growing awakening. An example of the remarkable coincidence of similar spiritual experiences was the conversions of Whitefield and Howell Harris of Wales. Even as Whitefield endured his Lenten travail of 1735, Harris went through a comparable ordeal in the village of Trevecka, about sixty miles west of Gloucester. Harris was a twenty-one-year-old schoolteacher, rather uninterested in spiritual matters until his parish pastor recommended Richard Allestree's classic *The Whole Duty of Man* (1658). In May 1735, at a communion service, Harris received salvation: "I was convinced by the Holy Ghost," he wrote, "that Christ died for me, and that all my sins were laid on him."[15]

The convert began to visit house to house, and village to village, proclaiming the message of God's grace to sinners. He immediately ran afoul of Anglican authorities, who cautioned him that laypeople had no authority to offer religious instruction beyond their own home and family. Harris prayed and received spiritual confirmation that his ministry was legitimate, and he resolved to proceed in the face of opposition, "not fearing," he wrote, "to have my guts torn in pieces, entirely relying on God for my qualification." In spite of the criticism he received, he wanted to stay within the Anglican Church as long as he could, seeking to reform the church from within.[16]

The Welsh revival surged in late 1737 through the preaching of Harris and his colleagues Howel Davies, Griffith Jones, and Daniel Rowland. (The latter two were Anglican ministers.) Refusing to heed Anglican warnings, Harris continued to itinerate, and also began the unusual tactic of preaching in the open air. Sometimes he did this at fairs, but at other times he preached impromptu in fields in order to accommodate the teeming crowds rallying to his sermons.[17]

Harris's innovative style and his Calvinist convictions drew Whitefield's attention. Like the Moravians, Whitefield wished to reach out beyond his immediate sphere of influence to strengthen the new evangelical network. In December 1738, Whitefield wrote to Harris. Encouraging him to keep preaching in spite of opposition, Whitefield reported that there was a "great pouring out of the Spirit, at London." Whitefield implored Harris to write him back, asking why they should not "tell one another, what God has done, for our souls."[18]

Harris was delighted and flattered when he received Whitefield's letter. Harris immediately replied and said that he had already read Whitefield's journal, which had suffused his soul with "uncommon influences of the divine presence." He was thrilled to hear of the London revival and returned news of awakenings in Wales, including a "great reformation in Cardiganshire through one Mr. Daniel Rowland." Harris hoped that Whitefield would soon visit Wales. Whitefield, although a year younger than Harris, had surpassed him in fame. But Whitefield did not necessarily see—or admit—this fact; he soon wrote to another correspondent that Harris "outstrips" him. "May I follow him, as he does Jesus Christ," Whitefield prayed.[19]

Whitefield also corresponded with Philip Doddridge, the influential Dissenting minister of Northampton, in central England. They exchanged letters at the same time that Whitefield and Harris did. Clearly, Whitefield had planned to contact these pastors as soon as he returned from Georgia. (Doddridge and Whitefield had become aware of each other's ministries at least two years earlier.) Doddridge had the same idea, since he composed a letter to Whitefield in mid-December 1738, but unexpectedly received one from Whitefield before he sent it. The irenic Doddridge believed in the religion of a converted heart, and that priority led him, like Whitefield, to de-emphasize denominational boundaries. Like Harris, Doddridge had read Whitefield's journals, which had "not a little comforted and edified" him. He prayed that the Methodists would renew the Church of England, since he loved that church, "notwithstanding our dissent."[20]

Whitefield would meet Harris and Doddridge in due course, but in the meantime he pursued the final step into priesthood. The Georgia trustees officially appointed him minister to the colony in December, and he traveled to Oxford in January 1739 to receive ordination. He and other assembled candidates went through the rituals confirming their readiness for pastoral ministry, but Whitefield "secretly prayed" for some of them, wondering whether they were all really converted believers with their "names written in the Book of Life."[21]

On Sunday, January 14, came the moment Whitefield had been waiting for since he went to Oxford: his entrance into the priesthood. It was a "day of fat things," Whitefield wrote. The service took place at Oxford's Christ Church Cathedral, a small, elegant twelfth-century sanctuary. As in his ordination as deacon, the bishop laid hands on the kneeling Whitefield, prayed for him to receive the Holy Ghost and to be a "faithful dispenser of the Word of God, and of his holy Sacraments."[22]

In spite of his surging popularity and ordination as priest, not all was well for Whitefield. His celebrity and penchant for controversy drew critics. One early anti-Whitefield tract, *Remarks on the Reverend Mr. Whitefield's Journal*, accused him of basing his faith on "perturbations of mind, possessions of God, ecstatic flights, and supernatural impulses." This would become the most enduring line of attack on Whitefield as some began suggesting that he was a fanatic and an "enthusiast."[23]

Another early opposition piece, *A Letter to the Rev. Mr. Whitefield*, written by the Anglican curate Tristram Land, showed that some of Whitefield's fellow priests were stung by the Methodists' criticisms of the established church. Land warned against "these young quacks in divinity, who are running about the city and taking great pains to distract the common-people, breaking the peace and unity of our excellent church." He suggested that the Methodists' were unwittingly serving the devil. The great spiritual enemy wished to turn people into enthusiasts, whose brief seasons of frenzy would eventually lead to burnout and disillusionment with Christianity.[24]

One might think that the disagreement between Anglicans such as Land and Whitefield was primarily about power in the church, and power was certainly a factor. But Land and Whitefield also had basic theological disagreements about the nature of salvation, the new birth, and regeneration. Land argued that Whitefield, in teaching that the new birth was an experience subsequent to baptism, was contradicting the baptismal liturgy in the Book of Common Prayer. In that ritual, the priest was to thank God (after sprinkling the child) for regenerating the infant by the Holy Spirit. Thus, to Land, those baptized in the church had already been regenerated and born again, and there was no need for them to be "born again a second time." The bishop of London likewise said that Whitefield's notion that the new birth must be "instantaneous, and inwardly felt" was not biblical. Whitefield strictly differentiated between infant baptism with water and the subsequent baptism with the Holy Spirit that accompanied salvation. "Many are baptized with water" as infants, he said, "which were never, effectually at least, baptized with the Holy Ghost." True spiritual baptism, to him, was not external washing, but internal transformation by the Holy Spirit.[25]

Whitefield read a tract written against him, probably Land's, the day after his ordination. The criticism wounded him, but he wrote in his journal that he had found strength to pray for the author. The next day, Whitefield prayed for Land publicly. He was coming to realize that his popularity would necessarily generate disapproval. But controversy also meant more popularity, and a bigger audience for the gospel.[26]

Whitefield went out of his way to show Tristram Land that he harbored no ill will toward him. The Sunday following his ordination, he attended Land's church, the Christopher Wren–built St. James Garlickhythe, in London, and received communion from Land himself. Whitefield subsequently wrote in his published journal that he loved Land and believed that the priest had a "zeal for God, though, in my opinion, not according to knowledge." Land apparently did not think much of this sentiment, for he wrote a second, even angrier letter against Whitefield in 1741.[27]

Whitefield and John Wesley held an important meeting with a group of their Anglican critics in late January 1739. Whitefield tried to explain the new birth to them theologically and told them about his conversion experience. Disappointed with their reaction, he said that they viewed him as a "madman." Whitefield may have at first hoped to convince some Anglican authorities to support the revivals, but after the meeting he concluded, "There is a fundamental difference between us and them." They had divergent understandings of regeneration, but more importantly, Whitefield believed, many of his opponents had no *experience* of regeneration: "They believe only [in] an outward Christ, we further believe that he must be inwardly formed in our hearts also." Expecting that many pastors and bishops would oppose him, Whitefield took their hostility as a sign that they had never personally tasted the grace and power of God.[28]

Even as Whitefield wrestled with growing opposition, large crowds appeared wherever he preached. And he preached often: on the afternoon and evening of the Sunday he attended Land's church, Whitefield spoke four times. At one of those assemblies, he estimated that almost a thousand souls pressed into the churchyard.[29]

He wrote later that this meeting was the moment at which he began to contemplate "preaching without doors" as a normal part of his ministry. Outdoor preaching would allow Whitefield to accommodate many more listeners than would fit in the limited confines of most sanctuaries. It would also allow him to preach in places where he was banned from the pulpit. It is not clear how many ministers had refused him because of opposition to his teaching. Some may simply have hesitated to open the church to the young priest, wishing to avoid needless controversy.[30]

In addition to preaching in the open air, he now began speaking without notes. Whitefield had given extemporary addresses before, practicing the method even before his first public sermon. But now he began to do so routinely, by design. Often-repeated, memorized sermons were essential components of his mature preaching. As he gained experience, he could also respond on the fly to an audience's mood. Sometimes he did not know what he would say until he ascended the field scaffold. He picked texts and biblical stories based on the feel of the moment and matched his remarks to the crowd's emotions.[31]

By all accounts, Whitefield was a passionate preacher, pleading with audiences to respond to the gospel. He regularly shed tears, and there is no compelling reason to see such tears as inauthentic or simply theatrical. Whitefield was utterly certain about the Christian gospel, the delights of divine grace, and the horrors of divine judgment: these truths understandably elicited strong feelings. But his emotions also flowed from his conviction that true religion—and excellent public speaking—engaged the heart, not just the head. You could go to any number of parishes in England and hear dry recitations of traditional doctrine. His background in the theater, the dramatic setting of the field sermon, and the freedom of the extemporaneous mode helped the young preacher shake people out of complacency.[32]

Whitefield was also a physically striking man, which helped fuel his popularity. Most of the surviving portraits of Whitefield show an older, genteel pastor who is balding and overweight. But in 1739 he was twenty-four and regarded as quite attractive (see figure 4.1). Some described him as angelic. Portraits usually depicted his crossed eyes too, and some caricatures ridiculously exaggerated them. (Later Whitefield would receive the epithet "Dr. Squintum.") He developed this ocular ailment during a childhood illness. In eighteenth-century British culture, however, some regarded crossed eyes as a sign of mystical power.[33]

Whitefield's surging popularity not only provoked criticism in print, but also sometimes precipitated altercations, such as a February 1739 incident at St. Margaret's Church, Westminster. (St. Margaret's is the parish church of the British House of Commons. A number of famous people are buried there, including Sir Walter Raleigh, who was beheaded in 1618 after running afoul of King James I.) No one at St. Margaret's that day seemed to know whether Whitefield had permission to preach. He almost left the building, but then a man he assumed was the parish officer or warden took him to the pulpit, where he proceeded with the sermon. A hostile account in the *Weekly Miscellany*, however, claimed that Whitefield's supporters had locked in a pew a minister who was scheduled to preach, and had had several strapping "lusty fellows" stand guard while Whitefield spoke. This seems unlikely—Whitefield called the charges lies—but he may not have taken every step possible to defuse a volatile situation.[34]

Shortly after the St. Margaret's incident, Whitefield set out for a tour of western England, including Bristol. During this period, Whitefield was raising money for Georgia and his proposed orphan house, which was the chief justification for his itinerant preaching. His controversial reputation followed him from London, with hecklers appearing nearly everywhere he spoke. In Basingstoke, southwest of London, people tried to shout him down. Some even pelted the church windows with stones.[35]

Whitefield's letters make clear that he found this open hostility both troubling and bracing. As usual, he filtered the experience through scripture, writing, "Wherever I go, many indeed wait for my halting and shoot out their arrows, even bitter words [Psalm 64:3], but I know in whom I have believed [2 Timothy 1:12] and am persuaded that neither death nor life, principalities nor powers, shall ever be able to separate me from the love of God, which is in Christ Jesus, my Lord [Romans 8:38]." Whitefield gave no chapter-and-verse references in this letter—he had so deeply internalized the scriptures, and so ingrained were they in the surrounding culture of English rhetoric, that verses flowed naturally from his pen.[36] The young minister seemed to feed off the attacks. An Anglican minister reportedly told one of Whitefield's friends that the "Devil in hell" was in the Methodists, and that Whitefield had set England ablaze with the devil's flames. Whitefield countered: "It is not a fire of the Devil's kindling, but a holy fire that has proceeded from the Holy and Blessed

Spirit. Oh, that such a fire may not only be kindled, but blow up into a flame all England, and all the world over!"[37]

Whitefield needed this kind of resolve. From Bath to Bristol, Whitefield found more priests and officials unwilling to open their churches to him. But he was prepared to preach in alternative locations. For several days, following the traditional Methodist practice, he preached at Bristol's notorious Newgate prison. John Wesley would later campaign for reform at the whitewashed jail, which one critic called "white without and foul within." Prisoners were packed into a basement dungeon there, sleeping in "putrid hotbeds of disease." Whitefield did not comment on the abuses at Newgate (he was likely aware of the jail's reputation from his childhood), but he was pleased with the results of his preaching, hoping that the "power of the Lord was present" to awaken some of the destitute prisoners to Christ.[38]

Greater preaching opportunities lay in the fields, however, so Whitefield went to the coal-mining district of Kingswood, just east of Bristol. The coal mines fueled England's early industrial revolution, with thousands of men, women, and children—"colliers," as they were called—toiling in the coal pits. Residents of towns like Bristol viewed the coal miners with suspicion, sometimes for good reason. In 1753, the Kingswood colliers were so enraged by soaring grain prices that two thousand of them marched under colors into Bristol, demanding relief. When none was forthcoming, they broke windows at Bristol's council house and occupied the city. A military detachment sent from Gloucester forced them out of Bristol a week later, but not before they took thirty captives in hopes of a prisoner exchange.[39]

The typical collier in eighteenth-century Britain earned relatively high wages, but only because, as the Scottish philosopher Adam Smith wrote, of the "hardship, disagreeableness and dirtiness of his work." Their diet consisted mainly of beer, tea, bread, and cheese, with meat a luxury that was enjoyed maybe once a week. The Church of England had never opened a parish church in Kingswood, leaving the devout with few options other than a lengthy trip into Bristol. For Whitefield, the colliers seemed like an attractive, untapped audience. (Methodism generally thrived in mining villages, where rapid growth drew in rootless folks and disrupted traditional parish organization.) "My bowels have long since yearned toward the poor colliers, who, as far as I can find, are very numerous and as sheep having no shepherd," he wrote.[40]

Upon arrival, Whitefield and William Seward went to the pits, calling the miners "out of their dens and holes in the earth." Then he ascended a nearby hill and spoke to about two hundred curious onlookers. "Blessed be God that I have now broken the ice!" he wrote in his journal. To a Methodist friend, he wrote, with a touch of amusement, "Where do you think I have been preaching? Upon a mount at Kingswood." Whitefield considered the setting reminiscent of that of the Sermon on the Mount: Christ "had a mountain for his pulpit, and the heavens for his sounding board; and who, when his Gospel was refused by the Jews, sent his servants into the highways and hedges."[41]

Repeatedly returning to Kingswood, Whitefield preached to crowds that were exponentially larger at each appearance. In late February, he spoke to a crowd he estimated, "at a moderate computation," to be about ten thousand people. Onlookers climbed trees (like Zaccheus in Luke 19) to see and hear him. He recorded in his journal: "All was hush when I began; the sun shone bright, and God enabled me to preach for an hour with great power." He spoke as loud as he could, projecting his voice as taught by his acting instructors in Gloucester. All could hear him; many responded. Whitefield saw some faces with "white gutters made by their tears, which plentifully fell down their black cheeks, as they came out of their coal pits." His critics spoke right, Whitefield decided: "The fire is kindled in the country; and, I know, all the devils in hell shall not be able to quench it."[42]

Crowd estimates that ran into the tens of thousands drew almost immediate criticism as gross exaggerations. Whitefield's publicist, Seward, had previously not tried to estimate crowds in newspaper reports, but now demanded that printers include them, chastising James Hutton for not publishing "the success of the Gospel here in the papers" and admonishing him: "Pray put in the 10,000 and the 15,000." Seward presumably believed that these were reasonably accurate numbers, and he told Hutton that if they did not report the astounding figures, "the stones will cry out against us." The crowd counts, to them, demonstrated the remarkable blessing of God on Whitefield's ministry. By May 1739, specific numbers began to appear in the newspapers, and Whitefield included them in new editions of his journals.[43]

The itinerant found field preaching exhilarating and liberating: "The open firmament above me . . . with the sight of thousands and thousands, some in coaches, some on horseback, and some in the trees, and at times all affected and drenched in tears together . . . was almost too much for, and quite overcame me." Neither parish boundaries nor church buildings, neither traditions nor pastoral recalcitrance, confined him. Using a saying often attributed exclusively to John Wesley, Whitefield wrote: "The whole world is now my parish. 'Tis equal to me whether I preach in field or in a church."[44]

Still, Anglican officials tried to corral the brash preacher. The chancellor of Bristol virtually banned him from the diocese and prohibited him from preaching in private meetings too. Whitefield asked why; the chancellor replied that he taught "false doctrine." He threatened Whitefield with excommunication should he continue his unlicensed preaching in Bristol. That evening, as was his practice, Whitefield prayed publicly for the chancellor, and the congregation "said most earnest amens to all the petitions I put up for him."[45] Whitefield also wrote to the chancellor's superior, Bishop Joseph Butler of Bristol. Butler was one of the Church of England's most influential apologists against Deism; his best-known book was *The Analogy of Religion* (1736). Butler's reply to the itinerant offered some encouragement, but when Whitefield showed the bishop's letter to the chancellor, the chancellor chastised him again and sent him away. So Whitefield wrote back to Butler, assuring him that he desired only to promote the glory of God. Whitefield again compared his trials to Christ's: "My Master was long since spoken evil of before me."[46]

His followers saw the controversy the same way. One concluded that Whitefield was preaching true "evangelical principles in an age swallowed-up so much by apostasy." Doing so provoked "the old serpent," the devil, and now the devil's "baleful eyes send forth a hellish glare and a wrathful hiss is heard." Both sides in the growing rift over Whitefield's ministry accused the other of succumbing to demonic influence. This kind of talk made reconciliation unlikely.[47] Indeed, Whitefield and his friends routinely used the rhetoric of "spiritual warfare," as William Seward put it. They understood his successes, and the opposition to his ministry, in terms that would be readily familiar to many charismatic or Pentecostal Christians today. Seward wrote of their "common cause of pulling down the kingdom of darkness" and advancing Christ's kingdom. Whitefield reported to a correspondent that as he preached in Wales and England, upon coming to the entrance of any town, "I said I came in the name of King Jesus, and if the Devil would not surrender, I should by the sword of the spirit . . . pull down his strongholds." He said that seeing so many repenting and believing reminded him of nothing so much as "Joshua passing on from city to city to destroy the devoted Canaanites."[48]

Fulfilling the request of Howell Harris, Whitefield left Bristol and took a ferry across the Severn estuary to Cardiff, Wales. There he met Harris face-to-face. They instantly warmed to one another and stayed up late talking and praying. He and Harris, Whitefield wrote, "joined hands and hearts and were so loving that I believe Satan envied us, but by the help of God, we intend to make his kingdom shake." Seward marveled that Harris routinely preached two-, three-, or four-hour sermons, sometimes going all night long. Here was a true collaborator for Whitefield.[49]

Antagonism toward Whitefield and Harris was growing, and sometimes opponents adopted clever means to disrupt their sermons. Denied the Anglican pulpit in Cardiff, Whitefield began preaching at the town hall, where Seward had a connection. Whitefield spoke from the judge's bench in the hall court-room. During one of these sermons, Whitefield noted with amusement, "Somebody did me the honor of getting a dead fox and hunting him with the hounds all round the hall," hoping that the dogs' howls would drown out the evangelist. But Whitefield pressed on, shouting above the din. That night "there was such a prodigious power that all were melted into floods of tears by the love of Jesus Christ."[50]

Whitefield could have easily stayed longer in the Bristol area. He enjoyed a response there surpassing even that in London. He was near new friends in Wales, as well as home and family. But he intended to go back to America as soon as possible. Whitefield was already assuming the true itinerant mode: preaching in one place for a time, but always leaving follow-up and consolida-tion to pastors in longer-term residence. By March 1739, Whitefield had begun to urge John Wesley to come to Bristol, and especially to Kingswood, where "there is a glorious door opened among the colliers." "You must come," Whitefield told Wesley, "and water what God has enabled me to plant."[51]

Whitefield's relationship with Wesley was changing. Wesley was still enjoying great successes in his own ministry, but Whitefield had clearly surpassed him in popularity. Even though Whitefield still called himself Wesley's "son," he was adopting a more assertive stance, and even treating Wesley as something of a lieutenant. Though Wesley was interested in following up the work in Bristol, he was a bit annoyed by Whitefield's newfound independence.[52]

Later that month, Wesley rebuked Whitefield for recruiting William Seward and John Cennick to work for him without formally securing the permission of other Methodists. Speaking to Whitefield as a co-leader of the movement, Wesley chided him, "Is it well for you or me to give the least hint of setting up our will or judgment against that of our whole society?" But Wesley insisted that he meant only to address a concern he had; he did not wish to break off their friendship.[53]

Confronting a brother's sin was a Methodist hallmark, and Whitefield received Wesley's correction. He meekly thanked Wesley for the "kind rebuke." Moving past that topic, he asked Wesley again to come to Bristol. (Wesley wrote that he asked "in the most pressing manner.") Could Wesley arrive by "the latter end of next week," before Whitefield left town? In a follow-up letter, he told Wesley that a Bristol newspaper had already announced Wesley's imminent arrival.[54]

Wesley cast lots and opened a Bible to random passages, but these efforts did not settle his mind about going to Bristol. The lot and the Bible did not give the same advice. The Bible passages frightened him: they repeatedly indicated that his life would be in jeopardy if he went. Nevertheless, he decided to go to Bristol.[55] Upon arrival, Wesley began to realize what a sensation "dear brother" Whitefield's preaching had created. That Sunday morning, Whitefield preached at a bowling green to a crowd, according to Wesley's estimate, of up to seven thousand. At noon he preached to the same-sized audience in Kingswood; at five, Whitefield drew a titanic throng of thirty thousand to a mount at Rose Green. The next day, the itinerant left Bristol. "I have seen none like him," wrote the flabbergasted Wesley.[56]

Before Whitefield departed, he proclaimed that Wesley would give his inaugural open-air sermon the next day. He sought to smooth the way for Wesley as best he could, telling supporters in the modified words of John the Baptist that "there was one coming after him whose shoe laces he was not worthy to unloose." It is not clear whether Whitefield had gotten Wesley's permission to make the announcement, for Wesley remained uneasy at the prospect, writing frankly, "I could scarce reconcile myself to this strange way of preaching in the fields, of which he [Whitefield] set me an example on Sunday, having been all my life (till very lately) so tenacious of every point relating to decency and order that I should have thought the saving of souls almost a sin if it had not been done in a church."[57] Wesley broke through his reluctance to "be more vile," as he put it, and on April 2 he spoke at a local brickyard to about three thousand people. He spoke on Luke 4:18–19, "The Spirit of the Lord is upon me, because he hath anointed me to preach the gospel to the poor." But he complained to Hutton that his clerical robes had not yet arrived with his luggage. "I want my gown and cassock every day," he said. Preaching outdoors was one thing, but he did not intend to give up all sense of propriety.[58]

Not all of Whitefield's followers were happy with his replacement. Wesley could not match Whitefield's preaching brilliance, and some had already begun to balk at Wesley's Arminian doctrine, which held that all people had free will to accept Christ's offer of salvation or to refuse it. A woman identified as "Jenny, a servant maid at Bristol," knew Whitefield's sister, Elizabeth Greville, who was going through her own conversion travail and being counseled by John Wesley. Jenny wrote a remarkable letter to Whitefield with concern about his sister's struggle to accept Christ. This letter not only gives us an all too rare perspective of an evangelical woman of modest background, but also reveals growing discontent with Wesley's anti-Calvinist theology, a discontent that would eventually help precipitate Wesley and Whitefield's split.[59]

Jenny noted that belief in the eternal security of a Christian believer (meaning that once saved, a person cannot lose his or her salvation) was "very great encouragement" to new believers. But Wesley taught against the doctrine. He told people that "the best may finally fall away." Apparently, Jenny personally confronted Wesley with her objections, telling him that "God's promises were as firm as his throne."[60] She objected also to Wesley's notion that everyone could be saved. He taught that instead of Christ dying just for the elect, "all the world is elected alike." Wesley had debuted this teaching, after some hesitation and prayer, on April 26, 1739. The confrontation with Jenny almost certainly happened on the day she wrote the letter, when Wesley wrote of meeting a woman who opposed the notion that "God 'willeth *all men* to be saved'" (I Timothy 2:4). Wesley jotted "Jenny Worlock comforted" in his personal diary for the date; this must be the Jenny of the letter to Whitefield, but she was hardly "comforted." Instead, she assured Whitefield that she would countenance no theological error from Wesley or anyone else, and that she would "dash out the brains of [the devil's] Babylonish brats against the stones."[61]

Before his return to London, Whitefield preached in Wales, Gloucester, and Oxford. In Gloucester, he learned of rumors circulating that he had gone entirely mad, that he claimed to be the Holy Ghost himself, and that he had "walked bareheaded through Bristol streets singing psalms." Whitefield certainly had not claimed to be the Holy Spirit, but he did emphasize the distinction between those who had received the Spirit, and those who had not. At one meeting, he observed, "Some were so filled with the Holy Ghost, that they were almost unable to support themselves under it. This, I know, is foolishness to the natural and letter-learned men." William Seward told a Methodist friend that "Brother Whitefield has had joy in the Holy Ghost without intermission for three years."[62]

Whitefield's emphasis on the indwelling Holy Spirit alienated some potential allies. For example, Bishop Joseph Butler became increasingly uncomfortable with what he heard about the Methodists' ministry, and in August 1739 he met with John Wesley and upbraided him for enthusiastic excesses. He singled out Whitefield in particular: "Mr. Whitefield says in his *Journal* [for February 11, 1739], 'There are promises still to be fulfilled in me.' Sir, the pretending to extraordinary revelations and gifts of the Holy Ghost is a horrid thing, a very horrid thing." Wesley told the bishop that he was not responsible for what Whitefield said, and insisted that, for his part, he claimed "no extraordinary revelations or gifts of the Holy Ghost."[63]

At the same time, the Dissenting pastor and celebrated hymn writer Isaac Watts of Stoke Newington, a neighborhood in London, wrote to the bishop of London, Edmund Gibson, expressing similar concerns about Whitefield's claims of special revelations from the Holy Spirit. In personal conversation, Whitefield had confirmed to Watts that he occasionally received impressions in his mind—thoughts or messages, often in response to prayer—that, he knew with certainty, came from God. Watts warned him against the "danger of delusion."[64]

Moderate evangelical leaders such as Watts rejoiced as great numbers of new converts came to believe in Christ for salvation, but they hesitated as Whitefield, Seward, and others emphasized the Holy Spirit's operations in the modern age. Most Protestant theologians believed that miracles and special revelations had "long since ceased," as Bishop Gibson put it in a pastoral letter against Whitefield, with the end of the time of Christ's apostles and the assembling of the New Testament canon. Miracles and revelations, such as those seen in the book of Acts, verified Christ's messianic claims, and special revelation was needed in the absence of a codified New Testament. But for many Protestants, contemporary claims of revelations from the Spirit were symptoms of enthusiastic madness or, worse, part of the deceitful repertoire of the Roman Catholic Church, which routinely reported healing miracles and divine signs such as bleeding icons. Most Protestants wished to confine the Spirit's operations to those available to all believers, such as comfort, encouragement, and conviction of sin. But early Methodists became convinced that astonishing operations of the Spirit had not ceased. In both John Wesley's and Whitefield's published journals, works of the Spirit seemed to confirm the authenticity of the new Methodist ministry. Whitefield had not yet determined, however, how to distinguish between the promptings of the Spirit and the workings of the flesh. Watts, Gibson, and other critics saw the risks that came from focusing on the gifts of the Spirit, especially the dangers of spiritual arrogance and deception. In 1739, Whitefield saw the Spirit's work as the means to break out of the churches' spiritual lethargy.[65]

Nevertheless, Whitefield had his limits regarding evidence of the Spirit. Sometimes John Wesley and other Methodists tested those limits. Wesley was more open than Whitefield to the extreme manifestations of the Holy Ghost, such as those seen among the French Prophets. Wesley regularly witnessed people thrown into violent convulsions, and some who exhibited signs of demonic possession. In May 1739, Wesley reported that an unconverted man was reading one of his sermons, and upon "reading the last page he changed color, fell off his chair, and began screaming terribly and beating himself against the ground." When Wesley came to visit the man, others were pinning him to the ground. The man fixed his eyes on Wesley and seemingly began casting demons out of himself, roaring out, "O thou devil! Thou cursed devil! Yea, thou legion of devils! Thou canst not stay. Christ will cast thee out." The penitent flailed against the floor, sweating profusely, and Wesley and his followers surrounded him, praying until he calmed down and his "body and soul were set at liberty." Whitefield cautioned John against encouraging such excessive displays. Doing so would give credence to the radical charismatics in their midst and would make new converts "depend on visions, convulsions, etc., more than on the promises and precepts of the gospel."[66]

Whitefield also became more circumspect about claiming inspiration from the Holy Spirit as Anglican authorities began criticizing him in mid-1739. In Whitefield's response to Edmund Gibson's pastoral letter, he explicitly denied that he had experienced any "extraordinary operations of working miracles, or of speaking with tongues." In a letter registering concerns about the Moravians' activities at the Fetter Lane Society, he noted dubiously, "I hear there is a woman among you, who pretends to the spirit of prophecy." He encouraged them to follow the counsel of scripture and "try the spirits," because he feared that the "devil is beginning to mimic God's work." Similarly, the itinerant had heard that some of the Moravians expected a resumption of the power to work miracles reminiscent of those seen in the book of Acts. What need did the church have of spectacular miracles such as bodily healings, he asked, "when we see greater miracles every day," most notably spiritual healings in salvation? Nevertheless, Whitefield maintained that any true Christian should expect "to feel and discern" the work of the Spirit living within, just as Whitefield himself felt the Spirit moving. He did not let the charge of enthusiasm dissuade him, for he believed that "every Christian, in the proper sense of the word, must be an enthusiast—that is, must be inspired of God, or have God in him."[67]

When Whitefield returned to London in late April 1739, eager crowds waited to hear him. In one case, some "Arch Wags" falsely advertised his return and first preaching engagement, drawing a disappointed group of hundreds. The skeptical *Country Journal* concluded that "Mr. Whitefield has many fools." Nevertheless, Whitefield was coming back to the metropolis, where he intended to implement what he called the "mad trick" of field preaching. When he was banned from preaching at one of the churches on his usual London circuit, St. Mary's Islington, Whitefield took it as confirmation that he should "go out into the highways and hedges, and compel harlots, publicans, and sinners to come in, that my Master's house may be filled" (Luke 14:23). He began preaching regularly in two open-air locations: Moorfields, an eighteen-acre park near the Fetter Lane meetinghouse, and Kennington Common, a twenty-acre open area south of the Thames, where the city kept a permanent scaffold used for executions. Anti-Methodist writings highlighted Kennington's macabre setting: one print pictured Whitefield preaching with bodies hanging from the Kennington gallows in the foreground and a whiskey seller hawking his goods underneath. A ditty printed in the *Daily Post* put it this way: "And if his frantick sermons miss their aim, / It's hoped the gallows will their lives reclaim." Whitefield often spoke at Moorfields on Sunday mornings and at Kennington Common on Wednesday evenings, reporting crowds in the tens of thousands.[68]

Whitefield was an extraordinarily creative religious entrepreneur, leading critics to label him a huckster or a "pedlar in divinity," as the historian Frank Lambert has noted. Whitefield became the first celebrity pastor of the modern era, which raised questions—as it has for his many successors—about the line separating marketing from piety. Whitefield might have told us that the gospel is so important that it warrants innovative techniques to reach the largest possible audience. Whether Whitefield always handled the "fiery trial of popularity" without succumbing to the temptation of self-aggrandizement is hard to say; surely there were ways in which the sensational responses went to his head. But we also know that Whitefield largely avoided the most obvious signs of trouble associated with celebrity pastors today, including scandalous sexual affairs and financial improprieties. Whitefield funneled most of his income into charity; he did not become especially rich, in spite of his phenomenal popularity. Indeed, he struggled for much of his early career with personal debt, even though he showed few signs of frivolous consumption.[69]

Not surprisingly, other, more secular entrepreneurs saw financial opportunity in the legions whom Whitefield attracted. A newspaper reported, for example, that once when Whitefield was delayed in arriving at Kennington Common, a notorious medical vendor named Richard Rock showed up, "took the advantage of [Whitefield's] absence, and talked so pathetically to the multitude of the efficacy of his [medicinal] packets, that he disposed of abundance of them." The hostile writer concluded that "the quack for the body made greater profit that afternoon than the quack for the soul." This association between Rock and Whitefield's "quackery" became a staple of anti-Whitefield writings and prints (see figure 4.2).[70]

A more famous (and more reputable) entrepreneur in Philadelphia took note of the young evangelist, too. Benjamin Franklin, the publisher of the *Pennsylvania Gazette*, soon began reporting on Whitefield's phenomenal meetings at Kennington. Or rather, he began printing extracts of stories about those meetings from London's *Daily Advertiser,* extracts originally supplied by William Seward.[71]

Franklin was a native of Boston, Massachusetts, about nine years older than Whitefield, and like Whitefield, he came from a relatively modest background. Unlike Whitefield, Franklin found no path to anything more than an autodidactic education. After falling out with his older brother, James Franklin, the printer of the *New-England Courant,* Benjamin made his way to Philadelphia, where he began publishing the *Pennsylvania Gazette* in 1729. Franklin was no traditional Christian, but he knew a good news story when he saw it. So when reports began to emerge that the boy preacher was returning to America in late 1739, Franklin began wondering how he could hitch his publishing wagon to Whitefield's star. By the end of the year, Franklin had become Whitefield's key publicist in America. They also became lifelong friends.[72]

Whitefield seized upon new opportunities in the religious marketplace, yet his sermons could also have a distinctly anticommercial edge. He especially criticized London's obsession with fashion. One report mockingly noted that several "fine ladies who used to wear French silks; French hoops of four yards wide," and other luxurious clothes had now turned into Methodist "followers of Mr. Whitefield." Their conversion, and Whitefield's preaching on the new birth, convinced them to wear only plain clothes and simple hairstyles.[73]

Whitefield continued to cultivate a broader British evangelical network, and in May 1739 he traveled about seventy miles northwest of London to Northampton, where he finally met the Dissenting pastor Philip Doddridge. Preaching on the town common, he concluded that nothing assured him more of God's plans to do a great work in England "than to find how his children of all denominations everywhere wrestle in prayer for me." When Whitefield returned to London, he received a letter from the brothers Ebenezer and Ralph Erskine, leaders of the secessionist Associate Presbytery in Scotland, who had also begun experimenting with outdoor preaching. The Erskines had seen audiences numbering in the tens of thousands. "Blessed be God!" wrote Whitefield, "there are more field-preachers in the world besides myself."[74]

Back in London, Whitefield kept preaching before gargantuan audiences. Reading his journals, the enormous crowds start to seem routine: ten thousand here, twenty thousand there. On one occasion, June 1, he claimed to have spoken to eighty thousand people. Historians have long debated whether to take these estimates seriously. There can be no doubt that Whitefield and Seward exaggerated the numbers of people, and in later editions of his journals,

Whitefield reduced some, but not all, of the highest totals. But with so many people present, how could either man have formed a reasonable estimate anyway? Conversely, it is difficult to envision how, in an age without electrical amplification, tens of thousands of people could hear Whitefield, or even physically jam into spaces to catch a glimpse of him. Yet a recent study by acoustic scientists on his intelligible speaking range has largely confirmed Whitefield's claim that crowds of twenty thousand or even thirty thousand could hear him.[75]

We need not assume that everyone at an assembly could actually hear Whitefield, either, or needed to do so in order to stay. Perhaps some could just faintly hear him speaking far off in the distance, and were satisfied with that. Whitefield noted at times that his audiences maintained "deep silence" during his sermons, and he typically ascended a hill or a scaffold in order to project his voice. Those who wished to hear would undoubtedly have pressed in as close as possible, while others may have hung around the periphery, chatting with friends or selling their wares. An outdoor Whitefield meeting, we must remember, was as much a festival as a formal church gathering.[76]

Many thousands regarded their attendance at Whitefield's sermons as a spiritual milestone, however. One who undoubtedly attended Kennington meetings in 1739 was Mercy Good, the seventeen-year-old daughter of a "hair seller" in Southwark, south of the Thames. She told Whitefield that his preaching gave her hope of forgiveness "by the power [of] the word by you tho' in a field." Her conversion was unexpected: "I went out of curiosity but came home with joy . . . I have done 17 years of age and not knew Jesus Christ 'til now." She sheepishly apologized for her writing, "for it is not spelt proper at toll," but implored him to write her back.[77]

His sensational London sermons in May and June of 1739 drew the harshest criticism against him yet. A burlesque, misogynist poem titled *The Methodists* portrayed Whitefield literally as the devil in disguise, charging that he was intent upon charming and seducing weak-willed women—perhaps those such as Mercy Good?—with rapturous talk of heaven:

What maid wou'd not be holy kist? Or who her teacher can resist?
Or when he tells her of her H—-n, what blessings thence to all are giv'n,
Which after death she's sure to meet; the dear temptation is so sweet.
In those soft moments, (all the soul unbent), the maid on heavenly joys intent,
Who could withstand the pleasing proffer, or withstand the pious lecher's offer?
Say wou'd she not in her New Birth, know some part of Heav'n on Earth?[78]

Whitefield had his defenders, too. *The Conduct and Doctrine of the Reverend Mr. Whitefield Vindicated* was as zealous to defend Whitefield as *The Methodists* was to ridicule him. *Conduct and Doctrine* presented Whitefield as a "Moses-like man" sent by God to "stand in the gap" (Ezekiel 22:30) and turn the British away from their sins before the judgment of God fell. His fiercest critics, the tract asserted, were the most "careless and debauched" members of the Church of England clergy, timeservers who delivered stultifying sermons a couple times a week and spent the rest of their time in "gaming, drinking, horse-racing, hunting and bowling about in quest of fresh diversions and merriment." This kind of assertion touched a raw nerve among Church of England clergymen, especially senior ones, who did not appreciate young Whitefield or his followers making blanket characterizations of their character. As the rhetoric became more heated, it became difficult to maintain a moderate position on the Methodists.[79]

The anti-Whitefield tracts attracted a sizeable audience. Joseph Trapp's *The Nature, Folly, Sin, and Danger, of Being Righteous Over-Much* went through four editions in 1739. In April, Whitefield heard Trapp preach a version of this sermon and concluded that "with all his learning, [Trapp] knew nothing yet as he ought to know." He prayed that God would rebuke Trapp's spirit. Trapp was quite learned: an Anglican clergyman as well as Oxford's first professor of poetry, he represented the Methodists as charlatans peddling faux religion. To Trapp, Methodism succeeded only because "the generality, the main bulk of the people, are injudicious, and easy to be imposed upon." And charmed by novelty: "They are wonderfully struck with every thing that is new and unusual . . . never considering, that truth is the oldest thing in the world; and that in religion and morality whatever is really new, is certainly false." Trapp earned a rejoinder from a pro-Whitefield author who wrote as "A Lover of Truth" and published the pointedly titled *Doctor Trapp Vindicated from the Imputation of Being a Christian.* The *London Daily Post and Daily Advertiser* likewise scoffed at Trapp and other clerical critics as "Reverend Papguns."[80]

By mid-1739, the literature for and against Whitefield had reached flood tide. Whitefield, Hutton, and the Methodists had already transformed the British publishing world with the preacher's sermons and journals, and now the anti- and pro-Whitefield titles began to crest, too. By one count, 154 anti-Whitefield titles appeared in 1739–40, which represented three-quarters of the total volume of anti-Methodist publications overall in those two years.[81]

By June 1739, Whitefield was preparing for his return to America. As he waited for passage, his relationship with John Wesley began to disintegrate. Wesley had decided to declaim against predestination and Calvinism, and to teach that Christians could achieve a state of sinless perfection in this life. Wesley began preaching on "free grace" in Bristol by the end of April, and soon correspondents apprised Whitefield of Wesley's theological turn. Whitefield wrote to an English pastor that he "by no means" approved of Wesley's teachings on perfection. Later he explained to a Scottish minister that he was "no friend to sinless perfection," for he believed that "relics" of the sinful nature always remained in Christians' hearts. In the succeeding months, Whitefield still encouraged his old mentor to preach alongside him. But their breakup was imminent.[82]

Behind the scenes, Whitefield wrote to Charles Wesley and pleaded with him to try to avoid a public split: "If your brother will be but silent about the doctrine of election and final perseverance, there will never be a division between us. The very thought of it shocks my soul." But John had made a firm decision. He told James Hutton that via the casting of lots, God had not only confirmed his teaching against Calvinism, but also told him to publish his views.[83]

Whitefield and Wesley's divide over predestination reflected a larger, long-term split among Anglicans on this question. (It also represented an ancient Christian debate. In the early fifth century, Augustine and Pelagius—who may have been born in the British Isles—had engaged in theological debates over election, free will, and people's need for grace.) By the beginning of the eighteenth century, Calvinism had few strong Anglican advocates, even though the church's Thirty-Nine Articles explicitly affirmed predestination and taught against free will. The Wesleys' mother, Susanna, had brought them up with hostility to Calvinism, telling John in 1725 that rigid predestination "charges the most holy God with being the author of sin." Whitefield, conversely, became convinced that a recovery of robust Calvinist teaching was essential to a renewal of pure gospel preaching. The theological controversy became an outlet for John Wesley and Whitefield to vent their personal frustrations with each other. Whitefield would never question Wesley's salvation (as he did with latitudinarians), probably because of their personal relationship, and because he knew that Wesley had a clear testimony of conversion. Still, their theological rift would become vicious.[84]

On June 25, 1739, Whitefield addressed Wesley directly, telling him that he had heard of Wesley's intention to "print a sermon against predestination." The prospect saddened him: "It shocks me to think of it. What will be the consequence but controversy?" Whitefield implored him to maintain silence and reminded him that there were already public rumors about animosity between them. A week later, Whitefield asked him again not to distribute the sermon, but glumly noted that Wesley had cast the lot. "Oh! my heart in the midst of my body is like melted wax!" Whitefield exclaimed.[85]

But the die was already cast—literally. Wesley published the sermon in Bristol. Although Wesley opened with an appeal for civility, he left no doubt that he considered the doctrine of election to be abhorrent and blasphemous. Limited atonement—the notion that Christ died only for the elect—suggested that "God condemned millions of souls to everlasting fire . . . for want of that grace he will not give them." Surely, God would not willingly "doom his creatures whether they will or no, to endless misery." With Whitefield and other Calvinistic Methodists directly in his sights, Wesley stubbornly declared, "Here I fix my foot. On this I join issue with every asserter of it. You represent God as worse than the devil."[86]

With his "fixed foot," Wesley *intended* to cause a public rift with Whitefield. The doctrine of predestination certainly caused consternation among its opponents, and Wesley joined a long line of Arminian theologians who had begged Calvinists to consider the logical implications of their theology, and the awful light in which it ostensibly presented God. It is hard to resist the conclusion that Wesley had also determined, for whatever reason, to use such inflammatory language that it would inevitably cause a split. It was a perennial theological dispute playing out between two strong personalities. The clash over Calvinism badly damaged not only Wesley and Whitefield's relationship, but also the British evangelical movement. (American evangelicals' feuding over Calvinism largely came later, after the Revolution.) One of Wesley's biographers notes that "the Calvinist controversy would be a running sore in the bowels of the Revival."[87]

Whitefield did not immediately take Wesley's bait. He continued to speak of Wesley as his "honoured friend" and wrote to Wesley in March 1740, saying, "Provoke me to it as much as you please, I do not think ever to enter the lists of controversy with you on the points wherein we differ." But Whitefield's printed reaction to Wesley would eventually come, in late 1740, after Whitefield had spent a year in America, where effectively all his revivalist allies were Calvinists.[88]

Whitefield was doubly frustrated as the break with Wesley unfolded: he should have already sailed for America. The British navy, however, had placed an embargo on outgoing commercial shipping until they could recruit (or forcibly impress) sailors needed for its ongoing conflict with Spain, the descriptively named War of Jenkins' Ear. Thomas Carlyle popularized this moniker in the nineteenth century: the war's name came from an ill-fated English captain,

Robert Jenkins, whose ship the Spanish boarded near Florida in 1731. Accusing Jenkins of smuggling, Spanish sailors slashed his head with a sword, nearly cutting off his ear. Finally, according to newspaper reports of the incident, "they made a last assault on Jenkins; clutched the bloody slit ear of him; tore it mercilessly off; flung it in his face," and said, "Carry that to your King, and tell him of it!" Jenkins kept the severed ear and apparently produced it during hearings before the House of Commons when he testified about his ordeal in 1738. Britain declared war against the Spanish in 1739. The naval war convulsed ports in Central and South America and the Caribbean. Whitefield's ally James Oglethorpe led a British force out of Georgia in a failed assault against St. Augustine, Florida, in 1740.[89]

So Whitefield waited and preached. On June 22 came sensational news about the itinerant: "The famous Mr. Whitefield," the *Daily Post* and other outlets reported, had "dropt down dead." The (still-living) Whitefield found the rumor annoying. He preached at Blackheath, south of the Thames, on June 23, to an audience unusually small because of the report, he wrote, "that I was dead." Whitefield admitted that he longed to be with Christ in heaven, yet he believed his time on earth was not up yet. He recorded his resolution in his journal: "I shall not yet die, but live, and declare the works of the Lord" (Psalm 118:17). But the report frightened his followers; Ralph Erskine's family heard the news in Scotland. They were devastated until they "heard other accounts." It was not the last instance of a false report of his demise—they were part of his trials of popularity.[90]

Throughout his time in England, Whitefield had raised money for the Georgia orphanage. The papers reported in June that Whitefield had accumulated £1,193 for his charitable projects. Nevertheless, critics questioned what Whitefield actually intended to do with that money, and lamented the gullibility of the (ostensibly) working-class audiences who gave it to him. The *Daily Post* of London said that many bosses were glad to see him go to America so that the lazy employees who flocked to the preacher would return to work. The article implied that Whitefield would visit Philadelphia to great personal advantage, spending the "fools pence he has talk'd out of the pockets of his lunatic audience."[91]

Threats of violence and arrest accompanied the printed attacks against him. Hostile sheriffs could not find legal justification for detaining Whitefield, although some tried to frighten him by raising the prospect. In July, Whitefield engaged in a particularly nasty exchange with the mayor of Basingstoke, where an angry innkeeper refused to house him, crowds jeered him, and hooligans shot fireworks at his door. The nervous mayor tried to forbid him from preaching in the town, fearing a riot.[92] Whitefield demanded to know on what legal basis the mayor intended to ban him. Furthermore, Whitefield reminded him that the town was simultaneously hosting a "revel," which included cudgeling and wrestling matches. Wrestling, boxing, and cudgeling were spectator sports that people would travel for miles to see. Those were presumably more a threat to the public peace than an assembly of God worshippers, Whitefield reasoned; why not ban the revel instead of his revival? If the mayor did not comply, Whitefield bluntly warned the magistrate that he would "rise up against you at the great day [i.e., Judgment Day], and be a swift witness against your partiality."[93]

On the appointed evening, Whitefield preached with little incident other than a few boys calling him "strange names." But Whitefield decided that he had to confront the revelers, so he went to the "stage, erected for the wrestlers, and began to show them the error of their ways." Some youths shouted him down with cries of "huzza," and one of the brawlers accosted him and hit him with a cudgel. Whitefield, fearing for his life, left the stage, pushed through the shouting crowd, and escaped on his horse. It was a frightening experience, but in his published journal, he reckoned it a great success. He resolved to mount "an offensive war with Satan," whatever the risks.[94]

Finally, in August 1739, the navy lifted the embargo. As Whitefield prepared to depart, he spent much of his time at Blendon Hall, the estate of Thomas Delamotte, a London sugar merchant who traded with Caribbean slave plantations. The estate lay down the Thames toward Gravesend and other ports from which Whitefield might ultimately depart. The Delamottes had become something of a second family for him. Of particular interest to him was the Delamottes' daughter, Elizabeth, whom Whitefield had met through Charles Wesley in the fall of 1737. Elizabeth had experienced conversion in 1738, becoming a zealous Methodist. Whitefield did not reveal in his writings exactly when his acquaintance with her grew into a romantic interest, but he certainly did not forget about Elizabeth as he traveled in the colonies.[95]

As he waited to sail, he tidied up his remaining affairs, hastily penning a response to Bishop Gibson's recent pastoral letter. Whitefield could not possibly respond to the avalanche of writings against him, but given Gibson's prominence as the bishop of London, Whitefield felt it necessary to reply to his missive. The itinerant tried to paint his view of the Holy Spirit as the moderate, biblical position, instead of an example of enthusiasm, as the bishop had charged. In his published journal, Whitefield suggested that Gibson had made good works a necessary condition of salvation, a theological error that Whitefield saw as the root of many of the Anglican Church's problems.[96]

Appropriately, he preached his Kennington farewell sermon on Paul's parting address to the elders of the church of Ephesus in Acts 20. In that passage, Paul concluded by saying, "Behold, I know that ye all, among whom I have gone preaching the kingdom of God, shall see my face no more." Acts records that the elders then "wept sore, and fell on Paul's neck, and kissed him, sorrowing most of all for the words which he spake, that they should see his face no more. And they accompanied him unto the ship." The crowd at Kennington did not accompany Whitefield to the ship, but many did weep sore.[97]

When Whitefield finally boarded the *Elizabeth* on August 13, he wrote, "Blessed be God for detaining me in England by the embargo." He resolved, as best he could, never to question God's timing. He set out again for America. Before, he had gone as a relatively unknown missionary to Georgia. Now he was the sensation of the British Atlantic world.[98]

5

"A Tour Round America": The American South and the Bethesda Orphanage

Benjamin Franklin, who recognized a good business prospect when he saw one, had never seen a better prospect than George Whitefield. The twenty-four-year-old preacher came to Philadelphia on November 2, 1739. Primed by news reports of his triumphs in England, the city received him eagerly. Although Philadelphia was the colonies' second-largest town, at about 13,000 residents, it remained something of a fledgling colonial outpost. The Scots traveler Alexander Hamilton (not to be confused with the future American patriot leader of the same name) said in 1744 that Philadelphia reminded him a great deal of "country market towns in England." The streets were unpaved and "full of rubbish and mire." He considered it "a degree politer than New York though in its fabrick not so urban." Philadelphia was bustling and growing, yet still marginal within the British Empire. Philadelphians, including Franklin, had never encountered anyone who caused a stir as Whitefield did.[1]

By the late spring of 1739, American newspapers, including Franklin's *Pennsylvania Gazette*, were buzzing with reports of England's star pastor. Skeptical by nature, Franklin puzzled at the reported throngs of tens of thousands. Could that many really hear him preach? Franklin thought one could answer most questions experimentally, as he would do by flying his electrical kite into a storm cloud thirteen years later. So when Whitefield came to town, Franklin set up an experiment during one of the itinerant's assemblies: "I had the curiosity to learn how far he could be heard, by retiring backwards down the street towards the [Delaware] River, and I found his voice distinct till I came near Front Street . . . Imagining then a semicircle, of which my distance should be the radius, and that it were filled with auditors, to each of whom I allowed

84

two square feet; I computed that he might well be heard by more than thirty thousand." To Franklin, this settled the question. The calculation "reconciled" him to the accounts of the mammoth crowds.[2]

Although Franklin never experienced the new birth of conversion, and later described himself as a Deist, he was convinced that Whitefield's ministry was legitimate. His preaching was incomparable, thought the printer, more like an "excellent piece of music" than the tedious recitations given by others. Publishing Whitefield's works became a bonanza for Franklin's print shop. Sometime before Whitefield's departure, the two men met at Whitefield's rented house on Second Street and struck a deal. Franklin announced shortly afterward, "The Rev. Mr. Whitefield having given me copies of his journals and sermons, with leave to print the same; I propose to publish them with all expedition, if I find sufficient encouragement." Thus began a business arrangement— and friendship—that lasted thirty-one years.[3]

At considerable financial risk, Franklin began releasing a flood of titles by or about Whitefield. Most took a favorable view of the preacher, although a few were critical. Between 1740 and 1742, Franklin printed forty-three books and pamphlets dealing with Whitefield and the evangelical movement. (In 1742 there was an uptick in titles specifically related to the Moravians and Count Zinzendorf.) Franklin produced editions of books recommended by Whitefield, too, including Ralph Erskine's *Gospel Sonnets* and Joseph Alleine's *Alarm to Unconverted Sinners*. Franklin's Philadelphia competitors William and Andrew Bradford published a number of Whitefield-related titles, as well. The Whitefield sensation helped the Bradfords and Franklin become the colonies' first omnibus printers, publishing and selling a range of genres. But only Franklin, the great entrepreneur, made this business profitable. He found that religion—and Whitefield specifically—often sold better than any other topic.[4]

As in Britain, media coverage buoyed Whitefield's American tour. By summer, reports appeared of Whitefield's massive meetings at Moorfields and Kennington. There was often a delay of about two months between reports in London and their reprinting in the colonies, but by the end of July, Americans had begun to read of Whitefield's imminent return to the colonies. (The *Boston Evening-Post* skeptically noted that Whitefield planned to bring some of his "methodically mad" supporters with him to work at the Georgia orphanage.) Reprinting commentary from London's *Daily Post*, the *New-York Weekly Journal* scoffed at the "giddy brain'd workfolks" who neglected their jobs in order to scurry after the preacher.[5]

As these reports were paving the way for his arrival, Whitefield enjoyed the respite of his Atlantic crossing. He told correspondents that the temptations of his "popular life" made him think of abandoning preaching, but he considered such thoughts to be whispers from the devil. It is unlikely that Whitefield ever seriously considered retiring to a more private life (such as becoming the resident director of the Georgia orphanage). But he recognized the "innumerable snares" that came with his celebrity status: pride, covetousness, and worldly pleasures.[6]

This ocean crossing was not nearly the ordeal that his previous voyage back from Georgia had been. He relished the company of his Methodist fellow travelers, whom he began to call his "family." Among the most important shipmates was his publicist William Seward, who would manage the coverage of Whitefield's American tour. Whitefield shared many hours of prayer and devotion with his companions, but also took time for private prayer, in which "the freeness and riches of God's everlasting love" so overwhelmed him that it occasionally rendered him speechless. He wrote a great deal, including the autobiographical *Short Account of God's Dealings with George Whitefield from his Infancy to His Ordination*, our most complete account of his early life and conversion.[7]

Whitefield continued to cultivate his Calvinist convictions; or, as Wesley later put it, he continued "warping towards Calvinism." (Whitefield, for his part, also worried about those "warping toward Arminianism.") The itinerant told Wesley that he had actually "never read any thing that Calvin wrote" and that he took his doctrine from the Bible alone, as God taught it to him. But of course, the Bible was not the only book Whitefield read. He was perusing books such as the Dissenting minister Jonathan Warne's *Arminianism, the Back-Door to Popery* (1738). Warne, quoting liberally from the Anglican Calvinist apologist John Edwards, argued that if the Anglican clergy were faithful to their own church's doctrines, they would embrace Calvinism. Whitefield affirmed Warne's convictions and thought they should "be written in letters of gold." He increasingly understood the value of publicly defending the Calvinist doctrines of grace, telling his Welsh friend Howell Harris that since they last met, "God has been pleased to enlighten me more in that comfortable doctrine of election . . . At my return, I hope to be more explicit than I have been." At some point he would need to confront John Wesley's Arminianism in print. Growing contemptuous of Wesley's notion of free will, Whitefield wrote, "Man is nothing: he hath a free will to go to hell, but none to go to heaven, till God worketh in him."[8]

Because of his familiarity with polemics for and against Calvinism, Whitefield knew that it was under assault in the eighteenth century as part of the intellectual revolution that historians often call the Enlightenment. (I prefer terms such as "liberal" or "humanitarian" thought to describe these new develop-ments, rather than the catchall term "Enlightenment." The concept of the Enlightenment, as many have noted, oversimplifies European intellectual trends of the time. Some Enlightenment figures were friendly toward tradi-tional faith, some not.) Pressure against Calvinist doctrine came from Arminians such as Wesley, who considered predestination irrational and unreasonable. Other critiques came from humanitarian voices who emphasized God's benev-olence rather than his sovereignty. Historians have also noted a growing senti-ment against "cruelty" in eighteenth-century thought, a development that would ultimately help birth the antislavery movement. To humanitarian critics such as Anthony Ashley Cooper, the 3rd Earl of Shaftesbury, notions such as eternal torment in hell, original sin, and predestination cast God as a merciless tyrant. To Shaftesbury, the Calvinist belief in a wrathful God spoke only to Calvinists' own disturbed, fearful psychology. He proposed that God was better understood as compassionate, loving, and "truly and perfectly good."[9]

In printed treatises and private reflections, Calvinist evangelicals such as Whitefield and Jonathan Edwards, along with less famous believers such as Sarah Osborn, of Newport, Rhode Island, defended Reformed doctrines in response to such humanitarian challenges. During the course of her life, Osborn suffered the early deaths of her husband and her son, as well as beset-ting illnesses, yet she remained convinced of God's providential sovereignty over each of these scourging experiences. She reminded herself that the Lord disciplined those he loved. The overcoming of doubts about election, predesti-nation, and the overarching authority of God featured prominently in many evangelicals' spiritual autobiographies.[10]

Whitefield may have adopted modern marketing and communication methods, then, but his message was traditional and Calvinist. Instead of soft-ening his view on the depravity of man in response to humanitarian critics, he emphasized original sin even more. Whitefield spoke regularly of how people in their lost state became "sunk into the nature of the beast and the devil." His hearers repeatedly noted this phrase in reminiscences about his preaching. One of them, Margaret Austin, found herself agreeing with the itinerant, writing that she really was "half a beast and half a devil." Another Methodist convert, Martha Claggett, recalled that she was in a state of spiritual despair: "I knew not what to do, having none to guide me till God sent Mr. Whitefield amongst us. He told me of Original Sin and man's fallen estate. This by sorrowful experience I had proved to be true." As Claggett recounted it, Whitefield's description of the dire weight of sin began her journey to spiritual relief because it resonated so accurately with her experiences.[11]

Befitting his far-flung travels and correspondence, Whitefield's Reformed influences ranged widely. He sought out a wider Anglo-American Calvinist network in travel, correspondence, and reading. In a letter to Ralph Erskine, Whitefield noted that he "exceedingly" liked the Scottish Presbyterian minister Thomas Boston, especially Boston's massive tome *Human Nature in Its Four-Fold State* (1720). The book had been "of much service" to his soul, Whitefield said. Boston's *Four-Fold State* portrayed sinful men and women as totally corrupt, with a "load of wrath" hanging over them. Boston insisted that the sinner also suffered from an "utter inability to recover himself." Salvation was entirely a work of God's grace. Through volumes such as these, Whitefield told Erskine, the Holy Spirit had convinced him of "our eternal election by the Father through the Son, of our free justification through faith in his blood," and other Calvinist precepts.[12]

Whitefield's advice to followers sounded increasingly Calvinist, too. If they had truly been saved, God would never turn away from them, he assured correspondents. Nor would God turn away from Whitefield himself, despite his own struggles with sin. "I fear not falling finally," he wrote to a friend during the Atlantic crossing, "for God I believe chose me in Christ before ever the earth and the world were made, as a vessel of his saving mercy." Whitefield still wrestled with his unnamed sin, which he called a "thorn in the flesh," echoing the Apostle Paul. These struggles did not represent anything more than obstacles on his path to final redemption, he assured himself, a state he was sure to reach because of God's grace and power.[13]

Whitefield disembarked at Lewes (Lewis Town), Delaware, where the Delaware Bay meets the Atlantic Ocean, on October 30. It had been a year and two months since he left Savannah, but it seemed much longer than that. Thanking God for another safe passage, he reflected: "As here's the same sun, so here's the same God in America as in England. I bless God all places are equal to me."[14]

All places were equally valuable, for all places had lost souls. But on this second visit he also began to understand how especially congenial America was. Everywhere he turned, he found allies. (In time, of course, he would also make his share of American enemies.) The revival in England was largely an Anglican-Methodist affair among English people. In America, Whitefield encountered friends of revival in many denominations: Presbyterian, Congregationalist, Baptist, Moravian, German Pietist, and occasionally Anglican, too. He also saw opportunities to bring the gospel to Africans in America (and, more distantly in Whitefield's experience, Native Americans). America remained a smaller venue, but one with major gospel potential and an enticing future.

Whitefield made his way up the Delaware River to Philadelphia. As was his habit, he met with Anglican leaders as well as Quakers, Presbyterians, and Baptists, attempting to ascertain potential friends and enemies. He found few supporters among the Anglican clergy. He needed to convince Anglican laypeople that "the generality of their teachers do not preach or live up to the truth as it is in Jesus," he wrote. Nevertheless, he assisted in services at Philadelphia's Anglican Christ Church before embarking on outdoor preaching. There was never any question that he would hold open-air meetings. Five days after his arrival, he spoke from the Philadelphia courthouse stairs to a crowd he estimated at six thousand. Reports said they "stood in awful silence" as they listened.[15]

Americans were more accepting of his outdoor preaching than the English, he concluded. In England, "the generality of people think a sermon cannot be preached well [outside a church]; here they do not like it so well if delivered within the church walls." Whether Americans (or Philadelphians) really were so different from English audiences is difficult to say; Whitefield had attracted legions to his open-air preaching in London and Bristol. But perhaps American audiences were more used to unconventional religious practices. Quakers founded Pennsylvania, of course, and they were among the most controversial of all Dissenters. Pennsylvania also had no official church. But he would receive an even more enthusiastic response in the New England colonies, where the Puritans had established the Congregational Church by law.[16]

While Whitefield maintained friendly contacts only with certain Dissenters in England and Scotland, in America he discovered that non-Anglicans were his most enthusiastic supporters. Among the first such supporters he met were members of the Tennent family. He enjoyed a visit from William Tennent, Sr., whom Whitefield called "an old grey-headed disciple and soldier of Jesus Christ." Tennent and his family were among hundreds of thousands of Scots-Irish immigrants to America in the eighteenth century, many of whom carried with them a cultivated tradition of Presbyterian piety. Although Tennent had received ordination as an Anglican, he felt more at home among Presbyterians. When his family arrived in Pennsylvania in 1718, he affiliated with the city's Presbyterian synod. In 1726 the family found a home in Neshaminy, Pennsylvania, where Tennent opened the so-called Log College seminary, a Presbyterian training school that was a precursor to the College of New Jersey at Princeton. Whitefield noted with delight that he and Tennent had common friends in the Erskine brothers of Scotland.[17]

Whitefield was even more impressed by Tennent's son Gilbert. Gilbert was eleven years older than Whitefield. For a time, Tennent became something of a replacement for John Wesley as the mentor for whom Whitefield longed.

Tennent served as the pastor of a Presbyterian church in New Brunswick, New Jersey, where Whitefield first encountered him. Although the Philadelphia Synod was divided over issues related to revivalism, it had allowed Tennent and several other evangelical pastors to form the revivalist New Brunswick presbytery in 1738. (In Presbyterian polity, a presbytery is a body of ministers and elders that governs the churches of a district; a synod is a larger governing body composed of presbyteries.) To Whitefield, Tennent and his circle of ministers were "the burning and shining lights of this part of America."[18]

Whitefield traveled with Tennent to Elizabeth Town, New Jersey, where they took a ferry to New York City, the colonies' third-largest city, with about 11,000 residents. It was a lovely place. One visitor remarked in 1748 that it was "extremely pleasant to walk the town, for it seemed like a garden." One could easily stroll from the wharfs and tightly bunched wooden buildings on the southern tip of Manhattan into the countryside that lay close by. The Anglicans' Trinity Church was one of the finest buildings on the continent. But the city also had a grittier side. It was a "slave city," as the historian Jill Lepore put it. One in five New Yorkers was enslaved.[19]

In the city, Whitefield listened as Tennent preached at Ebenezer Pemberton's Wall Street Presbyterian Church. He was impressed. Never before had he "heard such a searching sermon," Whitefield wrote. Tennent helped Whitefield see that they had to preach the gospel in its stark, offensive fullness. All people— including pastors—had to experience conversion. In salvation, religiosity did not matter. A preacher must have experienced the conviction of sin and the redeeming power of grace in his own heart, or else his preaching would inevitably be cold, moralistic, and misleading. Whitefield was invigorated. Tennent was a true collaborator, willing to press the issue of conversion, without any of Wesley's theological problems. Tennent was a "son of thunder," Whitefield reckoned. He did not "fear the faces of men."[20]

Whitefield soon met with, and offended, the minister of Trinity Church, the Anglican commissary William Vesey. (Commissaries were officials whom the bishop of London appointed to oversee affairs in the American colonies, where there was no resident bishop.) Forty years older than Whitefield, Vesey came into the meeting primed for a fight. He denied Whitefield the Trinity Church pulpit before Whitefield could request it. He charged Whitefield with breaking his ministerial oath and the church's canon by preaching without a license. Whitefield countered that he knew Vesey frequented taverns, and reminded him that the canon also forbade clergy from going to such places. "This, though spoken in the spirit of meekness," Whitefield drily noted, "stirred up his corruptions more and more."[21]

Once again, Whitefield would have to find somewhere else to preach other than an Anglican pulpit. He was, of course, prepared for Vesey's hostile reaction. That afternoon he began field preaching, attracting an audience of a couple of thousand people. In the evening, he preached to a packed house at Ebenezer Pemberton's church.[22]

One of the most detailed accounts of Whitefield's preaching, perhaps written by Pemberton himself, emerged from that day's appearances. The correspondent was friendly toward Whitefield's revival preaching, but was initially concerned that the itinerant might indulge in enthusiastic extremes. Observing Whitefield's outdoor meeting, the writer noted that Christians of all denominations, as well as a small number of Jews, gathered to hear him. Many attended out of genuine spiritual interest. Others, members of what the writer called the "Devil's Chapel," had other motivations. The godly pressed around the preacher; the skeptics hung around the periphery and spent most of their time in "giggling, scoffing, talking & laughing." Nevertheless, by the end of the sermon, Whitefield's powerful rhetoric had captured the attention of most, and a "solemn awe" fell over the crowd.[23]

After seeing his dazzling performance at the Wall Street church, the writer was convinced: "Every scruple vanished. I never saw nor heard the like, and I said within myself, 'Surely God is with this man of a truth.'" Of Whitefield himself, he wrote:

> He is a man of a middle stature, of a slender body, of a fair complexion, and of a comely appearance . . . He has a most ready memory, and I think, speaks entirely without notes. He has a clear and musical voice, and a wonderful command of it. He uses much gesture, but with great propriety; every accent of his voice, every motion of his body, speaks, and both are natural and unaffected. If his delivery is the product of art, 'tis certainly the perfection of it, for it is entirely concealed.

The correspondent regarded the evangelist's theology as solidly Calvinist. Although Whitefield did not make eschatology, or the study of the last days, a central point of his preaching, he did regard the current time to be the "midnight state of the church." A "Glorious Day," however, was approaching, when legions would come to new faith in Christ. Perhaps that day was dawning. Like many of his Reformed and evangelical colleagues, Whitefield prayed for the ultimate conversion of the Jews to Christianity. Perhaps this is why the correspondent noted that Jews were present at Whitefield's meeting.[24]

Catching his American stride in New York, the itinerant said that he had felt no "greater freedom in preaching" since he arrived. But Anglican opponents were mustering their forces. Soon, one of the first American anti-Whitefield publications appeared. The fusillade came from the pen of Jonathan Arnold, a missionary with the Anglicans' Society for the Propagation of the Gospel. Arnold confronted Whitefield in New York, charging him with teaching false doctrine and offering to debate him publicly. Whitefield declined, saying that he did not debate unregenerate men. The irate Arnold went to the newspapers, proclaiming that Anglicans should treat Whitefield "as he deserves, i.e. with neglect and contempt, as being the most irregular man in doctrine and manners," calling him also "remarkable for ignorance and confidence." One of Whitefield's defenders returned fire in a front-page letter in the *American Weekly Mercury*, saying that Arnold's lies proceeded "from the Father of Lies, the Devil."[25]

Nothing that Whitefield or Tennent did made opponents angrier than calling them unconverted. Both pastors would level general charges about the "dangers of an unconverted ministry," as Tennent's incendiary 1740 sermon would put it. Whitefield had also begun openly telling people like Jonathan Arnold that they were unregenerate. In one of the letters he wrote on board the *Elizabeth*, for example, Whitefield informed a British pastor that he did not think "that a thorough work of conversion was ever wrought upon your soul."[26]

This was a delicate issue, one that Whitefield did not handle delicately. Obviously, he and the new evangelicals believed that conversion was essential to salvation. Evidence such as opposition to revival, lax theology, or compromised morals could indicate that a person, even a minister, had not experienced the new birth. But, as he would later admit, Whitefield was incautious about turning disagreements over theology and tactics into a (literally) damning charge that a person was unregenerate. Long-serving ministers, in particular, did not wish to be indicted as hell-bound by a twenty-four-year-old.

Whitefield realized his potential for cockiness. After leaving New York City, he wrote a sheepish letter to Ebenezer Pemberton, suggesting that he might not have shown the humility to Pemberton "due from a babe to a father in Christ." (Pemberton was only nine years older than Whitefield, but had served at the Wall Street Presbyterian Church since 1727.) Whitefield frankly admitted that it was difficult to "not be puffed up" by the kind of success he had enjoyed. Pemberton was apparently not offended, however, since he wrote a positive letter to Whitefield, commending him for being used by God to start "a good work in this secure and sinful place."[27]

Whitefield did not clash with every older minister, of course. His rivalries did not run along simple generational lines, as could be seen in his quick appreciation for William Tennent. He soon met a longtime friend of the Tennents, Theodorus Frelinghuysen. Frelinghuysen, a Dutch Reformed pastor twenty-two years older than Whitefield, had immigrated to New Brunswick, New Jersey, in 1720. Frelinghuysen represented a trend among the German-Dutch churches of northwestern Germany (he had previously served a church near Emden) toward blending Reformed theology and revival. Frelinghuysen was known to make sharp distinctions between the converted and the unregenerate when addressing congregations. Gilbert Tennent, then a fresh Yale College graduate, began preaching in New Brunswick several years after Frelinghuysen, and Tennent learned a great deal about preaching heart religion from the Dutch Reformed minister. They held joint services together, with sermons delivered in both Dutch and English.[28]

Whitefield called Frelinghuysen a "worthy old soldier of Jesus Christ." He credited the Dutch minister with precipitating revivals in the 1720s that helped prepare New Jersey for Whitefield's arrival in 1739. To get a picture of early American evangelicalism's diverse, transatlantic qualities, especially in the Middle Colonies, one need look no further than the alliance of Frelinghuysen (Dutch), Tennent (Scots-Irish), and Whitefield (English). All three were immigrant (or itinerant) preachers laboring far away from the lands of their birth, all of different denominations, and all three proclaiming the need for personal transformation by the grace of God.[29]

After five days in New York, Whitefield and Gilbert Tennent preached their way through New Jersey and Pennsylvania, visiting key pastors such as Frelinghuysen along the way. They stopped at Neshaminy, Pennsylvania, to see William Tennent and his wife. Enjoying sweet fellowship, they stayed up late discussing coordinated tactics for "promoting our dear Lord's Kingdom." Whitefield admired Tennent's Log College, which he described as a "loghouse, about twenty feet long, and near as many broad." It reminded him of the "schools of the old prophets" referred to in 2 Kings 2. Such schools were critical for training up a new generation of pastors and evangelists who were converted and faithful to the true gospel.[30]

The small towns between New York and Philadelphia did not muster the phenomenal crowds of Whitefield's urban meetings. Nevertheless, he marveled at how people streamed from the woods to hear him preach. At Maidenhead, New Jersey, Whitefield mounted the back of a wagon to address fifteen hundred people. At Abingdon, Pennsylvania, he spoke out of a meetinghouse porch window to about two thousand. And at Neshaminy, where he addressed about three thousand in the churchyard, Whitefield also estimated that about one thousand horses were there. (He complimented the Neshaminy audience for tying the horses up at the hedges rather than sitting on them during the meeting.) He found it surprising that so many people "so scattered abroad" could be "gathered at so short a warning."[31]

Outside Philadelphia, Whitefield visited Germantown, a common destination for German immigrants to the colony. By the middle of the century, Pennsylvania's Germans probably numbered about one hundred thousand, or between a third and a half of the colony's population. Many of these came from Reformed and Pietist backgrounds. Whitefield met an eager response at Germantown, even though he did not speak German. Preaching from a balcony, he addressed six thousand people for two hours, and saw a powerful "demonstration of the Spirit." Many in the crowd wept bitterly. Again, the immigrant throng illustrated the transatlantic quality of the revivals. Whitefield marveled at the "different nations and professions" represented. He estimated that Germantown had perhaps fifteen different Christian denominations, all of them (no doubt overstating their relative harmony) agreeing "to hold Jesus Christ as their head, and to worship him in spirit and truth" (John 4:23–24).[32]

At the end of November, Whitefield said good-bye to his friends in Philadelphia, setting out to travel by horse to Georgia. As he proceeded through Delaware and Maryland, he continued to see large crowds primed to see him by news and word-of-mouth reports. (Whitefield reflected that even negative news reports helped him by exciting "people's curiosity.") Coming to Annapolis, he called it a "little town, but the metropolis of Maryland." Annapolis was a village seaport with perhaps seventy-five households and about eight hundred residents. It was the colony's primary slave market, with about a third of its people enslaved. Maryland began as a refuge for Roman Catholics, but by the 1740s it had become a more typical British colony dominated by Protestants.[33] Annapolis was also ethnically diverse, even among its Europeans. A historian of the town imagines its eighteenth-century waterfront sounding of "saw and hammer and caulking mallet, the slap of rigging and creak of wooden hulls, the voices of men in accents Irish, English, and Scots, Prussian and African." Smells of fish, hemp, sea breezes, spices, coffee, rum, and rotting trash filled the itinerant's nose.[34]

Whitefield received a cheerful welcome from Maryland's governor, Samuel Ogle. Launching a blistering attack on the town's propertied class, Whitefield warned them about the "folly and sinfulness of those amusements, whereby the polite part of the world are so fatally diverted." He may well have criticized Annapolitans' passion for horse racing, which by the 1740s had become a major spectacle, thanks in part to Governor Ogle, who even introduced thoroughbred horses to the town in 1747. Nevertheless, Ogle remained a supporter of Whitefield's ministry during his repeated visits to Annapolis.[35]

Not everyone in Annapolis shared Ogle's view. One of Whitefield's detractors was Stephen Bordley, a well-connected lawyer, legislator, and Anglican vestryman. In the wake of Whitefield's Annapolis visit, Bordley wrote a hostile yet evocative letter about his preaching. The "celebrated Whitefield," Bordley conceded, had a wondrous "delivery" and appearance: "His voice is strong and clear, but not musical, and he has a little of the west country twang" (the accent typical of those from the west of England). He admired Whitefield's "fine set of teeth," which he considered a "great ornament" for any public speaker. His natural good looks were sullied by the "prodigious squint with his left eye," however. Whitefield's voice was unforgettable. Bordley thought the man had mastered "the art of pronunciation."[36] Rhetorical talents aside, Bordley found Whitefield's doctrine appalling. Touching on common criticisms, Bordley concluded that the "doctrine of the [Holy] Spirit and his railing at and accusing the clergy in the manner before mentioned, are the great hinges" of his sermons. This sensational preacher was really just a "ranting enthusiast." Nevertheless, Whitefield had entranced some foolish followers in Annapolis, sending them on a "wild goose chase in quest of that degree of the Spirit which perhaps they will never find." In summary, Bordley determined that the English star had the "the best delivery with the worst divinity that I ever met with."[37]

Whitefield's party crossed the Potomac River from Maryland into Virginia about thirty miles south of today's downtown Washington, D.C. They marveled at the lonely, leafy stretches between Annapolis and Williamsburg. James Blair, the Anglican commissary, spoke for many when he wrote in *The Present State of Virginia, and the College* (1727) that Virginia was both "one of the best [and] one of the worst of all the English plantations in America." Blessed with incredible natural resources and a burgeoning but dispersed population, the colony had struggled to establish a key port to compete with Boston or Philadelphia. Travelers had to depend on the hospitality of scattered strangers to give them food and lodging. Occasionally, Whitefield's group happened upon a roadside "ordinary," or tavern, where they could spend the night or take a meal.[38]

Women often operated, or even owned, Virginia's ordinaries. At one of these taverns, Whitefield appreciatively noted that the "woman of the house" kept quiet some other patrons who had become "disordered in liquor." He and his companions slept peacefully in a bed that the host made for them in the kitchen.[39] Whitefield engaged this charming hostess in spiritual discussion, but to his disappointment found that she did not accept his view of the new birth.

She thought that term referred to the believer's transformation in heaven. He insisted that she needed to turn to God for forgiveness and conversion; she assured him that God was quite merciful. Maybe he did not need to worry so much about judgment and hell, she mused. "The devil loves to represent God as all mercy, or all justice," Whitefield glumly wrote. Thousands responded eagerly to Whitefield's message, but others, from Anglican critics to this unnamed tavern keeper, countered him with their own reading of scripture.[40]

A couple weeks after leaving Annapolis, Whitefield reached Williamsburg, "the metropolis of Virginia." (He arrived, without comment, on his twenty-fifth birthday.) Williamsburg, which had served as Virginia's capital since 1699, was about the same size as Annapolis. About half its residents were enslaved or free blacks. The *Virginia Gazette* kept close tabs on Whitefield's progress in America, printing fourteen news items about him before his arrival in that colony. When he came to Williamsburg, the paper reminded readers that the "celebrated preacher" had already dazzled tens of thousands in New York and Philadelphia. The *Gazette* was no doubt pleased that a luminary of such magnitude had come to Williamsburg.[41]

Commissary James Blair happily welcomed Whitefield, in contrast to the reception offered by other Anglican officials. Blair was the key leader in Virginia's Anglican Church. The octogenarian Scotsman had come as an Anglican missionary to Virginia in 1684, and five years later became the first Anglican commissary in the colonies. In 1693 he secured a charter for the College of William and Mary, a school founded so that the Anglican Church would have a proper "seminary of ministers of the gospel, and ... that the Christian faith may be propagated amongst the western Indians to the glory of Almighty God." He singlehandedly kept the college afloat through a series of early crises, from devastating fires to repeated feuds with Virginia governors.[42]

Whitefield hailed Blair— "by far the most worthy clergyman I have yet conversed with in all America." He also commended the work of the college and prayed that "learning Christ" would be the students' chief goal. While he was on the subject, Whitefield took a swipe at Oxford and Cambridge, asserting that most English schools and universities had become "mere seminaries of paganism." Since their curriculums were focused heavily on the classics of Greek and Roman antiquity, students' heads became "stuffed with heathen mythology" at the expense of the knowledge of Christ. (Whitefield himself knew the classics well, and often referred to them in his sermons and letters, so he was not opposed to classical education per se.)[43]

In spite of Blair's encouragement, Whitefield did not linger in Williamsburg. His Sunday-morning sermon at Bruton Parish Church went off without much notice. As he prepared to leave, he assessed the Anglicans of the Chesapeake region as "more dead to God" than those in the northern colonies, but "far less prejudiced." In the Chesapeake, "Satan seems to lead people at his will," he reported to Gilbert Tennent. The distance between the region's plantations made it more difficult for him to assemble large meetings. Moreover, the "commonality is made up of Negroes and convicts," including slaves and indentured servants, whose masters did not want them to attend religious meetings.[44]

The entourage moved into eastern North Carolina, the most desolate stretch of his overland journey. They arrived at Edenton, North Carolina, the colonial capital, on December 20, 1739. Whitefield called it "a little place, but beautifully situated by the water-side." From Edenton, he took a ferry across the wide Albemarle Sound. He estimated the journey across at twelve miles; it took them seven hours to reach the southern side. They proceeded to Bath, North Carolina, the colony's oldest town, incorporated in 1705.[45]

Whitefield would visit Bath four times in his career, earning a dubious place in local folklore. On one occasion, he reportedly became so frustrated with local opposition that while leaving, he shook the dust from his feet and placed a curse on the town, forever keeping it from major commercial development. (Among the reasons to doubt this story is that if Whitefield cursed every town where he encountered opposition, countless places would have endured Bath's fate.)[46]

From Bath they again took a ferry, crossing the Pamlico River. Traveling across North Carolina was arduous: abysmal roads, "wet and swampy" soil, and few people. The climate struck Whitefield as unusually warm—almost tropical—and flocks of strange birds flew squawking overhead. At night the travelers heard the howling of what they assumed were wolves.[47]

Whitefield celebrated Christmas in New Bern, North Carolina. Anglicans had established New Bern's parish only in 1715, and the church still met at the courthouse. Whitefield received communion there, but sadly noted that parishioners and the parson worshipped in an "indifferent manner." When he preached in the afternoon, however, he witnessed one of the most dramatic manifestations of the "Divine Presence" since his arrival. The people gave him rapt attention, and many wept. He considered the experience an "earnest of future and more plentiful effusions of God's Spirit in these parts."[48]

Up to this point, Whitefield had said little about slaves or slavery in his writings. He grew up in an area connected to the transatlantic slave trade: in the second quarter of the eighteenth century, Bristol was Europe's largest outfitter of slave ships, and its merchants had deep ties to Caribbean sugar plantations. But

Whitefield had minimal personal experience with chattel slavery. As he moved farther south, however, the realities of America's bound-labor system confronted him. At an ordinary south of New Bern, Whitefield visited with a slave family "belonging to the house." He prayed with two of their children and thought they spoke well. This chance personal encounter seems to have catalyzed Whitefield's thinking: what group was a more fitting subject for Methodist charitable ministry than slaves? He was convinced, unlike many southern slave masters, that white Christians could and should educate Africans in the ways of the Lord. Contemplating the creation of a "school of young negroes," he soon wrote to a London correspondent that America's slaves were much on his "heart."[49]

Slavery, both on plantations and in towns, was a seminal fact in American society, especially in the slave colonies of the South. From the Chesapeake southward, the culture was interlaced with slavery. In 1750, the Chesapeake colonies (Virginia and Maryland) had about 150,000 slaves, which represented about 40 percent of the population. South Carolina had a black majority by perhaps a two to one ratio, and the total slave population of the Lower South was about 60,000. But even in the North, whites owned about 33,000 slaves at midcentury. While slavery was not as central to northern colonial development as to southern, it could cause great anxiety among whites there. Around the same time as his colonial tour, a panic erupted in New York City over a reputed slave plot to burn the town. The frenzy resulted in the hanging of seventeen accused slave conspirators. New York authorities burned another thirteen slaves to death at the stake.[50]

South Carolina had also just endured the greatest slave rebellion in colonial American history. In September 1739, perhaps as many as one hundred slaves along the Stono River near Charleston stole firearms, killed twenty whites, and marched toward Spanish Florida, beating drums and chanting, "Liberty!" A white militia attacked the rebel slaves, soundly defeated them, and denied them quarter, executing most of them on the field of battle. The whites decapitated many of the rebels and placed their heads on pikes along the roads as a warning to other slaves.[51]

On New Year's Day 1740, Whitefield's party entered South Carolina, a colony reeling both from the Stono Rebellion and from the ongoing threat posed by the Spanish in the War of Jenkins' Ear. It was not long before he and his friends experienced the anxiety felt by whites there. On the night of January 2, the party lost its way in a moonless countryside. They could not find the plantation home where they had planned to stay. As they nervously wandered down the road, they saw a light in the distance, which upon investigation turned out to be a "hut full of negroes." Whitefield's friends asked them for directions, and the African Americans seemed to feign ignorance. The group suspected that these blacks might have participated in the recent rebellion (a suspicion that was probably wrong).[52] In any case, Whitefield's entourage hurried down the trail. Not long afterward, they saw a bonfire near the road and guessed that it had been lit by another "nest of such negroes." Their fears rising, they left the trail to avoid notice. Some thought they could see blacks "dancing round the fire." The panicked group was relieved when the clouds cleared and they could see again in the moonlight. Half expecting to encounter more runaway slaves, they finally found the house they were looking for. They breathlessly told the plantation owner about the blacks they had seen. He assured them that the slaves were no rebels, and nothing to worry about. Nevertheless, the party was relieved when they got to Charleston.[53]

Charleston (still spelled "Charles Town" in those days) was the most significant southern port in colonial America, and at about 6,500 residents it was one of the five most populous American towns. "A neat pretty place," as one observer called it, the town stood at the confluence of the Ashley and Cooper Rivers (named for Anthony Ashley Cooper, the 1st Earl of Shaftesbury, Carolina's founder and the grandfather of the humanitarian philosopher). The town faced out on Charleston harbor, beyond which lay the wide Atlantic. Charlestonians traded in rice, indigo (used for dyeing clothes), and enslaved human beings. Cotton was not much of a factor yet; the short-staple cotton that thrived in the South was easy to grow, but its sticky seeds made it difficult to process. (The invention of the cotton gin, which solved this problem, was still a half century away.) The majority of the Lower South's rice shipped from Charleston, and about 40 percent of slaves imported to the South between 1730 and 1780 disembarked there. The colony's governor once remarked that the Cooper River was like a "floating market," bringing crops from the Carolina interior and carrying back goods wanted on plantations. Many of those goods, of course, came from British companies.[54]

Whitefield attended the Anglican service at St. Philip's Church that Sunday morning, January 6. The church, completed in 1723 after twelve years of construction, illustrated the cosmopolitan sensibilities of elite Charlestonians. The massive brick building featured three porticoes with Tuscan columns, and an octagonal tower and dome over the church. City boosters compared the church to the great religious edifices of London.[55]

That afternoon, Whitefield preached at the Reverend Josiah Smith's Independent church. As in Annapolis and Williamsburg, he found the congregation too "polite" for his taste. He wondered how they could remain spiritually passive in light of "divine judgments lately sent abroad amongst them," including the Stono Rebellion and the War of Jenkins' Ear. Epidemics of yellow fever and smallpox had recently ravaged Charleston, too. During a yellow fever plague of the summer of 1739, pastors conducted multiple funerals every day. Doctors knew only to treat feverish patients with alcohol, plying them "burnt wine, hot punch, and strong juleps," which did little but ease the pain.[56] The next day, Whitefield preached to an overflow audience at the Huguenot (French Protestant) church. A number of French Protestants had fled their homeland in 1685 after the revocation of the Edict of Nantes and Louis XIV's brutal campaign to suppress the Protestant movement. Huguenots had a greater social and economic impact in South Carolina than in any other American colony. Whitefield's visit to the French church offers another reminder of the international character of early American religion and society.[57]

Whitefield's party had not yet reached its final destination, Georgia. Traveling overland in the South Carolina Lowcountry was prohibitively difficult, so Whitefield and his friends set out from Charleston by canoe. Five "civil, diligent, and laborious" slaves rowed them to Beaufort, around Hilton Head Island, and then finally to Savannah. Whitefield was delighted. He had now not only traversed the great Atlantic, but had trekked across the colonies from New York to Georgia. Few had made this trip.[58]

The end of the journey put him in a reflective mood, and he wrote a short essay reviewing the religious state of the colonies (leaving out New England, for the time being). He loved Pennsylvania the most. "The garden of America," as he called it, had seen the most powerful work of God, with the possible exception of "Northampton in New England," in Jonathan Edwards's church. He clearly meant to include New Jersey, as well, for he specifically mentioned the ministerial labors of Gilbert Tennent. Pennsylvania would be the ideal spot for his proposed "school for negroes." He especially commended Pennsylvania's practice of religious liberty, where even Dissenters could "worship God their own way." This allowed for the true friends of the gospel, regardless of denomination, to flourish in peace. Many of those friends were indeed Dissenters. Unfortunately, he thought the Church of England was at a "low ebb" in Pennsylvania.[59]

The South, to Whitefield, was more problematic. Religion among Maryland Anglicans was at a lower ebb even than that in Pennsylvania. Virginia offered more hope, but he reiterated that the high prevalence of slaves and indentured servants, combined with the scattered nature of the settlements, made consistent religious practice difficult for many. North Carolina was the least hopeful; in that sparsely settled colony, "there's scarce so much as the form of religion."

In South Carolina, he saw more formal religious commitment, but "no stirring among the dry bones" (Ezekiel 37) yet. But he would come back to Charleston in due course.[60]

One of his first tasks upon reaching Savannah was to buy land for the orphanage. This was a significant moment in Whitefield's institutional legacy. James Habersham, who stayed behind when Whitefield left Savannah fifteen months earlier, had picked out a tract of five hundred acres of sandy soil ten miles south of Savannah. Whitefield called the place "Bethesda," a Hebrew name mentioned in the Gospel of John, meaning "House of Mercy." The orphanage site was remote from the tiny town, selected intentionally so that the children would be free from "bad examples" and could work the farm he intended to establish there.[61]

Students would attend school for five hours a day; most would spend the remainder of their time "picking and carding cotton." (The cotton operation would bear little fruit because it was so inefficient, and under the British Navigation Acts, colonists were not supposed to be producing finished cotton anyway.) Whitefield immediately began gathering orphans to live in temporary housing until workers could build the orphan house. The place would become an enduring Savannah landmark; Bethesda Academy continues to operate on the site today, not far from Whitefield Avenue. The brick Whitefield Chapel, built in 1925, is now one of the most distinctive buildings on the property.[62]

Throwing himself fully into the project, Whitefield went to Frederica to "fetch the orphans" he could find there. He also wanted to visit General Oglethorpe, who was in Frederica planning an invasion of Spanish Florida (an action related to the War of Jenkins' Ear). Whitefield soon exasperated Georgia officials by taking some orphans without the trustees' express permission, including some children who seemed to be living in fairly stable environments with older siblings.[63]

A power struggle was emerging between Whitefield and certain trustees. They thought he worked for them, but Whitefield assumed that because he had raised so much money for the orphanage, he could run it as he saw fit. Some trustees were wary because Whitefield intended to take the children and "breed them up Methodist." (Whitefield certainly planned to "breed up for the ministry" any talented Bethesda boys who had experienced true conversion, as he wrote to a New England supporter.) The trustee Lord Egmont noted in his journal that even though he considered Whitefield an enthusiast, he was "willing to excuse the fool" for the time being. If the trustees angrily confronted the itinerant, Egmont feared that Whitefield might throw a fit and abandon the project altogether. Whitefield was also frustrated that the trustees had not yet arranged for a church to be built in Savannah. They talked as if religion was a major priority, but they did not act like it. By January 1740, Whitefield had begun threatening the trustees, via their accountant, Harman Verelst, that if Georgia authorities did not move quickly, he would "inform pious people in a public manner how little good has been done with their charitable contributions." The trustees told him he was "rash and uninformed" to "menace" them that way. By the time he left Georgia, three months later, Whitefield was so dismayed by the governance and moral state of the colony that he hinted he might shift his charitable focus to Pennsylvania.[64]

He had already decided he would not remain as Savannah's parish priest. Planning to stay in Georgia only long enough to set up the orphanage, he decided he could better provide for it financially from a distance. Fund-raising appeals would stay as regular features of his preaching. "When I have resigned the parish, I shall be at more liberty to take a tour round America," he noted.[65]

Whitefield returned to Charleston in March 1740. The Anglican commissary, Alexander Garden, had been out of town during Whitefield's visit in January. Garden was there this time and ready to put Whitefield in his place. Garden, thirty years older than Whitefield, had labored in South Carolina since 1720, becoming commissary in 1728. He and the itinerant met in Garden's parlor, and Garden charged Whitefield with enthusiasm and rash denunciations of the Anglican clergy. The commissary particularly resented a public letter that Whitefield had written to the bishop of Gloucester (published in Whitefield's journal), in which Whitefield averred that Henry Stebbing, a chaplain to King George II and a critic of the Methodists, knew "no more of the true nature of regeneration, than Nicodemus did when he came to Jesus by night" in the Gospel of John.[66]

When Whitefield refused to apologize, Garden declared that if he spoke at any church in the province, he would suspend him. Whitefield replied, "I shall regard that as much as I would a Pope's bull." Why did Garden worry so much about Whitefield's preaching, the itinerant asked, when Garden himself would not "exclaim" against the balls and dances so popular in Charleston? (Charleston was rapidly developing a reputation for lavish and lewd entertainments; as mentioned earlier, George Farquhar's bawdy *The Recruiting Officer* had been the Dock Street Theater's first play when it opened in 1736.) Garden indignantly replied that he saw no harm in those pastimes. If that was Garden's position, Whitefield retorted, then it was his duty to "exclaim" against Garden. The enraged commissary had heard enough. He told Whitefield and his friends, "Get you out of my house."[67]

Whitefield spent most of the rest of his Charleston visit communing with Dissenters. Two days after the altercation with Garden, he dutifully attended St. Philip's Church and heard Garden, as Whitefield put it, represent him as a "Pharisee." He spoke at Josiah Smith's meetinghouse the next evening and collected a remarkable £70 for Bethesda, the largest onetime gift he had yet received. Such continuing successes convinced him that a rift with Anglican authorities was unavoidable, and part of God's plan.[68]

Back in Savannah, Whitefield laid the first brick of Bethesda's great house and then made arrangements for returning to Philadelphia. It would have been easy for Whitefield to forget his concerns and friends back in Britain, which must have seemed far away as he stood on the cleared acreage at Bethesda. But two people back home especially stayed on the twenty-five-year-old's mind. One was John Wesley. Whitefield got a letter from Wesley when he returned from Charleston. Wesley had continued to push Whitefield to accept Wesley's views on perfectionism and to reject Calvinism. Pleading with Wesley to stop bringing up these topics, he said that they both had strong opinions and were unlikely ever to agree. Whitefield was "ten thousand times more convinced" of the doctrines of election and the final perseverance of believers than he was the last time they had talked. He still maintained that he did not want to go public with his objections to Wesley's theology. That determination would not last out the year, however.[69]

The other person on Whitefield's mind was Elizabeth Delamotte. Thoughts of this relationship were perplexing to the itinerant, who sought to mortify desires he considered frivolous or worldly, including romantic desires. But receiving a letter from Delamotte when he arrived in Savannah after his trans-colonial trek brought back the feelings that had stirred him while visiting with her as he waited out the embargo in England. In early February 1741, he wrote to her, sending mixed messages clothed in spiritual garb. The letter opened with standard Methodist spiritual advice. He confessed that he feared having his heart drawn away from Christ by "earthly objects." What room, he asked, "can there be for God, when a rival hath taken possession of the heart?" Asking about her family, he abruptly closed, saying, "My heart is now full. Writing quickens me. I could almost drop a tear, and wish myself, for a moment or two, in England. But hush, nature." He signed the letter "your sincere friend and servant in Christ."[70]

This episode has become fodder for speculation about Whitefield's psycho-logical turmoil regarding women generally, and Delamotte in particular. We need not go as far as the historian Harry Stout, who says that Whitefield was "obsessed with Delamotte and hating himself for the 'vile' passions" he felt for her. Even the pastor-historian Arnold Dallimore, however, depicted the itinerant as enduring "bitter" struggles in these months as he wrestled with his feelings about Elizabeth and confronted fears of what acting on those feelings might do to his ministry. It is tempting to read his agonized deliberations over Delamotte into the "unspeakable trouble and agony of soul" he experienced on March 30.[71]

In April, Whitefield took the ten-day sea journey back to Philadelphia. While on board, he anxiously prayed and decided to resolve his struggles over Delamotte by sending her a marriage proposal. And what a proposal! He composed two letters, one to Elizabeth's parents and one to her. The opening line of the letter to the Delamottes told them how one Methodist woman he brought from England had already died, and another was gravely ill. Then he told them that he needed a godly woman to take care of his affairs in Georgia; moreover, he had become convinced that the Lord wanted him to get married. Is "Miss Elizabeth . . . a proper person to engage in such an undertaking?" he asked. If so, could he have their permission to propose to her? Refusing the request was fine, he said, since he was "free from that foolish passion, which the world calls LOVE." If they declined, he would know that Elizabeth was not the one for him.[72]

He also sent the Delamottes a letter for Elizabeth; they were to deliver it only if they approved of his proposal. Was she willing to submit to the demands of being his wife, he asked? Could she manage the growing "family" at Bethesda? Would she willingly part with the itinerant, "even for a long season, when his Lord and master shall call him forth to preach the gospel, and command him to leave you behind?" His conscience was clean, for he desired to take her, "my sister[,] to wife, not for lust, but uprightly." Not offering any "passionate expressions" such as those used by "carnal courtiers," he would promise only to help her grow closer to the Lord if they married. He just loved her "for God."[73]

The nineteenth-century biographer Luke Tyerman put it well when he wrote that Whitefield "was one of the oddest wooers that ever wooed." Dallimore said that had he tried, Whitefield could not have written letters more likely to precipitate negative responses. Indeed, Elizabeth did not accept his proposal. In July, Whitefield received a letter from her that suggested to Whitefield that she was spiritually "in a seeking state only," and perhaps not even converted. Such an intermediate condition would "not do," he told William Seward: "I would have one that is full of faith and the Holy Ghost." He wept over receiving the news, but Jesus assured Whitefield that he would not let him "fall by the hands of a woman."[74]

The reference to Delamotte's seeking state may have reflected the fact that, in Whitefield's absence, the Delamottes had split with John Wesley and become Moravians. But Delamotte had another suitor, as well, a Moravian man whom she married less than a year after receiving Whitefield's proposal. The parents too seem to have sent a negative reply to the itinerant, but Elizabeth (whose letter we do not have) may have equivocated. As late as November 1740, Whitefield wrote, "Mr. and Mrs. Delamotte refuse to give their daughter, but yet I believe [Elizabeth] may be my wife." It was not to be.[75]

Upon his return to the Middle Colonies, he preached at Wilmington, Delaware, a river port of six hundred residents about thirty miles from Philadelphia. Whitefield estimated that three thousand people attended, and "God was pleased to be amongst us," he wrote, "as in the holy place of Sinai." He was glad to be back. As was typical at the end of his journeys, he paused to reflect. "The world is now up in arms," he said, aware of the progress of the war with Spain, in which his friend James Oglethorpe was on the front lines. "Blessed Jesus," he prayed, "whilst the kings of the earth are striving to extend their dominions, do thou secretly carry on thy Kingdom in believers' hearts, till the earth be filled with the knowledge of thee, our Lord, as the waters cover the sea" (Isaiah 11:9). And indeed, a new flood was on the rise. Soon he began preparing to visit New England.[76]

6

"TO REVIVE THE FLAME AGAIN":
WHITEFIELD COMES TO NEW ENGLAND

On an October Sunday morning in 1740, George Whitefield ascended the pulpit of the Northampton, Massachusetts, meetinghouse. Five years earlier, Jonathan Edwards's church had experienced what has become perhaps the most famous revival in Christian history outside of those recorded in the book of Acts. Now the great itinerant visited Northampton, at Edwards's invitation, in hopes of "reviv[ing] the flame again, even in the darkest times." Edwards thought that the new revivals in Britain and America might signal "the dawning of a day of God's might power and glorious grace." Having heard several years earlier about Edwards's 1734–35 revival, Whitefield eagerly made his way to the frontier town to call on the Northampton congregation to return to their first love. Edwards noted that the congregation was "extraordinarily melted"; almost everyone there wept. Among those deeply moved was Edwards himself. "Dear Mr. Edwards wept during the whole time of exercise," Whitefield noted. It was a remarkable meeting of the two greatest leaders of the Great Awakening.[1]

Upon returning to Philadelphia in April, Whitefield delivered three letters to Ben Franklin for publication, first in the *Pennsylvania Gazette* and then as a pamphlet. The letters confronted two of the most controversial topics imaginable: the faith of Anglican archbishop John Tillotson, and the state of American slavery. Tillotson, who died in 1694, was one of the most influential Anglican writers of the period, promoting a latitudinarian faith emphasizing rationality and morals. He was irenic but anti-Calvinist, and his prominence—which continued well after his death—fed into evangelical Calvinists' sense that biblical theology was under attack. In his travels, Whitefield routinely met

Anglicans who loved Tillotston's works. Whitefield often told these devotees that Tillotson was "natural" and unconverted. The archbishop, he believed, was one of the chief defenders of a polite, quasi-Christian moralism that Whitefield believed would lead its adherents to hell. It was time to expose the "mystery of iniquity" (2 Thessalonians 2:7) he saw woven into the man's writings.[2]

Archbishop Tillotson, Whitefield declared, "knew no more of true Christianity than Mahomet." (Whitefield noted that this comparison was not original to him; he had heard John Wesley make it first.) He cited Tillotson as saying that believers must "perform the conditions of the Gospel" in order to become partakers of its blessings. To Calvinists and also to Arminians such as Wesley, this belief was unadulterated works-righteousness. Tillotson understood nothing of a Christian's acceptance by God through faith in Christ, nor of justification by faith alone, Whitefield asserted.[3]

Critics were appalled. Did Whitefield mean to say that Tillotson was in hell? The attack on Tillotson would help turn Harvard College's faculty against Whitefield. Tillotson had helped Increase Mather secure Massachusetts's new charter in 1692, leaving a positive memory of the archbishop even among conservative New England pastors. The letter secured Anglican animosity toward the itinerant, nowhere more so than in Philadelphia. The Anglican commissary, Archibald Cummings, had allowed Whitefield to preach at the city's Christ Church on his initial visits, but once he learned of the anti-Tillotson publication, Cummings barred him from the pulpit. Some of the itinerant's Anglican supporters began attending Dissenting meetings because of the clash between Cummings and Whitefield. Cummings complained of some parishioners, "Several have refused to contribute to my subsistence which was bare and precarious" already.[4]

Cummings's reaction to Whitefield, published in a pamphlet titled *Faith Absolutely Necessary, But Not Sufficient to Salvation Without Good Works*, showed again that while the clash between the itinerant and his Anglican opponents was about power, it was also rooted in theological differences. Cummings rejected Whitefield's argument that salvation came by grace alone, through faith alone, and that good works were a by-product of true conversion. The difference between good works as the fruit of salvation, and good works as a condition of salvation, was "evasive and trifling," the commissary declared. Faith, to Cummings, had to include sincere obedience, or it was not saving faith. To Cummings, Whitefield and his fellow itinerants were fanatics "disgorging themselves in flames of fire and brimstone; threatening hell and everlasting damnation against all that would not implicitly believe their incredible rhapsodies."[5]

The theological feud between Whitefield and his critics had a broader popular resonance, since many laypeople readily recognized its significance. Did good works add anything to one's salvation? If not, what role did morality play in the Christian life? The *American Weekly Mercury* printed a snide ditty about Whitefield and his followers that raised just this point:

> WHITEFIELD to what end do you preach,
> Since you have no good works to teach?
> No man e'er preach'd so much as you;
> Yet, more good, many preachers do.
> None e'er such crowds of hearers had,
> And none so FEW, that were not MAD.[6]

Following his break with Cummings, Whitefield found most of his support (as in Charleston) among Philadelphia's Dissenting pastors. Given the nondenominational tendencies of modern evangelicals, it is difficult to appreciate the novelty of the Anglican Whitefield's impact on American Dissenters. Whitefield even admired certain Baptist ministers (many Anglicans and Dissenters disdained Baptists because of their refusal to baptize infants), regarding the Baptist pastor Jenkin Jones as the "only preacher that I know of in Philadelphia, who speaks feelingly and with authority."[7]

As Whitefield cooperated with Dissenting ministers and preached from their pulpits, some experienced conversion through his ministry. This may have been the case for the Welsh Baptist minister Abel Morgan, who was so affected by "Brother Whitefield's spirit" that he became an itinerant himself, going "forth preaching the glad tidings of salvation towards the sea coast in the Jerseys." And while Richard Treat, a Presbyterian minister of Abingdon, had taught the Calvinist "doctrines of grace" for years before hearing Whitefield preach, he realized that he had never "experienced them in his heart." Treat told his congregation that he had "deceived both himself and them" and asked that they pray for his conversion. (Whitefield reported in a later edition of his journals that Treat had indeed experienced "comfort" and had been walking with God for years.)[8]

In addition to its attack on Tillotson, Whitefield's *Three Letters* launched a salvo against slave masters in "Maryland, Virginia, North and South Carolina." Although public criticism of slavery was fairly limited in Britain and America at the time, Whitefield was not the first Methodist to comment upon its horrors. Charles Wesley had recounted a number of stories of the "diabolical cruelty" meted out against slaves for the slightest infractions. He said that white children were given slaves of their own age to abuse and tyrannize for sport. Wesley also recalled hearing of a dancing master in Charleston who whipped a female slave until she fell unconscious; then, with the assistance of a physician, he revived her and continued the whipping. He climaxed the torture by pouring hot wax onto her ripped flesh. "Her crime," Wesley wrote, "was over-filling a tea cup."[9]

Wesley jotted that passage in his journal, which was not published in his lifetime. For Whitefield to go on record publicly about the evils of American slavery was far more significant. As he passed through the South on his overland journey, Whitefield was "touched with a fellow-feeling of the miseries of the poor negroes," he confessed. White southerners' troubles, from the Stono Rebellion to disease and war, reflected God's "quarrel" with them for their "abuse of and cruelty to the poor negroes." He shuddered at the stories of vicious beatings by masters, who whipped and "ploughed upon their backs, and made long furrows [Psalm 129:3], and at length brought them even to death itself." Because of such severe treatment, the southern colonies had occasionally faced slave uprisings, such as the one at Stono. He wondered why the slaves did not revolt more often.[10]

Many masters also intentionally kept their slaves ignorant of the gospel and Christianity, Whitefield charged. They casually permitted slaves to violate the Sabbath by "dancing, piping, and such like," thereby putting their souls in jeopardy. Whitefield considered this neglect particularly ironic: if the slaves embraced Christianity, they would become more obedient. In a reflection of his interest in a possible school for African Americans, he averred that blacks and whites were both naturally sinful, but both also equally susceptible to moral and intellectual improvement.[11]

Whitefield was reacting to the treatment of American slaves in the same way that some earlier Anglican parsons had done when they arrived in the colonies in the past century. While Anglican officials in Britain assumed that ethnicity was no necessary barrier to conversion and baptism, many southern and Caribbean planters spoke as if evangelistic overtures were wasted on blacks and Indians. By the 1740s, white southerners had become increasingly reluctant to proselytize or baptize their slaves (or to allow their ministers to do so), fearing that Christian slaves might expect to be liberated. Under European law, when a slave or indentured servant became a Christian, he or she often had to be freed. New Virginia statutes in 1667 and 1705 explicitly stipulated that Christian baptism did not require emancipation. If colonial authorities had intended such laws to encourage planters to permit the baptism of Africans and Indians, that is not what happened. The Anglican minister Morgan Godwyn, who came to Virginia in the 1660s, was shocked to find many parishioners hostile to the notion of baptizing black slaves. One white churchgoer told Godwyn that baptism was no more beneficial to a slave than to a "black bitch" (a dog).[12]

In advocating the evangelization and baptism of slaves, then, Whitefield was battling against well-established white southern disregard for those Christian duties. Whitefield's missive against slavery made one critical caveat, however. He demurred on the question "whether it be lawful for Christians to buy slaves." He failed to call slavery itself sinful, leaving Christian ownership of slaves as a permissible option, one that Whitefield himself would come to accept.[13]

Indeed, Whitefield had already become convinced that introducing slavery into Georgia was essential to the colony's economic prospects and to Bethesda's welfare. Denying Georgians access to slaves (as well as to rum) was "little better than to tie their legs, and bid them walk," he wrote. The proprietors of the colony meant well, he believed, but their vision of a southern colony without slaves was "absolutely impracticable." When Whitefield sent William Seward back to England (he departed on April 28), he instructed him that the first item to discuss with the Georgia trustees was the "allowance of Negroes."[14]

In the meantime, acting on his newfound urgency about educating slaves, Whitefield purchased a five-thousand-acre tract about seventy miles north of Philadelphia, in the Lehigh Valley. (He did not comment on the fact that a sizeable Lenni-Lenape Indian town was located on the property.) Calling the place Nazareth, he intended to open a school there for "all such negroes, whether young or old, as shall be sent to me." He planned to buy some young slaves himself in order to send them to Nazareth, and hoped that some of his slave-owning supporters might sell prospective slave students to him at an "easy rate." It is not clear whether he hoped eventually to free these students from slavery.[15]

He arranged for the relocation of German Moravians to the Nazareth tract from Georgia, to help build the school. But plans for Nazareth fizzled because of theological squabbles between Whitefield and the Moravians. Moravian craftsmen did build the "Whitefield House" on the property, but a year after purchasing the land, Whitefield sold Nazareth to the Moravians. His dreams of a school for African Americans never materialized. Nazareth became a largely German community, forerunners of people often called the "Pennsylvania Dutch."[16]

Nevertheless, Whitefield reached out to free and enslaved African Americans in his ministry. In April 1740, for example, he preached in Philadelphia to a very large crowd, upward of ten thousand people. He spoke on the woman healed of chronic bleeding by Christ; as described in Luke 8, she received instantaneous restoration when she touched the hem of his garment. (This was one of the revivalist's standard sermons.) Whitefield then "invited the poor Negroes to touch Jesus Christ by faith" for spiritual healing. If they did, they "would gain freedom from the slavery of sin and Satan," he promised them.[17] Freedom from spiritual slavery, but not freedom from earthly slavery? Today, this seems an insufferable contradiction, but early evangelicals often maintained that tension without any obvious ethical reservations. Whitefield lived in a world of all kinds of hierarchies and inequalities. His Bible never conclusively told him that slavery was evil. He was left to interpret for himself passages that, on one hand, told slaves to obey their masters, and, on the other, proclaimed that in Christ there was neither slave nor free, "for ye are all one in Christ Jesus" (Galatians 3:28).

Reflecting a view shared by many Christians of the time, Whitefield believed that the Bible tacitly accepted slavery, but required masters to treat their laborers with kindness. Jonathan and Sarah Edwards kept household slaves. Jonathan had purchased "a Negro Girle named Venus" when he was in his late twenties, several years before the Northampton revival began. In 1741, at the height of the Great Awakening, Edwards found himself tasked with the awkward duty of defending one of his ministerial colleagues for owning a slave, even though that pastor, Benjamin Doolittle, reputedly had Arminian theological tendencies and did not embrace the revivals. Some of Doolittle's parishioners had attacked him for a range of issues, including a lavish lifestyle. (Owning slaves was a mark of gentility.) Although Edwards may have sympathized with Doolittle's critics on theological points, he did not approve of their complaints against Doolittle for holding slaves. Whites in the northern colonies were particularly touchy about this topic in 1741, since New York had just put down its rumored slave insurrection with mass arrests and public burnings of a number of African Americans.[18]

Edwards's ministerial association asked him to draft a response to the charges against Doolittle. The Northampton pastor regarded the antislavery argument as disingenuous. Why focus on the immorality of owning a slave or two when far greater enormities transpired in the Atlantic slave trade? New England's seagoing economy was deeply complicit in that human traffic. As for slave owning itself, Edwards thought that scripture accepted its existence, providing moral guidelines only for its practice. Nevertheless, Edwards signaled that the abuses and inequalities of slavery would vanish in the millennial era—the reign of Christ on earth—when, he expected, "many of the Negroes and Indians will be divines."[19]

Whitefield shared Edwards's ambivalence about slavery, but unlike Edwards, he felt glimmers of moral hesitation about the issue before, not after, becoming a slave owner. After 1740, Whitefield said little more about the widely known abuses within the slave system and never reflected at length on whether the actual practices of chattel slavery, with its mass transport of African captives, the cruel conditions of the Middle Passage across the Atlantic, the appalling death rates on plantations, and the frequent physical and sexual abuse, could be redeemed. To Whitefield, benevolence to slaves primarily entailed introducing them to the gospel. The itinerant adjusted his preaching when slaves were in the audience. He and his Methodist friends recorded numerous instances of speaking individually with African American seekers. Whitefield recorded that some even asked him, "Have I a soul?" Following the sermon on the healing of the bleeding woman, William Seward visited an African American woman and prayed personally with her, concluding that she had experienced divine grace in her heart. He found the experience "peculiarly sweet."[20]

Franklin was happy to have Whitefield back in town, but not as pleased to be subjected to Whitefield's fund-raising appeals: "His eloquence had a wonderful power over the hearts and purses of his hearers, of which I myself was an instance," the printer wrote. Franklin liked the concept of Bethesda, but he thought it made more sense to build it in Philadelphia than in remote Georgia. Whitefield disagreed, so Franklin "refused to contribute."[21]

Then Franklin attended one of the itinerant's sermons. Suspecting that he would ask for money, Franklin wrote: "I silently resolved he should get nothing from me. I had in my pocket a handful of copper money, three or four silver dollars, and five pistoles in gold. As he proceeded I began to soften, and concluded to give the coppers. Another stroke of his oratory made me ashamed of that, and determined me to give the silver; and he finished so admirably, that I emptied my pocket wholly into the collector's dish, gold and all."[22]

This passage from Franklin's autobiography poked fun at Whitefield's incessant requests for money. But Franklin was adamant that the revivalist had an impeccable character. Many spread rumors that Whitefield spent the charity's money on himself, but to Franklin, those charges were absurd, and he defended Whitefield in print: "He was in all his conduct a perfectly honest man. And methinks my testimony in his favor ought to have the more weight, as we had no religious connection." Franklin was no evangelical believer, despite Whitefield's pleas for him to accept Christ's offer of forgiveness. Whitefield wrote to Franklin in late 1740 and predicted that his friend would soon see "the reasonableness of Christianity." He urged the printer to "apply to God; be willing to do the divine will, and you shall know it." Looking back decades later, Franklin concluded that "ours was a mere civil friendship, sincere on both sides, and lasted to his death." There was more depth to their friendship than the description "mere civil" might indicate, however. Franklin once told his brother James that Whitefield "is a good man and I love him."[23]

In late April, Whitefield set out again for New York City. His return saw fairly large crowds but no notable response. New York would always be one of the toughest cities in America for Whitefield to reach. But from the eastern end of Long Island came enticing reports of "a most glorious work" led by two young ministers. One was Jonathan Barber of Oysterponds, who had begun to contemplate his own possible role in the unfolding work of God.[24] One Saturday night a couple months before Whitefield's visit, Barber had stayed up all night praying and reading his Bible. The next morning, he turned to Psalm 102, and the thirteenth verse jumped off the page at him. God himself seemed to say: "Thou shalt arise, and have mercy upon Zion: for the time to favour her, yea, the set time, is come." Barber was so ecstatic when he read this passage that he fainted. He woke up in time for church and spent the rest of the week telling the people of Oysterponds how he had been overcome when God revealed this word to him.[25]

Affecting the style of an apostle, taking no money or even a change of clothes, Barber walked the roads of Long Island, resolving that he would go only where the Holy Spirit told him to go. The Spirit immediately led Barber to Southold, to visit the second minister whom Whitefield mentioned, James Davenport. Davenport, one of the most perplexing characters of the whole American awakening, had met Barber as part of a Pietist student group at Yale College. (The colony of Connecticut had founded Yale four decades earlier as a training school for Congregationalist pastors.) Davenport and Barber began meeting around the same time that Whitefield entered Oxford and encountered the Wesleys. Critics of the Yale "club" said that they heavily emphasized "impressions and impulses," and that they sought guidance from the Holy Spirit, expecting God to impress scripture on their minds.[26]

The rambling Barber found that God had given Davenport a new passage of scripture, too. It was Psalm 115:12–14: "The LORD hath been mindful of us: he will bless us; he will bless the house of Israel; he will bless the house of Aaron. He will bless them that fear the LORD, both small and great. The LORD shall increase you more and more, you and your children." Davenport, bolstered by Barber's visit, entered an extraordinary new phase of ministry at his Southold church. He began openly naming church members that he regarded as unregenerate, and holding lengthy sessions with his supporters. At one point, he preached to them for almost twenty-four hours straight.[27]

Davenport had heard that Whitefield was coming to New York, and so he made the hundred-mile trip across the island to meet him. Whitefield was very impressed with the pastor. God had blessed Davenport's ministry with a number of conversions, Whitefield wrote, yet he was "looked upon as an enthusiast and a madman by many of his reverend pharisaical brethren." In private conversations, Whitefield reportedly said that he never knew someone who had a closer walk with God than Davenport. Indeed, one of Connecticut's key revivalists, Benjamin Pomeroy, asserted that Davenport surpassed Whitefield in "heavenly communion" with God. The charges of fanaticism against Davenport would only grow louder over time, however.[28]

In their work in New York and Philadelphia, both Whitefield and William Seward continued to be deeply affected by conversations they had with African American converts, and they recorded a number of such discussions in their published journals. The Methodist emphases on charity and conversion met perfectly in ministering to blacks. Britain had very few African residents, so there was real novelty in proselytizing the large African populations in America. Reaching this largely unevangelized group with the gospel was of keen interest to Whitefield's supporters. Seward told of an African American woman in Philadelphia who insisted that "Mr. Whitefield had been in a trance" as he addressed the city's blacks, meaning that "Jesus Christ had told him what to speak to the people, or else he could not speak as he did." Seward thought that such inroads among African Americans suggested that God was beginning a great new work. Perhaps it represented "the dawnings of the glory of the latter day" or the inauguration of the Kingdom of God on earth, Seward thought.[29]

Whitefield likewise noted personal interactions he had with blacks. In Philadelphia, he conversed with an African American woman who had experienced conversion through his preaching the previous autumn. She told him that she had struggled to attain assurance of salvation, but during a sermon preached by the Baptist evangelist Abel Morgan, "the Word came with such power upon her heart, that at last she was obliged to cry out." She kept shouting so much that Morgan stopped his sermon. Several in attendance urged her to be quiet, but Whitefield concluded that "she could not help praising and blessing God."[30]

There were not many settings in eighteenth-century America in which a black woman would interrupt a white man publicly. Whitefield, far from perturbed, thought her reaction was not only appropriate and godly, but "rational and solid." He said that when God was working in an extraordinary manner, pastors should expect some people to respond likewise. He reminded blacks of Galatians 3:28, which said that in Christ there was "neither male or female, bond or free." And "when the poor negroes are to be called," Whitefield predicted, "God will highly favor them, to wipe off their reproach, and to show that he is no respecter of persons [Acts 10:34], but that whosoever believeth in him shall be saved [Romans 10:13]." This was robust spiritual egalitarianism, but to Whitefield, the social implications of this belief lay in an indeterminate future, when God would "wipe off the reproach" of people of African descent.[31]

Abel Morgan was not the only one seeing unusual outbursts in his meetings. Whitefield witnessed a remarkable outpouring of spiritual fervor at a Methodist-style society of young women in Philadelphia. (A later report indicated that at least twenty-six of these societies began meeting in the city as a result of the revivals.) Even as he began to pray over the meeting, he choked up and could not continue. But "a wonderful power was in the room," he wrote, and "with one accord, they began to cry out and weep most bitterly for the space of half an hour." The cacophony continued after he left, and he heard that five of the women were "affected as those that are in fits." Unlike the African American woman's cries of joy, Whitefield regarded these convulsions as coming from the devil, who wished to cause distracting controversy about the revivals.[32]

Whitefield's dizzying experiences in Philadelphia continued the day after the young women's meeting. He preached that Sunday morning to a crowd of perhaps fifteen thousand people and then went to the Anglican church to hear Commissary Cummings denounce him and his followers as those who "have a zeal of God, but not according to knowledge" (Romans 10:2). Then he went outdoors again, preaching a farewell sermon to a mammoth assembly he estimated at twenty thousand. Supporters pressed around his rented house after the sermon. About fifty blacks were in the throng. Some, in spite of their apparent poverty, donated to Bethesda.[33] In his sermon, Whitefield turned again from spiritual ideal to social reality, expressing hope that "masters and mistresses will shortly see, that Christianity will not make their negroes worse slaves." For him, the first priority was always evangelism. From Whitefield's perspective, suffering on earth as a slave did not compare with suffering eternal torments in hell. While he indicted slave owners for their worst abuses, he still envisioned a kind of benevolent Christian slave owning, in which masters would educate slaves in the gospel, not unlike the way they should nurture their own children.[34]

Unless we understand Whitefield and his fellow evangelicals' conviction that heaven and hell were utterly real, we will struggle to fathom their apparent callousness toward slavery. A slave headed for heaven, Whitefield believed, was better off than a king headed for hell. Yet many younger British and American evangelicals, such as Whitefield's friend the former slave trader John Newton, the author of the hymn "Amazing Grace," later realized that supporting slavery compromised their credibility as gospel preachers.

Native Americans also drew Whitefield's evangelistic attention. But language barriers and the danger of travel into the interior made Native American evangelism difficult. So Whitefield was delighted to meet an "Indian trader," likely an Anglo-Pennsylvanian, who had experienced conversion under his preaching and had subsequently begun ministering to his Indian clients. Whitefield saw this trader's work as a hopeful sign that God was fulfilling his promises to give Christ "the heathen for his inheritance, and the utmost parts of the earth for his possession" (Psalm 2:8).[35] Whitefield wrote to this aspiring trader-evangelist and advised him on the methods most likely to result in authentic conversions. He warned the man not to discuss baptism or the Lord's Supper before the natives' sincere reception of grace. Otherwise, no doubt thinking of Catholic proselytes among the Indians, "they will catch at a shadow, and neglect the substance." He urged the trader to tell potential converts that real faith entailed the heart as much as the head, and that accepting Christ would make them truly happy. Real faith would also produce substantive change in their lives.[36]

Whitefield wrote a letter for the trader to pass on to the Indians of the Allegheny Mountains region. In it, he laid out the principles of Christianity and the "promises of the gospel that had especial reference to them." He gave a broad overview of the Bible's narrative of creation, fall, redemption, and the final return of Christ. Cautioning Native Americans to be wary of identifying all Europeans as Christians, he noted that "thousands of white people only believe in their heads, and therefore are no more Christians than those who never heard of Jesus Christ at all." Apologizing for not coming to them himself, Whitefield said his other business would not permit it. In his career, the itinerant would never devote sustained attention to Native Americans, in contrast to James Davenport, who attracted a number of Indians to evangelical piety in the early 1740s, or Jonathan Edwards, who spent six years ministering to the Stockbridge Indians in the 1750s.[37]

Whitefield continued to see remarkable awakenings in the Philadelphia area, preaching on consecutive days in May 1740 at Nottingham and Fagg's Manor, Pennsylvania, west of Philadelphia. Whitefield estimated the crowds at twelve thousand people. (Some of the same people likely attended both meetings, which were about twenty miles apart.) These areas had a deep Scots-Irish revival tradition, cultivated lately by the Tennent family and others in their circle. At Nottingham, thousands shouted and fainted, with some shrieking "as if they were in the sharpest agonies of death." Whitefield himself was overcome with emotion and entered a trancelike state, sweetly lying at the "feet of my Jesus."[38]

Coming out of this divine stupor, Whitefield moved on to Fagg's Manor. The scene there was even more intense: "Some were struck pale as death, others wringing their hands, others lying on the ground, others sinking into the arms of their friends; and most lifting up their eyes towards heaven, and crying out to God." Whitefield compared these sights to those he expected to see at Christ's return to earth.[39]

An unwelcome guest abruptly brought Whitefield out of his reverie. Francis Alison, a hostile Presbyterian minister, approached Whitefield even as many lay moaning on the ground, and challenged him to a public debate. Alison was irritated by Whitefield's teaching on assurance of salvation: the Presbyterian asserted that people could be true Christians without such confidence. Whitefield replied that he thought Christians might struggle with doubts concerning salvation, but that they should seek full assurance.[40] As this confrontation unfolded, some who had been caught up in the meeting's fervor became "exasperated" with the interloper, and one man began yelling at Alison. Whitefield rebuked his supporter for menacing Alison, but he also told Alison that it was inappropriate to seek a theological debate when "he saw the power of God so visibly amongst us." Alison, looking out on a sea of angry faces, thought better of it and withdrew. But Alison's appearance signaled increasing public opposition to Whitefield in the Middle Colonies.[41]

Hostility did not deter Whitefield, however: "The more I am opposed, the more joy I feel." Whitefield believed that the events in Philadelphia were part of a "general awakening" unlike anything seen before in America. Evangelicals did not use the term "*the* Great Awakening" in the 1740s, just as participants did not initially know they were part of "*the* American Revolution." But while England, Wales, Scotland, and the American colonies had seen local and regional revivals before, Whitefield's ministry was producing far broader effects. Newspapers and pamphlets helped link and publicize a common spiritual awakening on both sides of the Atlantic. Whitefield's presence at many centers of revival gave them a common leader. Especially in America, activity across denominational lines made this far more than an Anglican renewal. An unprecedented transatlantic awakening had begun.[42]

Whitefield boarded his ship, the *Savannah*, the next day, temporarily leaving Philadelphia behind. While on board, Whitefield sent John Wesley a letter addressing their growing theological rift. In the two months since his previous letter to Wesley, Whitefield had grown more confident. Before, he had asked Wesley only to stop bringing up Calvinism. Now, he boldly asserted that Wesley was wrong. His new certainty came partly from the relative theological unanimity among the American revivalists. In America, there were effectively no Arminian awakeners, at least not until Wesleyan Methodists began to arrive in the 1770s.[43]

Whitefield anticipated his return to England with trepidation because he knew it would require a confrontation with Wesley. He contemplated remaining in America, "where we all think and speak the same thing," in order to avoid the clash. But he and Wesley would reunite either in this life or the next, Whitefield believed. If they met again only in glory, Wesley would then have realized "that sovereign, distinguishing, irresistible grace brought you to heaven." More convinced than ever that they would not reconcile, Whitefield simply asked Wesley not to be angry with him. To the London printer James Hutton, Whitefield wrote, "For Christ's sake [would you] desire dear Brother W[esley] to avoid disputing with me."[44]

The orphanage, with about 130 residents, was thriving upon the itinerant's return to Savannah. More incredible outbreaks of revival transpired during his brief visit there in June 1740. Bethesda's children were particularly affected, as Whitefield noted: "The power of the Lord came as it were upon all. Most of the children, both boys and girls, cried bitterly." The scene was reminiscent of Pentecost, when the Holy Spirit surged "like a mighty rushing wind." In the meetinghouse, the children knelt and prayed in every corner, "begging of Jesus to take full possession of their hearts." Four or five girls wept uncontrollably for almost two hours, pleading for forgiveness and assurance of salvation. But Whitefield did not want just emotional reactions: immediately following his description of the children's experiences, he noted that he had hired a Latin instructor for Bethesda, and that he was making plans to expand the orphanage into a proper university. To Whitefield, head and heart went together in true piety.[45]

In early July, Whitefield returned to Charleston, where he found the Anglican commissary Alexander Garden ready to resume their feud. At Garden's church, Whitefield "heard the commissary preach as virulent, unorthodox, and inconsistent a discourse" as he had ever heard. Following the sermon Garden sent his clerk to Whitefield, telling him to withhold himself from communion until they could resolve Garden's complaints against him. Undeterred, Whitefield made the rounds at Dissenting congregations in the area, preaching and raising funds for Bethesda. Far from worrying about Garden's fury, he struggled much more with a besetting ailment exacerbated by the broiling heat of the Carolina Lowcountry. But a week later, he was back at Garden's church, where the commissary took aim at him again. "Had some infernal spirit been sent to draw my picture, I think it scarcely possible that he could have painted me in more horrid colours," Whitefield wrote. Whitefield found that the Spirit strengthened him during Garden's tirade, and he prayed for Garden's conversion, asking the Lord to let Garden "know that it is Jesus whom he persecutes," just as the Apostle Paul had persecuted Christians before his conversion.[46]

Yet Garden went even further. He brought Whitefield up for ecclesiastical trial, citing him for irregular preaching and for neglecting the Book of Common Prayer. The young cleric cleverly turned the trial into a debate about the South Carolina court's jurisdiction over Whitefield as an itinerant, and the propriety of Garden functioning as a judge when he had already publicly condemned Whitefield. Whitefield had a right to appeal these matters to London. Because he did so, Garden could take no additional actions for a year. After receiving no word from English authorities (who simply ignored the case) for twelve months, Garden declared that for Whitefield's "excesses and faults," the court was suspending him from preaching. By then, Whitefield was back in England, and no one, least of all Whitefield, paid attention to Garden's ruling.[47]

Even as Garden's case proceeded, Whitefield continued to ponder the possibilities of ministry to southern slaves. A turning point came when he befriended the brothers Hugh and Jonathan Bryan, South Carolina planters who converted under Whitefield's preaching. Hugh, formerly a nominal Anglican, had heedlessly left his slaves in "ignorance of the common salvation thro' Jesus Christ." He personally knew nothing of the new birth. His wife, Catherine, had a similarly superficial faith until a terrible illness frightened her about her eternal fate. Suddenly, "the light of God's Spirit darted in upon her soul," and she experienced conversion. Hugh marveled at her vigorous faith, but until he heard Whitefield preach, he did not understand that he too needed a new birth of salvation. Then he felt the illumining power of the Spirit, and received "assurance of God's favour" to his soul.[48]

As Hugh's friendship with Whitefield grew, they discussed the prospect of opening a "negro school" in South Carolina, like the one planned for Nazareth. In an extraordinary scene at Bryan's plantation, however, Whitefield fell deathly ill from his heat-induced ailment. He "stretched for immortality," he wrote, "and longed for the blessed angels to come and carry me to Abraham's harbour." Bryan sat by Whitefield's bedside and wept while (as Whitefield recorded it) "poor negroes crowded round the windows, and . . . expressed a great concern" for him. Hugh told them that Whitefield was their friend, too.[49]

Upon Whitefield's recovery, he returned to Savannah, where in early August 1740 the Bryan brothers and their brother-in-law Stephen Bull came to hear him preach. Before Whitefield had even finished his opening prayer, Bull swooned and "dropped down, as though shot with a gun." But he got back up and listened attentively to Whitefield's sermon. The next day, Whitefield met with Stephen and Jonathan, who was also struggling under conviction of sin and mourning his "misspent life." Whitefield asked Bull why he had fallen down during the service. "The power of God's Word," Bull replied. The group knelt together and prayed, and Whitefield was confident that Bull and Bryan would break through to salvation. A couple of weeks later, when Whitefield saw Jonathan Bryan in Charleston, the itinerant found that he was "much established" in his faith.[50]

In late August 1740, Whitefield set out from South Carolina for New England. New Englanders had begun hearing reports of Whitefield's ministry as early as the spring of 1739, when the *Boston News-Letter* included a story on his preaching to the Kingswood colliers. By mid-1739, news about Whitefield had become a staple of the Boston papers, and on November 20, 1739, the *New England Weekly Journal* reported on the itinerant's arrival in America.[51]

In November 1739, Whitefield began writing to key New England pastors. One was Jonathan Edwards. "I rejoice for the great things God has done for many souls in Northampton," Whitefield wrote. "I should rejoice to be instructed by you." Edwards wrote back in February, extending an invitation to visit. Whitefield wrote also to Benjamin Colman, the sixty-six-year-old minister of Boston's Brattle Street Church and the most influential pastor in Boston. Colman had much to teach him in ministry, Whitefield respectfully noted. But he soon wrote to Gilbert Tennent that he found Colman's published sermons "acute and pointed, but . . . not searching enough by many degrees."[52]

Colman, for his part, registered his own concerns in a reply to Whitefield, a letter subsequently published in Philadelphia. Colman was a key figure in the moderate wing of the emerging evangelical movement: he was delighted by the success of the gospel, but worried about maintaining sobriety and order. Whitefield was quite young, and some of his theology seemed unrefined, Colman noted. He also wondered about the propriety of Whitefield's endless travels. Did he really need to come to America when so many more needed the gospel in England? Nevertheless, Colman was sure that Whitefield and the Methodists heralded a renewal of the "right evangelical articles of faith upon which the church reformed from Popery."[53]

The newspapers in New England monitored Whitefield's movements throughout 1740. One hostile letter from Philadelphia, printed in the *Boston Weekly Post-Boy* in June, deplored the "vulgar" people who thronged Whitefield's field meetings. His assemblies subverted "all order and decency." Some in the itinerant's audiences were "terrified into despair," while others were "transported with passions which influence them to believe that they have had the beatific vision, and immediate intercourse with him who is invisible." And, the writer concluded, Boston could expect the zealot Whitefield to appear there in the autumn.[54]

Upon Whitefield's arrival in Rhode Island, he arranged for a letter describing the work at Bethesda to go in the *New England Weekly Journal*. "Philadelphia, New York, & Charlestown people have been very liberal" in supporting the orphanage, he wrote. Now he was in New England, eager to see their response to his preaching and charitable appeals.[55]

His first stop was in Newport. At about six thousand residents, it was one of the five largest towns in America and a center of the transatlantic slave trade. It was also one of the most diverse cities in America. As a thriving seaport that honored religious liberty, it was home to a variety of Christians as well as a small community of Spanish and Portuguese Jews. A visitor to Newport four years later described the town as centered on one mile-long street so straight that someone standing at one end could see the other. All of it sat perched overlooking the wharfs and harbor. Wealthy women and men strolled the street, some of them from prominent South Carolina families who vacationed in Newport during the summer.[56]

Whitefield had his usual chilly meeting with the local Anglican minister, James Honeyman, who privately complained about "the noisie Mr. Whitefield." Under pressure from congregants, Honeyman grudgingly gave Whitefield permission to preach at the spacious Trinity Church, erected in 1726. The itinerant estimated it could hold three thousand people. The sanctuary was packed beyond capacity for his services, attended by people from all denominations. Whitefield was far more impressed with the seventy-one-year-old Congregational pastor Nathaniel Clap than with Honeyman, calling Clap "the most venerable man I ever saw in my life." He "looked like a good old Puritan, and gave me an idea of what stamp those men were, who first settled New England."[57]

Rhode Island charmed Whitefield, but he knew that his primary destination lay seventy miles to the north. Boston in 1740 remained the largest town in the colonies at 17,000 residents. Founded in 1630 during the Puritans' Great Migration out of England, Boston was both a hive of churches and a hub of commerce. But it lagged behind Philadelphia, New York, and Charleston in commercial development, and its population would slowly dwindle over the next three decades as the American Revolution approached. An English traveler, John Bennett, writing the same year as Whitefield's visit, noted that "the town was not built after any regular plan" but still paid it several compliments: "The streets are well paved, and lying upon a descent. The town is, for the generality, as dry and clean as any I remember to have seen." For the colonies it was a large city, but to someone who knew London, it still seemed like a rustic outpost (see figure 6.1). Bennett, for one, complained that the taverns "have no good beer" and only a "sorry sort of Madeira wine," and he regarded their Sabbath keeping as unreasonably strict.[58]

Whitefield arrived in Boston on September 18 and paid an obligatory visit to the Anglican church and its commissary, Timothy Cutler. Cutler, a fifty-six-year-old native of Massachusetts, was one of the Anglicans' most formidable American leaders. The Harvard graduate became the rector of Yale College in 1719, but by then he had already begun to doubt the legitimacy of the Puritans' Congregationalism, cut off as it was from the traditions of the Church of England. In 1722 he detonated an ecclesiastical explosion at Yale when he concluded his commencement prayer with "let all the people say, amen." This was telltale episcopal language. The shocked audience realized that he was repudiating Congregationalism and affiliating with the Anglican Communion. Cutler soon sailed for London, where he received ordination, and upon his return he became rector at Christ Church, Boston.[59]

Cutler developed an extensive correspondence with Edmund Gibson, the bishop of London and one of Whitefield's most articulate opponents. Already in May 1739, Cutler had apprised the bishop of evangelical agitation in America, particularly the 1734–35 Northampton revival led by Cutler's former Yale student Jonathan Edwards. The skeptical Cutler highlighted the most enthusiastic aspects of that revival and concluded that while some good might have come of it, overall there was a "great deal fantastical and foolish in those shows" of religion.[60]

Cutler already had well-formed opinions of revivalists when Whitefield appeared in Boston. Their exchange, which Whitefield recorded at length, again revealed the fundamental theological rift between the new evangelicals and Anglican leaders. The key differences lay in their views of denominations and regeneration. Because Cutler saw the Church of England as having unique apostolic authority, he did not regard the Dissenting pastors' ordinations as valid. Indeed, he regarded his own Congregationalist ordination as illegitimate. Whitefield, in spite of his Anglican ordination, was not concerned about the particular authority of any one church. Why did Whitefield cooperate with Dissenters, Cutler asked? Whitefield answered that he "saw regenerate souls among the Baptists, among the Presbyterians, among the Independents, and among the Church folks [Anglicans], all children of God, and yet all born again in a different way of worship, and who can tell which is most evangelical?" When it came to conversion and regeneration, one's denomination (assuming, of course, that it was Protestant) did not matter.[61]

Whitefield's statement that he "saw regenerate souls" in all denominations frustrated Cutler. "Can you see regeneration with your eyes?" he asked.

Whitefield said that a true believer could perceive his or her own conversion, and others could see the "fruits of the Spirit" (Galatians 5:22–23) in their lives. Cutler said that regeneration came at baptism, when the Holy Spirit fell upon the baptized person (ordinarily an infant). Whitefield protested that if every child was born again in baptism, then every baptized child would be saved. "And so they are," said Cutler, unless they fell away from the grace conveyed at baptism. To Whitefield, this was nonsense—legions of people who had been baptized into the Church of England showed no more than nominal commitment to Christ as adults. Surely, baptism alone did not save them, without a subsequent experience of conversion.[62]

Although Cutler did not give Whitefield the rude reception that he got from Alexander Garden (Cutler even invited him to stay for lunch), their doctrinal differences were essential. To Cutler, those baptized in the Church of England could have a reasonable expectation of salvation if they led moral, obedient lives. To Whitefield, only a profound experience of grace, knowingly received by a sinner, could give legitimate assurance of everlasting life. Convinced that he would get no support from Cutler and his associates, Whitefield moved on to Colman's Brattle Street Church, where a crowd of four thousand assembled to hear him preach.[63]

There Whitefield initiated a rapid series of Boston sermons, hustling from one supportive church to another. One Sunday, he visited Brattle Street to hear Colman preach, then addressed a crowd at the Old Brick Church. "Immediately" following that, he went to Boston Common and spoke to a teeming throng he estimated at fifteen thousand. A report in Philadelphia said there was "at least 8000" there. In any case, Whitefield attracted a crowd comprising at least half of Boston's population.[64]

Perhaps it was inevitable that such overpacked rooms would precipitate a tragedy, and one transpired at the New South Church. In "a very sorrowfull accident," people had "crowded so thick" into the gallery ringing the sanctuary that they became claustrophobic. When a board on which they were standing broke with a terrifying crack, some began to shout that the gallery was collapsing. The room melted into ugly chaos as people jumped from the galleries to the floor. Others flung themselves out the windows. In the press to get out the doors, some women and children were shoved down and trampled without regard for "the terrible screeches and outcries" of those underfoot. The stampede crushed four women and a "servant lad" to death.[65]

The panic occurred before Whitefield arrived at the church. When he saw the horrible aftermath, including "two or three lying on the ground in a pitiable condition," he made a snap decision to go ahead with his sermon, but relocate it to the Common, a short walk away.[66] Colonial Americans lived in a world filled with "awful providences" such as this, and instead of canceling his preaching, Whitefield sought to "improve what had befallen" the congregation. The itinerant saw the episode as a satanic assault on him and his followers: "Though Satan in this bruised our heel, yet I doubt not but even this will be a means of bruising his accursed head" (Genesis 3:15). As pointless as the deaths seem in retrospect, to Whitefield they exemplified the fleeting quality of life and the urgency of salvation. As he once asked listeners, "How do you know but this may be the last opportunity God will favour you with? How do you know, but e're midnight, your soul must launch into eternity?"[67]

Harvard College, the oldest institution of higher learning in America, was just over a century old when Whitefield arrived in Massachusetts. It remained relatively small: about one hundred students, four tutors, and a president (Edward Holyoke). Although Yale College had emerged as an alternative, Harvard remained the primary training school for Congregational pastors in New England and elsewhere, such as Charleston's Josiah Smith. Its 1692 motto was not simply *"Veritas,"* as it is commonly shortened today, but *"Veritas Christo et Ecclesiae,"* or "Truth for Christ and the Church."

When Whitefield came to Cambridge to visit Harvard, he was less than impressed. It was not only considerably smaller than Oxford, but also "not far superior to our universities in piety and true godliness." This was an indirect way of saying that true godliness was in short supply. The tutors "neglect to pray with and examine the hearts of their pupils," he said. Many ran after fashionable authors such as John Tillotson rather than reading the Puritan classics of their New England heritage. Addressing the students, Whitefield spoke on 2 Corinthians 2:17, "We are not as many who corrupt the Word of God." President Holyoke treated him politely, but later became enraged when Whitefield's published journal described the college in unflattering terms. Indeed, Whitefield would later come to regret his "rash and uncharitable" characterizations of Harvard and Yale.[68]

Some at Harvard certainly responded to his preaching. A skeptical tutor noted in his diary that a number of the students were under "great concern for their souls" and that some had gone to radical extremes. One pupil supposedly "pretended to see the devil in shape of a bear coming to his bedside," and others spoke rapturously of great spiritual terrors and comforts. One of the tutors, Daniel Rogers, would soon leave Harvard to follow Whitefield, convinced by the itinerant's insistence that formal piety was worthless without the new birth.[69]

Jonathan Belcher, the Massachusetts governor and a Harvard graduate, also warmly received Whitefield, inviting him and the ministers of Boston to dine at his home. In a private meeting, Belcher emotionally thanked the itinerant for his ministry and asked for his prayers. In addition, the fifty-eight-year-old Belcher made his carriage available for Whitefield's use.[70]

An even more fervent assembly packed Boston Common to hear Whitefield on September 27. He estimated them at fifteen thousand people, many of whom were overcome with emotion. As he went back to his rented house, "the power and presence of the Lord accompanied and followed me," he wrote. As he continued to speak to those assembled at his house, many "wept bitterly, and cried out under the Word." A group stayed up praying with him, and Whitefield recorded the presence of the divine: "The Spirit of the Lord was upon them all. It made intercession with groanings that cannot be uttered." This is a tanta-lizing reference, using language directly from Romans 8. Were some there speaking in tongues, in the language of the Spirit (glossolalia), which has become a mark of the modern Pentecostal movement? We do not know, but later, more cautious editions of his journals excised this passage.[71]

Whitefield continued to fly from one remarkable scene to another: one morning he spoke at the Old South meeting, collecting the vast sum of £555 for Bethesda. In the afternoon he preached at Benjamin Colman's Brattle Street Church, collecting another £470. Colman pronounced it the "most pleasant time" he had enjoyed in four decades of ministry. After supper, Governor Belcher met privately with him. Going from the most elite to the lowliest of Boston society, Whitefield then visited with a group of African Americans, preaching on the conversion of the Ethiopian eunuch in Acts 8. Returning bone-tired to his house, he found yet another crowd waiting for him, and he obliged them with a brief exhortation.[72]

Whitefield was running himself ragged and becoming extremely ill, violently vomiting between sermons. He was feverish, dehydrated, and sweating profusely. Nevertheless, he was up and gone by seven the next morning, bound for Marblehead and Salem. During his weeklong tour of towns in Boston's northern hinterlands, he preached sixteen times and rode, he estimated, 178 miles. Yet he was not "in the least wearied or fatigued," he asserted. Rambling along the rocky seacoast seemed to do him good.[73]

Continuing his nonstop preaching in Boston, he held a particularly notable meeting at the Old South Church on October 8. Again, the specter of tragic death hung over the meeting, this time because of a child who fell gravely ill just after hearing Whitefield preach. The boy reportedly said he would "go to Mr. Whitefield's God," and soon passed away. Whitefield specifically directed his preaching and praying toward the children present at the meeting. "Little children," he said, "if your parents will not come to Christ, you [should] come and go to heaven without them." This exhortation brought many children and adults to tears. "The Word smote them," he reckoned. He had not seen a "greater commotion" since coming to Boston. The grateful audience contributed another £440 to the orphanage.[74]

The following day, Whitefield hurried to the Old South Church again. He had picked a passage of Scripture before leaving the house and had even folded down the text in his Bible. But as he drew near to the church, he found himself moved to switch and preach on Jesus's meeting with the Pharisee Nicodemus in John 3. Nicodemus was a religious leader among the Jews, yet Jesus famously told him that "except a man be born again, he cannot see the kingdom of God." A number of Boston area ministers attended the sermon. When Whitefield came to John 3:10, "Art thou a master in Israel, and knowest not these things?" he began to speak "boldly against unconverted ministers."[75] This was an inflammatory topic, one that Gilbert Tennent had broached in his March 1740 sermon "The Danger of an Unconverted Ministry." Tennent had likewise reviled Pharisee-preachers who "had a very fair and strict out-side; yet were they ignorant of the new birth: Witness Rabbi Nicodemus, who talked like a fool about it." Whitefield considered Tennent's sermon "unanswerable" and, in his published journal, concluded that "the generality of preachers talk of an unknown, unfelt Christ." Why have congregations been so dead, he asked? "Because dead men preach to them." Ministers squirmed at these claims, but most declined to contradict Whitefield openly.[76]

Whitefield's popularity was soaring, as abundantly illustrated on the day of his Boston farewell sermon. That morning he preached at the Old South Church to a congregation so packed that Whitefield had to enter the building through a window. Afterward he met privately with Governor Belcher, who took him in his coach to the Common. There Whitefield addressed a mammoth throng he initially estimated at thirty thousand (newspapers suggested twenty-three thousand; later editions of Whitefield's journal said twenty thousand). In any case, the crowd was larger than the population of Boston, and possibly the largest ever gathered in the history of the English colonies. Darkness began to settle over the Common as he concluded his sermon, and many wept as he spoke of departing.[77]

In his journal, Whitefield wrote that a "glorious work" had begun in Boston, but that the town had fallen far from the founding glory of the Puritans. Too many Bostonians were caught up in the things of the world. Their church meetings seemed more like fashion shows than solemn assemblies: "jewels, patches, and gay apparel are commonly worn by the female sex, and even the common people . . . dressed up in the pride of life." He encountered remarkably little opposition in the town. But he foresaw rising hostility if he became "more particular in [his] application to particular persons." Too many had only a head knowledge of religion, he thought, maintaining outward duties without a vital, inward commitment to Christ. One report said that a small group of Boston gentlemen attributed his success "only to the force of sound and gestures." But for now, criticism in New England remained minimal.[78]

Whitefield proceeded west from Boston, visiting towns of the Massachusetts hinterlands. The pastor at Sudbury, Israel Loring, had been waiting to hear Whitefield for almost a year. In his journal, Loring had noted Whitefield's arrival in America in November 1739. Loring met with his friend Benjamin Colman in Boston and "asked him what he thought of Mr. Whitefield." Colman told him that he "looked upon him as one under more than ordinary influence of the Holy Spirit, even such as Luther, Calvin, and the first reformers." Colman lent him a book of Whitefield's sermons, and Loring rose early the next morning to begin reading it. He copied into his diary the newspaper reports of Whitefield's successes in Philadelphia and New York, but he was never quite sure what to make of the itinerant. He dutifully recorded Whitefield's appearances in Concord, Sudbury, and Marlborough, noting that he did not attend the final sermon. Whitefield described Loring as a "man of God," but Loring was becoming alarmed by the radical tendencies of the revivals—especially the work of untutored exhorters, who by 1742 had routinely begun claiming to have visions and divine revelations. In denying itinerants access to his pulpit, Loring lamented that "such an enthusiastic, factious, censorious spirit was perhaps never more predominant in the land." Whitefield could not convince all New England pastors that his ministry—or the broader awakening—was of God.[79]

The itinerant was soon ferried across the Connecticut River to Northampton, where, as Whitefield wrote, the "pastor's name is Edwards." Whitefield was deeply impressed with the Edwards family, and the relationship between Jonathan and Sarah. Indeed, so taken was he with Sarah that she inspired him to reflect on his desire for a godly wife: "She is a woman adorned with a meek and quiet spirit [1 Peter 3:4], talked feelingly and solidly of the things of God, and seemed to be such a helpmeet for her husband [Genesis 2], that she caused me to renew those prayers, which, for some months, I have put up to God, that he would be pleased to send me a daughter of Abraham to be my wife." He asked that God would choose a wife for him, as God had chosen Rebekah for

Isaac. No doubt the difficulties in courting Elizabeth Delamotte had made him weary and wary of pursuing a wife by his own initiative.[80]

Whitefield preached four times at Northampton, extending his stay longer than usual for a town of its size. The meetings grew increasingly emotional until the Sunday morning when many wept openly, including Edwards. That afternoon saw an even more powerful meeting; "Our Lord seemed to keep the good wine to the last" (John 2:10), Whitefield observed. He preached on Genesis 3, likely his oft-repeated sermon "The Seed of the Woman, and the Seed of the Serpent." Speaking of the Last Judgment, he trumpeted: "Satan, the accuser of the brethren . . . shall then be cast out . . . then shall the righteous shine in the Kingdom of the Father, and sit with Christ on thrones, in majesty on high." In rapid-fire staccato, he assured the audience that "the Lord Jesus has engaged to make you more than conqueror over all—plead with your Savior, plead—plead the promise in the text—wrestle, wrestle with God in prayer . . . Be not any wise terrified by your adversaries—The King of the Church has them all in a chain."[81]

Whitefield hoped that he could help the people of Northampton recover "their first love," and the visit did help precipitate a new revival. "Mr. Whitefield's sermons were suitable to the circumstances of the town," Edwards wrote, "containing just reproofs of our backslidings, and, in a most moving and affecting manner, making use of our great profession and great mercies as arguments with us to return to God, from whom we had departed." By the end of the year, the church had awakened again, its young people showing particular interest in spiritual matters. Even some of Edwards's own children apparently experienced conversion. Edwards asked for Whitefield to pray that he would be filled with the Holy Spirit and "become fervent, as a flame of fire in my work."[82]

Edwards was delighted with Whitefield's ministry, but the two were not in complete accord about the revivals. Even as Edwards accompanied Whitefield from Northampton to his father's church in East Windsor, Connecticut, he told the itinerant (eleven years his junior) that he was giving too much credence to spiritual impulses, and that he should be more cautious about "judging other persons to be unconverted." Whitefield did not try to argue with Edwards about these matters, nor did he seem particularly offended. Still, Edwards thought the awkward discussion put a damper on what was otherwise a wonderful visit. In fact, Edwards decided, "Mr. Whitefield liked me not so well, for my opposing these things," and he believed that Whitefield kept their friendship at arm's length from that point forward.[83]

Shortly after Whitefield's visit, Edwards devoted a series of sermons to Christ's parable of the sower in Matthew 13, warning about those who warmly responded to the initial message of the gospel but then fell away. Edwards worried that some Northamptonites might be reacting more to the sensation surrounding the itinerant than to his proclamation of the new birth. Some, he cautioned, "are drawn to take some notice of what the minister says, either by the unusualness of the subject, or the unusual manner of treating it, or the loudness of his voice, or his extraordinary earnestness." They might even weep heartily, but still the seed of the gospel could fail to take root. Devotion to the messenger rather than the message could lead to deception and an even harder heart. Edwards would explain in *Religious Affections* (1746) that long-term commitment to Christ was the best test of one's spiritual experiences, not fleeting reactions to any one preacher.[84]

Although Whitefield would never have a spectacular schism with Edwards as he did with John Wesley, Edwards permitted his private correction of Whitefield in 1740 to be publicized in 1745—ironically, in a pamphlet in which Edwards defended Whitefield against his critics. Edwards tried to establish that although he disagreed with the itinerant on some points, overall Whitefield was a legitimate minister. As Edwards's biographer George Marsden has noted, it is striking that while Whitefield struggled to maintain friendships with fellow evangelicals such as Edwards and Wesley, he had no such difficulties with his skeptical friend Benjamin Franklin.[85]

The differences between Whitefield and Edwards may seem relatively minor in retrospect (the differences between Whitefield and Wesley were more significant), but both men knew that they were in the process of shaping a new evangelical movement. The importance of that opportunity magnified even small disagreements. Edwards and Wesley were both eleven years older than Whitefield, strongly opinionated, and inclined to correct the headstrong itinerant's perceived errors. But in the end, Edwards and Whitefield remained committed to the same goals: the salvation of souls, and the revitalization of the Reformed Protestant world. Though Wesley and Whitefield were committed to those goals, too, that shared sense of purpose could not prevent an estrangement between them that would last for decades. The evangelical movement was formidable, but its most important leaders struggled terribly to maintain interpersonal harmony.

7

---•—

"HEARING HIM PREACH, GAVE ME A HEART WOUND": CALVINIST PREACHING, CALVINIST CONTROVERSY

George Whitefield's preaching changed the life of Nathan Cole, a farmer in Kensington, Connecticut. Before the fall of 1740, Cole was a nominal Christian. As an "Arminian," the twenty-nine-year-old figured that if he were moral and pious, he would be saved. After reading reports about the sensational itinerant's travels, Cole wished that he would visit central Connecticut. He heard that Whitefield was at Boston; then closer, at Northampton. One morning a messenger rode into his field and announced that Whitefield was to preach later that day at Middletown, twelve miles away.[1]

"I dropt my tool that I had in my hand," Cole recalled, "and ran home to my wife telling her to make ready quickly to go and hear Mr. Whitefield preach." They galloped off, fearing they would miss him. As they approached the road that ran from Hartford to Middletown, he saw "a cloud or fogg rising." It took him a second to discover what was happening:

> I first thought it came from the great river, but as I came nearer the road, I heard a noise something like a low rumbling thunder and presently found it was the noise of horses' feet coming down the road and this cloud was a cloud of dust made by the horses' feet.

Everywhere he looked were determined riders on lathered horses. The countryside was emptying, the road funneling everyone toward Middletown.[2] Arriving just in time to see Whitefield ascend the platform, Cole recalled the scene:

> He looked almost angelical; a young, slim, slender youth before some thousands of people with a bold undaunted countenance, and my hearing how

God was with him everywhere as he came along it solemnized my mind; and put me into a trembling fear before he began to preach; for he looked as if he was clothed with authority from the great God; and a sweet solemn solemnity sat upon his brow. And my hearing him preach, gave me a heart wound; by God's blessing: my old foundation was broken up, and I saw that my righteousness would not save me.

This was only the beginning of Cole's conversion, not the end. For two years more he wrestled with God, especially concerning divine election and unmerited grace. From Whitefield, he understood these doctrines to be essential to authentic Christianity. Finally accepting them, he experienced conversion and assurance of forgiveness. For decades Cole was a key leader in Kensington's radical evangelical movement, separating from his Congregational church and eventually becoming a Baptist.[3]

Hearing Whitefield preach began a conversion ordeal for Hannah Heaton, too, a farm woman of North Haven, Connecticut. Whitefield delivered "preaching as I never heard before," she wrote, as he explicated the marks of an unconverted person. Did the audience members' minds ever wander to worldly business as they sat through long church services? Did they struggle to devote even one day exclusively to the Lord? "How could you endure to be in heaven with him forever where nothing but praises are?" he asked. Heaton, stricken with guilt, knew that her attention often drifted during Sunday meetings. "I began to think my nature must be changed but how to attain it I knew not," she wrote. She struggled for another eight months to discover the way to salvation. Finally, she received a brilliant vision of Christ, "a lovely God man with his arms open ready to receive me." Full of praise and thanksgiving, she knew that Christ would pardon her sins.[4]

Conversion took only weeks, not months or years, for the Harvard tutor Daniel Rogers. Rogers had grown up in a minister's family in Ipswich, Massachusetts, and he was under consideration for a ministerial position at Boston's New North Church when Whitefield arrived. A 1725 Harvard graduate, Rogers knew Christian doctrine and ethics, but had never experienced the new birth. Perhaps Whitefield could help him break through, he thought, and so he joined the evangelist's traveling cohort.[5]

Whitefield may have encouraged Rogers to start journaling. His diary began just as he set out with Whitefield from Boston, his spiritual struggles spilling onto the pages. The day before Nathan Cole heard Whitefield preach, Rogers wrote: "I am heart sick of the kingdom of sin and Satan, and want the Kingdom of God within me in righteousness peace etc. I hunger, I thirst. Lord Jesus, let me be filled, Lord help me to wait upon thee, to believe in thee, to hope in, rely upon thy promise. I find myself a lost damned creature without thee ... I hunger I thirst after an experimental knowledge of Jesus Christ."[6] Rogers received such "experimental knowledge" as they approached New York City. "It pleased God of his free and sovereign grace to come into my poor soul with power and so to fill me with peace," Rogers wrote, "yea with such joy in the Holy Ghost as I never experienced before. I could not forbear smiling nay laughing for joy and gladness of heart." He told Whitefield and his other happy companions that he had experienced the new birth.[7]

These three conversion accounts from the fall of 1740 show that certainty about salvation could come quickly to some evangelicals, though it was rarely secured during a single meeting. For some, like Cole, it could take years. Particular themes came up repeatedly: hearing a preacher, Whitefield or someone else, who delivered a focused message on the new birth was ordinarily a part of the story. Converts typically were already aware of their sinful nature, their particular offenses, and the divine judgment awaiting them if they did not find a way of escape. Personally discovering that way through Christ led to elation. Although others eventually fell away, for Rogers, Heaton, and Cole, conversion was the entryway into a long life of evangelical devotion.

Whitefield visited Yale College in October 1740 and found the environment there similar to Harvard's. Not yet forty years old, Yale had endured financial and religious struggles, not least the defection of Rector Timothy Cutler to Anglicanism in the 1720s. Whitefield noted that the school had "one rector [Thomas Clap], three tutors, and about a hundred students." He heard no reports of significant awakenings at Yale (those would come soon). As at Harvard, he spoke intently with the students, warning them of "the dreadful ill consequences of an unconverted ministry." He cautioned them that they could receive the best education available and still miss the most important qualification for a preacher: the new birth. As Whitefield prepared to leave New England, he wrote that Harvard's and Yale's "light is become darkness, darkness that may be felt" (Exodus 10:21). But he was nonetheless hopeful: "I pray God those fountains may be purified, and send forth pure streams to water the city of our God." This characterization (which soon appeared in print) stung the college authorities; they would bring it up four years later upon Whitefield's return.[8]

Whitefield's provocations regarding unconverted ministers irritated many, but to his sympathizers, they confirmed fears felt for some time. Some recognized that they had helped ordain ministers who did not show definitive signs of conversion. At Stamford, Connecticut, Whitefield wrote, "At dinner, the Spirit of the Lord came upon me again," enabling him to speak confidently against sending unconverted men into the ministry. Two of the ministers there began weeping and confessed that they had laid "hands on young men [in ordination services] without so much as asking them, 'whether they were born again of God, or not?'"⁹ Whitefield helped some ministers, such as Daniel Rogers, see that they had never experienced the new birth. An older minister visiting the itinerant at Stamford cried bitterly as he confessed, despite having "preached the doctrines of grace a long time," "I believe I never have felt the power of them in my own soul."[10]

At the end of October, Whitefield's tour of New England came to a close. Marked by remarkable crowds and fervor everywhere he went, his time in New England was arguably the greatest triumph among the many he enjoyed in ministry. Whitefield attributed much of New England's religious strength to its Puritan founders, but he believed that its devotion had grown cold, polite, and formal. "I like New England exceeding well," he wrote, "and when a spirit of reformation revives, it certainly will prevail more [there] than in any other place, because they are simple in their worship, less corrupt in their principles, and consequently easier to be brought over to the form of sound words, into which so many of their pious ancestors were delivered." Without saying so explicitly, Whitefield was conceding that the Dissenting origins of New England gave it a firmer basis for revival than the Anglican-dominated colonies or England itself.[11]

Whitefield enjoyed a pleasant reunion with friends in New York, including James Davenport. But he was also confronted with more published attacks, led by Alexander Garden's *Six Letters to the Rev. Mr. George Whitefield*, and *The Querists*, which had been produced by the antirevivalist New Castle Presbytery. Garden, whom Whitefield regarded as "angry overmuch," raged against Whitefield's "Mobb Harangues" and his contention that many Anglicans did not preach salvation by grace alone. Garden also took exception to Whitefield's attacks on Archbishop Tillotson. The commissary told Whitefield that Tillotson's fame would persist well after "you and your dirty pamphlets are sunk into oblivion."[12]

Whitefield generally ignored Garden, which compounded the commissary's rage. But *The Querists* touched a nerve, coming as it did from Presbyterians rather than predictably hostile Anglicans. *The Querists* combed Whitefield's writings for troubling passages. The authors cautioned readers that some of his ideas so strongly identified born-again believers with the divine that they smacked of "Antinomian reveries, of being god-ed with God, and christ-ed with Christ." Ironically, given Garden's attacks, *The Querists* charged Whitefield with implying that good works contributed to salvation. (At other points, the authors claimed he suggested that believers had no obligation to obey God at all.) Whitefield obviously did not believe in salvation by works, but these Presbyterians' accusations showed how easily an emphasis on obedience could imply that religious duties earned a sinner merit before God.[13]

Although he called it a "bitter pamphlet" in his journal, Whitefield's printed response to *The Querists* was uncharacteristically gentle. *The Querists* gave him an opportunity to correct some of the misleading "expressions that have formerly drop'd" from his pen, he said. Some of the mistakes had occurred before God gave him a clear understanding of the doctrines of grace. (He compared his apology to that of "St. Austin [Augustine]" before him, who, toward the end of his life, published the *Retractions*.) Whitefield readily conceded instances of poor phrasing and imprecise theological understanding, in most cases agreeing with *The Querists'* complaints.[14]

He was especially keen to distance himself from John Wesley's errors, with which *The Querists* connected him. (Whitefield's ministry, as well as the debates about it, proceeded in a thoroughly Anglo-American context, facilitated by the circulation of printed texts between Britain and the colonies.) Whitefield used his reply to *The Querists* to refute Wesley on the doctrine of perfectionism. *The Querists* especially noted that Whitefield had endorsed Wesley's edition of *The Life and Death of the Reverend Learned and Pious Mr. Thomas Halyburton* (1739), in the preface of which Wesley asserted that truly converted Christians could stop committing sin altogether. Having sloppily failed to read Wesley's preface, Whitefield said that he would not have endorsed it if he knew what Wesley had said. Indeed, he had begun ripping out that section of Wesley's preface before giving away copies of the Halyburton memoir.[15]

Although responding to *The Querists* kept Whitefield busy, what he really wanted was to see revival in New York. Whitefield put a great deal of emphasis on the audience's reaction to his sermons—probably too much emphasis. He commented on displays of the Word's and the Holy Spirit's power, or the absence thereof, at nearly every meeting. The subtle implication was that when there was no manifest reaction to his sermons, he had somehow failed. But audience's moods were fickle, and after all, was not the real work of revival up to God?

The day he finished his reply to *The Querists*, he preached twice to large crowds, "neither time without power." The next day, a Sunday, he spoke with "some power" in the morning, but felt "dejected" and weak before the evening meeting. He dragged himself to the pulpit, but once he began the sermon, he felt the Spirit take over. "At length [the Spirit] came down like a mighty rushing wind, and carried all before it," he wrote. "Shrieking, crying, weeping and wailing were to be heard in every corner." People collapsed into the arms of friends. "The like I never saw before," wrote Daniel Rogers. When the sermon ended, Whitefield went down among the people, finding one girl uncontrollably crying out, "Oh my Jesus, my Jesus!" A weeping little boy sprawled on the stairs leading to the pulpit. Someone asked why he cried, and the boy said that Whitefield's sermon had cut him to the heart.[16]

Whitefield was hardly immune to overwhelming experiences in the Spirit. That night, he participated in the wedding of Jonathan Barber, who soon would become superintendent of the Bethesda orphanage. The "Holy Ghost" was so powerfully present at the ceremony that afterward when Whitefield retired to his lodgings, he recorded: "Divine manifestations flowed in so fast, that my frail tabernacle was scarce able to sustain them." Friends gathered around his bedside, and he cried out in prayer for each of them, and was "pierced by the eye of faith, even within the veil" (Hebrews 6:19). He lay in this ecstatic state for thirty minutes. Whitefield explicitly linked this transcendent moment to publication of *The Querists*: "God has remarkably revealed himself to my soul, ever since I have seen the pamphlet published by the Presbyterians against me." By the conclusion of this visit to New York in early November, however, Whitefield had not seen a citywide awakening there to compare with the glories in Boston.[17]

On Staten Island, Whitefield met with Gilbert Tennent, whose wife had recently passed away, taking him briefly off the front lines of the revivals. (Whitefield noted that Tennent had bravely preached the funeral sermon with his wife's corpse lying in front of him.) They rode to Newark, New Jersey, where Whitefield gave an exhortation that precipitated another remarkable outpouring: "Oh how did the Word fall like a hammer and like a fire!" Many were overcome with weeping and lost their bodily strength. Whitefield was so physically taxed after the meeting that he vomited and collapsed on his bed.[18]

Whitefield's cohort moved on to Basking Ridge, New Jersey, where on November 5 they saw one of the most intense outbreaks of fervor during the entire Great Awakening. Basking Ridge was the home of the Reverend John Cross, who was achieving a status akin to Tennent's among evangelicals. James Davenport was also there, preaching in the morning to a crowd of several thousand. Once Tennent and Whitefield arrived, this may have been the most formidable assembly of preaching talent seen at one meeting during the American revivals.[19]

In the afternoon, Whitefield preached from the back of a wagon on the story of the blind beggar Bartimaeus, who cried out to Jesus and was healed in Mark

10. "The Holy Ghost displayed his power" as Whitefield exhorted the assembly to follow Bartimaeus's example and call on Jesus. As he often did in his most evocative sermons, Whitefield spoke as if the story of Bartimaeus was being replayed that very day: "Jesus, I trust, is passing by; I feel his presence, I hope many of you feel it too; O then, cry mightily to him, who is mighty and willing to save you . . . Jesus will answer you, he will not cast out your prayer . . . the more they charge you to hold your peace, do you cry out so much the more a great deal, 'Jesus, thou Son of David, have mercy on us.'" Daniel Rogers said that many in the audience took Whitefield's exhortation literally and "after the example of the blind man [began] to cry out after Jesus."[20] A little boy, seven or eight years old, began weeping and calling out "exceeding piteously." Cross brought the boy up into the wagon, and Whitefield stopped his sermon and called "upon the people to hear this lad preaching to them." Again, this created a burst of emotion among the people, and, as Rogers wrote, some fainted and seemed ready to "fall into fits."[21]

They took a short supper break, and then John Cross announced that there would be an evening meeting at his barn. Two hundred people pressed in there, among smells of livestock and sweat. Tennent preached first, then Whitefield prayed and gave an exhortation. The Holy Spirit surged. "I had seen great things before," Rogers wrote, "yet this exceeded them all." He struggled to represent the scene in his diary: people were "weeping, sighing, groaning, sobbing, screaching, crying out." After Whitefield preached for six minutes, one man began calling out, "I have found him, I have found him!" and "He is come!" The man pressed through the throng to embrace Whitefield, who began praying over the convert. Finally, at eleven o'clock the exhausted preacher left the barn and retired to Cross's house. The new convert accompanied Whitefield and remained in "an ecstasy" for an hour or two. The man spoke incessantly of Jesus, "his sweet Christ, his free-hearted Christ." Rogers and James Davenport returned to preach in the barn into the wee hours of the morning. Many stayed all night.[22]

This was an incredible high moment, but two of its key figures, John Cross and James Davenport, would soon fall into serious trouble. Cross was accused of sexual immorality and removed from the ministry in 1741. A published anti-revivalist letter said that Cross had seduced a young woman in his congregation, reportedly suggesting that she needed to experience grievous sin before she could properly receive Christ's forgiveness. (Tennent advised Whitefield of this debacle in early 1742.) Davenport, for his part, became the leader of the radical evangelical movement on Long Island and in New England. By 1742, the evangelicals of New England had begun to divide themselves bitterly into moderate and radical camps. A preacher's position was often determined by his opinion of Davenport. Connecticut officials arrested and deported Davenport for illegal preaching in May 1742, but not before calling out the militia to quell a near riot by his supporters in Hartford. The increasingly moderate Tennent broke with Davenport later that year, saying that he could not countenance Davenport's encouragement of independent revivalist congregations (which were illegal because of New England's Congregationalist establishment) and his focus on the immediate inspiration of the Spirit. Whitefield would never definitively break with Davenport, even though he began to shy away from his radicalism.[23]

We do not know how many African Americans or Native Americans attended revival meetings like the one at Basking Ridge, but we do know that at least one female servant, probably a slave, was at that assembly. The "poor Negroe-woman" approached Whitefield the next day and asked to join his traveling company. Remarkably, her master had consented to this proposal. But in a telling response, Whitefield instructed her to go back home, "with a thankful heart[,] to serve her present master." Whitefield had no interest in the immediate emancipation of slaves; instead, he believed in the evangelization and education of African Americans, the benevolent treatment of slaves, and the use of slave labor specifically to enhance the Bethesda project and the economy of Georgia. In this life, Whitefield thought the woman's faith would make her a better servant to her master, and a witness for Christ in her appointed station.[24]

From Basking Ridge, Whitefield's party moved on to Gilbert Tennent's church in New Brunswick, New Jersey. There the group made a critical decision, one that Whitefield had contemplated for some time: they would part ways. Tennent and Daniel Rogers would go back to New England to "blow up the divine fire lately kindled there." When it came time for them to say farewell, they prayed earnestly for one another. Tennent "was our mouth to God," Whitefield wrote. "He prayed in the Holy Ghost" (Jude 20).[25]

Back in Philadelphia again, Whitefield discovered that supporters had erected the "New Building," a commodious brick structure one hundred feet long and seventy feet wide, with a gallery ringing it. He had tried to discourage the construction of such a building in May, fearing that it would signal he was trying to confine the work of God to one place. But now that the edifice was mostly built, Whitefield seemed pleased to use it. Although the structure was not yet roofed, the builders boarded the floor and constructed a pulpit. Whitefield was eager to debut the facility, so he spoke under the chilly open sky, and "God's glory filled the house."[26]

In his Philadelphia sermons, Whitefield began to focus on the threat of Deism and natural reason. This new emphasis came partly through the conversion of Charles Brockden, a "notorious Deist." Brockden had grown up in a religious family, but in early adulthood he "began to doubt of, and to dispute [God's] very being." On Whitefield's first visit to Philadelphia, Brockden had attended a sermon out of curiosity. As Whitefield spoke on Jesus's conversation with Nicodemus in John 3, God struck Brockden's heart, and he soon experienced the new birth.[27]

Not long after learning about Brockden, Whitefield began preaching against Deism, perceiving that Philadelphia was a stronghold of skepticism. Deism could mean many things in the eighteenth century, but its proponents always emphasized human rationality as a reliable gauge of truth. This became Whitefield's chief point of attack. On November 15, he found himself ill and uncertain of his text for preaching, but when he began his sermon, he found himself energized—"I felt the Holy Ghost come upon me"—and he spoke out against "depending on our natural reason." This was a novel topic for him, and upon investigation (probably by asking Brockden), he learned that a "cluster" of Deists had been present at the meeting. "Then I knew wherefore I was so assisted," he wrote. Whitefield was testing new levels of reliance on the Holy Spirit for guidance in preaching.[28]

A correspondent wrote a poem for Franklin's *Pennsylvania Gazette* upon hearing Whitefield preach in the New Building, confirming the sense that the city's skeptics were among his key adversaries:

Though haughty Deists, Favorites of the Times,
Do all thy Actions construe into Crimes:
Though some who to Religion make Pretence,
Want only Power to send thee bleeding hence:
Though Earth and Hell should with united Force
Employ their Malice to impede thy Course:
Yet fear thou not, be to thy Master true;
He will direct thee, and preserve thee too.[29]

The day after speaking against the Deists, Whitefield prepared to leave Philadelphia. He collected £105 for Bethesda and held a baptismal service for five adult female converts (presumably, they had never received baptism as children). He preached his farewell sermon to a large, emotional crowd, though not nearly as large as the one he saw upon departing Philadelphia six months earlier. Whitefield proceeded through New Jersey and Maryland, meeting enthusiastic assemblies at every stop, before embarking from Reedy Island in

2.1 [Unidentified artist], after William Hogarth, *Scholars at a Lecture*, c.1736.
Harvard Art Museums/Fogg Museum, Gift of Belinda L. Randall from the collection
of John Witt Randall, R5692. Photo: Imaging Department © President and Fellows of
Harvard College.

2.2 "Cathedral from Church Tower, Gloucester, England," Snapshots of the Past (2007), Wikimedia Commons.

3.1 St. John's Chapel inside the White Tower at the Tower of London, England. Photo by Bernard Gagnon, 2007. Wikimedia Commons.

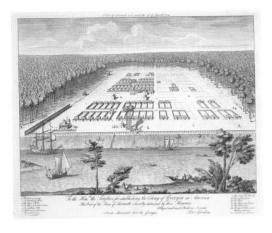

3.2 Peter Gordon, "A View of Savannah as It Stood the 29th of March, 1734," Toronto Public Library via Wikimedia Commons.

The Rev.ᵈ Mʳ. George Whitefield
of Pembroke College Oxford.

4.1 Frontispiece of George Whitefield, *The Christian's Companion: or, Sermons on Several Subjects* (London, 1738), [C 1394.28], Houghton Library—Hyde Collection, Harvard University.

4.2 *Dr Rock's Political Speech to the Mob in Covent-Garden* (London, 1743).
©The Trustees of the British Museum.

6.1 View of Boston, in *The American Magazine* (July,
1745). Beinecke Rare Book and Manuscript Library, Yale
University.

11.1 Countess of Huntingdon, from Theron Brown and Hezekiah Butterworth, *The Story of Hymns and Tunes* (New York, 1906), Moody Memorial Library, Baylor University.

12.1 George Whitefield, by John Russell, oil on canvas laid on board, 1770?, NPG 1792, © National Portrait Gallery, London.

CREDULITY, SUPERSTITION, and FANATICISM.
A MEDLEY.

Believe not every Spirit but try the Spirits whether they are of God: because many false Prophets are gone out into the World.
1 John. Ch. 4. V. 1.

Design'd and Engrav'd by W.ᵐ Hogarth.   Publish'd as the Act directs March y.ᵉ 15ᵗʰ 1762.

12.2 William Hogarth, *Credulity, Superstition, and Fanaticism* (London, 1762).
Wikimedia Commons.

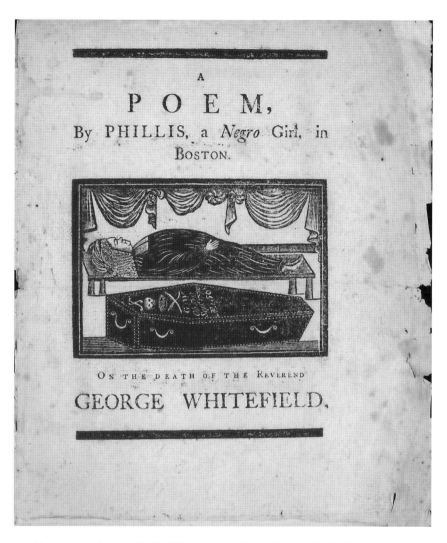

A

P O E M,

By PHILLIS, a *Negro* Girl, in
BOSTON.

ON THE DEATH OF THE REVEREND

GEORGE WHITEFIELD,

13.1 Frontispiece of Phillis Wheatley, *An Elegiac Poem: On the Death of That Celebrated Divine and Eminent Servant of Jesus Christ, the Reverend and Learned George Whitefield* (Boston, 1770). Beinecke Rare Book and Manuscript Library, Yale University.

13.2 Silver medal for George Whitefield, 1770. Transfer from the Yale University Library, Numismatic Collection, 2001, Gift of Charles Wyllys Betts, B.A. 1867, M.A. 1871. Yale University Art Gallery.

13.3 Wood, Enoch (1759–1846). George Whitefield. Bust. British, Burslem, Staffordshire, ca. 1790. Lead-glazed earthenware, H. 12 1/2 in. (31.8 cm). Gift of Francis P. Garvan, 1940 (40.171.6). Image copyright © The Metropolitan Museum of Art. Image source: Art Resource, NY.

Delaware to return to the South. He estimated that he had preached 175 times publicly since his arrival in Rhode Island in September, averaging more than 2 sermons a day. "All things concur to convince me that America is to be my chief scene for action," he concluded. He expected that God would soon remove the "candlestick" of favor from England (Revelation 2:5), and that America would become famous for the work of revival.[30]

Whitefield had reason to worry about England, for in his absence he had lost several of his key allies. His London publisher, James Hutton, had become more fully committed to the Moravians' theology after a visit to their congregations on the Continent. In contrast to the Methodists' emphasis on the spiritual disciplines of prayer and Bible reading, the Moravians taught a doctrine of "stillness." They emphasized nonaction, even to the point of disparaging taking communion, reading scripture, and attending church for those without certain faith. They believed that religious busyness could confuse works with salvation. Whitefield considered their "stillness" a perversion of Psalm 46:10 ("Be still, and know that I am God"), an exhortation not designed, as he wrote to a Moravian, to keep Christians from striving for faith. In London, the tension between John Wesley (whose troubles with Whitefield also festered) and the Moravians came to a head in July 1740, when Wesley renounced Hutton's Fetter Lane society.[31]

Whitefield too became increasingly troubled by the Moravians' theology, both because of what he heard from England and also because of discussions he had with Peter Böhler. Along with Hutton, Böhler had been one of the key leaders of the Fetter Lane society before migrating to Pennsylvania in 1740. He and Whitefield conversed about selling the Nazareth tract, and about their theological differences, including the Moravians' emphasis on perfectionism. They concluded that in order to avoid fruitless disputes, they would "carry on the work of God apart," as Whitefield told Hutton.[32]

Similarly, Hutton had begun to balk at printing Whitefield's works with which he disagreed. Whitefield told Hutton that he did not wish for him to print anything that would violate his conscience. And as with Wesley, he asked Hutton not to rashly denounce Calvinism. Whitefield craved a unified evangelical front, asking Hutton, "How can we build up a church unless we are like minded?" Whitefield, Wesley, and Hutton found that they were incapable of theological rapprochement. The strife made Whitefield long all the more for heaven, he said, where divisions between the brethren would cease.[33]

As Whitefield began to prepare for his return voyage to England, his trepidation about relationships there mounted. Before he left Philadelphia, he got the letter indicating that Elizabeth Delamotte's parents remained opposed to their proposed union, even though Elizabeth herself seems not yet to have given him a final no. Whitefield also wrote to Gilbert Tennent and said that he expected William Seward to return to America soon to help manage the affairs of the orphanage. Unbeknownst to Whitefield, Seward had tragically died a month earlier at the hands of a rock-throwing mob in Wales.[34]

When Seward returned from America, he took up preaching with Howell Harris. In September 1740, Seward had been nearly blinded by a rock-throwing hooligan. He wrote that the angry crowd came prepared for the confrontation, throwing "continual showers of stones, walnuts, dirt, a cat and also a dead dog" at them. Then came the fatal showdown in the town of Hay, where Seward received a deadly blow to the head with a heavy rock. He perished several days later, at the age of thirty-eight. In faraway Massachusetts, Jonathan Edwards was moved by Seward's martyr-like death to paste a page from Seward's printed elegy inside the front cover of his personal notebook titled "Faith." Edwards placed another page from it on the inside back cover of his Hebrew and Greek Bible.[35]

Newspapers paid little notice to the tragedy, mentioning only that the deceased was the "famous enthusiast Mr. William Seward, formerly belonging to the Treasury Office in the South Sea House, and lately very remarkable in being a disciple and close follower of Mr. George Whitefield." In his life, Seward had reportedly given more than £10,000 to Christian works, including Bethesda. But he apparently did not leave a will, leaving Whitefield "embarrassed," as he put it, with debts for the orphanage—estimated at £1,000—that he had expected Seward to pay. Whitefield faced arrest if he did not pay Seward's outstanding debts incurred for Bethesda, a risk averted only by a timely loan of several hundred pounds from an English benefactor.[36]

Meanwhile, the revivalist dealt with pressing difficulties in the South. On November 18, 1740, a terrible fire ravaged Charleston, South Carolina, engulfing a third of the town and destroying about three hundred houses, the Dock Street Theater, and the public library, among other structures. Such fires were not unusual in cities of the British Empire; the Charleston fire hardly compared to the horror of the Great Fire of London in 1666, which destroyed more than thirteen thousand homes and scores of churches, including St. Paul's Cathedral. Nevertheless, the fire devastated the southern port, with estimated losses of £250,000. Whitefield arrived three weeks after the fire, and at his first opportunity preached on Isaiah 1:9: "Except the Lord of Hosts had left unto us a very small remnant, we should have been as Sodom, and we should have been like unto Gomorrah." Perhaps the experience would help the city's residents escape the fires of hell, which "never shall be quenched" (Mark 9:43).[37]

Whitefield passed his twenty-sixth birthday and Christmas at Bethesda, bringing a much-needed infusion of more than £1,000 with him. Although the orphanage continued to struggle to cover its financial obligations and to maintain enough residents, Whitefield and his donors were happy with the project. A visitor wrote that the typical day for the fifty-four resident children consisted of a wake-up bell at sunrise, and "when the children arise, they sing a short hymn, and pray by themselves: then they go down and wash; and by the time they have done that, the bell calls to public worship." They studied a classical curriculum, learned trades, and took meals in a common room, where a "wholesome diet [was] provided." They attended worship services four times daily in summer; three in winter. The writer anticipated that if Georgia "allowed negroes, as it is thought must and will be," the orphanage could expand.[38]

Whitefield wished to challenge the religious authorities in South Carolina and Georgia, just as he had in New England and the Middle Colonies, calling on them to preach a pure gospel of God's grace. He and his allies had already discovered, via Alexander Garden's attempted suspension of Whitefield, that the southern establishment was willing to use disciplinary power to stop them. James Habersham and Jonathan Barber, the new spiritual director of the orphanage, elicited the wrath of Georgia authorities when they confronted the new Anglican parson of Savannah, Christopher Orton, with pointed questions about his spiritual state. "After abundance of uncharitable and scurrilous behavior [and] denouncing damnation to Mr. Orton for preaching false doctrine," they concluded that he was not a real Christian, wrote William Stephens, soon to be the governor of Georgia, with whom Whitefield had clashed over theology and the disposition of money for Bethesda. Although initially grateful for Whitefield's electrifying presence, Stephens began to complain about the revivalist: "Mr. Whitefield preached . . . [on] the doctrine of the new birth, and justification by faith, provided it be such, as to produce an evidence within ourselves, that the Spirit of God is working in our hearts; which he insists on, we may feel with a real sensation; and till that is wrought within us, we are in a state of damnation." After their confrontation with Orton, magistrates arrested Habersham and Barber for disturbing the peace, convicting and fining them at trial. Whitefield conceded that they should not have questioned whether Orton was a Christian, but he considered the arrests a fresh instance of "persecution."[39]

The South Carolina planter Hugh Bryan likewise ran afoul of Charleston authorities for writing a blistering letter, with Whitefield's assistance, about the spiritual lessons behind the city's fire. Bryan blamed the disaster on the colony's Anglican ministers, who were "deceiving precious souls and causing them to sleep in their sins to damnation." Legions languished in religious nominalism, casually identifying as Christians but never embracing its doctrines or practice. Such people needed their ministers to tell them of divine judgment and the necessity of the new birth. "The blood of such," Bryan warned, "will be required at their teachers' hands." He believed that the "dreadful fire of Charles-town hath spoken terror": "If we regard not this to lay it to heart, humble ourselves, and repent truly of our sins; the just God will yet pour out upon us more terrible vials of his wrath."[40]

Anglican officials did not take kindly to the letter, and constables briefly arrested Bryan and Whitefield for libeling the town's ministers. Far from being humbled by the experience, Whitefield saw it as more persecution and counted it an honor to suffer for Christ. Echoing Jesus's words on the cross, he prayed that God would be merciful to his antagonists: "They know not what they do." The following Sunday, Whitefield preached on King Herod sending the wise men to find the Christ child, ostensibly wanting to worship him, but really intending to murder him instead. "How dreadful it was to persecute under a pretense of religion," Whitefield warned.[41]

His brief detention did not interrupt his plan to sail for England. Charleston supporters showered him with so many provisions for the ship that he had to send most of them to Bethesda. Finally, on January 16, 1741, he boarded the *Minerva*; a week later the ship sailed. The journey took about six weeks, and was far easier than his previous return to England. It gave him some badly needed rest. He read, meditated, and prayed, regaining a "feeling possession" of God's presence even as he contemplated the trials awaiting him in Britain. Already eager to return to America, he planned to do so within four or five months.[42]

The chief unpleasantness he had to face in England, aside from his dashed hopes of marrying Elizabeth Delamotte, was a confrontation with the Wesleys. The conflict between the Wesleys and Whitefield's Calvinist allies reached a crescendo in Bristol while Whitefield was en route to London. John Cennick, the master of the Methodists' Kingswood school, clashed with the Wesleys as John worked to consolidate control of the Methodist societies and to marginalize Calvinists. Cennick wrote to Whitefield to apprise him of the crisis. Wesley acquired a copy of the letter and read it aloud to a meeting of the Bristol society. Cennick had written that he believed "no atheist can more preach against predestination" than did the Wesleys. "All who believe [in] election are counted enemies to God, and called so" by the Wesleys, he said. Cennick admitted that he wrote the letter and would not retract what he said. Therefore, John expelled him and his allies from the society for scoffing "at the preaching of Mr. John and Charles Wesley" and for speaking "evil of them behind their backs."[43]

Whitefield did not yet know about this episode as he penned another letter to Wesley while traveling to England. Why did John and Charles not remain silent about their disagreements with him, he asked? Charles had exacerbated the tension when he published an anti-Calvinist verse in *Hymns and Sacred Poems* (1740), declaring, "Horror to think that God is hate! / Fury in God can dwell! / God could a helpless world create, / To thrust them into hell!" Whitefield insisted that he could no longer preach the gospel without referring to predestination and election. He informed them that he had prepared a response to John's sermon "Free Grace," that he had left it to be published in Philadelphia and Boston, and that he would also publish it in London.[44]

Knowing that a definitive break with the Wesleys was imminent, Whitefield kept building a network of Calvinist evangelicals. One of the key links in that network was Anne Dutton of Great Gransden, England, where her husband led a Calvinistic Baptist church. Dutton, two decades older than Whitefield, was an insightful theological writer, and Whitefield came to depend on her to help strengthen his interdenominational Calvinist cohort. As he crossed the Atlantic, he wrote and asked her to write a substantial letter to Bethesda residents. Her book *A Discourse on Walking with God* (1735) had become a standard devotional text for Whitefield and his Bethesda colleagues. Telling her of troubles he expected to encounter back in England, he confessed that "it is an ease thus to unbosom one's self to a friend." Dutton was one of several key women — including the Countess of Huntingdon and his future wife, Elizabeth James — from whom Whitefield sought counsel and to whom he entrusted leadership responsibilities. For all but a few evangelical women of the time, formal pastoral roles were out of the question, although John Wesley did permit a number of female preachers (without ordination) to operate in his ministerial circuits. Whitefield never seems to have seriously entertained the possibility of allowing women to assume official pastoral positions. But he did not balk at enlisting women such as Dutton to help him bolster his revival network.[45]

It should be kept in mind that Methodism specifically and evangelicalism generally were predominantly women's movements, especially when considering the percentage of men and women involved. Critics of revivalism often focused on the behavior of female participants, raising the specter of sexual indiscretions: "The levees of Whit[e]field and Wesley used to be crowded with young women enquiring about their sensation," recalled one anti-Methodist writer, "and a number of grown females, widows, etc. were always coquetting in a song-of-Solomon way with these illustrious fathers." These negative associations of women with evangelicalism implicitly suggested the prevalence of women in the movement, and the anxiety it created for some. While some observers have painted evangelicalism as misogynistic, most modern historians realize that even without access to formal pastorates, many women found revivalism spiritually and socially satisfying. Evangelical leaders placed important restrictions on women's public roles, but the movement offered women vital social networks and outlets for expressing the "disciplined moral energy" that was essential to piety. Prominent women such as Anne Dutton, Elizabeth Whitefield, and the Countess of Huntingdon became pious exemplars, informal advisers, and trusted organizers for Whitefield and other male leaders.[46]

Whitefield arrived in London in late March 1741 and found the situation there as bleak as he had expected. The Methodists had fractured into Calvinist, Arminian, and Moravian factions. Whitefield saw large crowds—twenty thousand or more—on his initial return to Moorfields and Kennington Common, but follow-up meetings drew only a few hundred hard-core devotees. Finding out about Seward's death was a blow, as was the realization of the financial distress it had caused. He also lamented the Moravian defection of James Hutton, who had made hundreds of pounds sterling by selling Whitefield's sermons and journals, and who now refused to print his writings. Most bitter was discovering how many followers the Wesley brothers had turned away from him; "They will neither hear, see, nor give me the least assistance," Whitefield wrote. Some passed by as he was preaching, but stuck their fingers in their ears to block out the sound. Some even sent him threatening letters saying that God would "speedily destroy" him.[47]

Whitefield met with Charles to seek reconciliation, and their deep personal history temporarily broke the ice. They wept and prayed that the "breach might be prevented." Yet the split continued to widen. The Wesleys asked him to preach once at their new meeting place, the Foundry, but did not invite him again. Whitefield was devastated, fearing that all his earlier successes in London had come to naught. "All my work was to begin again," he wrote.[48]

Whitefield had many remaining London friends, of course, and some (as in Philadelphia) began to build him a wooden preaching structure they called the Tabernacle. It was not far from the Wesleys' Foundry. "A fresh awakening immediately began," Whitefield wrote, and he started sending for Calvinist allies, including John Cennick and Howell Harris, to share preaching duties.[49]

Finally, Whitefield met personally with John Wesley. The reunion was not so sweet as the meeting with Charles. Wesley wrote, "Having heard much of Whitefield's unkind behavior since his return from Georgia, I went to him to hear him speak for himself." Whitefield told him that they "preached two different gospels." He would no longer join with Wesley, the itinerant declared, nor even give him the "right hand of fellowship," but would publicly preach against him. Perhaps the conversation was not as unpleasant as it sounds, for the next night Whitefield and Cennick attended a love-feast with Wesley.[50]

Whatever the case, within a week of this meeting, Whitefield's *A Letter to the Reverend John Wesley: In Answer to His Sermon, Entitled Free-Grace* was published in London, with other editions appearing in the colonies. He professed profound hesitation in confronting Wesley publicly: "Jonah could not go with more reluctance against Nineveh, than I now take pen in hand to write against you." But Whitefield reminded his audience that Wesley had initiated the public controversy nearly two years earlier, having cast lots before publishing *Free Grace*. Whitefield wondered whether this method did not improperly "tempt the Lord." (The itinerant did not reflect on the extent to which casting lots differed from receiving unmediated guidance from the Holy Spirit.)[51]

Much of Whitefield's concern focused on Wesley's handling of the controversy, but he objected to Wesley's theology as well. Whitefield stated his own position succinctly: "I believe the doctrine of reprobation, that God intends to give saving grace, through Jesus Christ, only to a certain number, and that the rest of mankind, after the fall of Adam, being justly left of God to continue in sin, will at last suffer that eternal death, which is its proper wages." Wesley argued that if God offered saving grace only to the elect, then preaching was pointless. Whitefield countered that the preaching of the gospel was God's means of saving the elect. Pastors and evangelists could never know who in their audience was elect and who was reprobate, so they should "preach promiscuously to all" as a matter of obedience.[52]

Whitefield contested Wesley's concept that believers could achieve perfect holiness in this life. While he had total confidence in salvation through Christ, Whitefield knew that he sometimes still sinned. The Bible presented this as the common struggle of all Christians. Unfortunately, Whitefield set up a straw man by arguing that scripture and experience contradicted the notion that "after a man is born again he cannot commit sin." This was not Wesley's position, although Whitefield did occasionally encounter followers of Wesley who claimed to have reached such a state of sinlessness that it had become impossible for them to sin. Regardless, speaking personally to Wesley, Whitefield speculated that his "fighting so strenuously against the doctrine of election, and pleading so vehemently for a sinless perfection, are among the reasons or culpable causes, why you are kept out of the liberties of the gospel, and that full assurance of faith, which they enjoy, who have experimentally tasted, and daily feed upon God's electing, everlasting love." Whitefield counted himself among those who had "experimentally tasted" that love. The itinerant predicted that when they reached heaven, he would be proved correct and Wesley would cast his "crown down at the feet of the Lamb, and as it were, [be] filled with a holy blushing for opposing the divine sovereignty in the manner you have done."[53]

This was harsh talk. Wesley found the letter "imprudent" and "burlesque," and told Whitefield as much shortly after receiving a copy. It made "an open (and probably irreparable) breach between him and me," Wesley concluded. Citing Ecclesiasticus 22:22 from the Apocrypha (which at the time remained in the King James Bible), Wesley wrote, "for a treacherous wound, and for the betraying of secrets, every friend will depart."[54]

Whitefield soon went to review the Methodists' schools in Bristol and Kingswood, and was not pleased with the Wesleys' influence there. A number of the Methodists now professed to have experienced total freedom from sin. One woman said she had been sin-free for a year, but Whitefield was dubious: "Alas! she showed many marks of imperfection while I was with her," he wrote. In letters exchanged with John in late April, they bickered about expenses and management of the Bristol projects. But the real point of contention remained Whitefield's publication against Wesley. Wesley insisted that if Whitefield had stuck to the theological point, and not made the letter so personal, he could have avoided the breach. According to Wesley, "[Whitefield could] have answered my proofs without mentioning my name."[55]

Wesley tartly vowed not to "dwell on those things which have an immediate tendency to make [Whitefield] odious and contemptible," promising not to return Whitefield's attacks in kind. But if the Wesleys did not indict Whitefield and his associates by name, they made clear that their followers should avoid them and their Calvinism. John Cennick, for one, said that Charles "called Calvin the first-born son of the devil" and exhorted his audiences to despise even the proponents of predestination and election.[56]

These months, then, saw the opening of a bitter rivalry between England's Arminian and Calvinist evangelicals. Howell Harris told John Cennick that the "hellish infection" of Arminianism had not yet come to Wales, but it festered close by in Bristol. Not even Harris and Whitefield were in complete accord theologically: at the same time that Whitefield and Wesley clashed over Calvinism, Harris and Whitefield engaged in a pointed exchange over a believer's power over sin. As Whitefield countered Wesley on the "monstrous errors" of perfectionism, Harris wrote, he seemed to suggest that "there is no such thing as dominion over indwelling sin." Harris thought this went too far. A true believer would enjoy greater freedom from sin over time, but Whitefield thought that even the holiest saint would still occasionally struggle with temptation and fall into sin. Chastising Harris, he speculated that he had become "tinctured with the doctrine of sinless perfection." He hoped Harris would not become angry with him over the issue; he could not afford to lose another key ally.[57]

As Whitefield prepared for his first trip to Scotland, in June 1741, he was becoming chastened, having endured the pain of schism with his onetime spiritual father, John Wesley. He told Howell Harris that they needed to avoid the extremes of "party spirit," on one hand, and too much "positiveness," on another. "The farther we go in the spiritual life," he said, "the more cool and rational shall we be, and yet more truly zealous. I speak this by experience."[58]

Remaining committed to the defense of biblical doctrine (meaning Calvinism), Whitefield increasingly realized the value of maintaining a united evangelical front. The movement could not sustain another horrible breakup. And while Whitefield did not detach revival preaching from correct doctrine, he relished nothing so much as seeing lives transformed by the Spirit, through the proclamation of the gospel. Seeing people like Nathan Cole, Hannah Heaton, and Daniel Rogers experience the new birth was his real passion. He resolved to keep it his main business.

"Thy Maker is Thy Husband": Whitefield Goes to Scotland

In the spring of 1742, Whitefield enjoyed some of his most successful preaching ever at Moorfields in London. Some there did not enjoy his successes very much, however. The fields—ripe for "Beelzebub's harvest," the itinerant reckoned—were lined with booths of stage players, puppeteers, clowns, and other entertainers. Whitefield wanted to "lift up a standard amongst them in the name of Jesus of Nazareth." As he mounted a field pulpit, thousands of people left the players' booths to hear Whitefield's performance. The angry entertainers followed them, not to listen, but to accost the itinerant. Soon a hail of "stones, dirt, rotten eggs, and pieces of dead cats" pelted the preacher. A clown climbed upon a man's shoulders and tried to slash Whitefield with a whip. Every time he swung at Whitefield, however, the clown tumbled down instead of hitting his target. Another clown climbed a tree close to Whitefield's pulpit and "shamefully exposed his nakedness before all the people," eliciting a chorus of hoots and laughter. Every attempt to silence Whitefield failed, and he went on preaching, praying, and singing for three hours.[1]

The danger was hardly over, however. The next day, descending from his pulpit after preaching at Marylebone fields, Whitefield suddenly felt his wig and hat nearly come off. He turned in time to see a sword graze his temple, thrust at him by a prospective assassin. A bystander knocked the attacker's sword aside with his cane, and Whitefield narrowly escaped. Still, he would not stop preaching. Scores gave him notes expressing their spiritual progress and concerns. They were sinners, Whitefield wrote, "snatched, in such an unexpected, unlikely place and manner, out of the very jaws of the devil."[2]

When we see the images of an aging Whitefield in his clerical wig and gown, we may struggle to understand these kinds of vicious reactions to him. Whitefield was no quaint parson—his ministry was intrusive, entrepreneurial, and well nigh revolutionary. Thus, it sometimes generated scorn and violence. Whitefield *competed* for adherents, regardless of how his tactics irritated adversaries representing the established church, Moorfields' entertainers, or the stage actors of London's theater district. To him, the gospel was important enough to use the new means of the marketplace to deliver it effectively. To many who responded, the ancient message of Christianity seemed, in Whitefield's elocutions, fresh and new. One Methodist woman recalled that though she went regularly to church, she had never been "struck in such a manner" as when she heard the itinerant at Moorfields.[3]

Less than a year before the attempt on his life, Whitefield had arrived in Scotland, on July 30, 1741. He disembarked at Leith, Edinburgh's port, which was just a short, "agreeable walk" to High Street, in the center of the city. Into Edinburgh flowed a range of raw and refined products, among them whales taken in the waters of Greenland, tobacco, textiles, and tea. Edinburgh handled much of the Scottish interior's trade with London, hundreds of miles down the North Sea coast. Edinburgh was also the leading intellectual center of Scotland, graced by writers such as David Hume and Adam Smith.[4]

Although this was Whitefield's first time in Scotland, he already had deep connections there. While traveling across Britain and America, he recommended works by Scottish authors such as Thomas Boston and Ralph Erskine in his short list of essential evangelical readings. Erskine was understandably pleased, telling Whitefield: "If I travel by pen as far as you do in person, and contribute my mite for spreading of gospel light, I rejoice." Whitefield called Boston's *Human Nature in Its Four-Fold State* (1720) a book "worth its weight in gold." It was one of the best-selling Scottish books of the eighteenth century. Boston helped craft the evangelical emphasis on conversion, explaining, "We are once born sinners; we must be born again, that we may be saints."[5]

Thomas Boston, who passed away in 1732, did not live to see the revivals for which he had prayed. But Ralph and Ebenezer Erskine appealed to Whitefield to bring his remarkable ministry to Scotland. Whitefield reached out to Ralph in March 1739, telling him of the awakenings in England and Wales. The more the Erskines heard about Whitefield, the more they wished he would visit Scotland, and in April 1741 Ralph implored him to come. "There is no face on earth I would desire more earnestly to see than yours," he wrote. The Erskines resonated with Whitefield's revivalist Calvinism, and Ralph commended Whitefield for confronting Wesley's Arminianism. "To deny and defame divine election," Ralph wrote, "and ascribe to themselves sinless absolute perfection is in my view such blasphemy, one might tremble to speak of it . . . Surely they may be ready next to burn their Bibles."[6]

The Erskines and their allies advocated for renewal in the Church of Scotland, but authorities suspended them in the 1730s for criticizing the church. The Erskines, now representing the secessionist "Associate Presbytery," asked Whitefield not to affiliate with pastors remaining within the Church of Scotland. Whitefield could not honor this request, disdaining denominational factions. "I come . . . to preach the simple gospel to all that are willing to hear me, of whatever denomination," he told the Erskines. They grudgingly accepted his interdenominational bent, but asked that he at least do nothing to "strengthen the hands of our corrupt clergy." Ebenezer also added, parenthetically, that he was "truly sorry for the Wesleys."[7]

Even as Whitefield proceeded up the coast to Edinburgh, his thoughts returned to Bethesda. He sought means of helping the administrators and orphans from afar. Feverishly writing letters to Georgia (and elsewhere in Britain's American colonies), he encouraged trusted supporters to do so as well. During an earlier preaching tour of England, he had visited Great Grandsen, the home of Anne Dutton. He wanted Dutton to use her epistolary talents for the good of key American followers, asking her specifically to write to Jonathan Bryan's family and to James Habersham. He told Jonathan Barber at Bethesda that he was impressed with Dutton's character. "Her conversation is as weighty as her letters," he concluded. Whitefield was the key figure in the emerging "epistolary circuit" of Calvinist evangelicals, but many women and men across America, Britain, and the Continent played a vital role in it, too.[8]

Whitefield wrote personally to many residents at Bethesda, including some of the orphans. His counsel to these youths did not smooth the hard edges of his doctrines. To a Rebekah B., he confessed that his sole purpose in bringing her to Bethesda was that she might be "brought to Jesus." Sympathizing with her struggles against sin (which she had discussed in an earlier letter), the itinerant told her, "You may well wonder, that God has not sent you to hell long ago." (Whitefield wondered the same about himself, of course.) Similarly, Molly A. had confided to him that she was wrestling to maintain her passion for Christ, and he prayed that God would humble her by the experience. "You may now see," he wrote, "what a poor wretch you are, how proud, how earthly, how sensual, how devilish; and yet, stupendous love! Jesus Christ will still receive you."[9]

Letters went to friends in New England, too, where the revivals became more intense after his departure. Again, people in the midst of these events did not call it the "Great Awakening," but Whitefield did rejoice that "this great awakening" had not passed over the household of one correspondent. From Daniel Rogers and Gilbert Tennent, he heard that there was a "shaking among the dry bones" among students at Harvard and Yale, and Whitefield told them that he was sorry he had said the colleges' "light was become darkness." Reminding them that learning without piety only promoted the devil's interests, he urged Harvard and Yale students to study "not to get a parish, nor to be polite preachers, but to be great saints."[10]

In addition to personal correspondence, Whitefield bolstered his publishing efforts in England, adjusting for James Hutton's defection. In London, John Lewis was printing a struggling evangelical periodical called the *Christian's Amusement,* and upon his return to England in spring 1741, Whitefield began managing the paper, renaming it the *Weekly History; or, An Account of the Most Remarkable Particulars Relating to the Present Progress of the Gospel.* The *Weekly History* supplied revival news across the Anglo-American world and gave Whitefield's followers a sense of participating in one common transatlantic, interdenominational movement. The first issue, printed by Lewis in London, featured a sermon by the South Carolina Baptist pastor Isaac Chanler, prefaced by the Boston Congregationalist minister William Cooper. By controlling the content of the *Weekly History,* Whitefield could promote the work of Calvinist evangelical allies, who implicitly contradicted the Wesleys on election and perfectionism. As he itinerated, Whitefield sent letters to Lewis and to friends such as Howell Harris, asking that supporters read the letters in meetings and that they be printed in the *Weekly History.* The *Weekly History* and similar periodicals in Scotland and America helped overcome the disadvantages of relying exclusively on personal, unprinted correspondence to maintain the evangelical network. Magazine issues were easily reproducible and relatively cheap, and buying them meant that one did not need to correspond directly with any particular figure to know what was happening in far-distant corners of the evangelical world.[11]

Whitefield increasingly realized that preaching biblical truth alone did not satisfy his responsibility to communicate: he needed to use media, both old-fashioned (letters) and new (magazines), to get the word out. Every product should be used in multiple ways. He preached sermons repeatedly, then published them. Letters were to be circulated, read out loud, and printed in the *Weekly History.*

Upon arriving in Scotland, Whitefield sought out Ralph Erskine, taking a ferry across the Firth of Forth (the mouth of the river Forth) to Dunfermline. There he preached at Erskine's meetinghouse, and was pleasantly surprised that when he named his text, many in the audience began rustling the pages of their Bibles to read along with him. (He came to believe that this reflected a general Scottish pattern, telling a Glasgow audience that he thought the Scots "are better acquainted with your bibles than others are." Daniel Defoe had similarly noted on a trip to Scotland in 1707 that "when the minister names any text of Scripture, you shall hear a little rustling noise over the whole place, made by the turning the leaves of the bible.") Apparently in England, Wales, and America, fewer people brought Bibles to meetings.[12]

The Erskines and their allies told Whitefield that they, too, had seen great workings of the Holy Spirit in recent times. Ralph had earlier apprised Whitefield that they had hosted "sacramental solemnities . . . where vast multitudes of people were present at the tents, without doors as well as in the churches." He had never experienced God's presence more than on these occasions: "The Spirit was sometimes remarkably poured out, and the power of the Lord was present to heal many souls." These great outdoor celebrations of the Lord's Supper had deep roots in the Scottish Reformed tradition. At one meeting in Dunfermline in the late 1730s, about five thousand people took communion, with tables served in the fields from nine in the morning until midnight.[13]

Delighted to meet Whitefield, the Erskines eagerly anticipated seeing him preach. They did not drop the issue of his denominational affiliation, however. Although Whitefield had promised to return quickly to Edinburgh, they urged him to stay longer so that they could (as Whitefield put it) "set me right about church government." He assured them that he would return to discuss their concerns. In Edinburgh, Whitefield preached at the nonseceding Canongate Kirk, and Ralph Erskine attended and even went up into the pulpit with him. Others in the Erskines' Associate Presbytery found this development appalling, and they took Whitefield to task for fellowshipping with the Church of Scotland clergy. The "set of grave venerable men," the itinerant wrote, pressed him to announce an alliance with their presbytery. They also asked him to endorse the Solemn League and Covenant, an agreement dating to the 1640s and the English Civil War in which Parliamentarians formally committed themselves to promoting the Scottish Presbyterian model of church government. (England repudiated the Solemn League and Covenant in 1661 upon the restoration of Charles II.)[14]

Whitefield did not intend to ally exclusively with the Erskines' presbytery, nor did he intend to recommend the Solemn League and Covenant. He found that issue arcane, at best. Ebenezer Erskine reminded the Associate Presbyterians that as an Englishman, Whitefield really could not be expected to appreciate the significance of this covenant. Patience was in order. One pastor, however, said that Whitefield deserved no patience, because England "had revolted most with respect to church government." The itinerant tried to explain that he had not studied these issues closely, "being too busy about other matters, as I judged, of greater importance." That excuse did not go over well. ("I never met with such narrow spirits" as the militant seceders, he complained to Gilbert Tennent.)[15]

Some Associate Presbytery ministers agreed that he need not immediately subscribe to the Solemn League and Covenant, but they still demanded that he stop preaching at nonseceding churches. Whitefield, however, would never limit himself in such a way. "If the Pope himself would lend me his pulpit," he declared, he "would gladly proclaim the righteousness of Jesus Christ therein." They simply could not agree, and the end result, Whitefield regretfully noted, was an "open breach." Although he tried to maintain a friendly relationship with the Erskines, one of Edinburgh's Associate Presbytery pastors published in 1742 the pamphlet A *Warning against Countenancing the Ministrations of Mr. George Whitefield.* The pamphlet asserted that Whitefield was "no minister of Jesus Christ" and that his success was "diabolical" in origin. (Whitefield called this the "most virulent pamphlet [he] ever saw.") Another fractious episode between potential allies was not what Whitefield needed, but principles of theology and church government kept dividing his evangelical cohort. He wrote wistfully to a correspondent about how much more irenic American Presbyterians were than the Scots: "Our brethren in America, blessed be God, have not so learned Christ" (Ephesians 4:20)[16]

The creation of the transatlantic evangelical network was so remarkable that we might forget just how much its members struggled to stay unified. Everywhere, disagreements troubled the movement: in England, debates between Calvinists and Arminians and fights over Moravian piety; in Scotland, feuds between Church of Scotland pastors and the Associate Presbytery; in America, tensions between Presbyterians, Congregationalists, Moravians, Anglicans, and others, and questions about the role of the evangelical radicals. Everywhere, there were personality clashes between major leaders. And evangelicals constantly wrestled with how to interpret manifestations of spiritual fervor and the workings of the Holy Spirit. While we may speak of an evangelical movement that emerged in the late 1730s, centered on Whitefield, we should not overstate evangelicals' ability to maintain a united front.

In Scotland, Whitefield saw such large crowds that it was not safe to give public notice of his sermons. "Pressing invitations" to preach came from around the country, but many also wished to recruit him for one side or the other in Scotland's church controversies. He upbraided John Willison, the prominent pastor of Dundee, telling him, "I wish you would not trouble yourself or me in writing about the corruptions of the Church of England." There was no perfect church under heaven, and Whitefield insisted that the Scots allow him to preach the gospel freely and to raise funds for Bethesda.[17]

In mid-September 1741, Whitefield preached ten times in Glasgow, which, at seventeen thousand residents, was about the same size of Boston, and roughly half as big as Edinburgh, its counterpart to the east. The Glasgow printer Robert Smith took sermons from Whitefield's "own mouth" (as the title page advertised) and published them with the "outmost expedition." A nineteen-year-old convert deeply affected by Whitefield's Glasgow sermons testified that she could not "remember distinctly" whether it was hearing his sermons or reading the printed versions that made the deepest impact. Whitefield's pulpit delivery packed a punch, of course, but many found the experience of reading his sermons (or hearing them read) compelling as well.[18]

In the few cases in which we can compare evidence from delivered and published sermons, we can see how Whitefield's spoken rhetoric dazzled. The itinerant certainly felt more comfortable preaching sermons than publishing them—fewer critics could capture and attack his ephemeral spoken words, but they pored over every published sentence for hints of doctrinal error or enthusiasm. His printed works, therefore, tend toward verbal and theological moderation. For instance, a sixteen-year-old female Cambuslang convert recalled being thrown into "confusion and amazement" when Whitefield stated in his sermon "Thy Maker is Thy Husband" that if anyone refused Christ as a spiritual husband, the devil was their husband instead. Indeed, they "sleep all night in the devil's arms." (Cambuslang was a village about five miles southeast of Glasgow.) When you compare the printed text of the sermon, however, the line is not nearly as striking. There Whitefield states: "If you are not married to Jesus Christ, you are married to the law, the world, the flesh, and the devil." It said nothing about sleeping in the devil's arms.[19]

His sermons paired principled theology with passionate persuasion. In one of the Glasgow sermons, "The Lord Our Righteousness," Whitefield defended the doctrine that Christ's moral character was imputed to believers for the purpose of judgment. Quoting Martin Luther, Whitefield argued that by the principle of imputation, "the Reformation was brought about." Two-thirds of the way through his address, Whitefield changed to a more emotional appeal, saying, "I have been too long upon the doctrinal part. To preach to your head without preaching to your heart is doing you no good." He asked whether his listeners had felt Christ's imputed righteousness in their hearts: "Can ye say *The Lord is your Righteousness?*" Looking out over Glasgow's High Church yard, which included the burial ground, he declared that most of the gathered throng could not say that Christ was their source of holiness. Evocatively, he advised that if they died without Christ's righteousness, "Ye may have a pompous burial, but while your friends are carrying your bodies to the grave, your soul may be in hell." One previously passive attendee noted that this sermon gave her "clear and heart-affecting views . . . of the wonderful inconceivable glories and match-less beauty and excellency of God in Christ." She could scarcely keep herself from crying out in the middle of the address.[20]

Often when retelling Bible stories, Whitefield set scenes with the thoughts, feelings, and appearance of characters. A key word he used to introduce such extrapolations was "methinks." For example, in a Glasgow sermon on Saul's (the Apostle Paul's) conversion in the book of Acts, Whitefield re-created Saul's journey to Damascus: "Methinks I see the young zealot riding along, pleasing himself with the thought with what triumph he should ride back to Jerusalem with the people of this mad way [Christians] dragged after him." But the resur-rected Christ confronted Saul on the Damascus road, leading to his remarkable conversion. When Saul first met the disciples at Damascus, having experienced that transforming grace, Whitefield said, "Methinks I see him breaking into floods of tears, and weeping over them, saying, alas my brother, can you forgive me? . . . Can ye forgive me that I intended to imbrue my hands in your precious blood?" Whitefield also applied biblical scenarios to modern events. In the same sermon, Whitefield said that Saul persecuted Christians because he saw them as a "company of enthusiastic mad men that talked of inward feeling, of the new birth, [and] of imputed righteousness." Those apostolic Christians sounded much like the new evangelicals.[21]

Whitefield also meant to shake the people of Scotland out of their nominal Christianity. Many believed that since their parents had had them baptized, and they had grown up in an overwhelmingly Christian land, and they had attended church and taken communion, they were real Christians. But Whitefield doubted their authenticity; he thought that many of these so-called Christians were little better than "baptized heathens" who "have not so much faith in the Lord Jesus Christ as the Devil himself." Many in the audience, he posited, would say that they had believed since early childhood, since before they could remember. This, to Whitefield, was dubious: When had they real-ized the damning gravity of their sin? When they had turned to Christ for rescue? Too many "mistake an historical faith for a true faith wrought in the heart by the Spirit of God," he warned.[22]

It was a "dreadful thing to fall into the hands of an angry God," Whitefield proclaimed. Just two months earlier (likely unbeknownst to Whitefield), Jonathan Edwards had preached his celebrated "Sinners in the Hands of an Angry God" sermon in Enfield, Connecticut, heralding the same danger, based loosely on Hebrews 10:31. (Although the King James and Geneva Bibles spoke in that verse of the "living God," the phrase "angry God" was used frequently in English Protestant circles.) In another Glasgow sermon, Whitefield also warned, Edwards-like, that the unconverted were "hanging over the fiery furnace, over hell-fire, by a single thread of this life." Whitefield painted a horrifying scene of the damned being raised to judgment: "Methinks I see the poor wretches dragged out of their graves by the Devil, methinks I see them trembling, crying out to the hills and rocks to cover them. But the Devil will say, 'come I will take you away,' and then they will stand trembling before the judgment seat of Christ. They shall appear before him to see him once, and hear him pronounce that irrevocable sentence, 'Depart from me, ye cursed' [Matthew 7:23]. Methinks I hear the poor creature saying, 'Lord, if we must be damned, let some angel pronounce the sentence.'" But no, Whitefield thundered, "The God of Love, Jesus Christ, will pronounce it."[23]

Whitefield certainly appealed to listeners' hearts, but he also referred regularly to weighty matters of doctrine and church history. In one of the Glasgow sermons, he mentioned in rapid succession the church fathers Ignatius of Antioch, Tertullian, and Polycarp, as well as Martin Luther, assuming that his audience would be familiar with each. Whitefield and his audiences lived in a world in which even modest home- and church-based educations centered on theology and Christian history. For those who know Whitefield only as a powerfully emotional preacher, the intellectual heft of his sermons may come as a surprise.[24]

Both Whitefield's rift with John Wesley and his desire to marry continued to weigh on him in Scotland. He received word that Howell Harris had recently engaged in promising conversations with the Wesley brothers, and that he "saw room to hope, that the Lord would bring us together in truth." Whitefield quickly wrote to John, taking the opportunity to apologize for publishing the report that Wesley had cast lots before publishing *Free Grace*. Suggesting that their theological differences need not divide them, Whitefield reminded Wesley that in practice he offered "Jesus freely to every individual soul," even though he believed that only the elect would receive Christ as savior. Whitefield assured Wesley that he could go as far as he liked with teaching sanctification, but Whitefield would never agree with the notion that "the in-being of sin is to be destroyed in this life."[25]

Somehow the blessedness of peacemaking had stirred Whitefield while visiting Scotland. The same day he wrote John Wesley, he also wrote Peter Böhler, the Moravian leader with whom he had split in 1740. Whitefield told Böhler that he was sorry he had brought up his name in his published letter against Wesley (he had suggested that Böhler taught that the damned in hell would eventually be saved). They both had made mistakes, Whitefield said. Dropping the apologetic tone, however, he emphasized that Böhler had "not acted simply in some things." Nevertheless, Whitefield hoped that they could heal their public rift.[26]

The itinerant discovered that the bad feelings between him, the Moravians, and the Wesleys would not heal easily. He did not know that Charles had written John two weeks before Whitefield did, insisting that there could be no reunion with Whitefield until he denied predestination. Perhaps John had begun to waver about whether they needed to hold the line against the Calvinists, but Charles asked how they could ever "trust [Whitefield] while the wound he has made is yet unclosed?" Charles demanded that John assure him that he was warning his Methodist flock against the "Other Gospel." If he did not, Charles would, "on the first preaching night[,] renounce [Whitefield] on the housetop." Both Wesleys rebuffed Whitefield's overtures, and Whitefield told Howell Harris in December 1741 that the Wesleys' attitudes were "worse than ever" toward them. Nevertheless, Whitefield kept communicating with them, included positive letters about them in the *Weekly History*, and even recommended some of their works to his followers. In his letters, he advised associates to pursue unity with other believers wherever possible, saying he thought it best "not to dispute, when there is no probability of convincing."[27]

While conflict with the Wesleys ground on, Whitefield's marital status took a surprising turn. Whitefield left Edinburgh in late October, traveling hundreds of miles south by horse, through northern England to Abergavenny, Wales. There lived Elizabeth James, an evangelical widow who was ten years Whitefield's senior. After arrangements made by Howell Harris, she was now Whitefield's fiancée. Whitefield's marriage to Elizabeth James concluded his troubled pursuit of matrimony. Harris had been aware that the revivalist wished to find a wife, in spite of his disastrous courtship of Elizabeth Delamotte. For his part, Harris felt drawn to celibacy, yet he became attracted to James, a follower of his ministry, in 1739. She had "no beauty, youth or riches," Harris wrote in his diary, but they became spiritually close. James told Harris that "God had owned [him] to her," which gave him a "great sweetness."[28]

It was not the Lord's will for Harris to marry Elizabeth, however. By the fall of 1740, Harris had begun to think that perhaps she would be a suitable wife for

Whitefield. Giving Elizabeth up was a great test for Harris; he called her his "Isaac" (referring to Abraham's sacrifice of his son in Genesis 22). After Whitefield returned from America, he and Harris began to discuss the possibility of his marrying Elizabeth. Harris broached the topic with Elizabeth in July 1741. Elizabeth chided him, saying that even her own father would not have the right of "disposing" of her against her will. Her chaotic feelings about shifting suitors from Harris to Whitefield caused her to lose both sleep and appetite. Nevertheless, she found it flattering to become the object of attention of the Lord's "two greatest favorites in this nation."[29]

James was conflicted, yet here was Whitefield, offering her the prospect of immediate marriage. She had deeper feelings for Harris, but he seemed set against marrying. Harris declared that Whitefield was "more holy & more able to make her happy & she more worthy of him than vile me." To make things even more complicated, Harris had another love interest besides Elizabeth James, a woman named Anne Williams, whom he would eventually marry in 1744. Five days after Whitefield and James married, Harris wrote to Williams, imploring her to marry him and assuring her that he wanted to marry not to gratify fleshly lusts but to gain her assistance in his ministry. In a subsequent letter, he confided that he had loved Anne for three years (a fact he also divulged to Elizabeth James), but that he regarded those feelings as a temptation while he still thought he might marry Elizabeth. Harris had surrendered his feelings for James so that she could marry Whitefield, but Whitefield, surprisingly, did not support Harris's marriage to Williams. Whitefield thought Williams should marry a man named John Syms, who had replaced William Seward as Whitefield's bookkeeper. Harris became irritated with Whitefield, telling him that he was being "selfish." It was an extraordinary display of relational intrigue—one might say foolishness—by two extraordinarily effective ministers.[30]

The circumstances of Whitefield and James's union—arranged by others, and happening quickly after an initial meeting—were not unusual in British culture, especially among wealthier classes. Either George or Elizabeth could presumably have scuttled the marriage had they found the other unacceptable during their brief courtship. But their emphasis was on the religious propriety and functionality of their union, not on affectionate feelings, which Britons were only beginning to see as an indispensable ingredient of marriage. The Whitefields' marriage did not begin with romance, but with a mutual sense of "matching religious temperaments," to use one historian's phrase.[31]

They must have found each other acceptable, for after a few days of visiting, George and Elizabeth wed in Caerphilly, Wales, on November 14, 1741.

Attendees took communion and sang a John Cennick hymn on marriage. "Jesus was present" at the wedding, Whitefield recalled. Afterward he preached on a decidedly nonmatrimonial text, Matthew 9:12, in which Jesus said, "They that be whole need not a physician, but they that are sick." A few months later, Whitefield described Elizabeth to Gilbert Tennent: "A widow, of about thirty-six years of age . . . neither rich in fortune, nor beautiful as to her person, but, I believe, a true child of God, and would not, I think, attempt to hinder me in his work for the world. In that respect, I am just the same as before marriage." It was common for a widow of middling financial status with children to remarry in Georgian England, and though Elizabeth was not rich, she was probably not poor either. Whitefield considered her a promising match mainly because of her piety and maturity. She was the sort of woman who would understand the unique demands of his traveling ministry. Some in eighteenth-century Britain and America might have begun to embrace a more romantic ideal of marriage, but if Elizabeth ever dreamt of a constant companion for a husband, George repeatedly disappointed her. A week after their wedding, he left to preach in Bristol and London. Long trips away from his wife, and from his new step-daughter, Nancy (whose name was almost entirely absent from his subsequent correspondence), became the norm.[32]

Methodist itinerants, especially John Wesley, were ambivalent about marriage. Autobiographies of Methodist preachers from the era commonly say little about the itinerant's wife or children, but highlight the camaraderie among the bands of brother pastors. The ideal Methodist minister was hard-working, self-controlled, and constantly traveling away from home. For decades, Wesley made no provision for the wives or widows of his network's preachers. Charles entered into a happy marriage with Sarah Gwynne and had given up itinerancy by the mid-1750s, which helps explain the friction that grew between the brothers in those years. John would get married, too, but it was a miserable, fraught union. In his attitude toward marriage, Whitefield seemed to stand in between John and Charles: his marriage to Elizabeth was pragmatic, and would be marked with suffering and terrible misunderstandings. In the long run, however, George came to depend on Elizabeth as an organizer and a communication link for his work. In his way, he loved her, but their marriage was not cozy or sweet. And he would always remind followers that in Christ, God became the believer's true spouse.[33]

Some in Whitefield's circle found the marriage abrupt: one minister wrote that although he had heard of the wedding, "[I] did not believe it till I received your letter." Critics scoffed that the preacher had hastily married a woman "old enough to be his mother." No one in Whitefield's family seems to have attended the wedding; indeed, his communication with his family had become quite limited since his emergence as an itinerant. He occasionally mentioned them in letters, and he visited his mother when he passed through Gloucester. We also know that his brother Richard continued to run the Bell Inn. Even as Whitefield's revival preaching proceeded in 1742, a note in the *London Evening Post* advertised "A Great Cock Match" to be held at Richard Whitefield's inn, "in a pit just built for that purpose."[34]

By the time of his marriage, Whitefield's ministry had fully recovered from the break with the Wesleys. There was a "very great awakening" in Scotland, Wales, and New England and in English cities, including London and Bristol, he told correspondents. Others told him of packed assemblies and dramatic conversions all over the Anglo-American world. It was a work the likes of which, according to Whitefield, "neither we nor our fathers have heard of." Whitefield continued building his evangelical network as much as he could: though his popularity and talent generated intense interest, it was impossible for him to travel and preach more than he was already doing. He had the *Weekly History* printing accounts of far-flung revivals, and he "earnestly recommended" new evangelical texts, such as Jonathan Edwards's *The Distinguishing Marks of a Work of the Spirit of God*. This sermon, given at the Yale College commencement in 1741, was published in Boston in 1741 and in Edinburgh and London in 1742. (John Wesley published an abridged edition of the sermon in 1744—with Edwards's Calvinist theology removed.)[35]

In the midst of the burgeoning awakenings, Whitefield probed the limits of what he might expect as he experienced the Holy Spirit at greater depths. Echoing Christ's phrase in Matthew 9:17, he routinely spoke of believers being filled with "new wine." He sometimes wondered, during intense revival meetings, whether he was "in or out of the body." For those who felt the deep "comforts of the Holy Ghost," he advised humility. "It is a good thing," he wrote, "to know how to manage a manifestation aright," navigating a middle course between frenzy and spiritual torpor. Believers could tangibly apprehend the work of the Spirit, he insisted, but he and his followers mostly eschewed claims of miraculous works such as healings or speaking in tongues. The Scottish pastor John Willison, for example, wrote, "I have myself been witness to the Holy Ghost falling upon [Whitefield] and his hearers oftener than once, I don't say in a miraculous, though observable manner."[36]

Despite his conflicts with Peter Böhler, Whitefield continued to see the Moravians as having unparalleled insight into the mysteries of spiritual experience. Increasingly, Whitefield spoke in the Moravians' distinctive phrases of

"blood and wounds" theology. Count Zinzendorf and other Moravians meditated on the wounds of Christ's scourged body in order to appreciate personally
the depth of his love. In typical Moravian language, Whitefield told a correspondent that he desired to "lie as a poor, very poor sinner at the feet of the
wounded Lamb," and he advised another to let Jesus's "blood, his wounds be
continually before you." In a letter to John Cennick, who would eventually join
the Moravians, Whitefield said he found all his happiness "in the wounds, and
blood of a dying God." John Gillies, the eighteenth-century editor of Whitefield's
papers, apparently regarded that statement as indiscreet, and edited it to say
Whitefield found all his happiness "in a crucified God."[37]

In the winter of 1741–42, Whitefield explored the viability of closer union
with the Moravians, perhaps as a bulwark against the Wesleys. In March 1742,
he chastised John for his prejudice against the Moravians and declared, "Jesus
Christ fights for the Moravian Brethren. They will insensibly increase."
Although he gravitated toward a Moravian alliance, Whitefield had to be
careful not to alienate American colleagues, including the increasingly
moderate Gilbert Tennent, who opposed the Moravians. Tennent saw them as
rank enthusiasts who promoted passion over correct doctrine. In late 1742,
Whitefield spread the word among his American supporters that he had not,
in fact, "joined with the Moravian Brethren." He wanted to emphasize evangelical unity, but still recognized that some of his principles—especially those
related to Calvinism—differed from the Moravians' as far "as the east is from
the west."[38]

Whitefield longed to return to America, but following up his work in Scotland
seemed more pressing. God had wrought a great renewal in the wake of his
visit; exuberant Scottish Calvinist pastors told him that the "Lord Jesus is a
picking up his elect vessels from among the herd that are reserved to a day of
slaughter!" Particularly intriguing news came from the small parish of
Cambuslang, where he had not yet preached. Cambuslang's fifty-one-year-old
pastor, William McCulloch, reported to Whitefield that three hundred people
(in a town of less than a thousand) had come under conviction of sin, and that
of those, perhaps two hundred had experienced authentic conversion. Many
more descended on the town on Sunday mornings, and he estimated that
crowds had numbered as many as ten thousand on recent Sabbaths. McCulloch
pleaded with Whitefield to come to Cambuslang as soon as possible. Arriving
in Edinburgh in early June, Whitefield told McCulloch, using language from 1
Kings 18: "The cloud is now only rising as big as a man's hand; yet a little while,
and we shall hear a sound of an abundance of gospel rain."[39]

Whitefield finally came to Cambuslang in early July. Many at Cambuslang had heard Whitefield preach before: one Cambuslang convert—a nineteen-year-old seamstress from Glasgow—recalled rejoicing when she heard Whitefield was returning to Scotland, for it was by his preaching that she had "first fallen under soul distress." News of Whitefield heightened the Cambuslang excitement, but his presence had not first catalyzed it.[40]

Whitefield played a unique role in the emerging Anglo-American evangel-ical movement, but we should remember that most conversions and revival meetings of the Great Awakening happened *without him*. One New England minister noted explicitly in 1742 that Whitefield never saw the kind of outpouring of revival that had happened since the itinerant "left this land." Cambuslang was another example: it tapped into deeper resources within Scottish Presbyterianism, assisted by the interest generated by reports of awakenings else-where. Whitefield's arrival marked a crest of the spiritual surge at Cambuslang, but McCulloch and other leaders played a longer-term pastoral role.[41]

McCulloch was, like Whitefield, a learned man, having graduated from the University of Glasgow in 1712 with expertise in classical languages. A published sermon, delivered on Guy Fawkes Day, November 5, 1726, revealed McCulloch as a man of scholarly Reformed sensibilities and of strident but typical anti-Catholicism. (November 5 commemorated the foiling of the Catholic conspir-ator Fawkes's plot to blow up Parliament in 1605.) McCulloch bluntly titled the work *A Sermon against the Idolatrous Worship of the Church of Rome*. His goal was to boost the "interest of Reformed Religion, in giving people a just impres-sion of the evil of Popery." This was an anti-Catholic rant, but not one born out of ignorance: during the course of the sermon, McCulloch referred to the orig-inal Hebrew and Greek texts as well as to the Septuagint (the Hebrew Old Testament in Greek) and Latin translations. Apparently, some at Cambuslang found this learned style—one lacking Whitefield's flair—less than compelling. McCulloch was what Scots called an "ale-minister," meaning that when he got up to preach, some in the audience headed for the pub.[42]

Whatever McCulloch's deficiencies as a public speaker, he and many of Cambuslang's laypeople earnestly wanted to see revival in the parish. By early 1742, at the request of ninety heads of families in the church, he began preaching on the new birth, and on Sunday evenings he read accounts of Whitefield's revivals, especially the remarkable news from New England. He was delighted to meet Whitefield, who preached repeatedly at Cambuslang in July 1742, from the afternoon until late in the evening. Sometimes McCulloch kept on preaching after Whitefield had finished. The "commotion" that ensued surpassed even the most remarkable revival scenes in the colonies, Whitefield said: "For about an hour and a half there was such weeping, so many falling into deep distress, and expressing it various ways, as is inexpressible." Military metaphors seemed to best explain the sights: "The people seem to be slain by scores. They are carried off, and come into the house like soldiers wounded in, and carried off a field of battle." Some stayed in Cambuslang's fields all night, singing and praying.[43]

Whitefield returned to Cambuslang a week later to help with an outdoor sacramental occasion, like ones he had heard about from Scottish correspondents. Over a long weekend, throngs gathered in a natural amphitheater setting, on a hillside the Scots called a "brae," near McCulloch's church. Congregants built two wood-framed preaching tents and set up communion tables in the fields. On consecutive days, Whitefield preached to crowds he estimated at twenty thousand. The twenty-one-year-old John Erskine, who would go on to become one of Scotland's leading evangelical ministers, described the brae as "the most commodious [place] for hearing ever I saw." Although the number of attendees was disputed, Erskine was "certain a voice near as good as Mr. Whitefield's could have reached a greater number had they been there."[44]

On the Sabbath, it came time, for those who qualified, to take communion. Church members, meaning those who had made a convincing profession of faith in Christ, received small lead tokens with which they gained admission to the tables. Churches from Scotland to Ulster to the Scots-Irish settlements in America had designed different shapes for these tokens. Some were plain circular pieces with the minister's initials; those used at the great Dunfermline revival featured two hearts becoming one, just as the believer united with Christ.[45]

McCulloch estimated that perhaps seventeen hundred of the tens of thousands of attendees received tokens at the July assembly. Whitefield attempted to help serve the communicants, but as he moved down the line, people got out of their seats and pressed around him, thanking him for coming and sharing prayer requests. Rather than become a distraction, he left the tables and allowed the other ministers to finish.[46]

Once everyone had been served, the whole assembly gathered before a tent, where Whitefield preached on Isaiah 54:5, "Thy Maker is thy husband; the Lord of hosts is his name." Ralph Erskine published a frequently reprinted 1708 poem on this verse, which was also a favorite of the Moravian leader Nikolaus Zinzendorf. Although Whitefield preached numerous sermons at Cambuslang, this is the one that converts remembered best. There was considerable variation between the preached versions and the published one, since Whitefield seems to have used a memorized skeleton outline, but in the estimation of an early

Scottish church historian, he delivered it each time "as his own feelings and a sense of duty prompted."[47]

In the published version of the sermon, Whitefield emphasized his simple preaching method. "I came not here to shoot over people's heads," he declared, but "to reach their hearts. Accordingly, I shall endeavor to clothe my ideas in such plain language, that the meanest [lowliest] Negro or servant, if God is pleased to give a hearing ear, may understand me." He spoke directly to the correct practice of the communion many had just taken, urging ministers to serve the Lord's Supper only to those who had united with Christ in spiritual marriage. Those who received communion in a worthy manner, he exclaimed, were "one with Christ, and Christ with them," and "they dwell in Christ, and Christ in them."[48] Going to the matrimonial metaphor of his text, Whitefield insisted that the "poorest and most illiterate person here present [may] easily know, whether or not he is really *married to Jesus Christ.*" Furthermore, he or she could often (though not always) know the time and circumstances under which that union occurred. "The day of our espousals is, generally, a very remarkable day; a day to be had in everlasting remembrance," he noted. Most true believers, he contended, could remember the moment of their conversion, just as they would remember their own wedding.[49]

Christ was the spiritual husband of every believer. Therefore, if earthly wives were to be "subject to their own husbands in everything, how much more ought believers, whether men or women, be subject to Jesus Christ." They were Christ's possession, body and soul. Whitefield's comparison of the believer's union with Christ to earthly marriage was common among early evangelicals; many preachers went further than Whitefield and used language of "ravishment"—a word with sexual overtones—to describe one's experience with Christ. As seen in Isaiah 54:5, the Song of Solomon, and a number of other scriptural passages, the theme of marital union between God and his people frequently appeared in scripture as well.[50]

Still, one is struck by how evangelical men readily accepted the metaphor of a bride's relationship with her husband to describe their relationship with Christ. Whitefield and other revivalists consistently promoted it, and men and women seem to have employed it with similar frequency in their conversion testimonies. In the absence of identifying biographical information, it is often difficult to tell whether a given evangelical testimony in this era was written by a man or woman. Some scholars suggest, however, that women emphasized the physicality and intimacy of the marital metaphor more than men did.[51]

For example, borrowing from the Song of Solomon, Newport's Sarah Osborn spoke of Christ as a lover who "stood knocking till his head was filled with the dew and his locks with the drops of the night," waiting for admission into her stubborn heart. (Her pastor and editor, Samuel Hopkins, deleted this passage from the published version.) After losing her first husband, who died at sea, the young widow seized upon the promise of Isaiah 54. In a critical moment of her conversion process, Osborn (apparently at random) turned to this passage and received it as words directly from God to her: "Thou shalt forget the shame of thy youth, and shalt not remember the reproach of thy widowhood any more. For thy Maker is thy husband, the Lord of Hosts is his name." This was in 1737, before the text had become a staple of Whitefield's preaching.[52]

William McCulloch compiled a remarkable collection of 109 testimonies from the Cambuslang revival. He may have intended them for publication, but McCulloch's two bound manuscripts have appeared only recently in modern print editions. The interviewees offered remarkable accounts of how they experienced Whitefield's revival preaching. But even as the testimonies confirm Whitefield's powerful influence, they suggest that neither Whitefield nor the other ministers could fully control laypeople's responses to revival preaching.[53]

William Baillie, one of the converts, found that Whitefield's "Thy Maker is Thy Husband" sermon helped him achieve assurance of salvation. Baillie had sought clear evidence of God's work in his life for some time before the Cambuslang revival. His faith soared at Cambuslang's communion tables, as he testified: "I was . . . enabled to receive Jesus Christ by faith, as exhibited in that ordinance, under the broken bread and poured out wine . . . I looked upon his body in that ordinance as broken for me."[54] That evening, Baillie heard Whitefield, "a stranger minister," preach "Thy Maker is Thy Husband." Baillie found himself cheered by Whitefield's description of the believer's marital responsibilities to Christ, "agreeing to every one of them, as ever bride did to the articles of a contract with one to be her husband." Baillie hardly balked at the marriage metaphor, but instead found it full of spiritual comfort. Similarly, a twenty-year-old unmarried man said that he "greatly rejoiced" at the thought that he stood "in such a relation to Christ."[55]

Dramatically concluding the sermon, Whitefield asked whether anyone wished "to take Christ for their husband." If they did, he extended an invitation: "Come and I'll marry you to him just now." This resonated biblically with the Apostle Paul's statement to the Christians at Corinth that he had "espoused" the church to "one husband" so that he might present it "as a chaste virgin to Christ" (2 Corinthians 11:2). A twenty-one-year old male convert said that when Whitefield "laid out the terms" of the union with Christ, he found his "heart made sweetly to agree to those terms." Another convert ran to embrace a friend, exclaiming that the minister had "married my soul to Christ." Then he lay down on the brae, wishing that he could die on the spot and go to be with Christ. Whitefield wrote that many "were married to the Lord Jesus that night."[56]

Margaret Lap, an unmarried twenty-nine-year-old who heard Whitefield preach first on his initial visit to Scotland in September 1741, found that his evocation of the dangers of hell summoned "great confusion" in her. She also attended his preaching of "Thy Maker is Thy Husband." The message lodged in her mind, staying with her for months or even years afterward. She frequently had Scripture passages impressed on her as she gained assurance, but early one Friday morning, while she still lay in bed, "these words, 'Thy Maker is thy Husband,'" came rushing into her thoughts, along "with several notes of a sermon of a certain minister." She became physically overwhelmed—"sick," she said—with love for Jesus, and the Spirit made her believe that Christ was indeed her spiritual husband.[57]

Another McCulloch interviewee, Anne Wylie (thirty-two and also unmarried), experienced conversion during a sermon by McCulloch, but Whitefield's printed sermons still played a role. Her experience was so awe inspiring that she fell into a kind of spiritual trance that lasted for an hour. Friends told her afterward that during this time she began repeating almost the whole text of a Whitefield sermon on Elijah "multiplying the widow's oil" (1 Kings 17), which she had read earlier. She applied the sermon to herself: "I was the empty soul the Lord was filling and pouring the oil of His grace into." It was not Whitefield alone who saw these kinds of effects: one convert testified that he had received many spiritual impressions of phrases and scriptures during his struggle for assurance of salvation. During one of Whitefield's sermons, the phrase "a God of love" rushed into his mind, but he noted specifically that this was *not* something Whitefield had said. The words came directly from the Holy Spirit. He was immediately "swallowed up" in worship and adoration, scarcely knowing "whether [his] soul was in the body or out of the body." Similarly, a Glasgow man testified that while he was listening to Whitefield, a text that McCulloch had preached on earlier struck him with such ferocity that he began crying out amidst the crowds on the Cambuslang hillside.[58]

Margaret Clark, a married forty-two-year old, saw one of the most remarkable visions described by any Cambuslang convert. For some time, she had experienced deep consternation over her sins, thinking she could never be forgiven. But as she listened to one of Whitefield's sermons, a powerful image appeared before her: "I verily thought I saw with my bodily eyes, Christ as hanging on the cross, and a great light about him in the air, and it was strongly impressed on my mind; that he was suffering there for my sins." Evangelical pastors like McCulloch were cautious about visions seen with "bodily eyes" (as opposed to visions occurring in the mind or spirit). Clark noted, probably with McCulloch's prompting, that she never saw the cross again, nor did she desire to see it again, and that she never "laid any stress of [her] salvation upon . . . seeing this sight."[59]

For some converts, hearing Whitefield brought their spiritual struggles to a conclusion. For others, hearing the preacher initiated their travails. Twenty-one-year-old John Wier testified that he had contemplated his eternal fate before, but kept putting such thoughts aside until he began listening to Whitefield. Night after night at Cambuslang, and elsewhere around the Glasgow area, Wier sought to hear as much of the itinerant's preaching as possible. The sermons did not bring joy, but fear, because he thought that he would go to hell. Indeed, Wier began to have visions of hell, once seeing it, "as it were," as a fiery pit where the "wicked were frying." During one evening sermon, he felt a crushing dread of damnation. Wier envisioned that when he was "at the top of the brae, that hell was just at the foot of it, and that [he] was ready to drop into it." Casting his eyes about the packed hillside, he imagined that "all the brae was on fire."[60]

Adding to his turmoil, Wier endured threats from antievangelical mockers. Wier was a tenant farmer, and the overseer of his rented plot thought the revival was enthusiastic nonsense. The overseer threatened to confiscate his crops and kick him off the land if he went back to the assemblies. He justified this penalty by suggesting that the revival was keeping Wier and another farmer from work, and that if they would go less frequently to Cambuslang, "we might pay our rent better, and work better." The overseer "particularly abused a certain minister," presumably Whitefield, "calling him a mountebank and damned rascal, who was putting all the people mad." Even Whitefield's clerical garb had a malevolent purpose: "he put on a black gown, to fright people out of their wits," the overseer proclaimed, and "when he put on his black gown and black cap at night he frighted them terribly." The overseer was apparently no anti-Christian skeptic, however: he advised Wier that reading the catechism was all the religion he needed.[61]

Whitefield's ministry continued to generate hostility in personal encounters like this one as well as in print. The work at Cambuslang only deepened his rift with the Associate Presbytery, some of whom published the floridly titled "Declaration, Protestation and Testimony of the Suffering Remnant of the Anti-Popish, Anti-Lutheran, Anti-Prelatick, Anti-Whitefieldian, Anti-Erastian, Anti-Sectarian, true Presbyterian Church of Christ in Scotland" against the itinerant and his Scottish supporters. Whitefield was "an abjured prelatick [Anglican] hireling, of as lax toleration-principles as any that ever set up for the advancing of the Kingdom of Satan." He was a "limb of Antichrist" and a "boar and wild beast from the Antichristian field of England." Cambuslang was a "mere delusion of Satan." Instead of leading participants to reject the apostate churches of England and Scotland, this faux revival birthed corrupt interdenominational cooperation and false shows of enthusiastic ecstasy, the seceders insisted.[62]

Even the relatively irenic Ebenezer Erskine reportedly condemned Whitefield and the Cambuslang awakening. A Whitefield supporter testified to Erskine, "I have . . . found the Gospel he preached to be the Word of God with power to my soul," at which the indignant Erskine threw up his hands and cried, "God save me from Cambuslang conversion and Mr. Whitefield's doctrine!" Whitefield noted that Erksine's "people" held a fast to pray against the Cambuslang work. (For their part, McCulloch and his allies also prayed for the seceders, that God would "open their eyes [and] remove their prejudices.")[63]

Undeterred by the attacks, McCulloch and other area ministers scheduled another sacramental observance for mid-August, which Whitefield also attended. By McCulloch's reckoning, the second event surpassed the first, not only in numbers of attendees, but also in "the power and special presence of God." Whitefield estimated that thirty thousand people attended, with twenty-five hundred communicants at the sacrament. McCulloch noted that Whitefield, while serving at the communion tables on Sunday evening, "appeared to be so filled with the love of God, as to be in a kind of ecstasy or transport." At ten o'clock that night, Whitefield preached through a heavy rain. "There was a great awakening," he concluded.[64]

Whitefield's American friends and opponents eagerly followed news of the Cambuslang revival. In a letter to William McCulloch, Jonathan Edwards marveled at the news of this "glorious work of God" and noted that the awakening had "spread into many other towns and parishes in that part of Scotland." Edwards had read accounts of the Cambuslang stir in the *Glasgow Weekly-History* and in the Kilsyth minister James Robe's narrative of the revival, which was printed in London, Glasgow, Boston, and Philadelphia in 1742. Kilsyth had also seen a major revival, and Robe published an account of that awakening which he titled, with a nod to Edwards, *A Faithful Narrative of the Extraordinary Work of the Spirit of God.*[65]

Thomas Fleet, the editor of the *Boston Evening-Post*, printed a front-page excerpt from the seceders' "Anti-Whitefieldian" rant in May 1743, dubiously attributing the document to the Erskines. This elicited a defensive rejoinder from Thomas Prince, Jr., in the *Boston Gazette*. The squabble over the Scottish revivals continued for weeks. New Englanders were keenly aware not only of the revivals in Scotland, but also of the debates surrounding them.[66]

Whitefield's correspondence and publishing networks worked well. The message was getting out. With the establishment of revival newspapers, the assistance of friendly printers such as Franklin, and the unpublished letters written by associates such as Jonathan Edwards, William McCulloch, and Anne Dutton, Anglo-American evangelicals believed they were serving a common movement spanning the Atlantic, part of the broader work of the Kingdom of God on earth. But letters were not enough: Whitefield longed to return to America, to see friends in person, and to check on Bethesda. He would have to wait two more years.

"Close Attacks, but Strong Consolations": The Return to America

On a summer evening in 1744, a weary Whitefield settled down for the night at an inn in Plymouth, in the far southwest of England. For the past two years, he had endured a number of "close attacks" but had enjoyed "strong consolations," too. He longed to return to America, a place that always seemed like a fresh start to him.[1]

Whitefield booked passage on a ship departing from Plymouth, the place from which the Pilgrims had departed for the New World 124 years earlier. International affairs delayed him again: England and France had gone to war, making it difficult for ship captains to get permission to sail.

That evening, while he waited, the woman of the house tapped on his door: a well-dressed gentleman was waiting downstairs to see him. Whitefield figured that this was a "Nicodemite" (like the Pharisee Nicodemus, who had visited Jesus by night). He invited the visitor up to his room.[2] All seemed well at first as the gentleman congratulated the itinerant on his triumphs. But then the stranger jumped up, started cursing at Whitefield, and began beating him about the head and shoulders with a gold-headed cane. The preacher immediately "underwent all the fears of a sudden violent death."[3] As he screamed for help, the woman of the house and her daughter ran up the stairs, burst into the room, and grabbed the assailant by the collar. Hitting Whitefield a few more times, the attacker got spooked and ran out the door. The woman shoved him down the stairs, but another assailant appeared. Meeting the innkeeper halfway up to the room, he grabbed her by the heel and cast her down to the first floor, nearly breaking her back. Neighbors had heard the commotion by now, and both attackers vanished into the night.[4]

Whitefield learned later that the miscreants had plotted the attack at a local tavern. He considered having the conspirators arrested and prosecuted, but instead just went about his normal preaching duties. The next time he spoke outdoors in Plymouth, two thousand more people than usual showed up, to "hear a man, that had like to have been murdered in his bed," Whitefield wrote. God could use evil to further the gospel, he reminded himself.[5]

Thankfully, most attacks were just printed, not physical. Although he did not answer each critic—doing so would have taken too much time—he did respond in a couple of pamphlets before his return from Scotland in November 1742. First, since antagonists routinely hinted at malfeasance related to the Bethesda orphanage, he produced A *Continuation of the Account of the Orphan-House*, which updated progress there. He noted that the orphanage had experienced several awakenings "much resembling" the one at Cambuslang, and he reprinted letters from Jonathan Barber and James Habersham detailing the work. Whitefield appended a detailed record of donations and expenditures related to the orphanage, but acknowledged that no amount of information about finances would silence rumormongers.[6]

A postscript to the Bethesda account contained news that Spanish forces had invaded Georgia in an action related to the War of Jenkins' Ear. When Georgia settlers learned that Spanish ships lay off the colony's coast, Habersham hastily arranged for Bethesda's evacuation, sending residents to Hugh Bryan's plantation in South Carolina. On July 5, 1742, the Spanish governor of St. Augustine, Florida, brought five thousand troops ashore at St. Simons Island, down the coast from Savannah. General James Oglethorpe's forces confronted the Spanish on July 7. When Oglethorpe learned that a Spanish detachment was proceeding up the island's Frederica road, he mounted his horse and attacked: "I charged [the Spanish] at the head of our Indians, Highland men, and rangers and God was pleased to give us such success that we entirely routed the first party," he wrote. The Spanish sent reinforcements, whom Oglethorpe's troops fired upon from brushy cover in one of the island's swamps.[7]

This British victory became known as the Battle of Bloody Marsh, which transpired in a marsh but was not extraordinarily bloody, with about fifty deaths, mostly on the Spanish side. Nevertheless, the demoralizing loss led the Spanish to abandon the island. It was the last major Spanish attempt to invade Georgia; Bethesda was preserved. The worried Whitefield wished he could have been there to comfort the orphans, and told Habersham that he "could willingly be found at the head of you kneeling and praying, though a Spaniard's sword should be put to my throat." When he learned of Oglethorpe's victory,

Whitefield said it was a miraculous deliverance on par with Israel's great triumphs in the Old Testament.[8]

Critics were hardly deterred by Whitefield's responses to their charges. The anonymous pamphlet by "A.M." titled *The State of Religion in New England, Since the Reverend Mr. George Whitefield's Arrival There* was published in Glasgow in August 1742 and may have been written by New England's key antirevivalist pastor, Charles Chauncy. It called the New England revivals a "superstitious panic," and Whitefield a "bold and importunate beggar" who "took all ways imaginable to persuade people to give him money." Whitefield published *Some Remarks on a Late Pamphlet* to defend himself, Gilbert Tennent, and other participants in the "great and marvelous work in New England." He especially recommended Jonathan Edwards's sermon "The Distinguishing Marks," which "answers all the objections that Mr. A.M. or others can make against it"; he added, "If any work has all marks of a divine signature, this undoubtedly has."[9]

Some reports from New England did trouble the itinerant, especially news related to his friend James Davenport, the dynamic, controversial Long Island preacher. An increasingly moderate Benjamin Colman told Whitefield that Davenport and other radical preachers were "too much under the impressions of a heated imagination, and no doubt often preached under actual fevers." Davenport declared enemy pastors unconverted, and led crowds singing through the streets of New England towns. Expelled from Connecticut for illegal preaching, Davenport went to Boston in the summer of 1742 and began praying publicly for the conversion not only of antirevivalists such as Charles Chauncy, but also of moderate evangelicals such as Colman himself. Authorities arrested Davenport and charged him with slander, but a Boston court declared Davenport mentally unfit for trial and released him. Whitefield wrote to Colman in November that although the "confusion" in New England concerned him, he was not sure that Davenport's incautious words warranted arrest and imprisonment. As a rift began to open between America's moderate and radical evangelicals, Whitefield tried to smooth over their differences.[10]

Whitefield's friends and opponents continued reading about his ministry in Britain, too. One anonymous anti-Whitefield tract published in Boston, *A Letter from a Gentleman in Scotland,* mirrored *The State of Religion in New-England* by characterizing the Scottish revivals as gross enthusiasm. McCulloch and other ministers had stoked an emotional frenzy even before Whitefield's second visit, the skeptical author noted, but the "screamings and hysterical affections which had been frequent there before, were now considerably increased by Mr. Whitefield's manner of preaching to them . . . the more wild and raving they were, they had the greater effect upon the illiterate crowd."

Whitefield, the "giddy fanatical hero," deemed it all an outpouring of the Spirit.[11]

An anti-Whitefield ditty published in England in 1742 captured central themes in opponents' attacks, targeting his Calvinism, overwrought emotions, and humble background:

> With face and fashion to be known,
> With eyes all white and many a groan,
> With arms outstretched and sniveling tone,
> And handkerchief from nose new-blown,
> And loving cant to Sister Joan.
> *'Tis a new teacher about the town . . .*
> With tap-house breeding and intrusion;
> With Scripture saws for elocution;
> With Calvin's methods and conclusion,
> To bring all things into confusion,
> And far-fetched sighs for mere illusion.
> *'Tis a new teacher . . .*[12]

Whitefield did not want to spend much energy battling his adversaries. It was time to move on from Scotland, so he preached a farewell sermon in Glasgow on Psalm 105:45, "That they might observe his statutes and keep his laws." (Whitefield would also preach on this text for his 1746 sermon "Britain's Mercies, and Britain's Duty," concerning the suppression of the 1745 Jacobite rebellion.) Calling it a sort of "national sermon," Whitefield addressed the responsibilities required by the Scots' religious heritage. He proclaimed: "Jesus Christ, has carried on Reformation farther in this land, than among any other people. And, I really believe, the Church of Scotland, is the best constituted church in the world." Although the Scots had their share of struggles, both earthly and spiritual, the Lord had given them an "extraordinary out-pouring of the blessed Spirit." Whitefield affirmed that he had "in no place, seen the Redeemer reign more in his power, than in this land." Yet immorality still dominated many places in Scotland, not least Glasgow, where swearing and drunkenness, "whoring and debaucheries," were rampant.[13]

Whitefield cautioned new converts to stay faithful to the Lord, even when enemies mocked their faith. According to his adversaries, Whitefield taught "only enthusiastical raptures" and was "always preaching up imputed righteousness, and . . . cry[ing] down good works," but he knew that he could call on his "dear friends . . . to witness, this is a slander." Many said that he came only for money, or that he was in league with the devil. Indeed, he wrote, "I think more calumny has been thrown on me in Scotland, than any other place where I have been." They would all have to wait until Christ's return to see who was right, he concluded.[14]

Whitefield returned to London in early November 1742. He discerned that God's presence for revival—the "cloud," he called it—was again moving across the Atlantic. But he found his way "blocked up from going abroad" for the time being. In London, Whitefield resumed preaching at the Tabernacle, where John Cennick and Howell Harris had been sermonizing in his absence. The Tabernacle had grown to 1,200 members, whom Harris helped organize into prayer and discipleship "bands" divided according to gender and marital status. (Elizabeth Whitefield, who returned from Scotland a few weeks before George, remained in contact with Harris, telling him that she was quite happy with Whitefield.)[15]

Whitefield had begun to attract as followers a number of British aristocrats, none more significant than Selina Hastings, the Countess of Huntingdon, who would become Whitefield's key patron. The countess, seven years older than Whitefield, had embraced Methodism in 1739. She and her husband regularly attended meetings at the Tabernacle, as did occasional guests such as the Duke of Cumberland, the youngest son of King George II. Having such supporters was socially and financially valuable to Whitefield, and may have steered him toward a more genteel, less controversial style.[16]

The itinerant began to recognize that he needed organizational structures to give stability to converts, lest they slip back into former patterns of sin and complacency. He told Harris that "there are so many living stones, it may be time to think of putting them together." Never John Wesley's equal in organizing, Whitefield told Wesley that he did not want to lead a denomination, nor did he want people "to be called after [his] name," adding, "If Jesus lives, I care not if the name of G.W. die forever." Yet they still needed to consolidate the revivals' successes.[17]

Harris warned him that the revival in Wales was in danger of sliding into chaos and infighting. Not that organization was entirely lacking, as Harris and other key leaders had established monthly meetings to help regulate the evangelical "societies" there in 1740. Whitefield had especially encouraged converts to form these home-based cohorts—little churches of "living stones"—in a 1740 publication, *A Letter to the Religious Societies*, which was soon translated into Welsh. Nevertheless, Whitefield wrote to the "brethren in Wales" at the end of 1741, warning them that the sheep (converts) there had no shepherd, and that they were "everywhere bleating for food." He recommended that they set up a

Methodist organization "without a formal separation from the Established Church." A year later, Whitefield convened meetings in Wales with Harris, Cennick, Daniel Rowland, and other key ministers. They finalized Welsh preaching districts and formed a union of Welsh and English revival leaders known as the Calvinistic Methodist Association. Whitefield was appointed moderator of it.[18]

Whitefield was satisfied that Wales had become more organized. He and Howell Harris preached at a series of meetings through southern Wales that spring, Harris speaking in Welsh, Whitefield in English. After making a four-hundred-mile westward circuit through Wales and Gloucestershire, the itinerant returned to London in May. In tiny towns throughout Wales he saw huge audiences: in the hamlet of Jefferson, he spoke to "several thousand souls, very like the Kingswood colliers," and at Llaffivran, he had "as it were a Moorfields congregation." Whitefield was still amazed at these scenes; he felt as if he were in "a new, but very unthought of pleasant world."[19]

In the spring of 1743, Elizabeth and George learned that they were going to have a baby. As the time for the child's arrival drew near, Whitefield continued preaching but took only short trips away from her. One fall evening, he learned that God had blessed them with a son. He hurried off to London to be with Elizabeth and the child. Thousands came to the Tabernacle for the baby's baptism. There Whitefield gave the boy "up to that God, who gave him to me." They named the boy John, after John the Baptist. Assuring correspondents that he would quickly return to preaching after baptizing the child, Whitefield asked for prayer that God would teach him "how to order the child aright."[20]

Even before his birth, Whitefield had become convinced that the child would be a boy, who would in turn become a great preacher. He publicly claimed the promise of the angel Gabriel to John's father and mother (also named Elizabeth) in Luke 1: "Thy wife Elizabeth shall bear thee a son, and thou shalt call his name John. And thou shalt have joy and gladness; and many shall rejoice at his birth. For he shall be great in the sight of the Lord." Elizabeth believed that the boy had already begun to display signs of true piety, even at his baptismal service, since he frequently clasped "his little hands," suggesting that he had a "sweet thought or something from the Lord."[21]

Because of ongoing financial struggles (which belied accusations that Whitefield unduly profited from his ministry), Whitefield decided to relocate the family to Elizabeth's home in Abergavenny. It was just too expensive to continue renting in London. In January, she and the baby set out for Wales, stopping over in Gloucester to stay at the Bell Inn. He told a friend that

Elizabeth and the "little one are brave and well." "But why talk I of wife and little one?" he asked. "Let all be absorbed in the thoughts of the love, suffering, free and full salvation of the infinitely great and glorious Emmanuel."[22]

While in Gloucester, the baby became severely ill, suffering at least one seizure. Whitefield's brother Richard, still the proprietor of the inn, summoned a doctor. In the cruel conventions of early-modern medicine, the doctor ordered that the baby be blistered. Physicians in Britain and America often used blistering, as well as other means of purging, to try to bring the body's fluids into balance. One of Whitefield's panicked friends in Gloucester, John Grace, wrote to Howell Harris and confessed that he did not know how to contact the itinerant to advise him of his son's dire condition.[23]

By the time Whitefield received word of his son's plight, it was too late. John passed away in late January, dying where Whitefield was born. Whitefield returned to Gloucester and learned the awful news. He wrote, "I was called to sacrifice my Isaac; I mean to bury my only child and son." His ambitions for his son had given the devil an opening to deceive him with "wrong impressions," he concluded. He had misapplied scripture to the child's destiny. Now all his "ill-grounded expectations" were destroyed by the child's sudden death.[24]

John was buried at Gloucester's St. Mary de Crypt, where Whitefield had been baptized, taken first communion, and first preached. At the funeral, George and Elizabeth knelt, prayed, and wept. Elizabeth told Howell Harris that John was now "as a little cherub made white in the blood of his and our dear Lord." George said less about John's fate, but noted that he took comfort in the story of the resurrection of a dead boy by Elisha's prayers in 2 Kings 4. George told Benjamin Colman that although God had called them to give up the "lovely boy," they were "enabled to make him a free-will offering." Whitefield returned to preaching as soon as he could. Indeed, he had already started preaching again before the funeral, and after burying John, he returned to London. Elizabeth went on to Abergavenny. Quoting the Bible commentator Matthew Henry, the itinerant told himself that "weeping must not hinder sowing."[25]

Whitefield did not say much about his feelings regarding John's death, but we can reasonably assume that the experience tested his faith in God's sovereign, benevolent rule over his life. He had scripture passages ready at hand to help him understand the staggering loss: Job lost his family to the "great wind" at the outset of that classic book of divine tribulation. God asked Abraham to sacrifice his son, Isaac (which Whitefield cited explicitly), and God the Father had given up his only begotten son, Jesus. Whitefield must have wondered, too, what the experience revealed about God's guidance through the Spirit—

Whitefield was sure that the boy would have grown up to become a powerful preacher, but he now regarded that certainty as devilish deception. He had no inkling that the Lord would take the boy away, and before he knew it, the boy was gone. Well might the itinerant and Elizabeth have returned repeatedly to Job's confession: "The Lord gave, and the Lord hath taken away; blessed be the name of the Lord."

Nothing soothed Whitefield more than preaching, even in the midst of such tragedy or when enduring ongoing harassment from local antagonists. Whitefield was hardly alone among evangelicals in receiving such treatment, which the Wesleys, Howell Harris, and other evangelicals also encountered. Outdoor preaching made the itinerants particularly attractive targets. The Welsh Anglican preacher Daniel Rowland reported that while preaching near the seaside in Cardiganshire, a "company of ruffians" armed with guns and clubs accosted him, beating him mercilessly and wounding him in the head. John Wesley likewise wrote that in Wednesbury, near Birmingham, mobs dragged him through the town, some shouting, "Knock his brains out, down with him, kill him at once!" Thankfully, most hooligans intended only to frighten or make fun of the preachers. Few suffered serious harm or met with William Seward's fate.[26]

The common experience of harassment helped broker a truce between Whitefield and John Wesley. The thaw had begun in late 1742, when Whitefield received a "kind letter" from Wesley, and Whitefield replied, asking that they "bear with, and forbear one another in love." Some months after Wesley's dangerous encounter at Wednesbury, Whitefield went to the town as well, noting that "much mobbing had been there against Mr. Wesley's friends." A smaller crowd accosted Whitefield. "Several clods were thrown," he wrote, "one of them fell on my head, and another struck my fingers, while I was in prayer." When he returned to London (shortly after his son's funeral), Whitefield held a fast and took an offering at the Tabernacle for the Methodists in the Birmingham area. Rather than renewing their former alliance, however, Wesley and Whitefield decided (as Whitefield put it) that they would "go on best when [they] only preach the simple gospel, and do not interfere with each other's plan." Their public feuding subsided, but their correspondence also became less frequent.[27]

Whitefield renewed his clash with Anglican authorities—or rather, they renewed it with him—with the anonymous publication of *Observations upon the Conduct and Behaviour of a Certain Sect, Usually Distinguished by the Name of Methodists*. This pamphlet, widely attributed to Whitefield's old nemesis Edmund Gibson, the bishop of London, accused Whitefield and the Wesleys of subverting church and state and indulging in wild enthusiasm. Citing Whitefield's journals, Gibson asked "whether a due and regular attendance on the public offices of religion" was not better evidence of the work of the Holy Spirit than the "sudden agonies, roarings and screamings, tremblings, droppings-down, ravings and madnesses" into which the Methodists had fallen?[28]

Anglican critics also implied that the Methodists were potential rebels against the king. Their meetings attracted tens of thousands of people, who were "subject to no control or examination." This represented a ready-made opportunity for "seditious persons to raise disturbances." These were serious charges, given that England had just entered the War of the Austrian Succession (the part of it fought in America was known as King George's War) against France, Prussia, Spain, and other European powers. Just before the bishop's publication, France had attempted a seaborne invasion, launched from Dunkirk, but terrible storms had stopped the attack. The French had hoped to depose George II and install the Catholic "Old Pretender," the son of James II (who had been removed in the Glorious Revolution) as the new British monarch. Confirming British Protestants' sense that a larger Catholic conspiracy was at work, the Old Pretender had been living comfortably in Rome on an annuity supplied by the pope. A March 1744 edition of the *London Gazette* advertised the publication of the bishop's anti-Methodist tract; that issue also bristled with Britons' proclamations to the king regarding the horror of "an invasion to extirpate our religion, laws and liberties, to set the pretender upon your Majesty's throne, and ourselves to be made tributaries and slaves to France."[29]

Whitefield published a reply to Gibson with a pointed quote from Psalm 35:11 on the title page: "False witnesses did rise up; they laid to my charge things that I knew not." The bishop should have titled the pamphlet "Misrepresentations of the Conduct and Principles, of Many Orthodox, Well-Meaning Ministers and Members of the Church of England, and Loyal Subjects to His Majesty King George," the itinerant chided. He was a "zealous friend" to the king and routinely prayed for and preached on obedience to him. In light of the crisis with France, Whitefield assured readers that he would continue warning audiences "against the dreadful effects of Popish principles, and exhort them to exert their utmost endeavours to keep out a Popish Pretender from ever sitting upon the English throne." This rejoinder went through three editions in London (as did Gibson's pamphlet), as well as one in Boston.[30]

Whitefield had been absent from America for three and a half years when his ship finally slipped out to sea in August 1744. The *Wilmington* joined a convoy of 150 British military and merchant ships, whose massed presence made the passage more secure during a troubled time. Elizabeth came with him, and the passage was tense and exhausting for them both. On one occasion, the sight of unidentified ships sent the crew into frenzied battle preparations. Elizabeth began making gunpowder cartridges. George admitted that he wanted only to "go into the holes of the ship, hearing that was the chaplain's usual place." A devout sailor pleaded with him, however, to come on deck and address the men before the fight. Whitefield complied, and for the first time in his life he "beat up to arms by a warm exhortation." Once the ships came into range, however, the crew realized that they were flying the Union Jack. They were safe.[31]

When Whitefield landed at York, Maine, he became so ill that he felt he was at the "mouth of the heavenly harbor." His "nervous cholic," as he described it, threw him into convulsions. After convalescing for three weeks at the home of a key supporter, Colonel William Pepperrell, the itinerant attempted a ferry ride across the Piscataqua River to Portsmouth, New Hampshire. Doing this was a mistake, and he relapsed. But his followers had already announced his intent to preach, so the gaunt twenty-nine-year-old proceeded with his sermon, which he thought he might simply deliver and die. That evening, friends laid him on a pallet near a fire to keep the fall chill at bay. (Elizabeth said that he had become "as cold as a clod.") Alarmed by his ghostly appearance, they whispered among themselves, "He is gone." But Whitefield reported that an African American woman sat beside him and said, "in broken language, 'Master, you just go to Heaven's gate. But Jesus Christ said, get you down, get you down, you must not come here yet; but go first, and call some more poor negroes.'" Indeed, he regained his health, and figured it was not yet his time.[32]

Great revival had shaken many parts of the colonies, especially New England, since Whitefield's last visit. He had heard so many reports of wondrous awakenings in America, he wrote, that "one would have imagined the millennium was coming indeed." Beginning in 1742, however, the Great Awakening spawned fierce debates not only between evangelicals and nonevangelicals, but also between friends of the revivals. In particular, the radical exploits of revivalists such as James Davenport and Whitefield's South Carolina convert Hugh Bryan brought an avalanche of criticism against radical evangelicals.[33]

The culmination of Davenport's radical career had come in March 1743 when, defying orders, he returned to preach in New London, Connecticut. Davenport was suffering from a "lame leg" that required his followers to carry him about in a chair. He later blamed this infirmity, caused by a "cancry humour," for producing a feverish daze that explained his behavior in New London. The Lord revealed to Davenport that his followers should burn the books of questionable authors, including some, such as Benjamin Colman, who had supported Whitefield. Davenport also called on them to torch the "idols of their gay clothes," including "scarlet cloaks, velvet hoods, fine laces, and everything that had two colors." Davenport himself cast a pair of "plush breeches" into the pile, but a brave young woman, thinking this was all too much, pulled his pants out and threw them in Davenport's face. Her bold gesture sobered the crowd; they realized that their zeal had become mindless frenzy. Davenport lost many of his followers and began making amends among pastors whom he had offended.[34]

Likewise, in the months following his conversion, Hugh Bryan came to believe that God was raising him up as a liberator of South Carolina's slaves. He sent a book of prophecies to the South Carolina legislature in Charleston, including the prediction that Charleston would be "destroyed by fire and sword, to be executed by Negroes before the first day of next month." Lawmakers promptly called for Bryan's arrest. But before they caught him, Bryan had already failed a test of his prophetic calling. A report printed in Boston said that he had taken up a rod and, Moses-like, attempted to part the waters of a Lowcountry river. He tumbled into the river with the staff in hand, "smiting, splashing and spluttering the water about with it," and nearly drowned.[35]

Moderate evangelicals remained thankful for the abundant conversions, but worried about spectacular embarrassments like the Davenport and Bryan affairs, and about more common excesses. These included the advent of "exhorters," whom critics described as "children, boys and girls, sometimes women; but most commonly raw, illiterate weak and conceited young men, or lads . . . [who] take upon them what they imagine is the business of preaching." Many worried about subversive effects on the slave population, too. Would the revivals' enthusiastic extremes give blacks notions of equality and liberty? One Anglican minister contended that Whitefield's *Three Letters* (1740) and its criticism of slaveholders "gave great countenance" to the supposed slave conspiracy in New York City in 1741, which led to the execution and deportation of hundreds of the city's slaves. Antirevivalists such as Boston's Charles Chauncy pointed to the evangelicals' extremes and said that they represented the essence of the revivals, which he regarded as ungodly chaos.[36]

In Whitefield's absence, many colonists had begun blaming him for the revivalists' radicalism. A report of Hugh Bryan's failed river parting, for instance, concluded that this episode represented "the workings of Whitefieldism in its native tendency." A survey of periodicals during his time away shows that ninety-three letters about him appeared in colonial newspapers. More than half were negative, twice the negative coverage that he received during his first American preaching tour. Whitefield had become used to charges of enthusiasm, but he found these attacks especially galling: how could he be guilty for American evangelicals' extremes when he was not even in the colonies in 1742 and 1743? He readily admitted that some of the radical preachers had gone too far: "Wild-fire will necessarily blend itself with the pure fire that comes from God's altar." In the ecstatic furor of the awakenings, some had mistaken their own imagination for God's revelation. But Whitefield would not accept responsibility for the imprudent behavior of Bryan, Davenport, and others. He unfairly received all the blame, he wrote, "as being the *primum mobile.*"[37]

Yet only the radical evangelicals seemed genuinely pleased by his return to New England. Daniel Rogers, the Harvard tutor who had experienced the new birth under Whitefield in 1740, was among a group of ministers who welcomed the ailing Whitefield in York, finding the itinerant "in bed very ill of a nervous cholic."[38] These friends and Davenport allies only confirmed critics' suspicion that Whitefield had not really turned over a new leaf. The itinerant had promoted "the same disorders in Scotland, and elsewhere, since he went from America," wrote one antagonist in the *Boston Evening-Post,* and now the church-rending radicals had served as his welcoming party in York. Some of his defenders, the writer noted, suggested that Whitefield would tone down his divisive rhetoric, but could he really "pull down a building which is the work of his own hands?"[39]

There was a real possibility that moderate evangelical leaders might turn against Whitefield if he could not convince them that he had repudiated his previous indiscretions. In late November 1744, Whitefield had recovered sufficiently to go to Boston, where he held a critical meeting with four leading pastors, including Benjamin Colman of the Brattle Street Church. Before sitting down to dinner, they had a frank exchange about some of his earlier mistakes and some enthusiastic passages from his journals. They expressed concern that while New England had seen a massive revival, a "chill" had come over the religious climate in the past couple years because of the "imprudence" of Davenport and other radicals. Some radicals had separated from existing congregations and illegally formed their own.[40]

Colman and his moderate colleagues pressed Whitefield: did he approve of these separations? Many radicals had cited Whitefield as having tacitly endorsed them when he denounced unconverted ministers and when he declared that the "generality of preachers preached an unknown Christ." The itinerant said that if anything he wrote or said had encouraged church divisions, he regretted it. In any case, he had come back to New England to "preach the gospel of peace . . . and promote charity and love among all." His divisive days were in the past. They could trust him to disrupt the churches no more. The Boston ministers clearly had come with an intention of asking for—and receiving— such assurances, and having done so, they "dined very comfortably" together. Colman invited Whitefield to speak the next day at his meetinghouse. Soon the irenic Colman had Whitefield assist him in serving at a communion service, as well.[41]

Whitefield had to secure the support of these moderate pastors in order to maintain access to New England's prominent congregations. The fact that they stood behind him, however, hardly ended the controversy. More than a half dozen pastoral associations publicly registered concerns about Whitefield and the effects of his ministry. Harvard and Yale, stung by his earlier comments about them, also weighed in against Whitefield. Harvard's faculty painted him as a troublemaking outsider whose preaching tended toward the "entire destruction of the order of these churches of Christ, which our fathers have taken such care and pains to settle." They highlighted his itinerancy and enthusiastic tendencies as particularly dangerous, chiding his devotees for following a man who "conducts himself according to his dreams, or some ridiculous and unaccountable impulses" of his mind. He implied, the professors lamented, that he had "as familiar a converse and communion with God as any of the prophets and apostles, and such as . . . all acknowledge to have been under the inspiration of the Holy Ghost." They warned against accepting any such claims of special access to God in the centuries since the passing of the apostles and the closing of the biblical canon.[42]

Yale's rector, Thomas Clap, went further, accusing Whitefield of planning to replace many of New England's ministers with his allies. This was a ridiculous charge—Whitefield retorted that "such a thought never entered [his] heart." But Clap claimed to have gotten the information from none other than Jonathan Edwards. Clap and Edwards had a history of conflict dating to 1741, when Edwards challenged Yale officials for failing to support the revivals in his commencement address "The Distinguishing Marks of a Work of the Spirit of God." Clap said that Edwards had confided in him in 1743 that Whitefield "designed to turn the generality of ministers in the country out of their places, and bring over ministers from England, Scotland and Ireland" to replace them. Edwards was incensed and "exceedingly astonished" by Clap's account, explaining that all he had said was that Whitefield expressed interest in bringing promising candidates from Britain to study at the Tennents' Log College. Edwards asked Clap "publicly to correct your mistake in this." Clap refused. Edwards and Clap engaged in a heated exchange of pamphlets that endured through the first half of 1745.[43]

Although Edwards admitted that he had had some earlier disagreements with Whitefield—especially over Whitefield's judging ministers as unconverted—he thought those conflicts were not exceptionally problematic. He attributed the mistakes to Whitefield's youth. Edwards considered the attacks on the itinerant, especially Clap's, to be mean-spirited and baseless. He lamented that Whitefield would be "pursued with so much violence, and appearance of inveterate opposition, and indefatigable endeavours to blacken him to the utmost; and with such artifices, as it would be mean to use, with respect to the basest miscreant." Clap, of course, had engaged in the worst of such "artifices."[44]

Whitefield quietly passed his thirtieth birthday by preaching in and around Boston. He saw large crowds and continuing signs of awakening, although it would have been difficult for the fervor to match that from his initial appearance in New England. Many who came admired him, but they had seen him speak before. At the end of December he preached in Bridgewater, south of Boston, at the church of John Porter, one of the Massachusetts pastors who had experienced the new birth under Whitefield's preaching four years earlier. Echoing Romans 5:5, he told Whitefield that he had never experienced true spiritual peace until he "felt the love of God shed abroad abundantly in his heart by the Holy Ghost." Whitefield preached and assisted with communion at Porter's church, and reckoned that Jesus "filled his people as with new wine" during the service. Some people cried out, but Whitefield did not try to restrain them, since "it did not give offense" and since he thought "country people could not so well restrain themselves as those of a more polite education in the town." The penitents were not drowning out Whitefield's sermon, anyway.[45]

Although Whitefield still permitted outcries such as these, he had moved into a moderate phase, emphasizing unity and sobriety rather than division and zeal. He did not back off his Calvinist theology, yet he now preached "little terror," he wrote. The avalanche of criticism he had received in England, Scotland, and America had stung him, especially when it came from influential allies such as Colman and Edwards. Whitefield sought to soothe grievances and build bridges with the alienated.[46]

Whitefield increasingly found that imperial politics and military affairs presented him with opportunities to build those bridges. He never stopped preaching the new birth, of course, but war and politics became more salient. These themes could help him win over critics and supply fresh material for his sermons. The year 1745 offered two ripe occasions for such material. One, as we shall see, was a Jacobite rebellion in Britain. The other was an American colonial expedition against Cape Breton Island. In both instances, Whitefield emphasized his role as a supporter of the Protestant British monarchy and as an inveterate foe of Catholic France. These were positions with which most Britons, including the colonists, would heartily agree (at least for the next couple of decades).

The French presence to the north of New England, especially at the Louisbourg fortress on Cape Breton Island, had become increasingly irritating to Massachusetts leaders. Louisbourg was the hub of a lucrative fishing trade, and the French had launched a raid from the fort on a British outpost at Canso, Nova Scotia, in 1744. The outbreak of King George's War in 1744 prompted the governor of Massachusetts to commission an expedition against the fortress. He raised several thousand men from the northern colonies and put the expedition under the command of Whitefield's friend William Pepperrell. Pepperrell asked for Whitefield's advice before he accepted the task, and Whitefield also supplied Pepperrell's forces with a motto, *Nil desperandum Christo duce* (No need to fear with Christ as our leader). Massachusetts held a public fast for the expedition, and Whitefield prayed for God to grant that Louisbourg would become a "garrison for Protestants." Another New Englander prayed bluntly in verse, "Destroy proud Antichrist, O Lord, / And quite consume the Whore."[47]

Pepperrell's forces proceeded up the Nova Scotia coast, landing on Cape Breton in early May and laying siege to the fortress. The New England troops dragged cannon over spring snow to bombard the French. The French soldiers were badly undermanned, and the British colonial forces captured a French supply ship that would have replenished their flour and meat rations. Instead, those supplies bolstered Pepperrell's men. The end came in mid-June, just before the New Englanders launched a direct assault on the fortress: a flag of truce appeared, and the French gave up Louisbourg.[48]

Whitefield and many other pastors, including his inveterate opponent Charles Chauncy, preached thanksgiving sermons on the happy news. The itinerant spoke from Psalm 41:11, "By this I know that thou favourest me, since thou hast not permitted mine enemies to triumph over me." Jonathan Edwards, whose congregation had supplied about twenty men for the expedition, wrote that Pepperrell's forces enjoyed one favor from God after another, making the victory "a dispensation of providence, the most remarkable in its kind, that has been in many ages." He concluded, "We live in an age, wherein divine wonders are to be expected."[49]

Louisbourg could not heal all disagreements, of course, and Whitefield found that he could not always successfully navigate the misunderstandings regarding the revivals. While he insisted that he opposed church separations, for instance, he not only still associated with Separate leaders, but also some-times preached in their breakaway churches. This practice led to a major show-down in Exeter, New Hampshire, with Pastor John Odlin. Odlin, who had served as the pastor of the Exeter church since 1706, was one of northern New England's most formidable antirevivalists, tangling repeatedly with Whitefield's convert Daniel Rogers, who itinerated in the area. The appointment of Odlin's son Woodbridge—who was also hostile to the revivalists—as the church's assis-tant pastor precipitated a split within the church, and the Separates erected a new building for their meetings.[50]

Whitefield visited Exeter in March 1745, intending to preach not just to the Separate congregation (he said), but to "all in general"—at the Separate meet-inghouse. Unsurprisingly, John Odlin was not convinced by this distinction. He denied Whitefield access to his pulpit and said that Whitefield was endorsing Separatism by appearing at the breakaway church. In a testy meeting, the Odlins proclaimed that Whitefield's itinerant ministry was illegitimate and forbidden by scripture. Whitefield countered that "the people had a right to private judgment and that [Odlin] could not, upon Protestant principles, deny the liberty of hearing for themselves." More antirevivalist pastors joined the debate, which became loud and heated. It ended with Whitefield saying that he had heard enough and hastily leaving "to prosecute his pernicious principle," as a hostile newspaper account put it. He trudged through fresh snow to the Separate meetinghouse, where he preached twice to packed audiences. There he "spoke of the things which make for peace," he noted. Daniel Rogers, trav-eling with Whitefield, jotted in his diary that Whitefield preached on 1 Peter 2:7, "To you therefore which believe he is precious: but unto them which be disobedient, the stone which the builders disallowed." Rogers said that he could feel God's power moving in the meeting.[51]

In August 1745, Franklin's *Pennsylvania Gazette* reported on Whitefield's travels, noting that the itinerant preached "for the Rev. Mr. Edwards of Northampton twice" on a mid-July Sunday. He delivered one of his Northampton sermons on the powerful text he had used at Cambuslang, Isaiah 54:5, "thy maker is thy husband." On the following Thursday, Massachusetts held a day of thanks-giving for the victory at Louisbourg, and Whitefield preached again at Northampton "at the request of the Rev. Mr. Edwards."[52]

This visit soothed misunderstandings between Edwards and Whitefield. Edwards's clash with Thomas Clap had aligned Edwards more closely than ever with the itinerant. The Northampton minister wrote to a Scottish corre-spondent: "Whitefield was reproached in the most scurrilous and scandalous manner . . . I question whether history affords any instance paralleled with this, as so much pains taken in writing to blacken a man's character, and render him odious." None of the attacks addressed any new problems; they all focused on his "old faults, without anything new worth speaking of," Edwards concluded.[53]

Edwards was pleased to host George and Elizabeth for almost a week in Northampton. Whitefield "behaved himself so, that he endeared himself much to me," Edwards told Scottish contacts. "He appeared in a more desirable temper of mind and more solid and judicious in his thoughts, and prudence in his conduct, than when he was here before." Following his visit to Northampton, Whitefield proceeded to eastern Connecticut, which had become a center of evangelical radicalism. Edwards happily noted that Whitefield spoke clearly against the extremes of the "wild and extravagant people there, and has there done a great deal of good." He had "reclaimed" a number of Connecticut's awakened from the dangers of enthusiastic frenzy. Whitefield also held a "great Indian meeting" with Mohegans, Pequots, and Niantics near Norwich, following up on their interest in Christianity, which had been stirred by the preaching of James Davenport and others. From eastern Connecticut he crossed over to Long Island, making his way to New York City and then to Philadelphia.[54]

A New London diarist, Joshua Hempstead, stopped stacking summer hay to hear Whitefield preach as he passed through eastern Connecticut. On the Sabbath, Hempstead listened to the itinerant as he spoke under an oak tree from a field pulpit carried by horse from town to town. Hempstead observed that "a great assembly perhaps twice so many as could possibly sit in the meetinghouse" was there. "An excellent preacher," Hempstead concluded.[55]

Whitefield was in New England for nine months, and despite the enormous controversy his visit precipitated, he had substantially repaired his reputation, at least among key leaders such as Benjamin Colman and Jonathan Edwards. He had more invitations to preach than he could honor. But comparisons with the spectacular results of his inaugural visit were inevitable. Edwards bluntly observed that the itinerant's "preaching in New England was attended with no such remarkable effects, in awakenings and reviving religion as before." Yes, he saw large, attentive crowds everywhere he went, but not many conversions. "The country in general remains in a great degree of stupidity, as to any work of conviction on the hearts of sinners," Edwards lamented. "I know of no such work going on anywhere in this land."[56]

As a Calvinist, Whitefield knew that whatever his mastery of preaching and print, he could not control the timing of revival. In spite of this conviction, he must have felt the sting of assessments such as Edwards's. The "remarkable effects" of his preaching in London in the spring of 1739, in New England in the fall of 1740, or in Scotland in the summer of 1742 would never return. Critics began painting him as a celebrity past his prime. The anonymous author of "Mr. Whitefield's Soliloquy" took on the voice of the itinerant, lamenting his downfall:

It must be so—unhappy man!
I'm sunk, I'm lost, do what I can.
Like Jonah's gourd, rais'd in a night,
I wither by noon-day light.
I build upon unconstant sand.
My fabric can no longer stand:
What shall I do? Where shall I go?
What course to take I do not know;
Shall I, whose tow'ring height surpassed
The mountain's top, for some years past,
And his my head among the clouds,
Stand level with the vulgar crowds?
. . . What would I give, could I redeem
The happy days that I have seen![57]

Of course, Whitefield never articulated such sentiments himself, but he faced a critical transition, one familiar in the twenty-first century. A young man or woman becomes an international media sensation and then spends the rest of his or her career coping with the memory of that season of celebrity. Some fall into obscurity or a spiral of self-destruction. Some accept a new, quieter reality and use their celebrity status for constructive purposes. In general, the latter path was the one that a less fractious, more moderate Whitefield took for his remaining twenty-five years. But moderation, too, can have its price.

"Hunting in the American Woods": Whitefield, Slavery, and Evangelical Radicalism

George Whitefield wrote thousands of letters in his life, but because of careless handling over the centuries, many original manuscripts have been lost. John Gillies's edition of his writings, published in the 1770s, included more than fourteen hundred letters. Even in Gillies's edition, however, there is a major gap between July 1745 and August 1746. Only a few scattered, unpublished letters in archives were able to help fill in that blank year. But in the early 1950s came a remarkable discovery: a whole Whitefield letter book, from precisely those missing months, was found in the personal papers of a colonial pastor from Delaware. The volume came to the attention of a Presbyterian historian, who transcribed and published the letters.[1]

One of the most remarkable—and disheartening—letters in Whitefield's corpus lies in that long-lost letter book. Whitefield traveled south in fall 1745 to check on the Bethesda orphanage. In December, he wrote to the Reverend William Hutson of the Stoney Creek Church in Lowcountry South Carolina, where the brothers Hugh and Jonathan Bryan served as deacons. Hutson had converted under Whitefield's ministry, and with the encouragement of the Bryans and Whitefield, he made slaves part of the church community, including some slaves whom Hutson or the Bryans owned. Slave conversions, to Hutson, entailed spiritual freedom, but not liberation in this life.[2]

At some point in 1745, Hutson offered to give Whitefield a "Negroe." This presented a unique temptation for Whitefield, who had earlier denounced southern slave masters' treatment of their bound workers and who had called for the evangelization and education of slaves. But he had never questioned slavery as an institution. Indeed, he called for its introduction into Georgia, where trustees had initially banned it. Now Whitefield had to make a personal decision about owning slaves, and about the related question of breaking Georgia's law against slavery. The legal question alone should have made the decision easy, but Whitefield thought that the ban on slavery was silly, and that it was only a matter of time before Georgia abandoned it. He also convinced himself that if he could just have a few slaves there, Bethesda would "more than maintain itself" financially.[3]

As for slavery itself, Whitefield was aware that some Quakers denounced it, but it was not until 1755 that the Society of Friends' Philadelphia Meeting decisively resolved to ban slave merchants from membership. Until that year, most Quakers' position on slavery was generally ameliorist; they wanted to make slavery more humane and Christian, not abolish it altogether. That was Whitefield's stance, too. New England Quakers did not ban slave traders from their meetings until 1770, the year of Whitefield's death. Few in the itinerant's own circles objected to slavery per se—John Wesley's *Thoughts on Slavery*, for example, did not appear until after Whitefield's death. The celebrated slave trader turned abolitionist John Newton, the author of the hymn "Amazing Grace," experienced conversion in 1748 and did not go public with his anti-slavery views until 1788.[4]

One exception to this silence on slavery among Whitefield's colleagues was Johann Martin Boltzius, a German Lutheran pastor of Ebenezer, Georgia, who was ten years older than Whitefield and had moved to Georgia in the mid-1730s. About the same time that Whitefield considered accepting a slave from Hutson, Boltzius met with Whitefield and expressed dismay at the revivalist's views on bound labor. Because Boltzius envisioned Georgia becoming a refuge for persecuted European Protestants, he thought that introducing slavery would depress the wages of white immigrants, making it difficult for them to live there. Whitefield told Boltzius that he thought the "Providence of God has appointed this colony rather for the work of black slaves than for Europeans, because of the hot climate, to which the Negroes are better used than white people." Boltzius thought this was a stereotype, however, and reminded the itinerant that some parts of Europe were as hot as Georgia during the summer. He was also dubious of Whitefield's claim that introducing slavery would allow for the evangelization of blacks; Boltzius thought slave masters were more likely to be worldly-minded and to "take advantage of the poor black slaves," raising the "sins of the land to a great height." The advent of slavery would be followed shortly by the appearance of mixed-race children in Savannah, he predicted, perhaps reflecting the tendency of some masters to prey sexually on their slaves.

Ministers who were truly worried about evangelizing African workers, Boltzius said, should simply cross the Savannah River and preach to South Carolina's burgeoning black population. Five years later (shortly before slavery's legalization in Georgia), Boltzius was still pushing Whitefield to explain how the "conversion of these poor creatures" would be furthered by expanding the brutality of slavery. By that point, Boltzius stood nearly alone in defending the colony's ban.[5]

Boltzius's pleas failed to convince the itinerant. In Whitefield's note to Hutson, he mentioned the recent arrival of traveling slaves, including "Bob," who worked as a teamster shuttling supplies from Charleston to Bethesda. Whitefield said that in spite of the prohibition on slavery in Georgia, no one noticed Bob or other slaves when they came to the orphanage. No one was interested in enforcing the preposterous law, Whitefield thought.[6]

"Therefore," he told Hutson, "if you think proper as you once said to give me a Negroe, I will venture to keep him." If some Georgia official did enforce the law and seize Whitefield's slave, he would just buy him back and send him back across the Savannah River into South Carolina. "I leave it to you to do as you find in your heart," he told the minister. But if he did send a slave, he told Hutson, he should make sure it was a *"sober one."* Then, before sending the letter, Whitefield jotted a hasty postscript: "upon 2d thots. you may Deferr sendg ye Negroe till I talk further abot. it." Whitefield still hesitated to break Georgia's law, but by 1747 he had acquired a South Carolina plantation, becoming a slave owner.[7]

By the time of his return to America in 1744, time and circumstances were turning Whitefield into a moderate man. He was stung by charges of fanaticism and subversion, and was weary of feuding with would-be allies over theology. Respectable, aristocratic followers appeared everywhere he preached, and he did not wish to alienate them. Whitefield maintained his core message of the new birth and the evangelical gospel, as well as his Calvinist absolutes. But his days of theological brawling, calling out unconverted ministers, fostering church splits, and reporting messages given him by the Holy Spirit were mostly in the past. Coming to terms with slave owning was also a part of his growing moderation. While he had never gone to the radical lengths of Hugh Bryan in prophesying the destruction of slavery, his 1740 address to slave masters certainly took an aggressive stance. Now slave owning and evangelism went together smoothly, at least in his mind.[8]

This journey to moderation was not unusual, and perhaps even expected, as Whitefield moved into his thirties, past the flush times of the early 1740s. Others experienced the same transition out of radicalism: James Davenport reclaimed some respect from moderate pastors after his book-and clothes-burning debacle, apologizing and swearing off his most controversial practices. When Whitefield arrived in Philadelphia, he found a subdued Gilbert Tennent, by then installed as the preacher at the New Building, which backers had initially erected for Whitefield's preaching. Regretting the "excessive heat" of his earlier behavior, Tennent had engaged the Moravians in a bitter exchange over their radicalism in 1742. By the time he accepted the position in Philadelphia, he had left much of his radical style behind. The man whom critics formerly painted as a dangerous enthusiast now railed against the "Moravian tragedy," which enticed naïve young converts with "enthusiasm, pride, error, and nonsense." Tennent had begun to wear typical ministerial attire—a wig and robes—and to read sermons from manuscripts instead of preaching extemporaneously.[9]

Gentlemanly supporters in Philadelphia tried to convince Whitefield to stay there, offering him an £800 salary if he would preach in Philadelphia for six months out of the year. The rest of the time, they said, he was free to itinerate. Whitefield turned them down. Agreeing to this arrangement would have effectively meant permanent relocation to the colonies. As much as he loved America, he was not prepared to make this commitment.[10]

Whitefield made his way south through Maryland and Virginia in the fall of 1745. In Hanover County, Virginia, a converted bricklayer named Samuel Morris had just missed seeing Whitefield on his earlier visit, but Whitefield's sermons had inspired him to lead his own local revival. Morris said that he had heard all the news about the "warm and alarming preacher" in the early 1740s, but not until 1743 did he receive direct exposure to the itinerant's work. It came through the 1741 Glasgow sermons "taken from [Whitefield's] mouth." (Morris remembered the printer's exact advertisement on the title page.) An immigrant from Scotland brought copies of these sermons with him, which Morris acquired. He liked them so much that he began preaching them himself. "I invited my neighbors to come and hear it," he recalled, "and the plainness, popularity, and fervency of the discourses, being peculiarly fitted to affect our unimproved minds, and the Lord rendering the Word efficacious, many were convinced of their undone condition, and constrained to seek deliverance." Many began to go to Morris's home meetings rather than attending Anglican parish services.[11]

The assemblies grew so large that Morris built a meetinghouse "merely for reading," he wrote. His recitations of Whitefield's sermons generated dramatic effects, with so many "crying out and weeping bitterly" that some regarded Morris's followers as "strange and ridiculous." Again, Whitefield's sermons could create a stir on their own. Even though Whitefield had been physically absent from Virginia for six years, his publications did a great deal of revival work in the interim, by Morris's initiative. Gilbert Tennent and other visiting Presbyterian pastors from the Middle Colonies began working with Morris's congregation. Strangely, by the time that Whitefield came to Hanover County in October 1745, his arrival did not seem to make an enormous difference to Morris. (Whitefield apparently declined an invitation to speak at Morris's meetinghouse.) The visit did give Morris's followers "farther encouragement" and helped them to recruit more Anglicans, who were more receptive to Whitefield than they were to the traveling Presbyterians.[12]

One Virginia correspondent noted that gentlemen and planters particularly responded to Whitefield's sermons. Any perceived threat that he posed to the institution of slavery had faded. One master came with a black indentured servant (workers who effectively served as slaves, but only for a contracted number of years). Curiously, this African laborer was a "Papist," a point the correspondent made sure to emphasize. A surprising number of slaves in America, especially ones from the Kingdom of Kongo (in modern Angola), had a Catholic background deriving from earlier Portuguese influence. The prospect of a Catholic African convert was worth mentioning. This man had three years left in his term of indenture, but his pious master apparently could not get him to church until Whitefield's arrival. Now the servant was so animated that "his master was in hopes he might be made use of if converted, to the conversion of other Negroes."[13]

Whitefield and his "dear yoke-fellow," Elizabeth, arrived in Charleston on November 8, 1745. The commissary, Alexander Garden, awaited him with a formal suspension from the Anglican ministry, but as before, Whitefield simply ignored Garden's sanctions. He repeatedly told correspondents that he pitied and prayed for "unhappy Mr. Garden."[14]

For half a year Whitefield shuttled between Charleston and Bethesda, trying to put the orphanage on a stronger footing. Though Bethesda always struggled to maintain sufficient funds and supplies, it struck visitors as an idyllic refuge cut out of the piney woods. One friendly visitor in 1748 wrote that the three-story main house, completed in 1742, "stands on a rising ground, having a descent on all sides—On the north and south, are yards about 120 feet long, planted with orange trees." The property had a lovely garden and orchard, and two enclosures for livestock; "on the east, is a water passage to carry you, to any part of Georgia [or] Carolina." Even a skeptical visitor in 1743 called the garden "one of the best I ever saw in America," and was impressed by the "genteel and friendly" welcome offered by Jonathan Barber and other Bethesda residents.

Although this traveler initially suspected that Bethesda was a haven for Whitefieldian fanatics, the visit disabused him of those concerns. In short order he "became a convert to the design."[15]

When Whitefield had departed in 1741, about a hundred people lived at Bethesda; now it was down to twenty-six. The remaining children's rigorous schedule of devotion and education had them studying evangelical standards such as Matthew Henry and Isaac Watts's edition of the Westminster Shorter Catechism as well as learning "Latin, arithmetick, writing, and reading." All lessons were accompanied by prayer. Whitefield said that the children benefited from their relative isolation: they did not have to contend with the temptations of cities, and Bethesda was more wholesome than southern plantations, "where children must necessarily be brought up with Negroes." Even though Whitefield urged the introduction of slavery in Georgia, he assumed that slaves, most of them uneducated non-Christians, were morally suspect.[16]

Soon after arriving at Bethesda, Whitefield began asking the South Carolina plantation master Jonathan Bryan for supplies. "I am obliged in conscience to keep [Bethesda] up," he wrote, and "I believe it may now be done with a little charge." He requested a hodgepodge of items for the farm and children: sheep, "pease," butter, a chaise and harness, salt, pork, corn, rice, shoemaker's thread, and flax. He wanted to do all he could for the project and to expand the residents beyond twenty-six people. "We have a house that will hold 100, and hearts that will hold 10,000," he told Bryan.[17]

Critics routinely indicted him for neglecting the orphanage, even suggesting financial malfeasance. The *Boston Evening-Post*, for example, printed a letter in 1743 that painted a much different picture of Bethesda than the rosy ones depicted by friends. A visitor claimed that the main house was dilapidated, the doors stood open at all hours, and cows ranged about the lower rooms, which the writer "perceived by the dung on the floors." He saw no evidence that any orphans actually lived at the place. People in the area told him that Whitefield was as bad as "a murderer, for enticing poor orphans to that place to starve."[18]

This sort of criticism pressured Whitefield to publish an independent audit of the orphanage's accounts, which he did in a letter to Ben Franklin printed in the *Pennsylvania Gazette* in May 1746. The auditors declared that it did not appear to them that Whitefield had "converted any part" of the donations to the orphanage to his private gain, and that the funds disbursed for Bethesda amounted to more than £5,500.[19]

One marvels at all Whitefield had to manage in his travels, from the supplies at Bethesda to the spiritual affairs of the London Tabernacle. Inevitably, slippages happened in his absence. In late 1744, he became concerned about reports of Moravian inroads among his English followers, inroads that would ultimately claim the allegiance of his key subordinates John Cennick and John Syms. For years, Whitefield had struggled to balance evangelical unity with his reservations about the Moravians' doctrines, especially their teaching on perfectionism. Even before he left England, he knew that Syms, his secretary, was thinking of joining the Moravians, and Howell Harris informed him in January 1745 that Syms had done so. A frustrated Whitefield wrote to Syms, noting that he had written him several times but had heard nothing back. He chalked up the silence to difficulty of mail delivery, given the ongoing war between France and England, and the associated Jacobite uprising in Scotland. Whitefield continued to use stock Moravian phrases in this letter and others, telling Syms that Jesus's "wounds and precious blood [are] a sure asylum and place of refuge in every time of trouble."[20]

By March 1746, Whitefield had also learned of Cennick's defection. Cennick specifically cited Whitefield's absence as a reason for the move, saying that the itinerant had "only gone to America because he foresaw that the whole affair would collapse," presumably meaning Whitefield's Calvinistic Methodist Association. Whitefield wrote a tense letter to Syms, saying that the divisions at the Tabernacle did not surprise him: "The fire lay under the embers and near ready to break out before I left England." He warned that Cennick and the other Moravian converts (he did not directly name Syms, but the implication was unmistakable) were verging toward "antinomianism." He figured that some of them would soon become "Ranters," an elusive species of radical heretic from the era of the English Civil War. These were ironic charges for Whitefield to make, since opponents had often associated Whitefield with antinomianism, and Alexander Garden had specifically drawn parallels between Whitefield and the "Ranters, Quakers, and French Prophets." But the epithets remained on Whitefield's mind: as he told John Wesley that antinomianism had become worse in New England than in Old England, and that many there had "turned almost complete Ranters."[21]

Whitefield, the paradigmatic "New Light," told Cennick to be wary of new light. He believed his former collaborator had an authentic, saving union with Christ, but he was concerned that Cennick would accept radical beliefs and lead the Calvinistic Methodists astray. "You and some others have imbibed antinomianism and under the notion of Christian liberty and new light—are really though unwittingly holding out a false light and bringing some into licentiousness of living . . . This has been always Satan's way after a great awakening—It is but the old story over again," Whitefield reckoned.[22]

Whitefield left open the possibility of godly new light if it brought "new love and lays the soul lower at the foot of Jesus." If it made people bitter and contentious, however, such inspiration did not come from God. In the end, Whitefield could yet not denounce Cennick or the Moravians, because of his latitudinarian principles. "I am a staunch Calvinist," the itinerant said, but "I cannot help loving [the Moravians] because I believe they love Jesus in sincerity." Many of Whitefield's English supporters followed Cennick and Syms into the Moravian fold, and ultimately, Whitefield estimated that he lost about 400 Tabernacle members in the schism. He called it the "Revolution at the Tabernacle."[23]

However moderate Whitefield was becoming, he would not cut off allies for theological radicalism or for former excesses and errors. For example, Whitefield reached out to Hugh Bryan and James Davenport, the two people who had brought the most notoriety to America's evangelical movement in the early 1740s. Kindly writing to Bryan, he indicted himself for making mistakes in the name of the Lord. "If blunders, frequent blunders ought to make a person silent, I am sure I ought to be dumb and open my mouth no more," he told the planter. He exhorted Bryan to receive Christ's forgiveness and to resume his ministry. Davenport had publicly recanted his errors two years earlier and had begun preaching in Hopewell, New Jersey. Davenport wrote to Whitefield in 1745, praying that "the Lord give you to take warning by my sad blunder and misconduct specified in my public retractions." In a congenial missive back to Davenport, Whitefield only hinted at the former radical's indiscretions, saying that he wished for the time when "corruption, infirmity, and error will be at an end."[24]

Aside from the Moravian defections, Whitefield was also troubled by reports of Britain's Jacobite rebellion. In July 1745, Charles Edward Stuart, commonly known as "Bonnie Prince Charlie" or the "Young Pretender," had invaded Scotland in hopes of reestablishing the Catholic rule of the House of Stuart. (His grandfather, James II, had been removed in the Glorious Revolution fifty-six years earlier. Jacobites supported a restoration of Stuart rule.) Charles Edward recruited a formidable army of Highland Scots, and by mid-September, Edinburgh had fallen to Jacobite forces. George II was not even in the country when the uprising began, and his best troops were occupied in fighting the French on the Continent. Charles Edward's army entered northern England, and for a moment it seemed as if he might march on London itself. Whitefield saw Jacobitism as part of a broader transatlantic Catholic threat, remembering Georgia's narrow escape from the Spanish, and the remarkable conquest of

Louisbourg. (He viewed these victories, along with the Glorious Revolution and other signal events in British Protestant history, as providential deliverances and "national mercies.") He wrote in November 1745 that the "threatened storm" was "breaking upon Scotland and England," adding, "I suppose ere long will reach us in America." Employing Moravian language, he prayed that his friends in Britain would "fly for shelter to a dear redeemer's wounds."[25]

The decisive battle of the Jacobite rebellion came at Culloden Moor in northern Scotland in April 1746, ending with a devastating defeat of Charles Edward's forces. Americans began receiving reports of the "bloody battle" at Culloden within three months. Whitefield, realizing the galvanizing potential of episodes such as Louisbourg and Culloden, delivered a well-publicized sermon, "Britain's Mercies, and Britain's Duty" in August 1746 at the New Building in Philadelphia. (He had left Charleston in May.) The sermon was "occasioned by the suppression of the late unnatural rebellion." Jacobitism had few supporters in America, especially in settled areas of the colonies. Just like anti-Catholicism, anti-Jacobitism helped soothe differences over Whitefield's previous excesses. A sermon like "Britain's Mercies" could also blunt charges that Whitefield and the Methodists had subversive designs themselves. An admiring report on the sermon said that Whitefield had never "met with a more universal applause; having demonstrated himself to be as sound and zealous a Protestant, as truly a loyal subject, as now he is a grand and masterly orator."[26]

In his sermon, the itinerant praised the "dread and rightful Sovereign King George the Second" for protecting Protestants' civil and religious liberties. The "horrid plot first hatched in hell" to remove George II and replace him with the Catholic Pretender would have surely ended those blessings. He speculated that in the Pretender's wake, "whole swarms of monks, Dominicans and friars, like so many locusts, [would] have overspread and plagued the nation." Oxford and Cambridge would have fallen to Catholics, and Anglican pulpits would have been "filled with those old antichristian doctrines, free will, meriting by works, transubstantiation, purgatory, works of supererogation [the doctrine that justified indulgences], passive obedience, non-resistance, and all the other abominations of the Whore of Babylon." (Including free will in that list was a swipe at the Wesleyan Methodists.) He also warned that the Jacobites would take away people's Bibles and deprive them of liberty of conscience.[27]

Along with his promotion of the Louisbourg expedition, "Britain's Mercies" reflected a growing political and imperial focus for the itinerant. Of course, he ended the sermon with an exhortation to repentance in light of continuing threats from the French, but the primary message was one of thankfulness to God for his providential interventions in British Protestant history, and of

Whitefield's confidence in the ultimate destruction of Europe's Catholic powers. Whitefield had the sermon published in Philadelphia, Boston, and London editions, and it became part of his sermon anthologies published in the 1750s and 1760s.

The itinerant still needed to reconcile with Gilbert Tennent, who had warred with the Moravians and had exchanged pointed letters with Whitefield in 1742 over the issue. Whitefield had accused Tennent of being overzealous for doctrinal precision, and Tennent responded angrily: "Your high opinion of the Moravians and attempts to join with them shocks me exceedingly and opens a scene of terror and distress. Oh my dear brother! I believe in my soul you never did anything in all your life of such dreadful tendency to the church of God as your favouring that sect of enthusiastical heretics." Managing such delicate matters via transatlantic mail (Whitefield was just preparing to visit Cambuslang as Tennent sent his letter) was less than ideal.[28]

Given the defections to the Moravians in London, Whitefield was eager to side with Tennent against them. Soon after returning to Philadelphia, Whitefield happily reported, "Jealousies and suspicions begin to vanish quite away and Mr. Tennent and we are very friendly." Elizabeth similarly wrote to Benjamin Colman: "Dear Mr. Tennent is getting alive again, and expresses great love to my dear Master, and says he loves him better than ever." No danger of a split with Tennent remained, and Whitefield and Ben Franklin arranged to have Tennent write the introduction for a new volume of Whitefield's sermons. (The first of the five sermons was Whitefield's standard "Thy Maker is Thy Husband.")[29]

Tennent's new moderation came out in this introduction, in which he endorsed Whitefield precisely because of his prudence. The itinerant's sermons, Tennent wrote, brimmed with "words of truth and soberness," adding "The style is easy and natural . . . grave and masculine." It was important to mention masculinity, which to Tennent implied rationality and emotional control. The sermons indicated a "sober, humble, well-informed mind, and a warm heart." No enthusiasm here, said Tennent, just trustworthy, grounded piety.[30]

Moreover, Tennent commended Whitefield's theology as reliable and as in agreement with the Anglican Thirty-Nine Articles and the Westminster Confession of Faith. He particularly praised Whitefield for speaking out against the "error of the Antinomians" (Moravians), namely, that "persons are actually justified before faith," which was the "first rise of all their abominations." This notion that the justification of believers happened at the cross, not at the moment of faith, was an extreme step beyond Luther and Calvin's teaching on salvation and justification as accomplished entirely by God. The Moravians de-emphasized the Ten Commandments and Mosaic law for Christians, which led critics to charge them with being antinomian (literally, "against the law").[31]

In addition, Tennent praised Whitefield's turn against "impulses," which Tennent defined as following "our own fancy, as a rule of conduct, without the written word, while the sober use of reason is rejected." Adversaries had routinely accused Whitefield of promoting spiritual impulses, especially in less prudent passages in his journals. But now, faced with the radical evangelical threat in America, Whitefield expressly opposed reliance upon such impressions. Tennent blamed the itinerant's earlier indiscretions on his "young years, strong passions, education in Arminian principles, and the continued hurry of his labors in preaching."[32]

Having reconciled with Tennent, Whitefield turned his thoughts to his estrangement from the Wesley brothers. He wrote them in September 1747 in anticipation of his eventual return to England, telling John that his heart longed "for an outward, as well as an inward union" with him and his followers. But doctrine was too important to Whitefield to overlook the disagreements that remained between them, especially on sinless perfection and the availability of Christ's atonement to all sinners. The itinerant had heard that the Wesleys were moderating their stance on perfectionism. "Time and experience I believe will convince you," Whitefield wrote, "that attaining such a state in this life, is not a doctrine of the everlasting gospel." On a universal offer of redemption, Whitefield was more pragmatic. He and Wesley already agreed that preachers should offer the gospel to "all poor sinners that will come and taste the water of life." Whether all were spiritually capable of responding to that offer was not immediately relevant. Whitefield advised preachers to give "a general offer and invitation; convinced of this, that every man's damnation is of himself, and every man's salvation all of God." A final resolution of these issues was difficult to achieve while an ocean separated him and Wesley. In any case, he told the Methodist leader that their ongoing disagreements need not prevent them from unity on their foundational conviction that Jesus was "the same yesterday, today, and forever" (Hebrews 13:8).[33]

In the midst of this fence-mending, Whitefield kept preaching. He told Wesley that he was happily "hunting in the American woods after poor sinners." During the summer of 1746, he preached for weeks in Maryland, which had only seen modest revival in the early 1740s. The itinerant repeatedly noted that he preached at crowded meetings, and concluded that there was a "prospect of a great and glorious awakening" there. Maryland did experience substantial revival in the mid to late 1740s. America's Great Awakening saw its peak in the early 1740s, but its effects continued for decades. The southern colonies witnessed their strongest revivals later than the northern ones. Cognizant that the South had not yet experienced the kind of awakening seen in the North, Whitefield strategically preached through each of the southern colonies from 1745 to 1747, praying that God would cause "these southern wildernesses to blossom like a rose."[34]

Writing to his mother, Whitefield said that he loved "to range in the American woods." (Phrases about hunting and the "American woods" appear regularly in his correspondence in these years.) He was beginning to think he might never go back to England, since well-connected people repeatedly asked him to settle in Philadelphia and Annapolis. Jesus kept him from "catching at the golden bait," however. He knew, as one English correspondent put it, that his followers there were "crying mightily" for his return. Elizabeth too was eager to go back. He and Elizabeth had continued to experience personal grief: he told his mother that she had recently miscarried (she would go on to endure several others, into her midforties). Nevertheless, Whitefield reported that he and his "dear yoke-fellow" were "happy in Jesus, and happy in one another." In the winter of 1746–47, George and Elizabeth split time between Charleston and Bethesda.[35]

Debt on the orphanage's construction and operating costs continued to trouble Whitefield, in spite of continuing contributions from British and American benefactors. Even Benjamin Franklin donated £75 in 1746. Whitefield personally thanked Franklin for the gift. Franklin apparently hoped to publish a list of donors (including himself) to help generate more funds for Bethesda, but Whitefield balked at that plan. He thought publishing the appeal would bring in more funds than he actually needed and might betray a lack of faith.[36]

In spite of these reservations, Whitefield widely publicized his 1747 acquisition of a South Carolina plantation—and slaves—as a breakthrough for the orphanage. "God has put it into the hearts of my South Carolina friends," he wrote, "to contribute liberally towards purchasing a plantation and slaves in this province; which I purpose to devote to the support of Bethesda." They called the place Providence. The 640-acre property, which had belonged to the Bryans and stood between their plantations, came with a house, outbuildings, and a barn; 60 acres were cleared for planting corn and rice. The Bryans also gave Whitefield "one negroe," and he planned to purchase more. Correspondents reported that "Mr. Whitefield has more friends in Charlestown among gentlemen, especially of distinction and substance, than ever heretofore," and that benefactors had raised upward of £300 for Bethesda.[37]

We might well echo the sentiments of Whitefield's nineteenth-century biographer Luke Tyerman, who saw the "odious act" of purchasing slaves as "one of the blots on [Whitefield's] distinguished life." But, blinded as he was by the prejudices of his time, and by the quest for financial stability, the itinerant did not see slave ownership the way we do. Instead, he viewed his plantation as another means of advancing the gospel among orphans, and among the slaves themselves. Soon he noted excitedly that "several negroes" at Providence had come under conviction of sin and were likely to experience conversion.[38]

The Whitefields spent summers in the northern colonies, and Elizabeth informed Howell Harris in May 1747 that they had returned to Philadelphia from Charleston after a four-hundred-mile journey during which George had preached about thirty times. The breakneck pace of travel caught up with him again, however, and he had a "great fever." The ravaging illness remained with him for weeks, and Whitefield wrote that his "whole frame of nature seems to be shocked" with convulsions and continuous fever. He also mentioned having the "gravel," or kidney stones (an ailment for which John Wesley once recommended taking wild parsley seeds). The itinerant agreed to take some breaks from preaching so that no one would charge him with "murdering" himself. Not surprisingly, Whitefield discovered that for him, it was "hard work to be silent." But the prospect of death—which meant being with his Lord—seemed pleasant. His body was "weak and crazy," he said, but "after a short fermentation in the grave, it will be fashioned like unto Christ's glorious body." He frankly hoped to die in the pulpit.[39]

William Shippen, a pioneering doctor in Philadelphia and friend of the itinerant, was not so enamored of the prospect of Whitefield's death, and even pleaded with one of Whitefield's associates to get their "dear friend" to slow down. When Whitefield did preach, Shippen requested that he "take pains to regulate his voice and so not strain himself, so much as he is wont to do." Shippen also prescribed him (unmentioned) medications and recommended that he ride out in the country on fair-weather days.[40]

Whitefield kept traveling and preaching, however, and in the summer of 1747 he took a northern tour through New York City and Boston, going as far north as York, Maine. Everywhere he reported crowds as large as ever, but the sensation of the early 1740s was largely gone. One Philadelphia diarist surmised that "the people's curiosity about him now seems so well satisfied that there is very little talk of him." His travels prompted little mention in the newspapers. That year, for the first time since 1738, there were almost no Whitefield-related publications in America, except for a solitary reprint of an antirevivalist sermon. His efforts to cast himself as an irenic moderate may have worked too well: news thrives on controversy, not the absence of it.[41]

In spite of letters clamoring for him to return to England, Whitefield decided to visit Bermuda. This British colony, more than six hundred miles off the North Carolina coast, was founded by the Virginia Company in 1609, only two years after Jamestown. It had become a vital port for trade between Europe and the Caribbean. Whitefield's Charleston ally Josiah Smith grew up in Bermuda and had served for a time as pastor of the island's Independent (Dissenting) congregation. Friends may have encouraged the visit to Bermuda, hoping to improve Whitefield's health, and he always found the prospect of preaching in new places enticing.

"Oh for a blessing upon the islands! Oh for a large draught of fishes!" the itinerant wrote to Howell Harris, who was no doubt frustrated by another delay in Whitefield's return. Harris had many questions he needed Whitefield to answer about the Tabernacle and the Calvinistic Methodist Association. Moreover, Harris was facing increasing criticism about what his Welsh colleague Daniel Rowland and others saw as his Moravian leanings. (Harris preached incessantly on the wounds of Christ in these months, saying that he had seen "deeper into the mystery of Christ's blood." At one meeting, he proclaimed that he would go as far as he could to "declare this fountain," and kept shouting "Blood, Blood, Blood, Blood!")[42]

Elizabeth was quietly frustrated with George, too; she stayed behind in Charleston, having already told him how much she wanted to go back to England. He preferred to leave her in America, however, in order to supervise Providence and Bethesda. "Should I bring her to England," he mused to Harris, "my two families must be left without a head. Should I go without [her], and unknown to her, I fear the trial will be too hard for her. But if the Lord calls, I can put both her and myself into his all-bountiful hands. Oh pray for me, my dear, dear man, that I may not err on the right hand, or on the left."[43]

Whitefield was struck by the lovely vistas when his ship sailed into the harbor of St. George's, Bermuda's oldest town. The beautiful "scene was quite new, and different from any [he] had ever beheld before." As usual, Whitefield received a mixed welcome from the Anglican clergy: one minister happily allowed him to preach in his parish churches, but two others kept their distance. A Presbyterian minister eagerly hosted him at his meetinghouse, where he preached on eight consecutive Sundays. In all, he found less opposition in Bermuda than in any "fresh place" he had ever gone. The island's air did boost his flagging health.[44]

Bermuda combined features normally associated with colonial northern seaports and Caribbean islands, being heavily focused on seaborne trade, but also had more slaves (by percentage) than towns such as New York or Boston. In the early 1720s, Bermuda's population stood at about 8,300 people, with whites outnumbering blacks 58–42 percent. As on the mainland, Whitefield arranged to address Bermuda's slaves directly. He held a May 1 field meeting "intended for the negroes," with perhaps a sixth of the colony's entire population in attendance. During the sermon, he asked whether they wanted to go to heaven, and one slave loudly replied, "Yes, sir." Whitefield said that this innocuous outburst "caused a little smiling," presumably among the whites. "But in general everything was carried on with great decency," the itinerant concluded.[45]

The large meeting put Whitefield in a reflective mood. He believed that God had helped him strike the right balance to reach the slaves, and "yet not to give them the least umbrage to slight, or behave imperiously to their masters." The circumstance called for perfect balance: "If ever a minister in preaching, needs the wisdom of the serpent to be joined with the harmlessness of a dove, it must be when discoursing to negroes." Whitefield heard that some of the Bermudan slaves did not think much of his preaching, though, because he "told them of their cursing, swearing, thieving and lying," and because he said "their hearts were as black as their faces." Some complained because they had expected he would say a word against the masters too, but Whitefield thought he should not do that in front of the slaves. A couple of the Afro-Bermudans walked out in the middle of his sermon. Others responded more warmly, showing signs of authentic conversion.[46]

Elizabeth waited for him on the mainland, but a ship was leaving Bermuda for England, so he decided to sail home without her. This was an extraordinarily callous thing to do, and suggests that—in spite of the suffering they had endured already in their marriage—the itinerant still saw Elizabeth as a ministerial assistant or employee as much as a wife. Perhaps he viewed his choice as a way to confirm that he would prioritize the work of the Kingdom over his family when circumstances warranted it.

Whitefield expected to come back to America in 1749, which is one of the ways he justified leaving Elizabeth (his "dear yoke-fellow") behind, even though they had agreed that he would go back to Charleston to retrieve her before departing for England. "O that I knew how it was with her," he wrote to one of her American friends as he sailed from Bermuda. "But I see that God will make those he loves, to live by faith and not by sense. Glorious privileges, though difficult to flesh and blood! As you are so dear a friend, I know you will do your utmost to comfort her." Not long after she realized that he had crossed the ocean without her, she advised him that she was returning to England. He did not seem too disappointed, conceding (as she passed the late summer in South Carolina) that the "climate will not agree with her." Soon he was telling friends that he would "persuade her" to settle in London. After some delays, she arrived in England in June 1749, bringing to an end any thoughts that she would remain as superintendent of his southern properties.[47]

By his return to England, Whitefield had become a slave owner and had successfully reconciled with moderate American allies. He had secured moderates' support without exactly denouncing most of the radical evangelicals. Of course, England had its own challenges, including the Moravian defections. And as always, there was his relationship with the Wesleys.

"AS I GREW MODERATE": WHITEFIELD MENDS RIVALRIES

Except for a brief chase by a French warship, the itinerant's journey from Bermuda to London was placid, giving him time to rest and think. He spent much of the voyage producing a new edition of his journals. This edition would not appear for another eight years, but during the Atlantic passage he wrote about his mindset as he tempered the journals' tone: "Alas! Alas! In how many things have I judged and acted wrong. I have been too rash and hasty in giving characters, both of places and persons. Being fond of scripture language, I have often used a style too apostolical, and at the same time I have been too bitter in my zeal. Wild-fire has been mixed with it, and I find that I frequently wrote and spoke in my own spirit, when I thought I was writing and speaking by the assistance of the spirit of God." He had given too much weight to spiritual impressions and experiences, including revelatory dreams. Nevertheless, he thanked God for carrying him through trials "both of popularity and contempt" and for "ripening [his] judgment a little more." His moderation went only so far, though: readers of the new version would still learn about the Spirit moving in his meetings, and about the importance of the "abiding witness and indwelling of the blessed Spirit of God" in their hearts.[1]

Here Whitefield was musing, as openly as he ever would, on the ministry of the Holy Spirit and on the way he should portray his spiritual journey. A decade earlier, Whitefield had so zealously embraced the promptings of the Spirit that he took little time to reflect on the risks of confusing the flesh with the Spirit. Jonathan Edwards and other revivalists had to evaluate this tension, too, and one of Edwards's greatest successes was to formulate a rubric for assessing a believer's experience in the Spirit, articulated in *The Distinguishing Marks of a*

Work of the Spirit of God, and especially *Religious Affections*, arguably Edwards's most important theological work.

In *Religious Affections*, Edwards explained how an emotional response to truth about God represented the core of authentic Christianity. "True religion," he proposed, "in great part, consists in holy affections." The tenets of the gospel—the threat of God's wrath, our inability to save ourselves by our works, and God's gracious gift of salvation through Jesus's death on the cross—will produce "lively" heart reactions when embraced by a sinner. Thus, dramatic manifestations of spiritual transport might be signs of real revival. Or they might not be. Emotions and transcendent testimonies could be fake or hypocritical. Viewing the revivals in retrospect, Edwards admitted that many of the intense experiences of the "late extraordinary season" came to nothing, leading some critics to disparage all expressions of spiritual zeal. But the only way to know the difference between godly affections and bogus ones, Edwards argued, was to test the fruit of revival. If those affective experiences enhanced the glory of God and the holiness of a believer, then one could assume they were of the Spirit. If the experiences drew attention only to the individual, and if that person showed no signs of long-term transformation, then one should question his or her claims.[2]

Looking back over the decade, Whitefield realized that he had not given enough thought to such distinctions between flesh and Spirit. He would never fundamentally question the role of the Holy Spirit in fostering revival. He was also cautious about denouncing even the most radical itinerants, such as James Davenport (who was on his own path to moderation). As we shall see, the Moravians were the only radical group he would openly condemn, in order to preserve his connection with Gilbert Tennent. But as he revised his journals, he knew that he needed to cast himself in a more moderate posture.

Whitefield's and John Wesley's published journals presented the preachers themselves as models for the Methodist movement. For an evangelical reader, Whitefield's journal provided an exemplary life of piety, though not one without fleshly struggles. Whitefield showed followers that he wrestled with sin, weariness, and illness, yet kept striving to give his all for Christ. Editing out more "enthusiastic" aspects of the initial versions implicitly conveyed to his followers that they should not put as much emphasis on impressions and dreams, and that they should not assume that their opinions matched the will of God. He also excised references, such as the comparison of his birth in an inn to Christ's, implying that God had uniquely raised him up as a latter-day apostle. Responding to the Spirit while maintaining humility about one's limits: that balance was a major theme of the rest of Whitefield's career.[3]

Whitefield's journals, then, had a pastoral function for his audience; they were not merely a chronological account of things that happened to him. Even a private diary typically has a literary perspective and leaves out most of what transpires in one's daily life. Whitefield's journals did include questionable factual details, such as the size of crowds. His cutting and revising years later also reminds us that Whitefield depicted his life as one that average readers could use as a model their own Christian devotion. By the late 1740s, Whitefield had become convinced that focusing on dreams, impressions, and quick spiritual judgments had caused many of his movement's early problems (seen most obviously in the career of James Davenport), and that he should no longer place them at the center of exemplary piety.[4]

The thirty-three-year-old Whitefield had not been forgotten in Britain during his nearly four-year absence. Public discussion about him waned, however, almost ceasing until 1748, when erroneous reports of his death appeared. One newspaper, under the heading "Tragical Occurrences," reported in March 1748 that Whitefield lay dying at Portsmouth, New Hampshire. Then in May, London newspapers announced the "death of the Rev. Mr. Whitefield, the famous itinerant preacher." Some may have been shocked on July 3 when, as London's *General Advertiser* reported, "the Rev. Mr. Whitefield (reported dead for some time since) arrived in town." His return made the *General Advertiser's* 1749 New Year's list of "Principal Events in the Year 1748."[5]

Supporters rejoiced to have their "spiritual father in Christ" back in England. The relieved editor of London's *Christian History* wrote that "a new face appears on things." Whitefield's work had certainly continued in his absence, fueled by print and less well-known preachers. One of these preachers wrote to Whitefield from Plymouth, telling how he became an exhorter. At a crowded Methodist meeting, this man wrote, "[I] sat about reading one of Mr. Whitefield's sermons as usual, but before I had scarce ended one page, the Lord opened my mouth to speak of my own experience, and just what he gave me I delivered to the people; so that our Savior's glory seemed to break forth, and his power to be manifested amongst them." The new evangelicals depended heavily on Whitefield, but their work was hardly confined to areas of his physical presence.[6]

The itinerant made significant ministry adjustments upon his return. First, he de-emphasized his role in heading the Calvinistic Methodist movement, feeling that it detracted from his preaching. While he still did not think that he and the Wesleys could bridge their theological differences, he did not want to build associations to compete against the Wesleys'. Longing to travel unfettered as the Lord directed, he sought to resign even his titular leadership of the Calvinistic Methodist Association and to find directors who permanently resided in Wales and England.[7]

Writing frankly to John Wesley a couple months after his return, Whitefield said that he feared that forming more Calvinistic Methodist societies would prove a "Penelope's web." This allusion, which recalled Whitefield's classical training, was to the *Odyssey*, in which Ulysses's wife, Penelope, in order to keep suitors at bay, perpetually wove and then unwove a funeral shroud ("web"), promising that she would choose her suitor once she finished it. Organization forming was a thankless task, one that did not suit Whitefield's talents anyway. Instead of building an Anglican renewal movement (or worse, in his mind, a Dissenting denomination), he simply wished to "go about preaching the gospel to every creature." Even if he and the Wesleys could not arrange a public reunion, he had no interest in fighting against their network. Encouraged by Howell Harris, Whitefield and the Wesleys continued to discuss possible union, and they met in Bristol in August 1749. Tangible improvements were elusive, however.[8]

Aside from such churchly affairs, Whitefield became involved in a peculiar conflict between the Wesley brothers over John's intention to marry Grace Murray, a committed Methodist widow. (Wesley and Whitefield shared similar struggles in establishing healthy relationships with women.) Charles became convinced that Murray was an unsuitable mate for John, and he hurriedly arranged for Murray to marry another Methodist instead.[9] The episode threatened to permanently damage the brothers' relationship. Whitefield, who happened to come to Leeds just as this marital drama peaked, managed to broker peace between John and Charles. John arrived in Leeds, in northern England, in early October 1749. He wrote, "I found, not my brother, but Mr. Whitefield. I lay down by him on the bed." They talked about what had happened, and Whitefield wept and prayed over him, trying to comfort John.[10]

The next day Charles arrived in town. John did not want to see him, but Whitefield implored him to do so. When the Wesleys met, Charles began to berate John, saying he would no longer have anything to do with him. But Whitefield and another pastor burst into tears at the prospect of the brothers' estrangement, pleading with them to be reconciled. Finally, the Wesleys embraced and agreed not to be angry with each other any longer. (John did ultimately get married, two years later, to another widow, Mary Vazeille.) The remarkable scene suggested that the Wesleys still trusted Whitefield, in spite of their long-standing rivalry. Charles exulted, "George Whitefield, and my

brother, and I are one,—a threefold cord which shall no more be broken."
Whitefield's tearful role in reconciling the brothers did not resolve all differences between the Calvinist and Arminian Methodists, however.[11]

Whitefield's ministry took another major turn with his appointment as a chaplain
to Selina Hastings, the Countess of Huntingdon (see figure 11.1). After losing her
husband in 1746, the forty-one-year-old countess suffered from grief and spiritual
uncertainty. By 1748, she had come down firmly on the side of Whitefield's
Calvinist faith and made the itinerant her chaplain and close confidant. In
August 1748 he preached four times at her London residence to "great company,"
including a number of nobles. Among those who would hear him preach at the
countess's home were the future prime ministers William Pitt (the elder) and
Frederick North. The countess gave him unprecedented levels of access to the
wellborn. To Wesley (who was disappointed by Whitefield's plum appointment),
Whitefield wrote that "the hour is coming when some of the mighty and noble
shall be called." Whitefield did not see his emphasis on aristocrats as a turning
away from common people; he saw the elites as a valued target audience who
had often resisted evangelical appeals. It must also have occurred to him that
wealthy benefactors could help him escape indebtedness over Bethesda.[12]

The turn to the aristocrats made sense to Benjamin Franklin, who told
Whitefield, "If you can gain them to a good and exemplary life, wonderful
changes will follow in the manner of the lower ranks." Franklin thought that the
wealthy needed Whitefield's ministry, for "there are numbers that perhaps fear
less the being in hell, than out of the fashion."[13]

Whitefield soon returned to Scotland, journeying overland to Edinburgh,
where he arrived in September. Complying with the countess's request, he sent
weekly updates about his travels. He confessed that he met with some "unexpected rubs" among the Scots. The Associate Presbytery continued opposing
him and clamoring for his endorsement of the Solemn League and Covenant.
His visit prompted them to pass a resolution vowing to use all lawful means "to
extirpate Popery, Prelacy, Arminianism, Arianism, Tritheism, Sabellianism, and
George Whitefieldism." Even some of the Church of Scotland's synods passed
resolutions banning him from their churches, an action reminiscent of the
hostile reception he had endured on his second visit to New England.[14]

He continued to see large crowds in Edinburgh and Glasgow, and also
enjoyed a visit to Cambuslang, where "the great awakening was about six years
ago." Whitefield stayed only six weeks in Scotland this time, returning to
London in late October. "I lead a moving life," he said, figuring that he would
have time for rest in heaven.[15]

To the extent that Whitefield maintained any interest in administration, it was focused on the Bethesda orphanage and Georgia. Upon his return to London, he wrote to the Countess of Huntingdon with news of what he regarded as a happy inevitability: "The negroes are allowed [in principle] by the trustees for Georgia," he reported. If they followed through and legalized slavery, the itinerant believed that "the province, under God, will flourish."[16]

He also began to think that the orphanage might serve as a "seminary of learning" for training pastors. Otherwise, how could the southern colonies have an adequate supply of evangelical ministers? It was not clear whether the pastors would be Anglican, and if so, how they could receive ordination aside from making the transatlantic trips that Whitefield considered routine. There was still no resident bishop in the colonies to perform ordinations.[17]

Writing to the Georgia trustees in late 1748, Whitefield exhorted them to legalize slavery so that the colony (and orphanage) could prosper. Bethesda was the largest civil employer in the province, and he implicitly threatened to refocus his efforts on South Carolina and the Providence plantation if they delayed legalization. "Georgia never can or will be a flourishing province without negroes are allowed," he chided. But he told them that he did not intend to bring slaves to Bethesda until he could "do it in a legal manner."[18]

By 1749, however, there were already at least five "negros" (presumably slaves) at Bethesda, as reported in a private letter from one of its white residents. The black workers were clearing land for a plantation. Whitefield apparently permitted the illegal introduction of slavery in Georgia after all. By the mid-1740s, many slaves had already been smuggled into the colony, and by 1749, Whitefield and many of Georgia's property owners were certain that the trustees would legalize their presence soon anyway.[19]

If they did introduce slavery, he wrote, it would bolster his intention to expand Bethesda into a "place of literature and academical studies." The Lower South badly needed such a school. Virginia's College of William and Mary (founded in 1693) was, thus far, the only institution of higher learning in the South. Benjamin Franklin had similarly proposed opening a Philadelphia academy, the precursor to the University of Pennsylvania. To house it, Franklin wanted to use the New Building, which supporters had erected for Whitefield's preaching. From the beginning, Whitefield had hoped the building could serve as a school. (Gilbert Tennent's congregation, which had been meeting there, was building a new meetinghouse.) In 1749, Franklin and wealthy trustees acquired the building and began developing plans for the academy, which would initially offer secondary education, and later, collegiate training.[20]

Franklin sent Whitefield a copy of his *Proposals Relating to the Education of Youth in Pennsylvania* (1749). Whitefield liked it very much, except for one problem: "There wants *aliquid Christi* [something of Christ] in it, to make it so useful as I would desire." Franklin had briefly noted that students would learn the value of public and private religion, and the "excellency of the Christian religion above all others." But Whitefield thought this was only a perfunctory reference. He pushed Franklin to make the academy fully Christian: "The grand end of every Christian institution for forming tender minds, should be to convince them of their natural depravity, of the means of recovering out of it, and of the necessity of preparing for the enjoyment of the supreme Being in a future state . . . Arts and sciences may be built on this, and serve to embellish and set off this superstructure, but without this, I think there cannot be any good foundation."[21]

This was a bracing vision of Christian education, but Franklin and the trustees were more concerned about the institution being nonsectarian than evangelistic. In 1751, the secondary academy opened, and in 1755, the College of Philadelphia was chartered as the first American institution of higher education with no denominational affiliation. Whitefield knew that Franklin's ecumenical vision would win out at the college, so he put more effort into assisting the fledgling College of New Jersey (now Princeton University), the solidly evangelical school founded in 1746. "It forbodes good for America," he wrote, "that such a spirit is excited in so many provinces for promoting a learned and religious education. God only knows how much my heart is on that side of the water."[22]

Whitefield remained mindful of his spiritual differences with Franklin, which he occasionally brought up in letters. In 1752, he commended Franklin for his growing fame related to his scientific experiments. "As you have made a pretty considerable progress in the mysteries of electricity," Whitefield said, "I would now humbly recommend to your diligent unprejudiced pursuit and study the mystery of the new-birth . . . One at whose bar we are shortly to appear, hath solemnly declared, that without it, 'we cannot enter the kingdom of heaven.'"[23]

The spiritual banter continued when Whitefield came across a copy of Franklin's personal epitaph, which the printer had written in his early twenties: "The body of B. Franklin, printer; like the cover of an old book, its contents torn out, and stripped of its lettering and gilding, lies here, food for worms. But the work shall not be wholly lost; for it will, as he believed, appear once more, in a new and more perfect edition, corrected and amended by the Author." Saying he had seen the epitaph, Whitefield urged Franklin in 1755 to "believe on Jesus, and get a feeling possession of God in your heart, and you cannot possibly be disappointed of your expected second edition, finely corrected, and infinitely amended." In spite of Whitefield's prodding, Franklin recalled in his autobiography: "[Whitfield] us'd indeed sometimes to pray for my conversion, but never had the satisfaction of believing that his prayers were heard."[24]

Nevertheless, the peculiar friendship endured. Franklin even speculated in 1756 about the two of them settling "a colony on the Ohio." He reflected,

> I imagine we could do it effectually, and without putting the nation to much expense. . . . What a glorious thing it would be, to settle in that fine country a large strong body of religious and industrious people! What a security to the other colonies; and advantage to Britain, by increasing her people, territory, strength and commerce. Might it not greatly facilitate the introduction of pure religion among the heathen, if we could, by such a colony, show them a better sample of Christians than they commonly see in our Indian traders, the most vicious and abandoned wretches of our nation?[25]

Why would Franklin care about such a project (which never came to pass), given his admitted skepticism? He gave part of the answer to the itinerant:

> Life, like a dramatic piece, should not only be conducted with regularity, but methinks it should finish handsomely. Being now in the last act, I begin to cast about for something fit to end with. Or if mine be more properly compared to an epigram, as some of its few lines are but barely tolerable, I am very desirous of concluding with a bright point. In such an enterprise I could spend the remainder of life with pleasure; and I firmly believe God would bless us with success, if we undertook it with a sincere regard to his honor, the service of our gracious King, and (which is the same thing) the public good.

Even though Franklin was older than Whitefield, he was not exactly in the last act of his long life, which had almost thirty-four years to go. The printer may have doubted some specifics of Christian doctrine, but he hardly questioned the merit of working for God's honor, the public good, and (in 1756) the service of the British monarch.[26]

Whitefield's growing circumspection helped him restore relations with a number of Anglican ministers in England, as it had with Dissenting pastors in America. For example, he received a warm response in his hometown of Gloucester when he preached there in December 1748. The bishop hosted him "respectfully" at the cathedral, where he took communion, and one of his old childhood tutors commended him for his change of attitude. "He said, as I grew moderate, the offense the governors of the church had taken against me, would lessen and wear off," Whitefield told the countess. Whitefield reflected that the "first zeal" of many preachers was often soiled with indiscretion. Yet those "first times have been generally blessed most, especially for awakening and converting souls." He may have wondered whether those abundant "first times" had now passed him by as he entered his midthirties.[27]

We must not overstate the decline in Whitefield's successes in the late 1740s. He continued to report large crowds, sometimes as large as twenty thousand. Still preaching tirelessly, he routinely put his health in jeopardy. In the summer of 1749, he toured southwestern England and southern Wales, estimating that he traveled a circuit of eight hundred miles, during which he preached to "upwards of a hundred thousand souls." In the summer of 1750 he preached twenty times on a visit to Edinburgh, and "thousands attended morning and evening." In mid-1751, he visited Dublin during his first preaching tour in Ireland, where he estimated one audience at ten thousand. He proceeded north to Belfast, and estimated that he spoke eighty times throughout Ireland altogether. Six weeks later he was in Edinburgh again, preaching fourteen sermons with as many as ten thousand attending each time. We inevitably grow less astonished at these repeated numbers, but his ability to draw massive crowds continued almost unabated in these years.[28]

A Whitefield visit still caused a sensation, especially in smaller towns. Traveling through northern England in 1750, he preached at tiny Haworth, England. The Anglican minister and Whitefield ally William Grimshaw of Haworth had experienced a dramatic conversion in the mid-1740s by reading evangelical classics such as John Owen's *The Doctrine of Justification by Faith* (1677). Grimshaw went through a trancelike experience in which he "saw a dark foul passage into which he must go; and being entered, saw a very high wall on the right hand, on the other side of which was heaven, and another on the left hand, on the other side of which was hell." He began to hear God the Father and Jesus discussing his fate: the Father said he should be damned because he still trusted in his own righteousness for salvation. But Jesus pleaded for him until the resolution arrived: "At last he evidently saw the Lord Jesus thrust down his hands and feet, as it were below the ceiling, while he remarked that the nail-holes were ragged and bluish, and streamed with fresh blood. Instantly he was filled with joyful assurance . . . [and] was filled with joy in the Holy Ghost." During his 1750 visit to Haworth, Whitefield reportedly preached to "upwards of 10,000" people and assisted Grimshaw in serving communion to about 1,200.[29]

Controversy still followed the itinerant's ministry, despite his efforts to defuse it. One Anglican official unconvinced by Whitefield's moderate turn was George Lavington, the bishop of Exeter. Lavington launched one of the most bitter anti-Methodist attacks in years with *The Enthusiasm of Methodists and Papists, Compar'd* (1749), printed shortly after Whitefield itinerated in Exeter. There was no more damning charge than associating Methodists with Catholics, especially in the aftermath of the Jacobite uprising. Lavington detailed alarming passages in Whitefield's and Wesley's writings and compared them side by side with similar ones from Ignatius Loyola and other Catholic figures. He concluded that Methodism was a "composition of enthusiasm, superstition, and imposture," and was "religion run mad." The sensational tract appeared in multiple editions into the nineteenth century.[30]

Disgusted by the "virulent pamphlet," Whitefield felt bound to respond, since Lavington was undermining Whitefield's self-refashioning as a moderate. Indeed, Whitefield used his *Some Remarks on a Pamphlet, Entitled, The Enthusiasm of the Methodists and Papists Compar'd* to reaffirm his new restraint. Lavington had criticized Whitefield's and Wesley's emphases on assurance of salvation and the inner witness of the Spirit, both of which the itinerant defended as biblical. Yet Whitefield readily conceded other youthful indiscretions. "My mistakes have been too many, and my blunders too frequent, to make me set up for infallibility," he said. Whitefield included a copy of his shipboard "wild-fire" letter of June 1748, in which he had described some of his earlier tactics as "rash and hasty."[31]

Howell Harris, however, told Whitefield that he thought he had apologized for too much, and that *Some Remarks* would "lessen his authority." Harris and Whitefield's relationship had grown increasingly strained since the itinerant's return to England, not least because of Harris's jealousy over Whitefield's appointment as the Countess of Huntingdon's chaplain. Fulfilling his wish to remove himself from administration, Whitefield formally named the thirty-five-year-old Harris superintendent of the Calvinistic Methodist societies. An awkward rift was simultaneously emerging between the two, however, especially over Moravian theology. Shortly after questioning him about *Some Remarks*, Harris challenged Whitefield's speaking out against Moravians. "I see they have the main and great thing," he told Whitefield, "the saving knowledge of Christ and his glory."[32]

Harris soon began feuding with Elizabeth Whitefield, too, whom he had once considered marrying. He wrote in his journal that he received some "sore stabs" from her "spiritual pride." The two of them apparently traveled together to Abergavenny in August, and Harris engaged in what he called a "home cutting reproving battle with Mrs. Whitefield about pride and self."[33]

Harris—who never enjoyed stable relationships with women—saw his personal life spin out of control because of his indiscreet dealings with a charismatic woman named Sidney Griffith. Harris and his wife, Anne, assisted Griffith when she became estranged from her abusive husband. The same week that Harris clashed with Elizabeth Whitefield, he wrote that he attended a private society meeting at which he experienced "such triumphing, singing, dancing, rejoicing and weeping for joy" as he had never seen. Griffith was there, and Harris stayed up late talking with her and another woman. The next day, he wrote in his journal that his wife had begun worrying that he "did not love her."[34]

The Welsh evangelist affirmed his commitment to Anne, but wrote in his journal that he had experienced a "total change" since meeting Griffith: he had been "raised to a new life, with God in everything." (This sounded suspiciously like a second new birth.) He construed his relationship with Griffith as pristinely spiritual, and even told his wife that while he loved her more than ever, he was sure she would "rejoice in seeing my heart running over with pure love to others according to the ties the Holy Spirit lays me under." Griffith had predicted that her own husband and Anne Harris would both soon die, a prophecy that Howell confided to Anne. On August 21, 1749, Anne wrote to Harris, complaining of a violent pain in her side and saying that she expected to perish soon. But she did not die, and a month later Harris noted a prayer that "Mrs. Griffith, my wife and I may be made as 3 cords in one." In December, the three of them traveled to London together, passing an evening at the Bell Inn in Gloucester.[35]

In London, Harris had another "dreadful combat" with Elizabeth Whitefield, who told him that everyone there considered him prideful. After the fight, Harris had a "long conference with Mr. Whitefield." Soon they began fighting, too, because Whitefield was not eager to have Harris preach any more. Harris told Whitefield that he was not growing in "the knowledge of Christ" and was preaching only "to the carnal and the weak, and to touch the affection." Finally, on December 30, 1749, Whitefield told Harris, "'tis over." He banned Harris from preaching at the Tabernacle. Harris glumly concluded that Whitefield had finally yielded to pressure from Elizabeth. "I think I am now hated by Mr. Whitefield," he wrote.[36]

Remarkably, Harris continued to agitate for a public union between John Wesley and Whitefield, even after Whitefield expelled Harris from the Tabernacle. This work soon bore fruit, since Whitefield agreed to preach at Wesley's chapel in January 1750 (Harris was still allowed to preach there, too). Wesley wrote that he and Whitefield took turns preaching and praying, and that the itinerant "preached a plain, affectionate discourse." Wesley gratefully noted that "one more stumbling-block" had been removed by the show of unity, and Whitefield said that the "Lord was with us of a truth." Whitefield and Wesley undoubtedly felt common indignation at Lavington's *Enthusiasm of Methodists and Papists Compar'd*, which had painted both revivalists as crypto-Catholic fanatics. But not all was settled between the old rivals. A week later Wesley jotted down a backward compliment about Whitefield: "Even the little improprieties both of his language and manner were a means of profiting many, who would not have been touched by a more correct discourse, or a more calm and regular manner of speaking." This section of Wesley's journal was published in 1756.[37]

Whitefield kept up a furious pace of preaching throughout England, Wales, Ireland, and Scotland, but he longed to return to America. The time came in August 1751. Elizabeth stayed behind, having recently endured a miscarriage. She wrote to the Countess of Huntingdon that she was so grievously ill with a "pleuritic fever" that the doctor refused to bleed her (in medical hindsight, this was likely to her benefit). But God still supported her "in and under all [her] trials and temptations," she said. Elizabeth and George corresponded while he was gone.[38]

The smooth journey to America was a welcome respite, since only a month earlier Whitefield had been throwing up blood. Upon arrival, he happily found the orphanage "in as good a situation as could be expected." At the beginning of 1751, slavery had finally become legal in Georgia, making Whitefield optimistic about Bethesda's prospects again (he soon began divesting himself of the Providence plantation in South Carolina). His acceptance of slavery had grown as he advocated its introduction. Whereas he had once denounced masters' treatment of slaves in the South, now he articulated a biblical defense of slavery that anticipated proslavery thought in the antebellum American South. He told a correspondent that in his reading of Scripture, slavery accorded with God's laws. Abraham and the ancient Israelites owned slaves, and in Joshua 9 "the Gibeonites were doomed to perpetual slavery." He further assumed that some of the "servants" mentioned in the New Testament were slaves.[39]

Whitefield acknowledged that the slave trade was immoral because it violated precepts such as the injunction against "mensteaters" in 1 Timothy 1. (Jonathan Edwards registered a similar objection against the slave trade, but not slave owning.) The itinerant figured that the slave trade would continue whether evangelicals liked it or not. He imagined making the best of the situation: "I should think myself highly favored if I could purchase a good number of them, in order to make their lives comfortable, and lay a foundation for breeding up their posterity in the nurture and admonition of the Lord." He never doubted Africans' spiritual equality to Europeans, writing later that "their souls are equally precious in the eyes of an all gracious Redeemer, as ours." Although race no doubt undergirded Whitefield's view of slavery, he did not make a primarily racial argument for it, instead believing that Africans' lack of civilization, education, and saving grace made them fit for slavery. He regarded other ethnic and regional groups as culturally inferior, too. Sometimes he spoke similarly of the "poor barbarous Highlanders" of Scotland and their resistance to the gospel.[40]

The itinerant strained credulity when he contended that he "had no hand in bringing [slaves] to Georgia," but acknowledged that he had long favored slavery's legalization. He noted, "I would not have a negro upon my plantation, till the use of them was publicly allowed." As we have seen, however, slaves seem to have been residing at Bethesda by 1749, two years before legalization. Now that slavery was legal throughout the colonial South, Whitefield thought he and his associates should redeem the institution, financially and spiritually. His planter associate Jonathan Bryan helped him acquire more slaves for Bethesda. Bryan expressed frustration to the itinerant about inexplicable delays in their purchase. "I don't know why they are not bought," Bryan fumed, "there has been several sales of Negroes . . . Your business can't go on well without them." Another correspondent who purchased slaves for Whitefield reported that the trade was competitive, describing how the planters at the slave market would "fight striving who shall get into the Negro yard first in order to get the first choice." The buyer acquired nine new slaves for Bethesda, including eight men and "a young wench."[41]

Whitefield's visit to America was surprisingly brief: he checked on the affairs of Bethesda and left. He cut short his trip for several reasons. The primary one was that he needed to return to England before the expiration of the Georgia trustees' charter in mid-1752 so that he could "apply for some privileges." He also learned that his mother had passed away during his visit. While he had remained in regular contact with her through these years, he left little indication of his reaction to her passing.[42]

Renewed problems with John Wesley seem also to have played a role in what he called his "sudden revolution to embark for England." In February 1752, Whitefield wrote from Charleston that Wesley was continuing to teach against the eternal security of believers, probably even among Whitefield's followers. After Whitefield's departure, Wesley published *Serious Thoughts upon the*

Perseverance of the Saints, in which he argued that Christians could fall away from God and "perish everlastingly." "Poor Mr. W[esley] is striving against the stream," Whitefield wrote. Believers should know, the itinerant averred, "that their stock is now put into safe hands; that the covenant of grace is not built upon the faithfulness of a poor fallible, changeable creature, but upon the never-failing faithfulness of an unchangeable God." He trusted that this truth would prevail at the Tabernacle; by May, Whitefield had returned to London to check on the congregation there. Elizabeth also defended George in his absence. She speculated that Wesley would grieve to see Whitefield "returned so soon, before [Wesley] had fulfilled his whole will."[43]

By the end of 1752, however, Whitefield was brokering peace again between John and Charles Wesley. The latter had written to Whitefield and implied that the brothers were close to another split. Whitefield told Charles that he wanted to do nothing to exacerbate the brothers' strained relationship. But he did seem to side with Charles, noting of John: "He is still jealous of me and my proceedings." Charles may have softened his opposition to Whitefield's Calvinism, but theological differences continued to chafe at Whitefield's relationship with John.[44]

Whitefield and the Wesleys whipsawed between friendly generosity and bitter criticism. In early 1753, Whitefield preached at the Wesleys' chapel in London while construction proceeded on a new brick building for Whitefield's Tabernacle. But then Whitefield spoke out against perfectionism again, calling it a "delusive dream" in a 1753 sermon, "The True Nature of Beholding the Lamb of God." That sermon stung John. The published version appeared shortly before a Wesleyan conference at Leeds in May 1753. The assembly recommended that "a loving and respectful letter be wrote to Mr. Whitefield, wherein he may be desired to advise his preachers not to reflect (as they have done continually, and that both with great bitterness and rudeness) either upon the doctrines, or discipline, or person of Mr. Wesley, among his own societies; to abstain himself (at least when he is among Mr. Wesley's people) from speaking against either his doctrines, rules, or preachers." They warned him "not to declare war anew, as he has done by a needless digression in his late sermon." John accordingly wrote to Whitefield and chastised him for promoting controversial doctrines among Wesley's supporters, including the eternal security of believers and the impossibility of sinless perfection. Full reconciliation between Wesley and Whitefield remained elusive, yet a month later Whitefield cheerfully wrote that he and the "Messrs. [Wesley] are very friendly."[45]

Whitefield and John Wesley's clash over Calvinism set a pattern among British evangelicals for a generation. The itinerants' feud would never again reach the public notoriety that it did in the late 1730s and early 1740s, but Wesley battled other Calvinist evangelicals in the subsequent decades. One of the most bitter clashes—one which also had a personal dynamic—occurred between Wesley and another Oxford Methodist, James Hervey, whose narrative dialogue *Theron and Aspasio* (1755) defended the doctrine of Christ's imputed righteousness to the regenerate. Wesley published a 1758 rejoinder against Hervey, whom he called a "deeply-rooted Antinomian." Hervey died at the end of the same year, before he could finish his reply to Wesley. John commented that Hervey had perished "cursing his spiritual father."[46]

Once he returned to England from Georgia, Whitefield kept preaching as if he had never left, taking a tour through southwestern England and Wales to keep offering "the gospel wine and milk to sale." In September 1752 he returned to Scotland by way of northern England, where he addressed audiences that were almost uniformly large and respectful (although some hooligans threw turnips at him in Leicester). At Edinburgh he "preached twice a day in the open air" with a number of aristocrats in attendance.[47]

Exactly how Whitefield determined his travel schedule is not clear. Of course, he preached more in summer than winter, and he received "continual calls" to visit and speak, more than he could accept. Certainly, he prayed over the requests, and he spoke often of going the direction the "cloud" was moving, referring to God's presence with the Israelites as they wandered in the wilderness. For example, he told his longtime supporter Jonathan Belcher (by then the governor of New Jersey) in late 1752: "It was no small self-denial for me to leave America without going to the northward; but the cloud moved towards England."[48]

Correspondents relentlessly pleaded with him to write and visit, sometimes professing to be "vexed" at the thought that he might not bring the gospel to their town. A "society of Christians at Sheerness" (east of London) wrote to Whitefield at length in 1752, outlining all the good effects his preaching could have in their village. They prayed that the lines of the letter might "have the same influence on you as the vision of the Macedonian had with St. Paul" (Acts 16:9). They even composed a brief verse: "The brazen doors, and iron bars shall yield, / When God Almighty speaks, by George Whitefield." He must have received countless requests like this, and he honored many of them. In fact, he visited Sheerness in 1753.[49]

Even as he kept preaching and mending other relationships, Whitefield concluded that he needed to break decisively with the Moravians. This move came in his *Expostulatory Letter* (1753) to Count Zinzendorf. Whitefield had long admired the Moravians' piety, but growing pressure from colleagues such as the Countess of Huntingdon and Gilbert Tennent, and increasing awareness of the Moravians' peculiar theology, led to the final rupture. In the late 1740s, some Moravians had plumbed the depths of pietistic radicalism. They began emphasizing the motherhood of the Holy Spirit and putting an intense focus on the wounds of Christ, especially the "side hole," where he was pierced on the cross. Moravian hymns (including ones in English translation published by Whitefield's old printer James Hutton, by then a Moravian) featured prayers to the side hole itself, speaking in vivid terms about it:

> Love's smart will I feel for ever,
> For the Side-hole I'll be sick;
> Other matters whatsoever
> Shall not to the heart me prick.
> O for ever blessed,
> Ne'er enough caressed,
> Side-hole's cavity so deep!
> I will weep
> After thee, and in thee creep.[50]

In early 1753, Whitefield told a correspondent that he had anticipated the Moravians' heterodox turn for some time. In a total reversal from his previous sympathy, he now regarded them as "antichristian in almost every respect." "Antichristian," to Whitefield, implied "Catholic," and he excoriated their use of images of people from Christ to Zinzendorf himself in worship. They were "introducing a whole farrago of superstitious, not to say idolatrous fopperies into the English nation," the itinerant wrote.[51]

His letter prompted angry responses from Zinzendorf, James Hutton, and John Syms, his former secretary, who said that he regarded Whitefield as "drunk with power and approbation." Elizabeth conveyed the "threatening" tone of Syms's letter to the traveling itinerant, who wrote back to Syms, regretting that "Moravianism leads us to break through the most sacred ties of nature, friendship, and disinterested love." Peter Böhler, the German-born Moravian leader, likewise told Whitefield that his missive was one big lie.[52]

While he broke ties with the Moravians, he kept cultivating his connection with Dissenters, especially in America. That connection was enhanced by the arrival in late 1753 of Samuel Davies and Gilbert Tennent, who had come to England to raise funds for the fledgling College of New Jersey, which would relocate to Princeton in 1756. Their visit indirectly highlights just how few of Whitefield's ministerial colleagues ever traversed the Atlantic. The Virginian

Davies found sea travel debilitating; he wrote in his diary, "I had no appetite, and the little I eat, I vomited up immediately; and the *smell* of the ship, whenever I entered the cabin was nauseous beyond expression. Now and then I forced a little cheerfulness, but it was wholly unnatural." He was delighted and relieved to sail into London on Christmas Day. The sights of the city—London Bridge, the Tower—as well as the pealing Christmas bells throughout the city, overwhelmed the American visitors.[53]

Whitefield immediately offered his home as a base during their stay. Davies, however, was ambivalent about that invitation, since he believed that the English Dissenters had generally become "disaffected" with the itinerant. (Whitefield's Anglicanism still made some Dissenters wary, while others had embraced Arminianism or even Nontrinitarianism.) Tennent was happy to reunite with his old friend, however, and Davies found Whitefield so generous and charming that he could not but help "admire the man, as the Wonder of the Age." When Davies went to hear Whitefield preach at the Tabernacle, he found the sermon "incoherent," but "better calculated to do good to mankind than all the accurate, languid discourses I have heard." Whitefield worked to connect Davies and Tennent with wealthy benefactors.[54]

The itinerant did not spend a great deal of time with his American guests, however, because in March he departed for the colonies again, with about a dozen orphans accompanying him to Bethesda. Leaving Elizabeth behind, he asked friends to visit her while he was away. He traveled by way of Lisbon, Portugal, where the ship's captain unloaded a cargo of wheat and where Whitefield spent the better part of a month. Whitefield preceded the English novelist Henry Fielding in the city by about four months. Fielding, desperately ill with gout, hoped to convalesce in the sunny, sprawling town of about 200,000 residents. But the writer was less than impressed by Lisbon at first glance, calling it the "nastiest city in the world." Two months after he arrived, Fielding died and was buried there.[55]

As in Whitefield's earlier visit to Gibraltar, the sights of Lisbon's Catholic devotion—its "ecclesiastical curiosities"— troubled him. He noted "the frequency of crucifixes, and little images of the Virgin Mary, and other real or reputed saints, which were placed almost in every street . . . to these [he] observed the people bow as they passed along." He watched as a procession of priests walked "two by two in diverse habits, holding a long and very large lighted wax-taper in their right hands—amidst these was carried, upon eight or ten men's shoulders, a tall image of the Virgin Mary, in a kind of man's attire; for . . . she had a very fine white wig on her head, (a dress she often appears in) and was much adorned with jewels and glittering stones." Similar ceremonies featured images of Christ and Saint Francis, and in some cases penitents flagellated themselves on their bare backs. Since he stayed through Lent and Easter, he even saw a great reenactment of Christ's Passion on Good Friday, a drama he considered a "tragi-comical, superstitious, idolatrous droll." Some scholars today regard these processions as evidence of the vital, participatory lay piety of the Catholic (or "Counter") Reformation. But Whitefield did not see them this way: "O for another Luther," he mused. "O for that wished-for season, when everything that is antichristian shall be totally destroyed by the breath of the Redeemer's mouth, and the brightness of his appearing!" (2 Thessalonians 2:8).[56]

A year and a half after Whitefield left Lisbon, it did indeed seem as if the apocalypse came upon the city. On the morning of All Saints' Day, November 1, 1755, the city was decimated by a massive earthquake and the resultant tsunami and fires, all of which killed tens of thousands. Many of those who died were attending mass in the city's enormous stone churches, which collapsed upon them. Undoubtedly, some victims were among those Whitefield had witnessed in Lenten processions. "Poor Lisbon!" he wrote, "how soon are all thy riches and superstitious pageantry swallowed up!" He thought the world had seen nothing like this calamity since Noah's flood.[57]

After a six-week journey, Whitefield arrived in South Carolina in May 1754. After settling his orphans at Bethesda, the itinerant prepared for a far longer American visit than his last. He found Bethesda in a "thriving situation," happily noting that the "family" there now included 106 people, counting both whites and blacks. Following about eight weeks in the South, he sailed for the northern colonies. In Philadelphia, he was pleased to preach at the New Building, which now housed the academy he had discussed with Franklin. Franklin printed an effusive description of Whitefield's preaching, saying that his "sermons have discovered a deep insight into human nature, and great skill in moral penciling; and these, with his manner of life, have gained him justly the character of an exemplary Christian, fine gentleman, and accomplished orator."[58]

On a somber occasion in New York City, he preached at the Presbyterian church before about two thousand people, speaking on Amos 4:12 ("Prepare to meet thy God, O Israel"). A newspaper reported that in the application of the sermon, "he was extremely pathetick with regard to the disturbances, not only on the frontiers of this province, but likewise on those of our neighbors." These "disturbances" heralded the beginning of the Seven Years' War (1756–63), a global conflict whose operations in America are known as the French and Indian War.[59]

Not long after Whitefield's arrival in the northern colonies, news had come of the French defeat of twenty-two-year-old Colonel George Washington at Fort Necessity, in western Pennsylvania. Washington had taken 160 men into the wilderness to confront French military garrisons there. During an initial fire-fight with the French, Washington's Native American guides set upon wounded French soldiers, scalping and killing them, which elicited French charges of a massacre. The Virginians hastily built a circular open-air stockade, covering it with animal skins and bark. The French attacked in the midst of a torrential rain that left the inexperienced troops wallowing in mud and the blood of fallen comrades. Washington's men abandoned the fort on July 4, 1754 (twenty-two years before the yet-unimaginable events of July 4, 1776). No one knew that Washington's unsuccessful venture would precipitate a true world war, one whose battles stretched from Asia to the Caribbean and Europe. America's frontiers churned with violence between French and British forces. Native Americans were allied mostly with the French at the war's beginning, but their growing disenchantment with the French helped turn the conflict in favor of the British in the late 1750s.[60]

The Seven Years' War made Whitefield even more sensitive to the fate of Protestant power, and to the danger of Catholic aggression, as represented by imperial France and Spain. The gospel of the new birth remained Whitefield's central concern, but he also realized that without the political and religious liberty afforded under British Protestant rule, the preaching of that gospel could be at risk. Wartime anti-Catholicism proved a potent source of British unity, and ministers offered assurance about the conflict's outcome. As one of Whitefield's correspondents put it, in the war against the "Whore of Babylon," God was "on our side."[61]

In October 1754 Whitefield returned to New England. The itinerant reported that he had never enjoyed such successes, estimating that thousands routinely came to his meetings, even those he held at seven in the morning at the Old North Church. He called the New England tour, during which he preached almost a hundred times in eight weeks, the "most important one [he] was ever employed in." His old ally James Davenport offered more sober analysis in a letter to Elizabeth. Certainly, the itinerant was "more flocked after than when last in America," but not as much as "we were favored with in the years 1740–41."[62]

It is challenging to interpret Whitefield's optimistic view of his New England circuit. There is no question that his preaching was not eliciting the same kind of reaction, positive or negative, as the height of his ministry had seen. So how do we account for his effusive assessments? One explanation is that he naturally wanted to paint as positive a picture as he could for correspondents, including benefactors such as the Countess of Huntingdon. If the crowd numbers he reported did not match the titanic throngs of his early career, they nonetheless remained quite large, certainly larger than those any other preacher could expect to attract. We might also imagine that Whitefield genuinely appreciated that he could preach now with relatively little controversy. "Enemies are made to be at peace, and friends are everywhere hearty," he happily wrote from Boston. His work from ten years earlier had substantially cleared his reputation from charges of fanaticism; supporters were delighted to see him, and opponents saw little harm in his visits. Whitefield remained remarkably popular, and much less controversial.[63]

Indeed, compared to his visit to New England in the mid-1740s, Whitefield's return generated little notice in the media. A supporter published a broadsheet poem about him, playing off the *Pennsylvania Gazette*'s encomiums to the revivalist as a "fine gentleman and accomplished orator":

Should we now offend the world,
We must and will declare
He is the man of whom there's none,
For us we can compare.

The poet trumpeted his inclusiveness:

The Negroes too he'll not forget,
But tells them all to come;
Invites the black as well as white,
And says of them there's room.[64]

Enemies were not entirely silent about the itinerant's visit—grumbling still came from Harvard, where the Hollis Professor of Divinity, Edward Wigglesworth, preached on the special calling of an evangelist after Whitefield visited Cambridge. Wigglesworth had been a formidable, learned presence at Harvard since becoming the inaugural holder of the Hollis chair (the first endowed professorship in America) in 1722. Wigglesworth regarded biblical evangelists as "a sort of officer peculiar to the apostolic age," which had gone out of existence once the canon of scripture came into place. Thus, he concluded that "the itinerants and exhorters, who have once and again overrun this, and the neighboring provinces and colonies, were no evangelists in the scripture sense of the word, as some of them pretended to be." Here he footnoted Whitefield's 1745 *Letter to the Rev. the President, and Professors, Tutors, and Hebrew Instructor, of Harvard-College in Cambridge,* in which Whitefield had affirmed that he did regard himself as an evangelist in the biblical sense, which justified his traveling ministry. Wigglesworth said that he had hoped that New Englanders had learned their lesson about the dangers of itinerancy and church separations. "But the length of a few years seems to have worn out all remembrance of past calamities," and crowds were eager to hear Whitefield preach once more. Wigglesworth also reminded the Harvard audience that the itinerant had never fully apologized for his rude comments about the college years earlier.[65]

Wigglesworth also condemned Whitefield's claims to speak with assistance from the Holy Spirit, saying such gifts had similarly been reserved for the apostolic period: "If any man pretends to speak as the Spirit gives him utterance, or to be under the immediate direction of the Spirit of God in his speech and preaching; you may conclude him to be a bold deceiver, or a man given over to strong delusions." Wigglesworth assumed that anyone claiming to preach under the direction of the Holy Spirit had to be claiming "infallible guidance," such as that given to the authors of the biblical texts. Whitefield never claimed infallibility, only that he had received assistance from the Spirit for courage and timely words. His critics failed to appreciate the distinction—if he spoke with the Spirit's aid, did that not imply that his words carried unquestionable divine authority? Wigglesworth advocated a strong distinction between the operations of the Spirit in the apostolic period and in the church era, a kind of theology that would come to be called "cessationism" in the twentieth century. Much of the controversy over Whitefield's ministry, and over the revivals generally, reflected clashing beliefs about the work of the Holy Spirit. That division persisted even after Whitefield had moderated his style.[66]

The chastened Whitefield passed his fortieth birthday as he proceeded south, heading back to Georgia. "I am now forty years of age," he mused, "and would business permit, would gladly spend the day in retirement and deep humiliation before that Jesus for whom I have done so little." Of course, nothing could be more incompatible with Whitefield's disposition than "retirement." But he was worn out, struggling with ailments that would mark much of his later decades. The arduous overland journey taxed him mightily, bringing his "old vomitings" back. Nevertheless, he briefly visited Bethesda and had the "orphan boys trained in weapons," in preparation for possible expansion of war from the north. Otherwise finding Bethesda's affairs in good order, he left for England again in March 1755. The journey went well, but he returned to the galling news that John Wesley had again stoked the flames of controversy against him.[67]

"This Pilgrimage Kind of Life": The End of Whitefield's Travels

"O this bigotry, this party spirit, this love of power, how doth it contract the heart and fill the soul with corroding jealousies and needless fears!" Upon his return to England in 1755, the lamenting Whitefield heard that at a recent conference of Methodists, John Wesley gave a sermon on self-denial and cited the itinerant as an example of one who neither preached nor practiced that virtue. (One attendee was so repulsed by this statement that he confronted Wesley, who promised to speak no more about Whitefield from the pulpit.) Wesley and Whitefield had known each other for two decades, yet they seemed no closer than ever to living at peace.[1]

The rivals exchanged tense letters in August when Whitefield spoke at a Norwich assembly led by a preacher whom Wesley had expelled from his conference. Whitefield declared that his time was "too precious to be employed in hearkening to, or vindicating of [himself] against, the false and invidious insinuations of narrow and low-life informers." These informers tried to cast Whitefield's Norwich appearance in factional terms, but the itinerant insisted that only Christ's glory motivated him. When Wesley and Whitefield saw one another, it seemed to help. During a personal visit with Whitefield in November, Wesley announced, "Disputings are no more. We love one another and join hand in hand to promote the cause of our common Master."[2]

After age forty, Whitefield became increasingly weary of personal conflict, illness, and traveling. Always sickly, he had never shied away from discussing his ill health. Now he was also gaining weight (reflected in drawings of the older Whitefield), which added to his lassitude (see figure 12.1). He told correspondents, "I dread a corpulent body. But it breaks in upon me like an armed man."

He was physically spent: "God knows how long I am to drag this crazy load along . . . I am sick of myself, sick of the world, sick of the Church and am panting daily after the full enjoyment of my God." News of the passing of friends came regularly. In 1758 he marked the "death of Mr. Jonathan Edwards." Edwards, who had recently assumed the presidency of Princeton, died of a smallpox inoculation gone awry. Whitefield himself kept preaching, usually about fifteen times a week.[3]

Although he remained absent from the colonies—the Seven Years' War would keep him away for eight long years—Whitefield waited eagerly for news of the conflict in America. The news that came was bad. In July 1755, General Edward Braddock perished in Britain's defeat at the Battle of the Monongahela, east of Fort Duquesne (Pittsburgh). The British had ordered Braddock's expedition as revenge for Washington's defeat at Fort Necessity. Benjamin Franklin helped British forces as they prepared to go to western Pennsylvania, securing dona-tions of eleven wagonloads of wine, chocolate, cheese, coffee, and tea. But Franklin also cautioned Braddock to watch out for the "ambuscades of Indians" and their unconventional fighting methods. Braddock scoffed at the printer's warning and proceeded to march his unsuspecting army into a furious attack by French and Native American forces, whom one British observer called "ravenous Hell-hounds." Inexperienced at making war in the woods, the British force melted into chaos and lost miserably.[4]

Braddock's demise galvanized Whitefield's turn toward political preaching. Learning of the debacle, Whitefield gave a sermon on Isaiah 59:19, "When the enemy shall come in like a flood, the Spirit of the Lord shall lift up a standard against him." The itinerant was confident that British Protestants would find this principle "true in a temporal and spiritual sense." Balancing the earthly and heavenly was becoming ever-more imperative. He routinely made temporal applications of such verses as Romans 8:37, praying of Braddock's death: "May the late defeat be sanctified; and then I doubt not but we shall be more than conquerors through the love of Christ."[5]

Whitefield sometimes blended the affairs of heaven and earth to the point of confusion. He told one correspondent that it was always his "bounden duty, next to inviting sinners to the blessed Jesus, to exhort [his] hearers to exert them-selves against the first approaches of popish tyranny and arbitrary power." But the root of such tyranny lay within all people, Whitefield explained, warning against the "opposition of Antichrist in our hearts; for after all, there lies the most dangerous man of sin." Even though he focused more on imperial concerns than ever before, he still tended to spiritualize political affairs. His turn to earthly matters did not escape the notice of critics: Samuel Johnson said that "he believed [Whitefield] sincerely meant well, but had a mixture of politics and ostentation."[6]

In early 1756, Whitefield penned *A Short Address to Persons of All Denominations*, which, along with *Britain's Mercies* (1746), was one of the two most popular sermons Whitefield had published since the early 1740s. Tellingly, both were on imperial topics. *A Short Address* quickly went through six editions published in London, Edinburgh, Boston, and New York. Whitefield personally sent the pamphlet to Franklin, who published it in Philadelphia. The address responded to a royal declaration warning of a possible French invasion of England. Defending the burgeoning conflict as a just war, Whitefield praised those Britons who were willing to draw their swords "in defense of our civil and religious liberties." He invoked Deborah's curse on Meroz from Judges 5:23, when, "under the immediate influence of the Holy Spirit," she condemned Meroz for not coming "to the help of the Lord against the mighty." As he had done during the Jacobite rising, Whitefield praised King George II as the preeminent defender of Britain's liberties, even proposing that the sovereign be called "GEORGE THE GREAT." Contemplating Britain's prospects if Catholics were to come to power, the itinerant recommended that readers consult the "shocking accounts of the horrid butcheries, and cruel murders committed on the bodies of many of our fellow-subjects in America, by the hands of savage Indians, instigated thereto by more than savage Popish Priests." He feared a similar fate for Britain, should the "Protestant interest" falter.[7]

His appeal to British Protestant patriotism did not appease all critics. In early 1756, Whitefield endured the worst antagonism he had seen in years. He had begun speaking twice a week at the Long Acre Dissenting chapel, in the West End section of London. The resistance to his preaching there was two-pronged: some came from the nearby theater community, which resented Whitefield's antitheater preaching. Hooligans sang and made "an odd kind of noise" outside the chapel, and occasionally heaved large stones through the windows. Opposition also came from local Anglican authorities, especially Bishop Zachary Pearce, the dean of Westminster. The sixty-five-year-old Pearce was, according to Luke Tyerman, "a feeble orator, an active prelate, and a hearty hater of the Methodists." The bishop tried to ban Whitefield from speaking at Long Acre because of its Dissenting affiliation, but the itinerant would not comply, writing lengthy missives asking the bishop whether he did not have more important things to do than restrict the preaching of the gospel. He chided Pearce for having misplaced priorities: "Ecclesiastical dissensions must be quite unseasonable, especially at this juncture, when France and Rome and hell ought to be the common butt of our resentment." Every true lover of liberty would see the righteousness of his cause, Whitefield predicted.[8]

Over weeks it became clear that the disturbances at Long Acre were "premeditated rioting." He suspected that someone was hiring the "baser sort" to cause a ruckus. Things took a dark turn in April 1756 when he began receiving death threats. Three letters promised "a certain, sudden, and unavoidable stroke" if he did not stop preaching or if he pursued legal proceedings against his tormenters. These frightening developments came to the attention of George II's court, which issued a royal proclamation condemning the threats and offered to pardon anyone involved who confessed and exposed his accomplices. This helped defuse the crisis, as did Whitefield's announcement that he would begin building a more suitable preaching venue nearby, on Tottenham Court Road. When completed, including a 1759 expansion, this new chapel sat more than four thousand people. An Anglican critic called the place "Whitefield's soul-trap."[9]

It was not certain who was behind the riots at Long Acre or the menacing letters. But the theater community certainly perceived Whitefield as a hazard to their livelihood, both because he denounced the theater and also because he was such a compelling, dramatic orator. One Methodist recalled that before his conversion, he could not "discern any difference between Mr. Whitefield's preaching and seeing a good tragedy." Similarly, the actor and anti-Methodist critic Tate Wilkinson wrote some of the most pungent criticisms of Whitefield, attributing the power of Whitefield's preaching to his background in the theater. Calling Whitefield the "first actor in the Methodist line," he cruelly mocked Whitefield's crossed eyes as a reason that he switched from acting to preaching. "As he liked tragedy, and found that a pair of squinting eyes . . . did not move the young ladies' tender hearts, but produced laughter instead of tears, he [damned] the stage," Wilkinson asserted, "but he often melted and squeezed to some purpose many a rich dowager, who felt the power of his feelings from their mutual sympathy." Wilkinson, a close observer of elocution, recalled that Whitefield's Gloucester "dialect was very particular," saying "*Lurd* instead of Lord, *Gud* instead of God—as, O *Lurd Gud!*"[10]

Any preacher, of any faith, must walk a fine line between effective oratory and sensationalism. The more talented the orator, the more pressing the quandary. How do you use your God-given speaking gifts without using dramatic artifice simply to get an emotional response? Few would recommend that a preacher give intentionally dull sermons in order to avoid melodrama, but many have chosen to avoid Whitefield's theatrical techniques. His was not a mode for every pastor. Whitefield was a phenomenally skillful speaker, and he used talents he cultivated in the theater to move his audiences. Some undoubtedly attended his meetings because of the emotions they felt there, but their experience had no lasting effect on their spiritual or personal lives. These facts alone, however, do not mean that Whitefield was insincere, and many did find that his preaching helped produce more enduring change. He would have been troubled by the notion that people in his audience did not gather the difference between his sermons and a "good tragedy."

Prevented from returning to the colonies, Whitefield continued promoting the British Protestant cause in the Seven Years' War. In late 1757, Whitefield delivered a celebratory sermon—thrice on one day in London—on Frederick the Great of Prussia's magnificent tactical defeat of the French and Austrian armies at the Battle of Rossbach. During a thanksgiving service for the Prussian victory, Whitefield spoke for three hours, reading letters from the Continent and America that gave accounts of "the sufferings and cruel persecutions of our poor brethren of the Protestant religion by their implacable and unrelenting enemies the French." He remained in contact with influential German Protestants such as Gotthilf August Francke of the University of Halle, whom Whitefield assured that thousands of Britons were praying daily for Prussian victory. After the Prussians suffered defeat by the Russian army at the Battle of Kunersdorf in 1759, Whitefield arranged for the London publication of a collection of letters titled *Russian Cruelty*, detailing the plight of refugee Protestants in Brandenburg, some of whom were receiving assistance from Francke. He also raised relief money for those "cruelly tortured and abused by the savage Cossacks."[11]

In June 1757, Whitefield had tried to take these sorts of sentiments to Dublin, Ireland. Dublin was a large city of about 140,000 with a fast-growing Catholic population that was much less sympathetic to the Protestant forces in the Seven Years' War, and to Whitefield's British patriotism. Whitefield preached at Oxmantown Green, where Catholic and Protestant mobs were known to clash. He did not realize the danger he was courting by doing so. Finishing a sermon on the green one Sunday afternoon, the itinerant tried to leave, but suddenly found himself surrounded by "hundreds and hundreds of papists," who began stoning him. Whitefield recorded the attack: "Every step I took, a fresh stone struck, and made me reel backwards and forwards, till I was almost breathless, and all over a gore of blood." Only a thick beaver hat he wore saved him from suffering fatal head wounds. He narrowly escaped into a nearby minister's house, where he waited until a Methodist colleague arrived with a coach. They sped away through the screaming throng of "Dublin rabble." Whitefield reckoned that they had tried to kill him not for speaking against Catholicism specifically, but "for exciting all ranks to be faithful to King Jesus, and to our dear sovereign King George."[12]

In spite of this harrowing experience, Whitefield continued making military and imperial topics staples of his preaching, far more so than earlier in his career. When he visited Scotland in August 1758, he delivered three thanksgiving sermons marking British and Prussian victories, including another victorious siege of Louisbourg in Nova Scotia, which the British had returned to France in 1748. The *Glasgow Courant* commended Whitefield's preaching on behalf of the "Protestant interest," which made the itinerant's visit "useful to the community in a civil, as well as a religious, light."[13]

Whitefield began announcing days of thanksgiving related to the Seven Years' War even before official royal pronouncements were made. This practice annoyed one Anglican critic, who scoffed that "being without law, [Whitefield] did not think it decency to wait till his Majesty appointed the day of thanksgiving." But Whitefield ignored such strictures. One of the most joyous occasions came on October 20, 1759, when Whitefield celebrated the news of the "late remarkable conquest" of the walled citadel of Quebec by the British general James Wolfe, which was the decisive British victory in the North American conflict. The itinerant preached twice at the Tabernacle and once at Tottenham Court, and though his topic was as martial as spiritual, the results strongly resembled one of his older revival meetings. "Hundreds were filled as with new wine," he told a New England correspondent. "Surely God is a wonder working, prayer hearing, promise keeping God."[14]

Whitefield's preaching remained so popular that it warranted an expansion of the Tottenham Court Road chapel, which reopened at the beginning of February 1760. "A great concourse of people" attended, hearing Whitefield preach on Jabez's prayer from 1 Chronicles 4:10, "Oh that thou wouldest bless me indeed, and enlarge my coast." But the blessings at the Tabernacle continued to raise the ire—and satire—of the theater community, resulting in the most memorable caricature of Whitefield ever: Dr. Squintum.[15]

Dr. Squintum was a character mentioned in Samuel Foote's wildly popular play *The Minor*, which opened in London in 1760. Foote, an associate of Tate Wilkinson and other seminal figures in the London theater scene, had emerged as an influential writer and actor in the 1740s. He played Othello a number of times at the Haymarket Theater in London. But *The Minor* caused a major sensation, generating numerous pamphlets and prints, and went through many editions into the 1790s.[16]

Within the play, Foote explicitly likened Whitefield and other Methodists to "public performers" like himself: "Whether we exhibit at Tottenham Court, or the Haymarket, our purpose is the same." It was a provocative charge, suggesting that Whitefield was essentially a theatrical performer who was cutting in on actors' business. Squintum does not appear in the play, but is repeatedly referred to by a former prostitute and (supposed) convert, Mrs. Cole. She provocatively spoke of how Dr. Squintum: "[He] stepp'd in with his saving grace, got me with the new birth, and I became, as you see, regenerate, and another creature." And she reported that Dr. Squintum taught that a "woman's not worth saving, that won't be guilty of a swinging sin." The play ends with a mimic named Shift (played by a leering and winking Foote) realizing that he could have "a thriving traffic in my eye—Near the mad mansions of Moorfields I'll bawl." Whitefield, in Foote's rendering, was an opportunistic fraud.[17]

This mockery of Whitefield, and the play's prurient use of scripture, unleashed a pamphlet war driven by years of pent-up resentment toward, as well as fascination with, Whitefield. Famous people attract mockers, sometimes simply because of their prominence. Virtually everyone in British towns had heard of Whitefield, thus they understood jokes made at his expense. The Countess of Huntingdon tried and failed to have the play banned, which only made it more popular. Some attacks on Whitefield and his supporters were quite vicious, such as the poem *Friendly Advice, For Dr. Squintum:*

'Do nothing and be saved,' he cries,
His stupid audience close their eyes,
And groan in concert, to the lies,
Of canting Dr. Squintum.[18]

The Squintum-related publications came in numbers surpassed only by those occasioned by Whitefield's initial rise to fame in the late 1730s. One of Whitefield's supporters told him that because of *The Minor,* there was "hardly a grown up person in this land but will sooner or later give their opinion either for or against you." Some missives against the play were satirical; one falsely claimed Whitefield as its author. *Memoirs of the Life of a Modern Saint* (1761), a mock biography of Squintum, was a takeoff on Whitefield's journals. *The Methodist* (1761), a play trying to emulate *The Minor's* success, included Squintum as an actual character, as did *The Spiritual Minor* (1763).[19]

William Hogarth's engraving *Credulity, Superstition, and Fanaticism: A Medley* (1762) followed the Squintum firestorm (see figure 12.2). Hogarth, a fiercely anti-Methodist artist, used *Credulity, Superstition, and Fanaticism* to play on key themes within *The Minor,* especially the dangers of deception and sexual license. The woman lying in the lower left—with baby rabbits running out from under her skirts—may suggest Squintum's devotee Mrs. Cole, but

Hogarth primarily based her on the remarkable "Rabbit Woman," Mary Toft, who in 1726 claimed to have given birth to seventeen rabbits. In his works, Hogarth repeatedly depicted the Toft fraud—and the initial inclination of some to believe her—as a species of medical enthusiasm, often paired with religious frenzy. The maniacal preacher "St. Money-Trap," whose appearance is not strictly based on Whitefield, foments the crowd into sectarian madness as his wig falls back to reveal a Catholic clerical tonsure. Hogarth draped the pulpit with lines from a Whitefield hymn, "Only love to us be giv'n." A foregrounded thermometer indicates the fruits of Methodist frenzy, from convulsions and lust to madness and suicide.[20]

Whitefield's own response to *The Minor* was muted. "I am now mimicked and burlesqued upon the public stage," he wrote. "All hail such contempt!" Perhaps after nearly dying in Dublin, mockery in the theater was relatively easy to absorb. During the fall of 1760, while much of the controversy convulsed London, he was away preaching in northern England, although Elizabeth sent copies of all the "low trash" published against him. In any case, the itinerant could not entirely avoid the Squintum frenzy: on at least one occasion after he returned to London, two young men interrupted Whitefield at the Tabernacle, loudly singing a "burlesque song of Doctor Squintum."[21]

Experience told Whitefield that controversy, however galling, was good publicity, and publicity brought attention to the gospel. A correspondent from Newcastle, in far northern England, informed Whitefield in September 1760 that Foote's "vile play" had been performed there, but God was using it for good. "I believe many would come to hear you now who never did before," the correspondent noted, because of the interest generated by *The Minor*. Several Newcastle gentlemen who previously had little interest in religion were "shocked at it." Maybe the play would become the means of opening people's eyes to the gospel, his friend suggested. He received similar reports of heightened interest from London.[22]

By late 1760, Whitefield had returned to London, but with a cold so besetting that by the spring of 1761 he was gravely ill. Indeed, another erroneous report announced that Whitefield was dead, leading an anonymous poet to quickly print an elegy. The elegy was a bit exuberant about the extent of his influence, claiming, "He went through Europe, and through Asia, / Thro' Afric also, and America. / 'Mongst Turks, and Papists, Mahomets, and Jews, / Pagans, and Heathens, he did preach glad news." Soon realizing their mistake, the newspapers noted that the itinerant was "dangerously ill, but not dead." (There was also a false report of Elizabeth Whitefield's death in early 1762.) The false death notice reached America, where it was printed in more newspapers than in England. One Philadelphia correspondent told Whitefield of her horror upon hearing the news of his demise, which made her go "cold all over." The illness kept him from preaching and traveling for much of the year, which frustrated him. He was "frequently tempted to wish the report of my death had been true, since my disorder keeps me from my old delightful work of preaching," he wrote.[23]

Whitefield's health improved enough that he was able to go to Holland briefly in the summer of 1762. Upon his return to Norwich, Whitefield gave a glowing account of the trip to his "dear old friend" Charles Wesley, telling him that the familiar "cloud of Divine Providence" had directed him across the North Sea. "Deep impressions were made by the word preached at Rotterdam among the English," he reported, although he lamented that he could not preach in Dutch. Nevertheless, he visited Dutch towns, including Amsterdam and Leyden, on his tour. Chiding Wesley, who had largely left off itinerating, Whitefield wondered what he would say to the offer of a sea voyage, perhaps to America? "Whilst you and yours lie at ease in London remember a poor pilgrim lying on a nasty stinking mat and bed and continually disturbed and bit by fleas at Norwich." No wonder Whitefield struggled to recover his health![24]

As his relationship with Charles grew sweeter, the itinerant and John Wesley continued to clash. Whitefield told Charles in March 1763 that John had written him "an angry letter without a cause" and that Whitefield thought it best not to reply. They remained on speaking terms, however; John visited Whitefield in Edinburgh in May, noting that "humanly speaking, [Whitefield] is worn out." While Whitefield was in America, John wrote him a friendly letter, and the itinerant responded in kind, wishing Wesley and all his preachers "much prosperity."[25]

In the late summer of 1762, Whitefield made his now-annual journey to Scotland, giving his departing sermon at Edinburgh on Aaron's blessing to the children of Israel in Numbers 6. The published text of the sermon, "taken in short-hand from his mouth," revealed that Whitefield had not muted his Calvinist convictions, though perhaps he emphasized them more before a friendly Scottish audience. He challenged those "who talk so much of the power of their free will": "A free will of one kind to be sure you all have. But a free will to what? To everything that is wrong." His old cadences and emotional phrases remained, but Whitefield also used his frailty, and Edinburgh's familiarity with him, as part of his rhetoric. He had been visiting the city for so long that some of the young adults he spoke with had not been born when he first toured Scotland. He and the other faithful Scottish preachers had told them often of the grace of Christ, he reminded the people. But still they were not heeded: "Alas! what a monstrous heap of gospel sermons will lie at some people's doors! This makes my heart bleed oftentimes when I come out of my chamber, not knowing but the sermon I would be glad to die in preaching, may rise up in judgment against some souls, for whose salvation I would be willing to spend every drop of my blood." Having spent himself for them, he pleaded with the people of Edinburgh not to refuse Christ in the end.[26]

Whitefield's growing moderation had not fundamentally changed his doctrine or his undergirding emphasis on the Holy Spirit. One of his most popular pamphlets written in the 1760s, published in London, Edinburgh, Boston, and Philadelphia, was *Observations on Some Fatal Mistakes, In a Book Lately Published, and Entitled, The Doctrine of Grace*. Responding to an angry anti-Methodist work by the bishop of Gloucester, William Warburton, the itinerant argued that in Warburton's effort to combat enthusiasm, he neglected the Spirit's role in the church and in believers' lives: "The Holy Ghost, like its almighty purchaser, is the same today as he was yesterday; [and] he is now, as well as formerly, in the use of all instituted means, appointed to convince the world of sin, of righteousness, and judgment" (John 16:8). Warburton ridiculed those vital operations of the Spirit instead of vindicating them. If it was fanaticism to pursue the "supernatural influences of the Blessed Spirit," then Whitefield hoped true believers would become more fanatical every day. "To be filled with the Holy Ghost," Whitefield averred several years later, "this is the grand point."[27]

Whitefield returned to Scotland in the spring of 1763, with a long-awaited twist to his itinerary: he would return to America from the north of Britain. The denouement of the Seven Years' War had come in 1762 as the British captured Havana, Cuba (and its £3 million in silver bullion), from Spain, and the Prussians scored their last major triumph at the Battle of Freiberg. (The peace treaties officially ending the war were signed in 1763.) Whitefield immediately realized that in spite of his faltering health, these favorable developments would open the door for another Atlantic crossing. Although most contemporaries regarded sea travel as fraught with danger, Whitefield still found it restorative. After all, his doctors had told him for years that he needed an extended break from preaching. An ocean voyage would do the trick, and he departed from Greenock, west of Glasgow, in June 1763 and headed for Virginia. "Jesus hath made the ship a Bethel," he wrote a week into the trip, "and I enjoyed that quietness which I have in vain sought after for some years on shore." The twelve-week journey did tax his health, but in August his ship cast anchor at the Virginia shore.[28]

Whitefield's return received wide press coverage, perhaps because of the long break since his previous visit. As he traveled north to Philadelphia, reports emphasized his poor health. Newspapers in Boston, New York, Portsmouth, and Newport printed an excerpt of his letter to a Boston friend, in which Whitefield confessed that the "voyage and journey have quite shattered me." Proceeding gingerly, in November he traveled to New York via Princeton. The College of New Jersey had suffered traumatic blows with the deaths of Jonathan Edwards and Samuel Davies, who had succeeded Edwards as president in 1759, four years after his fund-raising trip to England. When Davies died in 1761, the evangelical Presbyterian pastor Samuel Finley became the college's fifth president. In spite of the school's recent turmoil, Whitefield regarded Finley's Princeton as a "blessed nursery; one of the purest perhaps in the universe." He would preach at Princeton's commencement in the fall of 1764.[29]

In New York, Whitefield—with apparent spontaneity—preached at the city jail on Christ's words in Matthew 25, "Inasmuch as ye have done it unto one of these my brethren, ye have done it unto me." An admiring newspaper report noted that the itinerant promised to raise money to provide for the prisoners, and that he gave "out of his purse" to help imprisoned debtors buy wood for the winter, even bailing out some who were locked up for small debts. "What a pity," the report lamented, "that such a God-like man's constitution is almost worn out by apostolic labors!"[30]

Impromptu charitable work had become a hallmark of Whitefield's ministry in recent years; for instance, he raised money to assist Boston when the town suffered a devastating fire in 1760. During his New York visit, he raised £120 for the Congregationalist minister Eleazar Wheelock's Connecticut charity school for Native Americans (which would relocate to New Hampshire in 1770 and become Dartmouth College), promising Wheelock that he would also write to British benefactors on the school's behalf. Likewise, he helped Harvard—where the faculty had long disliked Whitefield—rebuild its library holdings after a recent fire. Here he had additional motives: he asked supporters to give "puritanical books" to replace Harvard's charred volumes of more dubious theology. Charitable acts not only fit the original Methodist mission, but also helped mute criticism that Whitefield was selfishly motivated. Raising money for projects other than Bethesda also deflected questions about how he spent money for the rural orphanage.[31]

Indeed, public criticism of Whitefield was almost entirely absent during this visit, in spite of the frequent newspaper pieces on his travels. One pamphlet, *Methodism Anatomized; or, An Alarm to Pennsylvania*, raised old fears of fanaticism and deception when he visited Philadelphia. "Beware! ye men of Pennsylvania! shun false doctrine, and false preachers;—the Arch-Deceiver is among you!" the Anglican partisan trumpeted. The writer scoffed at how the Methodists encouraged untutored men (and even women) to exhort and become ranting preachers themselves, their only qualification being "incoherent phrases, sham-crying, and distortion of phiz, with bawling out, 'The Lord Jesus Christ!' ten times in a sentence." ("Phiz," short for "physiognomy," meant one's facial expression.) Such fusillades against him had become rare and seemed somewhat out of date, given Whitefield's moderate turn.[32]

Whitefield and Benjamin Franklin exchanged letters, with Whitefield again imploring Franklin to accept evangelical faith. Replying with unusually serious sentiments, Franklin thanked Whitefield for his prayers. The printer expressed confidence that God loved him, adding, "And if he loves me, can I doubt that he will go on to take care of me not only here but hereafter? This to some may seem presumption; to me it appears the best grounded hope."[33]

The itinerant traveled to his beloved New England in February 1764, preaching on Long Island as he went. "A sweet influence hath attended the word at Easthampton," he noted. Samuel Buell, the pastor at Easthampton, stood at the threshold of the most intense season of revival seen in the region since the 1740s. It began a month after Whitefield's visit. Yet Buell, who had served as a young itinerant during the earlier revivals, failed to note Whitefield's presence in his published account of the revival. Similarly, John Cleaveland of Ipswich, Massachusetts, oversaw a major revival in his church that subsequently spread across northeastern Massachusetts. After visiting Ipswich, Whitefield told Eleazar Wheelock that "there is really a great awakening in those parts." But Cleaveland did not mention Whitefield's appearance in Ipswich in his narrative of the awakening, either. Younger American revivalists seemed to welcome Whitefield, but may have regarded him as a bit passé.[34]

Whitefield made a northern swing into New Hampshire, where he engaged in the most intriguing conversation of this American visit. He preached before thousands at the Portsmouth meetinghouses of Samuel Haven and Samuel Langdon, but before he left, the three met privately, and Whitefield told them a secret: "My heart bleeds for America. O poor New England! There is a deep laid plot against both your civil and religious liberties, and they will be lost. Your golden days are at an end. You have nothing but trouble before you. My information comes from the best authority in Great Britain. I was allowed to speak of the affair in general, but enjoined not to mention particulars. Your liberties will be lost." Three days later, across the sea, Parliament passed the Sugar Act, the first major new revenue act following the Seven Years' War. By August, leading Bostonians, led by Samuel Adams and James Otis, had begun to call for a boycott of British luxury goods.[35]

This was a remarkable moment in Whitefield's development as a political figure, and it places him as one of the earliest heralds of the Revolutionary crisis. However, the account of this conversation is historically questionable, since it comes from William Gordon's four-volume *The History of the Rise, Progress, and Establishment, of the Independence of the United States of America,* which was not published until 1788, twenty-four years after the reported exchange. Gordon was a Dissenting minister who moved to America in 1770, during the buildup to the Revolution. He became a Congregationalist pastor in Roxbury, Massachusetts, and for a time served as chaplain to the Massachusetts provincial congress. He went back to England in 1786, and completed his history two years later. For Gordon, the Whitefield anecdote represented a key turning point in the friendly relationship between Crown and colonists in the early 1760s, and the bitter feud that began to emerge in late 1764. Gordon said he got the information "in conversation" with Samuel Langdon, so we can probably assume that what Gordon reported was, at a minimum, not a direct quotation from Whitefield. How accurate it was beyond that is difficult to say.[36]

Whitefield likely had caught wind of British plans to raise new revenue from the colonists. He also realized that some in the Anglican hierarchy were thinking of introducing an American bishop. Ironically, Whitefield's own name had come up as a bishop candidate as early as the mid-1740s. Some of Whitefield's influential patrons, including those affiliated with Frederick, Prince of Wales, and the Countess of Huntingdon, entertained thoughts of having Whitefield made a bishop, but Frederick's untimely death in 1751 hampered that prospect. Still, American and British newspapers reported in 1765 that if one or more American bishops were appointed, Whitefield would certainly be one of them. Fear over the imposition of a bishop, and a concomitant loss of religious liberty, was one of the most provocative religious controversies of the Revolutionary crisis. However, we should not exaggerate the colonists' preparedness for revolution in 1764. The newspapers' repeatedly printed June article on Whitefield's farewell sermon in Boston opened with reports of Bostonians celebrating King George III's twenty-sixth birthday, which was observed with fireworks and "demonstrations of loyalty and joy."[37]

Leaving Boston to universal acclaim for his still-powerful preaching and emphasis on the "common cause of Christianity," Whitefield began another overland trek to Georgia. For a man in poor health, it was a remarkable (and perhaps foolish) journey to take. But Whitefield would have it no other way: "This pilgrimage kind of life, is the very joy of my heart," he wrote. Reports circulated that he intended to visit Bermuda again, or Spanish Florida, or even English settlements on the Mosquito Shore of Nicaragua, where Anglicans maintained a mission. But he traveled slowly, lingering in Philadelphia, then traversing the South to Charleston during November 1764. James Reed, an Anglican minister of New Bern, North Carolina, noted that the "surprising minister" was struggling with "an asthma, though fat and looks well." Whitefield "kept quite clear of enthusiastic rant and within the bounds of decency" until the end of his New Bern sermon, when he "got to raving," spoiling the sermon for many polite Anglicans. Nevertheless, Reed thought his visit helpful because he spoke against Separate Baptists, who had emerged from the revivals in New England and had begun to take root at Sandy Creek, North Carolina, in the mid-1750s. At New Bern, Whitefield "condemned the rebaptizing of adults" and endorsed infant baptism, in accord with the traditional practices of the Church of England.[38]

Whitefield was not altogether unhappy with the South's radical evangelicals, however. As he passed through eastern North Carolina, he happily noted meeting "what they call New-Lights almost every stage." Some of those itinerants received the sort of fearful response from critics that Whitefield himself had met with two decades earlier; one contemporary Anglican report described Virginia as a scene of "madness and enthusiasm": "The Methodists from the North come down upon us like a torrent." (Anglicans sometimes called the new evangelicals, including Baptists, by the catchall name "Methodists.") Whitefield, preparing to pass his fiftieth birthday, generated widespread interest and notice in the newspapers, but no longer elicited many charges of enthusiasm.[39]

The itinerant returned to Bethesda in December 1764. More than a year after Whitefield had last left the orphanage, the Lutheran pastor Johann Martin Boltzius wrote a detailed description of Bethesda, which was developing into a slave plantation as much as a school. About three miles away from the original orphanage, Whitefield established a "Negro farm," where around thirty slaves grew grain, beans, sweet potatoes, rice, and indigo. They also processed lumber into boards and shingles. Boltzius, who had criticized Whitefield's efforts to introduce slavery in Georgia, ruefully noted that the slaves' labors had not made enough money to keep up with the orphanage's expenses.[40]

The Bethesda students, according to Boltzius, were "healthy and merry," eating rice and grits and drinking a low-alcohol beer fermented from syrup, Indian corn, and hops. They raised some crops, too, but their attempts to make silk had produced few results. Students learned reading, writing, and arithmetic, and boys who seemed to be promising pastoral candidates studied Greek and Latin. All memorized the Westminster Catechism. "The Calvinist religion is the dominant religion in the orphanage," Boltzius said. Whitefield was pleased with what he found there. "Peace and plenty reign in Bethesda," he wrote. He sought to get as many of the residents placed in jobs as he could; by the time he left, there were as few as five orphan boys remaining there. Far fewer orphans remained than slaves. Indeed, newspapers reported that the orphan house had "ceased."[41]

The itinerant was planning another major transition for the orphanage. While in Georgia, he began the process of having a charter approved for a college at Bethesda that would educate white, black, and Native American children (presumably boys). But expanding Bethesda would also mean buying more slaves: he announced that he planned to spend substantial funds "in purchasing a large number of negroes for the further cultivation of the present orphan-house and other additional lands, and for the future support of a worthy able president, professors and tutors." The proposal easily won the approval of the Georgia governor and houses of assembly (his ally James Habersham was the president of the upper house). Whitefield worked for three more years on the charter, but Thomas Secker (the archbishop of Canterbury) and the king's council finally derailed the proposal. Whitefield envisioned the college as evangelical and interdenominational rather than distinctly Anglican, which was contrary to the wishes of the British authorities. Whitefield had his drawn-out correspondence with the archbishop of Canterbury published widely, including in the colonies, where the misunderstanding further soured colonists' views of the Anglican hierarchy as the crisis with Britain began to unfold. In the meantime, Whitefield made another accounting of Bethesda's finances, which showed that the itinerant had not profited personally from funds raised, and had in fact spent more than £2,000 of his own money on the orphanage. These occasional reports did not entirely defuse the old charges of financial impropriety, of course. One burlesque performance from 1765, calling Whitefield the "bell-weather of the flock," mocked that "with one eye he looks up to heaven . . . that's his spiritual eye; and with the other he looks down to see what he can get; and that's his carnal eye."[42]

Even if Whitefield had lost some of his novelty, many who attended his preaching for the first time were thrilled to see him. This was the experience in February 1765 of the memoirist Olaudah Equiano, a twenty-year-old slave who belonged to a Quaker on the small Caribbean island of Montserrat. His master encouraged Equiano to purchase his own freedom, which he would do the next year before going on to become one of the most compelling antislavery writers in England. Equiano was visiting Savannah on his master's business (he remembered the episode as happening in Philadelphia, but it seems clear that he was confused about the location). He "came to a church crowded with people; the church-yard was full likewise, and a number of people were even mounted on ladders, looking in at the windows." Equiano had never seen anything like the scene before, and he asked what accounted for it. Someone told him that the great itinerant Whitefield was there. "I had often heard of this gentleman," he recalled, "and had wished to see and hear him; but I had never before had an opportunity." Equiano pressed into the crowd and saw the "pious man exhorting the people with the greatest fervor and earnestness, and sweating as much as ever I did while in slavery on Montserrat beach." (Whitefield's sweaty preaching in clerical robes, and his frequent shedding of tears, account for his ever-present preaching handkerchief in portraits.) Equiano, who had never witnessed a minister so passionately engaged in speaking, assumed that this was why most other pastors spoke to relatively sparse crowds.[43]

In spite of his declining health, little evidence suggests that Whitefield lost his preaching vitality in his fifties. One of the best accounts of Whitefield's late-career preaching came from his assistant Cornelius Winter, who had experienced the new birth under Whitefield's ministry in 1760. Winter said that Whitefield would normally spend an hour or two in private prayer and reading before giving a sermon, and that he particularly depended upon study tools such as an annotated Bible published by the nonconformist minister Samuel Clarke, Alexander Cruden's concordance, and Matthew Henry's Bible commentary, which Whitefield called "unparalleled." Textual analysis confirms that Whitefield frequently employed Henry's commentary in composing his sermons. (Henry's and Cruden's books remain popular Bible study guides today.) All three writers stood outside the Anglican fold. Whitefield similarly continued to recommend the writings of evangelical Dissenters such as the Baptist John Bunyan, author of *The Pilgrim's Progress.* The itinerant wrote a preface to a new edition of Bunyan's works in 1767, praising Bunyan's "catholic spirit" and noting how the irenic author maintained fellowship with non-Baptist Christians. Whitefield's comfort with Dissenters emerged from alliances with them in Britain and, more importantly, in America. This interdenominational disposition damaged Whitefield's credibility among certain Anglicans, including the officials who rejected the proposal for Bethesda College because he would not make it exclusively Anglican.[44]

Beyond Whitefield's methods of preparation, Cornelius Winter emphasized the remarkable atmospherics of Whitefield's oratory: "It would be only by hearing him, and by beholding his attitude and his tears, that a person could well conceive of the effect . . . He had a most peculiar art of speaking personally to you, in a congregation of four thousand people." With a style polished by decades of practice, Whitefield almost never stumbled upon a word, and he exhibited deep emotion, often lifting his hands high, stamping his feet, and weeping. Critics saw the tears as stagecraft, but Winter thought this unfair. Sometimes he wept so bitterly that the audience wondered whether he could regain his composure, but he always did. Winter also noted the disturbing toll that preaching took on Whitefield in his later years; he routinely vomited "a vast discharge from the stomach, usually with a considerable quantity of blood," after stepping down from the pulpit.[45]

Given the state of Whitefield's health and his celebrity status, it is not surprising that he became crabbier and more inflexible in his later years, or at least Cornelius Winter thought he did. Although Winter loved Whitefield as his spiritual father, he felt that the itinerant did not always treat him or his servants reasonably: "He was very exact to the time appointed for his stated meals; a few minutes' delay would be considered a great fault. He was irritable, but soon appeased." Demanding that servants keep his house scrupulously tidy, he said he would not die in peace if he thought his gloves were laid out of place. He dined at a fashionably decorated table, but rarely enjoyed fancy foods. A loaf of bread and cheese were enough, but his favorite dish was cow's heel. "How surprised would the world be," the itinerant chuckled, "if they were to peep upon Doctor Squintum, and see a cow heel only upon his table."[46]

Satisfied with Bethesda's stability, Whitefield returned to New York, preaching along the way. He had already passed through Virginia when, on May 29, 1765, the twenty-nine-year-old Patrick Henry introduced resolves in the Virginia House of Burgesses against the Stamp Act, a new tax on printed goods, including newspapers, almanacs, and playing cards. In New York, plans had already begun for a colonies-wide meeting about the Stamp Act to transpire in October. By then, Whitefield had already returned to England, having crossed the Atlantic to pursue Bethesda's college charter. Following a quick four-week passage, he arrived safely in Plymouth in July 1765.[47]

News about resistance to the Stamp Act followed Whitefield across the ocean. James Habersham, a senior adviser in the Georgia government, opposed the tax in principle, but threats against royal officials tasked with collecting the tax troubled him. In a plaintive letter to Whitefield in January 1766, Habersham said that his hands shook as he considered "the madness of the people here." Agitators affiliated with the Sons of Liberty—leaders of the colonial resistance—had sent him a letter warning that they would tear down his home, should he attempt to enforce the Stamp Act. The frightened Habersham came to believe that the tumult of America's "giddy multitude" was more dangerous than British imperial policy.[48]

The itinerant was not so sure. On February 13, 1766, he attended Benjamin Franklin's testimony on the Stamp Act before the House of Commons, lending moral support to his longtime friend. Acting as an agent for the Pennsylvania Assembly, Franklin took questions from members of Parliament about the effect of the new taxes. "What was the temper of America towards Great-Britain before the year 1763?" they asked. "The best in the world," the printer replied. "They were governed by this country at the expense only of a little pen, ink and paper. They were led by a thread." But now, their temper was "much altered." They would never willingly submit to the Stamp Act, he warned. A month later, a frustrated Parliament repealed the act, but still asserted an unconditional right to tax the colonists. Whitefield wrote in his letter book, "Stamp Act repealed, Gloria Deo." A letter from "an eminent clergyman in London"—probably Whitefield—subsequently published in the *Pennsylvania Gazette*, assured readers that "Doctor Franklin spoke very heartily and judiciously, in his country's behalf."[49]

The erupting crisis between Britain and the colonies concerned Whitefield, but he remained occupied primarily with evangelistic and educational affairs. He never focused on America's controversy with Britain as he much as he did on the course of the Seven Years' War. The intra-Protestant, intra-British fracas in the colonies was a more delicate controversy for him to navigate than the great Catholic-Protestant clash of the 1750s and 1760s.

One of his first duties upon his return to England was dedicating the Countess of Huntingdon's new chapel at Bath, near Bristol. The countess had continued to recruit a network of evangelical Anglican ministers, and had begun to erect chapels at her residences throughout England, buildings that would effectively serve as churches exempt from Anglican oversight. One historian has characterized her construction of the chapels as "ecclesiastical subterfuge": she formally remained an Anglican but had functionally begun to separate (she would officially break with the Church of England two decades later). Whitefield wept openly as he preached at the new chapel, which he described as "extremely plain, and yet equally grand." A grumpy Howell Harris, however, regarded the place as lavish and popish.[50]

Whitefield also met with John Wesley upon his return, their repaired relations still holding. Wesley thought that Whitefield looked terrible, like an "old, old man." Despite being a decade older than Whitefield, Wesley thought he was doing better physically. Indeed, Wesley reckoned that his health was as good as it was when he and Whitefield first met at Oxford, except for his having fewer teeth and more gray hair. Wesley had not forgotten their past disagreements, however, since he blamed Whitefield for making the first "breach among Methodists." But he could not help noting of Whitefield: "He breathes nothing but peace and love. Bigotry cannot stand before him, but hides its head whenever he comes." Their longtime rivalry seemed to be cooling at last. By late summer, the Countess of Huntingdon and Whitefield had engaged the Wesleys in a more formal union by which the Wesleys could preach in the countess's chapels. The "quadruple alliance," as Charles called it, would tenuously last through Whitefield's death.[51]

In 1767, Whitefield attended one of John Wesley's conference meetings. "Love and harmony reigned" there, wrote a pleased Wesley. He told a correspondent, "God has indeed effectually broken down the wall of partition which was between us. Thirty years ago we were one: then the sower of tares rent us asunder: but now a stronger [one] than him has made us one again." Even the chastened Howell Harris attended, signaling that Whitefield and his old Welsh ally had quietly reconciled.[52]

Before Whitefield left for England, reports had indicated that the itinerant would bring with him a "Black, which he has converted." This "Black" (a common term for Indians as well as African Americans) was a Mohegan, Samson Occom, the most influential Native American evangelical preacher of the eighteenth century. Whitefield had met Occom during his 1764 tour of New England. Although he did not actually accompany Whitefield, Occom arrived in England soon after the itinerant. For years, Whitefield had carried on a correspondence with Eleazar Wheelock about his plans for the Indian charity school, and about Occom, his star pupil. Wheelock and Whitefield routinely clashed about strategies for the school and Occom's chronically underfunded missions to the Indians, whom Wheelock called the "most savage and barbarous [people] of the human race." Whitefield suggested that it would be easier to raise money if Wheelock came to England, but Wheelock sent Occom and Nathaniel Whitaker, a Connecticut colleague, instead.[53]

In the weeks following Franklin's interrogation at Parliament, Whitefield was busy hosting Occom, who preached "with acceptance" before leading Londoners, including Lord Dartmouth (who would become one of Wheelock's key benefactors) and George III himself. Occom and Whitaker briefly stayed at the Whitefields' London home and subsequently at lodgings the itinerant furnished for them. Occom found the sights of the metropolis overwhelming, with people "cursing, swearing, and damning one another," he wrote in his journal. "Others was hollowing, wrestling, talking, giggling, and laughing, and coaches and footmen passing and repassing, crossing and cross-crossing, and the poor beggars praying, crying, and begging upon their knees." Whitefield showed them around the city, and even took them to the Houses of Parliament on the day of Franklin's testimony.[54]

Occom, accustomed to more negligent treatment by Wheelock, appreciated Whitefield's generous hospitality. "He is a tender father to us," Occom wrote, "he provides everything for us, he has got a house for us, the Lord reward him a thousand fold." Occom also noted that Whitefield's charity did not extend just to America, but to Londoners as well: the Whitefields' home was "surrounded with the poor, the blind, the lame, the halt and the maimed, the widow, and the fatherless." The itinerant had Occom speak at the Tabernacle, regarding him as a "settled humble Christian" who "behaves well." But Whitefield worried that the lengthy visit to England might "spoil him for the wilderness."[55]

Occom and Whitaker's trip to the British Isles, which lasted two and a half years, was wonderfully successful, raising more than £12,000 as Occom preached more than three hundred times. But when Occom returned to Connecticut in 1768, he found his wife and children neglected and nearly destitute. Soon Wheelock relocated the Indian academy to Hanover, New Hampshire, obtaining a charter for Dartmouth College in 1769. He also gave up on the Indian school concept and began catering exclusively to white students. By 1771, the embittered Occom permanently broke with Wheelock. Whitefield had reportedly forecast Wheelock's betrayal: just before Occom returned to America, the itinerant said, "You have been a fine tool to get money for them, but when you get home, they won't regard you, they'll set you adrift." Occom doubted Whitefield's prediction then, but he told Wheelock in 1771 that he was "ready to believe it now."[56]

As Whitefield observed his fifty-third birthday, his relations with many evangelicals—Wesleyan Methodists, the Countess of Huntingdon's quasi-independent Calvinist network, and British and American Dissenters—were better than ever. But with Anglican officials, like those who scuttled his plans for Bethesda College, feelings were growing ever sourer, especially because of a 1768 incident in which Oxford officials expelled six Methodist students. The students reminded Whitefield of the Holy Club members of the 1730s. Their removal led him to question Anglicans' commitment to the toleration of Dissenters and of evangelicals (like himself) who remained within the Anglican fold. Other Anglicans thought the students got what they deserved: when James Boswell told Samuel Johnson that the students were good people, Johnson replied, "I believe they might be good beings; but they were not fit to be in the University of Oxford. A cow is a very good animal in the field; but we turn her out of the garden."[57]

Whitefield disagreed, and in defense of the students, he argued that the fundamental difference between Methodists and the Anglican establishment lay in their views of the Holy Spirit. Oxford administrators became suspicious of the students' society meetings, which featured hymn singing and extemporaneous prayers, neither of which struck Whitefield as offenses warranting expulsion. He reminded the officials that Anglican ordination candidates had to respond affirmatively to the question "Do you trust that you are inwardly moved by the Holy Ghost?" But Whitefield thought that if Oxford was going to banish students for such pious crimes, then the proper question should be "Do ye trust that you are NOT inwardly moved by the Holy Ghost?" A supporter of Oxford's actions countered Whitefield's "enthusiastic rants," asserting that in the postapostolic age, the Spirit's movements in a believer's life were "secret and imperceptible." Only manifest fruits, including love, joy, and peace, were a reliable gauge of the Spirit's work.[58]

In denouncing the expulsions, Whitefield reminded his audience of the ongoing controversy over appointing an American bishop, a firestorm fueled by fears that Anglicans did not really respect religious liberty. The affair at Oxford would surely "increase the prejudices of our colonists . . . against the establishment of Episcopacy," Whitefield predicted. (Indeed, an edition of Whitefield's letter quickly appeared in Boston, stoking fears about a bishop there.) He simultaneously dismissed any notion that evangelical faith undermined political loyalty, asserting that "every additional proselyte to true Methodism, is an additional loyal subject to King George the Third."[59]

Writing from Scotland in summer 1768, Whitefield asked one of his London assistants to send "tender love to all, particularly to my dear wife," who was in failing health. Shortly after Whitefield's return to England, a "violent fever" seized Elizabeth, and she died. Their union of almost twenty-seven years had seen suffering and trials, and in retrospect it is difficult to judge the quality of it. The most famous (and unfair) comment on Whitefield's marriage came from the evangelical preacher John Berridge, who said that matrimony "might have spoiled John [Wesley] and George if a wise Master had not graciously sent them a brace of ferrets." Whatever the truth of this comment about John Wesley's wife, Mary Vazeille, it does not apply to Elizabeth Whitefield. If anything, Elizabeth seems to have patiently endured the demands of being married to the ever-rambling Whitefield. (Berridge, a bachelor, was widely regarded as rude and eccentric.)[60]

Weightier was the testimony of Cornelius Winter, who wrote of Whitefield: "He was not happy in his wife . . . He did not intentionally make his wife unhappy. He always preserved great decency and decorum in his conduct towards her. Her death set his mind much at liberty." Winter, as we have seen, harbored grievances toward Whitefield, but there seems little doubt that George and Elizabeth did not enjoy an affectionate marriage. Yet he depended upon her as one of his key ministry coordinators, often referring correspondents to her for more information about his plans or mentioning that she had sent him information on various subjects. The darkest episode they endured was the death of their infant son in 1744, and Elizabeth also suffered the indignity of being left behind in South Carolina in 1749. After that point, she for the most part stopped traveling with him, helping operate Whitefield's ministry from their home base in London.[61]

Others recognized the demands that his itinerant ministry put on Elizabeth. James Davenport wrote her in 1754 and asked, "Shall I now sympathize with you, under the frequent and sometimes long absence of your dear husband? Or shall I not rather? Or shall I not withal, congratulate you on his being about his Master's business, and his success therein." Whatever else we can say about their marriage, Whitefield depended on Elizabeth and certainly grieved the "unexpected breach" of losing her. Three months following her passing, he wrote to an associate, "I seem as if I were some other person than myself since I lost my dear wife." Four months after that, he said he was still daily feeling her absence, as if he had lost his "right hand."[62]

In 1769, Whitefield still met occasionally with John Wesley, and they reminisced about their days back in Oxford, "the former times and the manner wherein God prepared us for a work which it had not then entered into our hearts to conceive," Wesley wrote. Wesley called the itinerant his "old friend and fellow-laborer." Most of their animosity was now healed. When Wesley related the history of Methodism in his sermons, he would favorably include Whitefield.[63]

Whitefield had also begun making plans for a return to America, where he hoped to check on an expansion of Bethesda, which he had ordered in spite of the disappointment regarding the college charter. In late summer he held farewell services at the Tabernacle and the Tottenham Court chapel. At a "parting general sacrament" at the Tabernacle, there were almost two thousand communicants. Everyone knew that this could likely be the last time they would see the preacher.[64]

In his farewell sermon on August 30, 1769, Whitefield spoke on a favorite passage of Calvinists, John 10:27–28: "My sheep hear my voice, and I know them, and they follow me: And I give unto them eternal life; and they shall never perish, neither shall any man pluck them out of my hand." London printers secured a transcript of the sermon and published it so quickly that Whitefield got a copy before he left for America. He regarded the publication as shoddy, "injudiciously paragraphed," and "wretchedly unconnected." But such was an "unavoidable tax upon popularity," he figured: people had long profited from his celebrity. A departing sermon, which could be his last ever delivered in England, was sure to sell copies.[65]

While the transcriber claimed that the farewell sermon was taken down "verbatim," even the printers admitted that it was "impossible for the press to convey an idea of that pathetic [i.e., emotional], moving manner, which is peculiarly his own." Regardless of Whitefield's frustration with the printed version of the sermon, we can see in it typical themes that endured throughout his preaching career. Although Whitefield still identified explicitly as a Methodist, he insisted that ecclesiastical labels were ultimately meaningless. There were only two types of people: the saved and the unsaved, the sheep and the goats: "Christ does not say, are you an Independent, or Baptist, or Presbyterian? or are you a Church of England-man? nor did he ask, are you a Methodist? All these things are of our own silly invention." Moreover, salvation came to the sheep by God's sovereign choice in election, "by the Father in a covenant passed from eternity."[66]

At the end of the sermon, Whitefield grew nostalgic and emotional, confessing that saying good-bye to London was "the hardest part I have to act" but was nonetheless necessary: "This is the thirteenth time of my crossing the water, and I find it a little difficult at this time of life. But I am willing to go. I am clear as light in my call." Whitefield ended the sermon with a reverberating appeal to the unconverted. "Take care, take care, if you never was among Christ's sheep, may you be brought into the number now. Come, come, see what it is to have eternal life! Haste! Haste! Haste away to the great, the glorious shepherd! . . . 'Come! Come! Come! Come!' said the Lord Jesus, 'Nothing shall pluck you out of my hand!'"[67]

In late September, Whitefield, accompanied by Cornelius Winter, embarked for America. (Whitefield had recruited Winter to come to Bethesda "to teach the negroes the way of salvation.") After about eight weeks, the anxious and seasick Winter happily noted, "By the good hand of our God upon us, we set our feet upon the American shore." Whitefield stepped off the boat at the waterfront in Charleston, South Carolina. He had returned to America for the last time.[68]

CONCLUSION: "JESUS CHRIST HAS GOT THEE AT LAST": GEORGE WHITEFIELD'S LEGACY

John Marrant, a free African American apprentice and musician, was living in Charleston when he first encountered George Whitefield, who was in the city on his final visit to America. Like many others, Marrant came to Whitefield's meeting not as a religious seeker, but to see what was happening and perhaps to have some fun at the itinerant's expense. "Passing by a large meeting house I saw many lights in it, and crowds of people going in," Marrant recalled. A companion told him that "a crazy man was hallooing there." His rascally friend said he would go in with him, but only on the condition that Marrant interrupt the meeting by blowing his French horn. "I liked the proposal well enough," Marrant said, so they pushed through the doors into the crammed audience. Marrant was taking his horn off his shoulder just as Whitefield named his text. Looking directly at Marrant, the aged itinerant pointed at him and quoted Amos 4:12, *"Prepare to meet thy God, O Israel."* The Word came with such ferocious power that it knocked Marrant down, and he lay "speechless and senseless" for half an hour.[1]

When he came to, people were giving Marrant smelling salts and throwing water on his face. Whitefield continued preaching. "Every word I heard from the minister was like a parcel of swords thrust into me," Marrant said. "I thought I saw the devil on every side of me. I was constrained in the bitterness of my spirit to halloo out in the midst of the congregation." This disturbed other listeners, so people carried Marrant into the vestry, where Whitefield came to see him after the service. The itinerant said, "Jesus Christ has got thee at last." Marrant soon broke through to conversion, becoming one of the most remarkable evangelical preachers of the era. Fifteen years after his encounter with Whitefield, Marrant received ordination at the Countess of Huntingdon's Bath chapel, and then went to Nova Scotia to minister to African Americans there. Insufficient support from the countess forced him to leave Nova Scotia, however, and ultimately he returned to London, where he died in 1791, the same year that the countess did.[2]

Perhaps Marrant's retrospective account is stylized, but there can be no doubt that Whitefield's preaching remained powerful. His meetings, as Marrant suggested, still attracted standing-room-only crowds: at another sermon in Charleston, his supporters had to "hoist" Whitefield in at one of the church windows because he could not get in at the door. His novelty may have worn off for many who, unlike Marrant, had heard him preach before. His style had moderated, and his health had declined, but that singular preaching prowess remained.[3]

In 1769, Whitefield passed his fifty-fifth birthday in Savannah, whose merchant shippers and planters had achieved economic prosperity (which Whitefield had predicted) after Georgia embraced slavery. "The increase of this colony is almost incredible," he exulted. Savannah's trade in everything from deerskins to rice had vastly expanded in the past fifteen years. Whitefield's old friend James Habersham frankly admitted, "I am loaded with business." The town boasted a population of about 2,000 people, about 1,200 whites and 800 blacks.[4]

In January 1770, Whitefield hosted Savannah's leading politicians and merchants for a service dedicating newly built wings of the orphanage, which he hoped would become the base of a new academy, even if not a college. In Oxford-like pomp, Whitefield wore his "university square cap" and processed with orphans, faculty members, and slaves to a reception with delicacies including "cold tongue, ham, tea, etc." Whitefield preached for forty-five minutes on Zechariah 4:9–10, "The hands of Zerubbabel have laid the foundation of this house," reflecting on thirty years of the orphanage's history. Bethesda's success was improbable, he mused, the isolated property standing in a "pine barren, and in a colony where the use of negroes was totally denied"—and widely expected: "All beholders looked daily for its decline and annihilation." But now, by the blessing of God, the orphanage and academy stood on a strong foundation. "The whole auditory seemed to be deeply affected," an observer wrote, "and his own heart seemed too big to speak, and unable to give itself proper vent." Following lunch, guests exchanged toasts. When James Wright, the royal Georgia governor, toasted George III, Whitefield added, "Let all the people say, amen," which elicited a hearty response across the room. By the eve of the Revolution, Whitefield had become America's spiritual founding father, but Bethesda was no patriot hotbed.[5]

The number of orphans in residence remained small in 1770: fifteen boys and only one girl. By contrast, there were seventy-five slaves at Bethesda's properties. Whitefield left extensive regulations for the white students, giving detailed guidance on their liturgical practices and topics of study. They were to translate the Thirty-Nine Articles into Latin, learn the history of ancient Greece and Rome, as well as of England and Georgia, and study evangelical standards such as Matthew Henry's Bible commentary, Philip Doddridge's *Rise and Progress of Religion in the Soul*, and the works of John Bunyan and John Owen. The itinerant provided cash prizes to be given for the best student lectures delivered on occasions such as Christmas, Easter, Whitefield's birthday, and November 5 (Guy Fawkes Day), when students would speak on "the Glorious Revolution, and the infinite mercy of God, in delivering Great Britain from Popish Tyranny and arbitrary power." Black boys, he briefly noted, were "to be baptized and taught to read," whereas black girls were "to be taught to work with the needle."[6]

Whitefield left Savannah in April and sailed for Philadelphia, spending the late spring and summer preaching throughout Pennsylvania, New Jersey, and New York. He said he felt better than he had in years, exclaiming that "a new scene of usefulness is opening in various parts of this new world!" In August he went to Boston, a town still unsettled by the "massacre" of five civilians in March 1770. British redcoats had opened fire on a crowd that had been taunting the soldiers and pelting them with snowballs. The patriot leader John Adams would successfully defend the soldiers in court three months after Whitefield's arrival. Shortly after the massacre, the British administration repealed most of the Townshend Duties, which had provoked this phase of colonial resistance. For about two years, the repeal defused much of Boston's patriot agitation, but the crisis boiled over again in 1773 with the passage of the Tea Act and the subsequent Boston Tea Party. Although Whitefield had only cautiously displayed his favor for the patriots, he expressed great sympathy for the colonists to an English correspondent, "Poor New England is much to be pitied; Boston people most of all. How falsely misrepresented!"[7]

Those lines appeared in one of the last letters the itinerant wrote. He had spoken of his declining health and of death for most of his adult life, and in this letter, written a week before his passing, he again predicted that his "day of release" would shortly come. His condition in precipitous decline, he missed an engagement at the Old South Church in Boston on September 21, leaving the assembled thousands disappointed. Regardless, he set out north of Boston, going as far as York, Maine. Returning to Newburyport, Massachusetts, on September 29, he stayed at the home of his ally, the Reverend Jonathan Parsons. Feeling ill, Whitefield retired early, but woke in the middle of the night complaining of an asthma attack. He was still well enough to talk and pray about his travel plans, debating "whether he should winter at Boston, or hasten to the southward."[8]

He slept a bit more, but then woke again with a tight chest, hardly able to catch his breath. Finally, he stopped breathing altogether, and despite the doctor's attempts to revive him, Whitefield died at six o'clock in the morning on September 30. Although offers to bury him immediately came from Portsmouth, New Hampshire, and from Boston's Old South Church, Parsons quickly arranged for Whitefield's interment in the vault of the Newburyport Presbyterian Church. (A delegation came from Boston to retrieve the body, but in a tense scene, "the people at Newbury-port would not allow the corpse to be brought away," Boston newspapers reported.)[9]

Whitefield's old friend Daniel Rogers of Ipswich, who had experienced salvation while traveling with Whitefield's entourage almost exactly thirty years earlier, prayed at the funeral. He said that "he owed his conversion to the labors of that dear man of God, whose precious remains now lay before them." Then Rogers began weeping and crying, "O my father, my father!" The congregation melted into tears.[10]

Word spread quickly through the colonies and Britain of the itinerant's passing. Cornelius Winter, who had remained at Bethesda while Whitefield went north, wrote, "You have no conception of the effect of Mr. Whitefield's death upon the inhabitants of the province of Georgia," noting that "all the black cloth in the stores was bought" to drape the churches for mourning. The news reached London on Guy Fawkes Day, and Whitefield's associates, acting on a previous agreement, asked John Wesley to give a funeral sermon at the Tottenham Court Road chapel. "An immense multitude" gathered there, Wesley wrote. "All were still as night."[11]

Given the occasion, one might have expected Wesley to give an admiring sermon about Whitefield's public ministry, and he did so, but Wesley also expressed gratitude for Whitefield as his friend. Indeed, Wesley identified Whitefield's generous friendship as "the distinguishing part of his character." Given the bitter lows their relationship had seen, this was a surprising and revealing assertion. Although Whitefield substantially contributed to his difficulties with the Wesleys, it is notable that he did not precipitate the first public split over Calvinism (John did), and that he remained committed to staying in contact with John and Charles over the years, even when misunderstandings kept buffeting their relationship. According to Methodist historian Gareth Lloyd, "the fact that their friendship managed to survive in the long term was due in large measure to Whitefield's willingness to forgive and forget." Wesley alluded to their past disagreements over "doctrines of a less essential nature," but said that he and Whitefield finally agreed on fundamental doctrines, which he summed up as "the new birth, and justification by faith." Whitefield's life—and now his death—reminded Wesley that Christians united by those essential beliefs should love one another and promote the common cause of the gospel.[12]

Charles Wesley likewise penned an elegy to Whitefield, recalling their first meeting at Oxford and how he walked with Whitefield through the itinerant's conversion ordeal until assurance of forgiveness came, by a work of the Holy Spirit.

> In the last extreme of hopeless grief,
> Jesus appear'd! and help'd his unbelief,
> Infus'd the faith which did his sins remove,
> Assur'd his heart of God's forgiving love,
> And fill'd with glorious joy, the joy of saints above.
>
> Who but the souls that savingly believe,
> The raptures of a faithful soul conceive?
> The joy unspeakable, the love unknown,
> The peace he felt is understood by none,
> By none but those who know their sins forgiven
> Thro' God the Holy Ghost come down from heaven.[13]

Other remembrances came from all over Britain and America, and none was more striking than that of Phillis Wheatley, a slave girl owned by an evangelical family in Boston, whose first published poem, appearing within two weeks of the itinerant's death, was an elegy to Whitefield (see figure 13.1). Wheatley would publicly criticize American slavery in a future editorial addressed to Samson Occom, but here she only praised Whitefield and his Savior.

> Thou didst, in strains of eloquence refin'd,
> Inflame the soul, and captivate the mind.
> Unhappy we, the setting sun deplore!
> Which once was splendid, but it shines no more.

Wheatley's Whitefield was unquestionably an American patriot:

When his AMERICANS were burden'd sore,
When streets were crimson'd with their guiltless gore!
Unrival'd friendship in his breast now strove:
The fruit thereof was charity and love.

Whitefield's Jesus succored both white and black Americans:

Ye thirsty, come to this life giving stream:
Ye preachers, take him for your joyful theme
Take him, "my dear Americans," he said,
Be your complaints in his kind bosom laid:

Take him ye Africans, he longs for you;
Impartial Savior, is his title due;
If you will choose to walk in grace's road,
You shall be sons, and kings, and priests to God.

A variant edition put that last line more pointedly: "He'll make you free, and kings, and priests to God." Wheatley's poem became a runaway success as broadside and booklet editions were sold in five American cities and in London.[14]

Writing from London, Benjamin Franklin said of his departed friend, "I knew him intimately upwards of 30 years: his integrity, disinterestedness, and indefatigable zeal in prosecuting every good work, I have never seen equaled, I shall never see exceeded." Whitefield worried about Franklin's salvation to the end, reminding him in a 1768 letter that "you and I shall soon go out of [the world]—Ere long we shall see it burnt—Angels shall summon us to attend on the funeral of time—And (oh transporting thought!) we shall see eternity rising out of its ashes. That you and I may be in the happy number of those who in the midst of the tremendous final blaze shall cry Amen—Hallelujah—is [my] hearty prayer."[15]

The work of remembering Whitefield began immediately, starting with the decision to bury him in Newburyport. The most significant publication immediately following Whitefield's death was the six-volume *Works of the Reverend George Whitefield*, which the itinerant had prepared with the Reverend John Gillies of Glasgow, a longtime correspondent who had already begun systematically preserving the history of the revivals in the 1750s. The *Works* remains the most comprehensive collection of Whitefield's letters, sermons, and tracts;

no complete scholarly edition of Whitefield's papers has yet appeared. Gillies meant for the documents to edify Christian readers rather than to establish a technically rigorous historical record. Unfortunately, he eliminated many names of letter writers and recipients, and he deleted phrases deemed embarrassing or of lesser interest. Many of the original manuscripts that Gillies worked from are now lost, so Whitefield scholars must largely rely on the *Works* in spite of its deficiencies. Accompanying Gillies's volumes was his *Memoirs of the Life of the Reverend George Whitefield*, an admiring biography compiled from the *Works* and other manuscripts in his possession.[16]

Pictures and engravings of Whitefield had been popular since the 1740s, and they remained popular after his passing. A collection of wax figures in New York City (a sort of precursor to Madame Tussauds) contained a life-size likeness of Whitefield. The proprietor of the museum, Patience Wright, took the image to London for display after the revivalist's death, along with statues of Benjamin Franklin and David Garrick. Wright's sister, also a wax artist, created an image of Whitefield that she donated to Bethesda. The likeness was "said to be so striking, that it astonishes all who have seen it."[17]

Just as there were visual representations of the itinerant, there were also postmortem political representations of him. Patriot leaders had begun casting Whitefield as an ally even before his death, even though Whitefield kept his sympathies for the colonists' cause fairly quiet and consistently affirmed that his followers should remain loyal to the king. (To be fair, exceedingly few Americans publicly supported independence or rejected George III until Tom Paine's *Common Sense* appeared in early 1776.) Still, publications such as Wheatley's elegy portrayed Whitefield as an advocate for America. One newspaper poem lamented that his devotees were "left behind to mourn the heavy loss, / Both to ourselves, and all AMERICA— / No Whitefield now with tears to plead our cause!" Another elegy envisioned the "bright Goddess" Freedom holding vigil around his tomb while "patriot torrents swirled around it" and New Englanders wept for their lost champion.[18]

Pastor Nathaniel Whitaker of Salem, Massachusetts, who would become one of the most militant patriot pastors in America, similarly eulogized Whitefield as a "patriot, not in show, but reality, and an enemy to tyranny." Whitefield opposed the imposition of an Anglican bishop in America and, more broadly, was "concerned for the liberties of America," Whitaker asserted. Most dramatically, Whitaker claimed that "under God it was in no small measure owing to him [Whitefield], that the Stamp Act, that first attack upon our liberties in these colonies, was repealed." Although Whitaker noted that Whitefield exerted influence on America's behalf during that time, he did not explain precisely how. Whitaker's testimony may indirectly corroborate Whitefield's 1764 conversations with northern New England pastors about the "deep laid plot" against America's liberties. It also suggests that Whitefield may have done more as an advocate for America than simply attending Franklin's parliamentary testimony against the Stamp Act and privately applauding the act's repeal. But exactly how much credit Whitefield deserved for opposing the Stamp Act remains a mystery.[19]

Perhaps these patriot claims on Whitefield were overstated, but they were hardly surprising. Whitefield was the best-known person to have traveled extensively in America. Overwhelmingly popular at his death, he had certainly left traces of his patriot sympathies after his turn toward politics, which began with the Louisbourg campaign and peaked during the Seven Years' War. American devotees may have simply assumed that Whitefield had strong patriot credentials: he was America's champion, and spiritual and temporal liberty were deeply connected. Upon the itinerant's death, the little-known poet Jane Dunlap produced a pamphlet of verses on Whitefield's sermons. (Among those she referenced was "Thy Maker is Thy Husband," which she held more dear because she had become a widow in the years since first hearing that sermon.) Dunlap's verses contained little overtly political content, mostly focusing on the itinerant's spiritual themes and the new birth: "Conversion's not an easy thing, / Though some may think it so; / From sovereign grace along it springs, / When God does it bestow," she wrote. Yet on the pamphlet's title page, below a drawing of Whitefield preaching above his casket, the publisher described Dunlap as a "Daughter of Liberty and Lover of Truth." No further political commentary was needed; poetry on Whitefield' sermons was appropriate for a true Daughter of Liberty.[20]

The most remarkable instance of Americans claiming Whitefield as a patriot came five years after the itinerant's death as Continental Army forces, led by the future turncoat Benedict Arnold, proceeded north on an expedition against Quebec in September 1775. They stopped at Newburyport on the Sabbath. After a sermon by their chaplain, Samuel Spring, Arnold and some of his officers went into the crypt and opened Whitefield's tomb. They found that the body had almost disintegrated (others who visited later reported that the body was almost perfectly preserved, however). The clothes remained, including his clerical collar and wristbands. These they took, cut into small pieces, and distributed among the men. The relics notwithstanding, the Quebec campaign went badly; perhaps this gave Spring and others pause about their "un-Protestant" act at the tomb.[21]

For evangelicals—and especially for Methodists—Whitefield's grave became a place of pilgrimage for thousands of admirers in the centuries after his death. The prominent Methodist itinerant Jesse Lee visited the tomb in 1790, and like Benedict Arnold, Lee opened the coffin, offering a clinical account of the body's condition: "They discovered his ears, hair, and a part of his nose had fallen off. His face was nearly in the common shape, though much contracted, and appeared quite destitute of moisture, and very hard. His teeth were white, and fast in their sockets. His breast bone had parted, and his bowels disrobed. His wig and clothes, in which he was buried, still remained; and were quite hard to tear. His flesh was black; and, as might be supposed, destitute of comeliness." Lee took "a small relic of the gown in which he was buried; and prayed that he might be endued with the same zeal which once inspired the breast of its wearer." Principled Protestants did not believe that spiritual power inhered in relics, yet just to be near the body, to gaze upon it, and perhaps to take a bit of the clothing inspired visitors like Lee. It gave them hope of acquiring some of Whitefield's passion and spirit.[22]

A surprising number of visitors to the tomb handled the remains of Whitefield's body, and, Hamlet-like, mused upon the itinerant's skull. A few, like Arnold's officers and Lee, went further and took bits of his clothing. Some even took pieces of the skeleton. In 1829, an English visitor bribed the sexton's son and stole Whitefield's right arm bone, mailing it to England. (The episode subsequently "caused the remains to be guarded with the strictest vigilance.") But in 1849, a guilty English correspondent, having come into possession of the bone, mailed it back to the Presbyterian pastor at Newburyport, who put Whitefield's arm back where it belonged. By the 1920s, Harvard Medical School had come into possession of a bone that was supposedly one of Whitefield's ribs. Similarly, in the Methodist Archives at Drew University there is a finger bone that may be Whitefield's, but no one seems to know how it came into the donor's possession. In 1933, the Newburyport church covered the tomb with slate tiles, making it much more difficult to purloin relics. Pilgrims today continue to visit the tomb by the hundreds every year. More visitors come now than a half century ago, longtime Newburyport church members say.[23]

Whitefield's death also produced religious collectibles and popular art, such as coins minted to commemorate him. Most depicted Whitefield in his wig and clerical gown on the front, but they had a variety of inscriptions and images on the back, including one with a cherub sitting next to a skull on top of an urn. Another was inscribed to the memory of Whitefield, "Who, with unreluctant grandeur, gave, not yielded up, his soul sublime, at Newbury P., N. America S.

30 1770, in the 56 year of his age, his conduct is a legacy for all." Another from London recalled Wesley's funeral sermon, and the text of that sermon from the Book of Numbers (see figure 13.2).[24]

Some continued to produce portraits and busts of Whitefield for sale well into the nineteenth century. One artist advertised to the "nobility, gentry, and others" in 1774 that he produced miniature portraits for bracelets, and particularly noted that "a fine miniature of the late Rev. Mr. Whitefield [is] to be disposed of." The prominent Staffordshire potter and Methodist Enoch Wood produced many busts of both John Wesley and George Whitefield in the first half of the nineteenth century. These busts' frequent presence in American and British art collections and at auctions testifies to their popularity (see figure 13.3).[25]

Whitefield's memory was a fixture of nineteenth-century evangelical culture, but journalistic and literary voices increasingly regarded him as an intellectually lackluster figure. An 1877 article from the *London Quarterly Review*, which the *New York Times* reprinted, asked "what was the secret of Whitefield's success?" The publication of the two-volume Whitefield biography by the English Methodist minister Luke Tyerman prompted the question. The review offered no definitive key to Whitefield's achievements, aside from his obvious preaching talent. Regarding Whitefield's publications, the writer sniffed, "We must agree with the opinion pretty generally passed on them by critics, and endorsed by the oblivion into which they have sunk, that they add nothing to the reputation of their author." Some thought that it would have been better if these publications had not survived, but in that case, the reviewer reckoned that Whitefield's devotees would have credited him with a "majestic intellect" that he clearly had not possessed.[26]

Even within evangelical and Methodist circles, Whitefield had fallen into relative obscurity by the time of his two-hundredth birthday, in 1914, just after the start of World War I. In London, a celebration of his birth held on Kennington Common saw only "small" attendance because of bad weather. One pastor recalled Whitefield's "magical power of speech" and David Garrick's story of Whitefield's command of the word "Mesopotamia." Others commended Whitefield's flexibility and open-air preaching. One noted that "with war in the air, people were thinking more deeply of spiritual things than in more peaceful times," and that like Whitefield, pastors should seize the opportunity. In America, the bicentennial generated relatively little comment. The *El Paso Herald* printed an editorial on the occasion, focusing on Whitefield's eloquence. "His sermons when printed out are meager and scanty. It was the man and his belief, soaring away into the infinite, that lifted people out of themselves," the writer noted.[27]

Although evidence is fleeting, a number of churches must have mentioned Whitefield's birthday during Sunday services on December 13, 1914. America's Federal Council of Churches recommended that member churches do so on that day. The pastor of Washington D.C.'s New York Avenue Presbyterian Church devoted his Sunday sermon to the evangelist, although the newspaper notice spelled his name "Whitfield" and explained that it was the "second anniversary" of his death. In Lordsburg, New Mexico, W. S. Huggett, the "Preacher in Charge" at the Lordsburg Methodist Church, put an ad in the paper for a Sunday-evening sermon titled "Bicentenary of George Whitfield [sic]: The Greatest Preacher of the Eighteenth Century." The *Kingston Gleaner* of Jamaica noted that Kingston's East Queen Street Baptist Church would observe the Whitefield bicentennial. East Queen Street was a congregation whose ministry dated back to the 1780s and the preaching of George Liele, a freed slave who had started a Baptist congregation in Savannah too five years after Whitefield's death.[28]

Perhaps the most enduring commemoration of the Whitefield bicentennial came at Franklin's University of Pennsylvania, where in 1914 the provost addressed students about the largely forgotten evangelist. Conversations began about erecting a statue to Whitefield, to complement the recently unveiled "Young Franklin" statue on campus. When Penn dedicated the Whitefield statue five years later, the provost gave special thanks to Penn's Methodist alumni and donors "for this reminder of the one who never failed to tell Dr. Franklin that his educational plan wanted *aliquid Christi* to make it as useful as was desirable." A choir performed a hymn titled "For Famous Men," which includes the lines: "For Whitefield, burning flame of God, / With golden tongue and vision clear, / Whose tender heart and charity / Inspired our first beginnings here." The statue remains a central feature on Penn's campus, though one wonders what current students might know about Franklin's preacher friend. A 2013 *Penn Current* article about the statue explained that "as Methodism was beginning, [Whitefield] held revivals in Philadelphia to introduce the Protestant denomination to America."[29]

In 1938, the two-hundredth anniversary of Whitefield's first arrival in America got more media attention than the bicentenary of his birth, primarily because of a remarkable joint commemoration by Princeton president Harold Dodds and former British prime minister David Lloyd George. Lloyd George had long cited Whitefield and Wesley as exemplars of the deep historical ties between Britain and America, ties that morally obligated America to assist Britain in times of need. In October 1922, Lloyd George had spoken at the Moorfields Tabernacle, commending Whitefield as "the greatest popular orator produced by the English race." No man did more for Anglo-American relations than Whitefield, claimed Lloyd George, and because of Whitefield, Wesley, and the Puritan fathers, "the moral training of America . . . is identical with ours." Lloyd George acknowledged Britain's heavy debt to America because of World War I, but those millions of dollars were "nothing to the debt which America owes" Britain, he told a cheering audience. In his view, the ledger showed the two parties even: "I should like to write the balance sheet: Debit, one thousand millions; credit, John Wesley and George Whitefield." Unlike patriot advocates of the eighteenth century, the former prime minister employed Whitefield in the cause of Anglo-American unity, remarkably claiming that "Whitefield and Wesley brought America into" World War I: "Their preaching moved America to come to our aid." He thought their moral legacy would bring the United States into the League of Nations too. Sixteen years later, Lloyd George and Dodds, hoping to rekindle Anglo-American unity in the face of a renewed German threat, held a joint broadcast. Dodds lauded Whitefield's commitment to Christianity and education, as illustrated by his early assistance to Princeton. These values would help defeat the greatest "heresies of the day," Dodds proclaimed, including communism and Nazism, or "the gospel that economic materialism dictates man's highest aspirations, and the pagan religion which commands us to worship the might and blood of the race."[30]

The most common way to capture the memory of someone like Whitefield, of course, is through writing history and biography. The scholarly and Christian pastoral study of Whitefield did not starkly diverge until the 1970s, with the publication of Arnold Dallimore's thoroughly researched and openly Christian biography. Academics who mentioned it at all (outside footnote references) tended to dismiss Dallimore's work. The Yale historian Jon Butler, writing before the release of his colleague Harry Stout's 1991 biography, said that a new treatment of Whitefield was needed and that Dallimore's was not it. The book was "thoroughly out of touch with modern scholarship and very much too long," according to Butler. In his biography, Stout spoke of Tyerman and Dallimore as "filiopietistic biographers" who portrayed Whitefield as a "time-less man," but he nonetheless commended their works as "indispensable" resources for research on the itinerant. Dallimore, for his part, excoriated Stout's biography as "false" and "painfully garbled." The prominent evangelical pastor John Piper similarly described Stout's book as "the most sustained piece of historical cynicism I have ever read."[31]

The tension between academic and confessional Christian approaches to Whitefield reflected some reawakening of interest in the itinerant, especially in Christian and conservative political circles. As of this writing, there are seven Twitter accounts representing Whitefield (not all actively tweeting, however). Jonathan Edwards has twelve. Two Facebook "Public Figure" accounts represent Whitefield, with thousands of followers each. As some readers may recall, I appeared, along with the Whitefield scholar Jerome Mahaffey, on an hour-long episode of Glenn Beck's Fox News television program in 2010 to discuss Whitefield, as part of Beck's "Founders' Friday" series. These cultural indicators all seem to point to an interest in Whitefield, tied to Americans' broader fascination with their national founding era and with American religious history and its political implications.[32]

With all these efforts to frame his image and legacy over the centuries since Whitefield's birth, what are we to make of him now? What was his significance? First, Whitefield was the most influential Anglo-American evangelical leader of the eighteenth century. His colleague and frequent rival John Wesley left a greater organizational legacy, and his ally Jonathan Edwards made a more significant theological contribution. But Whitefield was the key figure in the first generation of evangelical Christianity; of the three, he linked, by far, the most pastors and leaders through his relentless travels, preaching, publishing, and letter-writing networks. Without him, Anglo-American evangelicalism would have hardly represented a coherent movement. From his first remarkable meetings at Moorfields to his last tour of the colonies, he saw and met more people in Britain, Ireland, and America than any other person of the era. His labors, above any other factor, virtually invented a sense of common transatlantic evangelical identity.

He also indelibly marked the character of evangelical Christianity, even through the present day. Whitefield pioneered evangelicals' masterful use of media, the premium they place on preaching, and their devotion to the Bible and doctrine. He revolutionized the use of print media to promote his ministry and eagerly enlisted partners such as Benjamin Franklin in the effort. Some might think that because Whitefield cleverly used media, he was insincere about his message, but just the opposite was true. To him, the gospel message was so critically important that he felt compelled to use all earthly means to get the word out.

Likewise, Whitefield was the first internationally famous itinerant preacher and the first modern transatlantic celebrity of any kind. With apologies to the Beatles, George Whitefield was the first "British sensation." But again, his celebrity need not suggest vacuity or shallowness. His mastery of media combined with an innate rhetorical genius to make him a remarkably recognized figure. Sometimes people become famous because they are extremely good at what they do.[33]

Indeed, Whitefield's reputation for shallowness has been exaggerated for a long time, beginning with critics in his own lifetime and continuing with what became the conventional view of critics in the nineteenth and twentieth centuries. Many have commented that there was a substantial gap between his ostensibly dull, confused printed works—which one biographer called a "mingle-mangle"—and the evident power of his sermons as delivered. To the contrary, Whitefield's sermons and other writings generally reflected the fruit of his Oxford education and comprehensive knowledge of the King James Bible. He knew scripture so well that he often reflexively spoke in its idioms. His sermons also routinely alluded to ancient Greek and Roman history as well as to the history of the church, both Catholic and Protestant, and a wide range of Christian authors. He did not match the soaring brilliance of Jonathan Edwards, and has many companions in failing to do so. But Whitefield was not shallow, even for his time. Instead, he was a learned and theologically precise gospel preacher.[34]

Part of the evidence for his theological substance was the fact that he held closely to his doctrinal convictions throughout his career, often to the point of provoking schism. Denominational boundaries mattered little to him, but he marked out well-defined convictions on key points of Protestant theology. In particular, as a principled Calvinist, he had robust, practical theologies of conversion, the Lord's Supper, and the Holy Spirit's role in the believer's and the church's life. If he had not had strong views on these subjects, he could have saved himself the time and emotional energy spent on repeated fallouts with the Wesleys, Moravians, Anglican adversaries, Scottish seceders, and others. But he felt that he was defending the best of the Reformed theological tradition in taking his positions, so he would accept doctrinal conflict if necessary.

More problematically, Whitefield contributed to evangelical Christians' troubling record on race relations and ethnic inequality. Whitefield was one of the earliest Anglo-Americans to make serious efforts to reach African Americans like John Marrant with the gospel, yet he did not see all that his gospel required of him in the temporal realm, especially with regard to slavery. (In this failure, one could compare Whitefield to America's other Founders—Thomas Jefferson, Patrick Henry, James Madison, and others—who preached liberty and human equality but did not liberate their own slaves.) Whitefield not only agitated for the introduction of slavery, but also permitted the presence of slaves at Bethesda before they were legal. He did not even liberate Bethesda's slaves at his death. Instead, he deeded the "buildings, lands, Negroes, books, furniture," and all other possessions there to the Countess of Huntingdon, who, following Whitefield's intentions, increased the number of slaves at the orphanage, even acquiring one "woman-slave" they named Selina. The orphanage would continue to struggle—the expanded building was struck by lightning and burned in 1773. Georgia officials, convinced that the countess and her successors could not manage the property from afar, took custody of Bethesda not long after the countess died.[35]

Whitefield was criticized for many things during his lifetime, but slavery was not prominent among them. Perhaps if he had lived a generation later, or had come under more public attacks, he might have scrutinized his use of slave labor more closely. During his career, white antislavery sentiment was rare, and organized activism against the institution was even rarer. The American Revolution was the engine that produced widespread—even if still regionally limited and disorganized—white hostility toward slavery. In America, many black and white evangelicals appropriated the rhetoric of universal liberty to criticize slavery. In England, many (including John Wesley) highlighted the colonists' hypocrisy in agitating for liberty even as they denied the most fundamental rights to their slaves. Whitefield died just before these new indictments of slave owning began to emerge.[36]

In early 1770, a Boston newspaper editorial did revile Whitefield for owning slaves, but it was one of the first such attacks he ever received, and it heralded the beginnings of more active American antislavery agitation. The writer rued how Whitefield intended to buy more slaves in order to build Bethesda and the prospective college there. "As the slave trade is evidently founded on murder and manstealing; this is only doing evil that good may come of it," the essayist declared. "Can we think the blessing of God will follow this college, if it must owe its existence to a trade that is accursed?" Memory of this piece lingered in 1832 when William Lloyd Garrison's radical abolitionist newspaper the *Liberator* quoted it with regret. (Garrison was born in Newburyport, yards away from Whitefield's tomb.) "Our surprise is great that he who thus eloquently denounced the system of slavery in 1740, should so far lose sight of the principles of justice in 1770 as to advocate a speculation in the bodies of the blacks for the benefit of a literary institution," the *Liberator* lamented.[37]

Whitefield also typified the evangelical blending of politics, war, and religion, especially during the Louisbourg expedition and Jacobite Rebellion of 1745, and the Seven Years' War. This move toward politics was a stark departure from Whitefield's exclusive message of the new birth, which had guided his preaching in the late 1730s and early 1740s. The politics of British Protestantism and anti-Catholicism offered a point of unity for Whitefield and many potential critics once the furor aroused by the early revivals had subsided. Whitefield also sincerely believed that Catholic imperial power represented a dire threat to the religious and political liberty upon which his preaching depended.

Although he showed signs of privately supporting the early patriot movement, it is difficult to say how Whitefield would have handled America's independence. One imagines that while he sympathized with the colonists' grievances, he would have worried about the consequences of losing a large piece of the British Empire. Whatever the case, Whitefield knew that there was a risk that focusing on politics and war could displace or corrupt the gospel witness—a danger that evangelicals continue to grapple with today.

On a stormy spring night in April 1786, the Reverend Samson Occom dreamed about his deceased friend, George Whitefield. "I thought he was preaching as he used to, when he was alive," Occom wrote. "I thought he was preaching at a certain place where there was a great number of Indians and some White People." Whitefield came to him and clasped his right hand. "He put his face to my face, and rubbed his face to mine and said 'I am glad that you preach the excellency of Jesus Christ yet.'" He exhorted Occom to go on in strength, and prayed, "The Lord be with thee, we shall now soon done." Whitefield was now done, but his memory, and the movement he inspired, lived on in Britain and America and even in the dreams of those who looked to him as a spiritual father. A man of his time, Whitefield had serious faults, which contemporaries pointed out and which are even easier to see from the vantage of three centuries. And yet he was a gospel minister of substantial integrity, spiritual sincerity, phenomenal ability, and indefatigable energy. Whitefield was the first great preacher in a modern evangelical movement that has seen many. Perhaps he was the greatest evangelical preacher the world has ever seen.[38]

NOTES

INTRODUCTION

1. George Whitefield, *A Continuation of the Reverend Mr. Whitefield's Journal, From a Few Days after his Return to Georgia to his Arrival at Falmouth, on the 11th of March 1741* (London, 1741), 41, 43.
2. Ian Clary, who is writing on Dallimore for his doctoral thesis at the University of the Free State (Bloemfontein), shared this biographical information with me.
3. Frank Lambert, *"Pedlar in Divinity": George Whitefield and the Transatlantic Revivals, 1737–1770* (Princeton, N.J., 1994), 6; Harry S. Stout, *The Divine Dramatist: George Whitefield and the Rise of Modern Evangelicalism* (Grand Rapids, Mich., 1991), xvi.
4. Jerome Dean Mahaffey, *The Accidental Revolutionary: George Whitefield and the Creation of America* (Waco, Tex., 2011), 188; Alan Heimert, *Religion and the American Mind: From the Great Awakening to the Revolution* (Cambridge, Mass., 1966), 148. See also Mahaffey, *Preaching Politics: The Religious Rhetoric of George Whitefield and the Founding of a New Nation* (Waco, Tex., 2007). Nancy Ruttenburg has also argued that Whitefield's "revolutionary" preaching represented the "democratic personality in its first American instantiation"; see Ruttenburg, "George Whitefield, Spectacular Conversion, and the Rise of Democratic Personality," *American Literary History* 5, no. 3 (Autumn 1993): 431.
5. George Whitefield, *The Full Account of the Life and Dealings of God with the Reverend Mr. George Whitefield* (London, 1747), 4.
6. Luke Tyerman, *The Life of the Rev. George Whitefield* (New York, 1877), 2:323n4.

CHAPTER 1. "THE CIRCUMSTANCES OF MY BEING BORN IN AN INN"

1. George Whitefield, *A Short Account of God's Dealings with the Reverend Mr. George Whitefield* (London, 1740), 8; D. Bruce Hindmarsh, *The Evangelical Conversion Narrative: Spiritual Autobiography in Early Modern England* (Oxford, 2005), 104–5.

2. Jonathan Barry, "South-West," in Peter Clark, ed., *The Cambridge Urban History of Britain*, Vol. 2: *1540–1840* (Cambridge, 2000), 70–71; George W. Counsel, *The History and Description of the City of Gloucester* (Gloucester, UK, 1829), 47, 72.

3. David Harris Sacks, *The Widening Gate: Bristol and the Atlantic Economy, 1450–1700* (Berkeley, Calif., 1991), 353; Kenneth Morgan, *Bristol and the Atlantic Trade in the Eighteenth Century* (New York, 1993), 7.

4. John Sawyer, *The Story of Gloucestershire* (Cheltenham, UK, 1908), 198.

5. Ibid., 200; Mary Anne Everett Green, ed., *Calendar of State Papers, Domestic Series, of the Reign of Charles II, 1661–1662* (London, 1861), 447.

6. *The Absolute Necessity of Standing by the Present Government* (London, 1689), 3.

7. Linda Colley, *Britons: Forging the Nation, 1707–1837* (New Haven, Conn., 1992), 47.

8. George Burton Adams and H. Morse Stephens, eds., *Select Documents of English Constitutional History* (New York, 1916), 475.

9. Thomas Bradbury, *The True Happiness of a Good Government*, 2nd ed. (London, 1714), 21; *Daily Courant*, Dec. 13, 1714.

10. The Book of Common Prayer and Administration of the Sacraments (London, 1717), 90.

11. Ibid., 89.

12. Whitefield, *Short Account*, 8–9.

13. John Calvin, *Institutes of the Christian Religion: The First English Version of the 1541 French Edition*, trans. Elsie Anne McKie (Grand Rapids, Mich., 2009), 52–53.

14. *Articles Agreed upon by the Archbishops and Bishops of Both Provinces, and the Whole Clergy, in the Convocation Holden at London in the Year 1562* (London, 1720), 9th article; Catherine A. Brekus, *Sarah Osborn's World: The Rise of Evangelical Christianity in Early America* (New Haven, Conn., 2013), 55–56.

15. Andrew Crichton, *The Life and Diary of Lieut. Col. J. Blackader* (Edinburgh, 1824), 352; Geoffrey Treasure, *The Making of Modern Europe, 1648–1780*, 3rd ed. (New York, 2003), 175.

16. Whitefield, *Short Account*, 9.

17. Arnold A. Dallimore, *George Whitefield: The Life and Times of the Great Evangelist of the Eighteenth-Century Revival* (Carlisle, Pa., 1970, 1980), 1:45; Whitefield, *Short Account*, 9.

18. Augustine, *Confessions*, ed. Albert Outler (Philadelphia, 1955), bk. 2, 32, available at http://www.ccel.org/ccel/augustine/confessions.pdf, accessed May 30, 2013; Whitefield, *Short Account*, 10; James P. Gledstone, *The Life and Travels of George Whitefield* (London, 1871), 3n.

19. Dallimore, *Whitefield*, 1:52–55; Whitefield, *Short Account*, 12; Whitefield to John Wesley, July 11, 1735, Duke University Special Collections.

20. Whitefield, *Short Account*, 12.

21. Ibid.; Thomas Ken, *The Manual of Prayers for the Scholars Belonging to Winchester College, and all other Pious Christians* (London, 1723), 4, 17.

22. Philip Stubbes, *Anatomy of Abuses* (1583), quoted in Margot Heinemann, *Puritanism and Theatre: Thomas Middleton and Opposition Drama under the Early Stuarts* (New York, 1980), 20.

23. Augustine, *Confessions*, bk. 3, 38–39.; see the reference to Augustine, for example, in Whitefield to Mr. M— — A— —, July 26, 1742, in *Letters of George Whitefield for the Period 1734–1742*, ed. S. M. Houghton (Carlisle, Pa., 1976), 411.

24. Whitefield, *Short Account*, 13.

25. "Country Clergyman," *Of Luxury, More Particularly with Respect to Apparel* (London, 1736), 10–11; Dror Wahrman, *The Making of the Modern Self: Identity and Culture in Eighteenth-Century England* (New Haven, Conn., 2004), 48, 80–81.

26. Percy Fitzgerald, *The Life of David Garrick* (London, 1868), 1:12.

27. Whitefield, *Short Account*, 13; Garrick quoted in Robert Philip, *The Life and Times of the Reverend George Whitefield* (London, 1838), 575.

28. Whitefield, *Short Account*, 14.

29. Ibid., 15.

30. C. Roy Huddleston, "George Whitefield's Ancestry," *Transactions of the Bristol and Gloucestershire Archaeological Society* 59 (1938): 222, 225; Whitefield, *Short Account*, 15.

31. Whitefield, *Short Account*, 15–16.

32. Ibid., 16.

33. Ibid., 16; Book of Common Prayer, 11.

34. Whitefield, *Short Account*, 16; W. R. Ward, *The Protestant Evangelical Awakening* (New York, 1992), 48; *The Works of the Reverend John Wesley*, ed. John Emory (New York, 1831), 5:133.

35. Thomas à Kempis, *The Christian's Pattern, or, A Treatise of the Imitation of Jesus Christ* (London, 1714), 281.

36. Peter Marshall, "Evangelical Conversion in the Reign of Henry VIII," in Peter Marshall and Alec Ryrie, eds., *The Beginnings of English Protestantism* (New York, 2002), 20.

37. David Ceri Jones, *"A Glorious Work in the World": Welsh Methodism and the International Evangelical Revival, 1735–1750* (Cardiff, 2004), 69; W. R. Ward, *Early Evangelicalism: A Global Intellectual History, 1670–1789* (New York, 2006), 24–39.

38. Whitefield, *Short Account*, 17.

39. Ibid., 17; Whitefield diary, Apr. 24, 1736, British Library; Misty G. Anderson, *Imagining Methodism in Eighteenth-Century Britain: Enthusiasm, Belief, and the Borders of the Self* (Baltimore, 2012), 89.

40. Whitefield, *Short Account*, 17; "R— —ph J— —ps— —n," *The Expounder Expounded* (London, 1740), 37–40; Albert M. Lyles, *Methodism Mocked: The Satiric Reaction to Methodism in the Eighteenth Century* (London, 1960), 131–32; Anderson, *Imagining Methodism*, 88–90.

41. Whitefield, *Short Account*, 18.

42. Ibid., 18.

43. Ibid., 18–19.

CHAPTER 2. "THE DAY STAR AROSE IN MY HEART"

1. Whitefield, *Short Account*, 39.

2. Ibid., 45, 47.

3. Ibid., 48–49.

4. Ibid., 49.

5. Ibid., 19–21.

6. Ibid., 21; Charles Drelincourt, *The Christian's Defense against the Fears of Death* (London, 1675), 6, 19.

7. Whitefield, *Short Account*, 22; Phyllis Mack, *Heart Religion in the British Enlightenment: Gender and Emotion in Early Methodism* (New York, 2008), 222–23.

8. Whitefield, *Short Account*, 23

9. Ibid., 22–23.

10. Verse quoted in Douglas Macleane, *A History of Pembroke College, Oxford* (Oxford, 1897), 325; Stout, *Divine Dramatist*, 16–17.

11. James Boswell, *The Life of Samuel Johnson* (Philadelphia, 1878), 1:55n2.

12. Boswell, *Life of Johnson*, 1:62–63, 65.

13. Whitefield, *Short Account*, 24; Whitefield diary, Mar. 23, 1735, Dr. Williams's Library (London; the library owns ten leaves from what was presumably a longer diary); Whitefield, "The Good Shepherd," in John Gillies, *Memoirs of Rev. George Whitefield* (New Haven, Conn., 1834), 604; Stout, *Divine Dramatist*, 18–19.

14. Whitefield, *Short Account*, 24–25.

15. Thomas Secker, *Fourteen Sermons Preached on Several Occasions* (London, 1766), 23; R. Greaves, "Religion in the University, 1715–1800," in L. S. Sutherland and L. G. Mitchell, eds., *The History of the University of Oxford*, vol. 5:*The Eighteenth Century* (Oxford, 1986), 402.

16. Whitefield, *Short Account*, 25.

17. Ibid., 25; William Law, *A Serious Call to a Devout and Holy Life*, 3rd ed. (London, [1733]), 1–2, 4.

18. John Wesley, *The Works of the Rev. John Wesley* (London, 1811), 10: 430; John Wesley, *A Serious Call to a Holy Life. Extracted from a Late Author* (Newcastle upon Tyne, UK, 1744).

19. V. H. H. Green, "Religion in the Colleges, 1715–1800," in Sutherland and Mitchell, *History of the University of Oxford*, 5:438–39.

20. John Wesley, *The Works of the Rev. John Wesley* (London, 1809), 1:276; Richard P. Heitzenrater, *Wesley and the People Called Methodists* (Nashville, 1995), 43; Josiah Tucker, *A Brief History of the Principles of Methodism* (Oxford, [1742]), 7.

21. John R. Tyson, *Assist Me to Proclaim: The Life and Hymns of Charles Wesley* (Grand Rapids, Mich., 2007), 16.

22. Heitzenrater, *Wesley and the Methodists*, 47–48; Richard P. Heitzenrater, ed., *Diary of an Oxford Methodist: Benjamin Ingham, 1733–1734* (Durham, N.C., 1985), 4n3, 8–9.

23. Heitzenrater, *Diary of an Oxford Methodist*, 122–23.

24. John Wesley, "The Circumcision of the Heart," in Albert C. Outler, ed., *The Works of John Wesley: Sermons I, 1–33* (Nashville, 1984), 1:402–3.

25. Whitefield, *Short Account*, 26–27.

26. Tyson, *Assist Me to Proclaim*, vii–1.

27. Whitefield, *Short Account*, 27; Vicki Tolar Burton, *Spiritual Literacy in John Wesley's Methodism: Reading, Writing, and Speaking to Believe* (Waco, Tex., 2008), 1–2.

28. Whitefield, *Short Account*, 27–28; Henry Scougal, *The Life of God in the Soul of Man* (London, 1677), 3, 5.

29. Whitefield, *Short Account*, 28; Scougal, *Life of God*, 7; George Whitefield, *The Kingdom of God* (Glasgow, 1741), 20–21.

30. Whitefield, "All Mens Place," in *Eighteen Sermons Preached by the Late Rev. George Whitefield* (Newburyport, Mass., 1797), 290–91; the title page describes this volume as "taken verbatim in Short-Hand, and faithfully Transcribed by Joseph Gurney." See also Dallimore, *Whitefield*, 1:73.

31. Whitefield, *Short Account*, 28, 33; Whitefield to Mr. H., Sept. 17, 1734, Whitefield to Mr. H., Feb. 20, 1735, Whitefield to Mr. H., Mar. 6, 1735, in *Letters of George Whitefield for the Period 1734–1742*, 4, 6, 7. Notes by the volume editor, S. M. Houghton, identify "Mr. H." as Gabriel Harris (likely Harris, Sr.) of Gloucester, a bookseller and civic leader (521). *Letters* is an edited facsimile edition of the first volume of John Gillies's *The Works of the Reverend George Whitefield* (London, 1771–72). Gillies's *Works* contains by far the largest collection of Whitefield's letters—more than fourteen hundred—many of which are no longer extant. Because Gillies sometimes modified the letters, obscuring personal names and smoothing out controversial phrases and details, I use unedited versions of extant manuscripts when possible.

32. Whitefield, *Short Account*, 32, 37.

33. Brian P. Levack, *The Devil Within: Possession and Exorcism in the Christian West* (New Haven, Conn., 2013), 210–11.

34. John de Castaniza, *The Spiritual Combat*, 2nd ed. (London, 1710), 5.

35. Whitefield, *Short Account*, 40.

36. Ibid., 41–42.

37. Ibid., 42.

38. Ibid., 43–45.

39. Ibid., 45; Whitefield to Mr. H, Feb. 20, 1735, in *Letters of Whitefield*, 7.

40. Whitefield, *Short Account*, 46.

41. Ibid., 47–48.

42. Whitefield diary, Apr. 3 and 4, Dr. Williams's Library (London); Whitefield, *Short Account*, 49.

43. Whitefield, *The First Two Parts of His Life, with His Journals, Revised, Corrected, and Abridged* (London, 1756), 17.

44. Whitefield to John Wesley, May 8, 1735; John Wesley to Whitefield, [May 13?, 1735], in Frank Baker, ed., *The Works of John Wesley: Letters I, 1721–1739* (Oxford, 1980), 25:426–27.

45. Whitefield, *Short Account*, 54.

46. Ibid., 57.

47. Ibid.

48. Richard Baxter, *A Call to the Unconverted to Turn and Live* (London, 1692), 29.

49. Joseph Alleine, *An Alarm to Unconverted Sinners* (London, 1703), 17, 19.

50. Whitefield to John Wesley, Apr. 1, 1735, in "Letters of George Whitefield," *Proceedings of the Wesley Historical Society* 10, no. 1 (Mar. 1915): 17–18; Whitefield to John Wesley, [approx. summer 1735], in *Letters of Whitefield*, 484; Whitefield to John Wesley, July 11, 1735, Duke University Special Collections.

51. Whitefield, *Short Account*, 60, 62–64.

52. Mack, *Heart Religion*, 232.

53. Whitefield, *Short Account*, 64–65.

54. Whitefield diary, Mar. 3, 6; Apr. 6; May 6, 30, 31; June 23, 1736, British Library. On Whitefield and the Holy Spirit, see also David Jull, "George Whitefield and the Great Awakening: A Pentecostal Perspective," *Asian Journal of Pentecostal Studies* 14, no. 2 (July 2011): 256–71. On the primacy of the Holy Spirit among evangelicals, see Timothy Larsen, "Defining and Locating Evangelicalism," in Timothy Larsen and Daniel J. Treier, eds., *The Cambridge Companion to Evangelical Theology* (New York, 2007), 10–12.

55. Thomas S. Kidd, *The Great Awakening: The Roots of Evangelical Christianity in Colonial America* (New Haven, Conn., 2007), xiv.

56. Ibid., xiv; David Bebbington, *Evangelicalism in Modern Britain: A History from the 1730s to the 1980s* (Grand Rapids, Mich., 1992), 3.

57. Whitefield diary, May 14, 1736, British Library; see also in Dallimore, *Whitefield*, 1:90–91. Dallimore transcribed some passages of this diary, but I am using the original.

58. Whitefield diary, May 31, 1736, British Library.

59. Whitefield diary, June 20, 1736, British Library; Dallimore, *Whitefield*, 1:95; Book of Common Prayer (Cambridge, 1701), n.p. ("The Ordering of Deacons"); Whitefield to Mr. S., June 20, 1736, in *Letters of Whitefield*, 15.

60. Whitefield, *Short Account*, 69.

CHAPTER 3. "GOD IS PREPARING ME FOR SOMETHING EXTRAORDINARY"

1. Whitefield, *A Further Account of the Lord's Dealings with the Reverend Mr. George Whitefield* (London, 1747), 5.

2. Whitefield to Mr. H., June 30, 1736, in *Letters of Whitefield*, 18–19.

3. Ibid., 18; Stout, *Divine Dramatist*, 28.

4. George Whitefield, *The Necessity and Benefits of Religious Society* (Boston, 1740), 12.

5. Ibid., 23–24.

6. Ibid., 14.

7. Whitefield to Mrs. H., July 7, 1736, in *Letters of Whitefield*, 19.

8. Whitefield to John Wesley, Sept. 2, 1736, in *Letters of Whitefield*, 486–87; Dallimore, *Whitefield*. 1:103.

9. L. S. Sutherland, "The Curriculum," in Sutherland and Mitchell, *History of the University of Oxford*, 5:482–83.

10. Whitefield, *Further Account*, 6–7.

11. Ibid., 7.

12. Ibid., 8; Philopolites, *The Present State of the Prison of Ludgate* (London, 1725), 65.

13. Whitefield, *Further Account*, 8–9.

14. John Wesley to the Rev. George Whitefield and the Oxford Methodists, [Sept. 10, 1736], journal fragment likely incorporated into a letter, in Baker, *Works of John Wesley*, 25:471–73.

15. "Charter of Georgia, 1732," in Francis N. Thorpe, ed., *The Federal and State Constitutions* (Washington, D.C., 1909), 2:765, 773; Frank Lambert, *James Habersham: Loyalty, Politics, and Commerce in Colonial Georgia* (Athens, Ga., 2005), 26–27.

16. *A New Voyage to Georgia* [London, 1735], 6; Harold E. Davis, *The Fledgling Province: Social and Cultural Life in Colonial Georgia, 1733–1776* (Chapel Hill, N.C., 1976), 33–34.

17. Betty Wood, *Slavery in Colonial Georgia, 1730–1775*, pb. ed. (Athens, Ga., 2007), 5–7.

18. James Oglethorpe to John Wesley, Sept. 9, 1735, in Baker, *Works of John Wesley*, 25:432.

19. John Wesley to John Burton, Oct. 10, 1735, in ibid., 25:439.

20. Ibid.

21. *The Journal of the Rev. John Wesley* (London, 1827), 1:21.

22. W. Reginald Ward and Richard P. Heitzenrater, eds., *The Works of John Wesley: Journal and Diaries I, 1735–1738* (Nashville, 1988), 18:412–13.

23. *The Journal of the Rev. Charles Wesley* (London, 1849), 1:34; Henry D. Rack, *Reasonable Enthusiast: John Wesley and the Rise of Methodism*, 3rd ed. (London, 2002), 115–16; Tyson, *Assist Me to Proclaim*, 29–36.

24. Richard P. Heitzenrater, ed., *The Elusive Mr. Wesley: John Wesley His Own Biographer* (Nashville, 1984), 78–80; Ward and Heitzenrater, *Works of John Wesley*, 18:436.

25. Rack, *Reasonable Enthusiast*, 127–28.

26. Ibid., 128–30; Ward and Heitzenrater, *Works of John Wesley*, 18:483.

27. Heitzenrater, *Elusive Mr. Wesley*, 91; Egmont cited in Rack, *Reasonable Enthusiast*, 133.

28. Whitefield, *Further Account*, 10–11.

29. Ibid., 11.

30. Whitefield to Charles Wesley, Dec. 20, 1736, Drew University, United Methodist Archives; Whitefield to Charles Wesley, Dec. 30, 1736, in *Letters of Whitefield*, 487–88.

31. Whitefield, *Further Account*, 12.

32. Ibid., 13; Whitefield to Mr. H., Feb. 10, 1737, in *Letters of Whitefield*, 24.

33. Phinizy Spalding, *Oglethorpe in America* (Athens, Ga., 1984; orig. 1977), 2–3, 28–29, 64–65.

34. Whitefield, *Further Account*, 15–16.

35. Ibid., 16.

36. Ibid., 17.

37. Ibid., 17–19.

38. Whitefield, *The Nature and Necessity of our New Birth in Christ Jesus*, 3rd ed. (London, 1738), v, vii–viii; Whitefield, *Further Account*, 24.

39. Alleine, *Alarm to Unconverted Sinners*, 82; Stout, *Divine Dramatist*, 38–39.

40. Whitefield, *Nature and Necessity*, 1, 4.

41. Whitefield, *Further Account*, 19; Whitefield, *Nature and Necessity*, front matter.

42. *Weekly Miscellany*, Apr. 1, 1737; *Daily Gazetteer*, July 29, 1737.

43. D. Bruce Hindmarsh, *The Evangelical Conversion Narrative: Spiritual Autobiography in Early Modern England* (Oxford, 2005), 73–75; Paul Langford, *A Polite and Commercial People: England, 1727–1783* (New York, 1989), 404.

44. *Daily Advertiser*, Sept. 19, 1737, quoted in Lambert, "Pedlar in Divinity," 53n4. On Seward, see Lambert, "Pedlar in Divinity," 52–69, and W. R. Ward, "Seward, William (1711–1740)," *Oxford Dictionary of National Biography*, at http://www.oxforddnb.com/view/article/40213, accessed Apr. 20, 2012.

45. Whitefield, *Further Account*, 21; Whitefield to Mr. H., Oct. 25, 1737, in *Letters of Whitefield*, 29; Lambert, "Pedlar in Divinity," 54–55.

46. John Scote to Whitefield, Jan. 17, 1738, in George Whitefield Papers, Library of Congress.

47. *Read's Weekly Journal or British Gazetteer*, Dec. 31, 1737; Whitefield, *Further Account*, 26; Charles Wesley to John Wesley, Jan. 2, 1738, in Baker, *Works of John Wesley*, 25:526.

48. George Whitefield, *A Journal of a Voyage from London to Savannah in Georgia* (London, 1738), 14.

49. Whitefield to Daniel Abbot, Jan. 9, 1738, in Graham Thomas, ed., "George Whitefield and Friends," *National Library of Wales Journal* 26 (1990): 369; Whitefield, *Journal of a Voyage*, 19, 21.

50. Whitefield interpreted Wesley's letter as saying that the lot instructed Whitefield to return to London, but Wesley probably was only inquiring about his own return to the city; see Baker, *Works of John Wesley*, 25:527–28n2; Whitefield, *A Letter to the Reverend Mr. John Wesley* (London, [1741]), 7.

51. S. T. Kimbrough, Jr., and Kenneth G. C. Newport, eds., *The Manuscript Journal of the Reverend Charles Wesley* (Nashville, Tenn., 2008), 108; Rack, *Reasonable Enthusiast*, 138–44.

52. Whitefield, *Journal of a Voyage*, 27.

53. Ibid., 33.

54. Stephen Constantine, *Community and Identity: The Making of Modern Gibraltar Since 1704* (Manchester, UK, 2009), 21; Whitefield to Mr. _____, Feb. 25, 1738, in *Letters of Whitefield*, 38.

55. Whitefield, *Journal of a Voyage*, 34.

56. Ibid., 41.

57. "Mezotinto" ad in *London Evening Post*, Jan. 28, 1738; Thomas Cooper in the *Daily Post*, Aug. 5, 1738; James Hutton in the *London Evening Post*, Aug. 5, 1738; Tyerman, *Life of Whitefield*, 1:118n1; Lambert, "Pedlar in Divinity," 77–78; Hindmarsh, *Evangelical Conversion Narrative*, 107.

58. Whitefield, *Journal of a Voyage*, 46–47.

59. Ibid., 47–49; Hindmarsh, *Evangelical Conversion Narrative*, 95–96.

60. Whitefield, *Journal of a Voyage*, 56–57; Whitefield to — —, May 6, 1738, in *Letters of Whitefield*, 43.

61. Mack, *Heart Religion*, 176–77, 182.

62. Ibid., 176–79.

63. Whitefield to Mr. H, June 10, 1738, in *Letters of Whitefield*, 44; Gillies, *Memoirs of Whitefield*, 28.

64. Julie Anne Sweet, "Bearing Feathers of the Eagle: Tomochichi's Trip to England," *Georgia Historical Quarterly* 86, no. 3 (Fall 2002): 341, 344, 353.

65. George Whitefield, *A Continuation of the Reverend Mr. Whitefield's Journal, From his Arrival at Savannah, To his Return to London* (London, 1739), 3.

66. George Whitefield, *The Eternity of Hell Torments* (London, 1738), vi; Michael J. McClymond and Gerald R. McDermott, *The Theology of Jonathan Edwards* (New York, 2011), 571; Tyerman, *Life of Whitefield*, 1:360; John Tillotson, *On the Eternity of Hell-Torments* (London, 1708), 10–12.

67. Norman Fiering, *Jonathan Edwards's Moral Thought and Its British Context* (Chapel Hill, N.C., 1981), 232.

68. Whitefield, *Eternity of Hell Torments*, 17, 21; Brekus, *Sarah Osborn's World*, 145; Fiering, *Jonathan Edwards's Moral Thought*, 207.

69. Whitefield diary, Mar. 8, 1736, British Library; Kimbrough and Newport, *Manuscript Journal of Charles Wesley*, 1:93; Gillies, *Memoirs of Whitefield*, 26; Whitefield, *Journal, Savannah to London*, 6–7; Whitefield to Mr. H., June 10, 1738, in *Letters of Whitefield*, 44; Johann Martin Boltzius to Gotthilf August Francke, Aug. 26, 1738, in Russell C. Kleckley, ed., *The Letters of Johann Martin Boltzius, Lutheran Pastor in Ebenezer, Georgia* (Lewiston, N.Y., 2009), 1:244; "Daily Reports of the Two Ministers Boltzius and Gronau," Jan. 16, 1740, in George Fenwick Jones and Don Savelle, eds., *Detailed Reports on the Salzburger Emigrants* (Athens, Ga., 1983), 7:19. See also Whitefield to G. A. Francke, [1738], in George Fenwick Jones, ed., "Two 'Salzburger' Letters from George Whitefield and Theobald Kiefer II," *Georgia Historical Quarterly* 62, no. 1 (Spring 1978): 51–52.

70. George Whitefield, *The Great Duty of Charity Recommended* (London, 1740), 24; Brekus, *Sarah Osborn's World*, 224–28.

71. Lord Egmont quoted in Edward J. Cashin, *Beloved Bethesda: A History of George Whitefield's Home for Boys, 1740–1800* (Macon, Ga., 2001), 12.

72. Whitefield, *Journal, Savannah to London*, 17–18.

73. Gillies, *Memoirs of Whitefield*, 28.

74. Whitefield to the Inhabitants of Georgia, Oct. 2, 1738, Whitefield to Mr. — —, Nov. 16, 1738, in *Letters of Whitefield*, 45, 490.

CHAPTER 4. "THE FIERY TRIAL OF POPULARITY"

1. *Daily Post*, June 24 and Dec. 6, 1738.

2. Whitefield, *Journal, Savannah to London*, 21–22, 25.

3. Ibid., 28–29.

4. Ibid., 31.

5. Whitefield, *A Continuation of the Reverend Mr. Whitefield's Journal, From his Arrival at London, To his Departure from thence on his Way to Georgia* (London, 1739), 1.

6. Colin Podmore, *The Moravian Church in England, 1728–1760* (Oxford, 1998), 5–7; Aaron Spencer Fogleman, *Jesus Is Female: Moravians and the Challenge of Radical Religion in Early America* (Philadelphia, 2007), 119.

7. Böhler quoted in Podmore, *Moravian Church*, 38; see also 38–44 for the forming of the society.

8. Whitefield, *Journal, London to Georgia*, 2; Kidd, *Great Awakening*, xiv; Whitefield to John Bray, Jan. 5, 1738, in Thomas, "Whitefield and Friends," 369; Whitefield, "The Indwelling of the Spirit, The Common Privilege of All Believers" (1739), in Whitefield, *The Christian's Companion: or, Sermons on Several Subjects* (London, 1739), 244.

9. Whitefield, *Journal, London to Georgia*, 2.

10. Ibid., 3.

11. W. Reginald Ward and Richard P. Heitzenrater, eds., *The Works of John Wesley: Journal and Diaries II, 1738–1743* (Nashville, Tenn., 1990), 19:29; Rack, *Reasonable Enthusiast*, 187–88; Whitefield, *Journal, London to Georgia*, 4; Gillies, *Memoirs of Whitefield*, 34.

12. Rack, *Reasonable Enthusiast*, 184–85, Ward and Heitzenrater, *Works of John Wesley*, 18:270, 280.

13. Edwards quoted in Kidd, *Great Awakening*, 13.

14. Kimbrough and Newport, *Manuscript Journal of Charles Wesley*, 1:156.

15. Howell Harris, *A Brief Account of the Life of Howell Harris* (Trevecka, Wales, 1791), 13–14; Mark A. Noll, *The Rise of Evangelicalism: The Age of Edwards, Whitefield, and the Wesleys* (Downers Grove, Ill., 2003), 79. Since Harris signed his name "Howell," I use this spelling instead of the more conventional Welsh "Howel"; see David Ceri Jones, Boyd Stanley Schlenther, and Eryn Mant White, *The Elect Methodists: Calvinistic Methodism in England and Wales, 1735–1811* (Cardiff, 2012), xv.

16. Geraint Tudur, *Howell Harris: From Conversion to Separation, 1735–1750* (Cardiff, 2000), 22–23.

17. Ibid., 42–43.

18. Whitefield to Howell Harris, Dec. 20, 1738, in Harris, *Brief Account*, 110–11.

19. Howell Harris to Whitefield, Jan. 8, 1739, in Harris, *Brief Account*, 112–14. This letter is dated Jan. 10 in Thomas, "Whitefield and Friends," 74, and I have used that version for quotations here; see also Whitefield to Mr. H., Jan. 27, 1739, in *Letters of Whitefield*, 47.

20. Philip Doddridge to Whitefield, Dec. 12 and 16, 1738, in Thomas, "Whitefield and Friends," 66–68. In an April 1736 journal entry, Whitefield noted that he had heard Doddridge was praying for the Methodists; see Dallimore, *Whitefield*, 1:88.

21. Whitefield to Mr. H., Dec. 30, 1738, in *Letters of Whitefield*, 46; Whitefield, *Journal, London to Georgia*, 8.

22. Whitefield, *Journal, London to Georgia*, 9; The Book of Common Prayer (Cambridge, 1701), n.p.

23. T. G., *Remarks on the Reverend Mr. Whitefield's Journal* (London, [1738?]), 2. This tract was advertised at least as early as January 16, 1739, in the *London Evening Post*.

24. Tristram Land, *A Letter to the Rev. Mr. Whitefield* (London, 1739), 5–6, 8–9.

25. Book of Common Prayer, n.p.; Land, *Letter to Whitefield*, 28; Edmund Gibson, *The Bishop of London's Pastoral Letter to the People of His Diocese* (London, 1739), 46; Whitefield, "The Nature and Necessity of our New Birth in Christ Jesus," in Whitefield, *Christian's Companion*, 9–10.

26. Whitefield, *Journal, London to Georgia*, 9.

27. Ibid., 10–11; Tristram Land, *A Second Letter to the Rev. Mr. Whitefield* (London, [1741?]).

28. Whitefield, *Journal, London to Georgia*, 15.

29. Ibid., 11.

30. Whitefield, *First Two Parts of His Life*, 118.

31. Whitefield, *Journal, London to Georgia*, 16; Whitefield diary, May 17, June 5, 1736, British Library; Stout, *Divine Dramatist*, 43.

32. Stout, *Divine Dramatist*, 41.

33. Ibid.

34. Dallimore, *Whitefield*, 1:228–29; Whitefield, *Journal, London to Georgia*, 17–18, 25; Tyerman, *Life of Whitefield*, 1:174.

35. Whitefield, *From his Arrival at London to his Departure*, 22.

36. Whitefield to Mrs. J. Mathews, Feb. 2, 1739, in Thomas, "Whitefield and Friends," 76.

37. Whitefield, *Journal, London to Georgia*, 28.

38. Ibid., 29; John Taylor, *A Book about Bristol* (London, 1872), 304.

39. T. S. Ashton and Joseph Sykes, *The Coal Industry of the Eighteenth Century* (1929; rept., New York, 1967), 121.

40. Ibid., 147–49; David Hempton, *Methodism: Empire of the Spirit* (New Haven, Conn., 2005), 27; Whitefield, *Journal, London to Georgia*, 31.

41. Dallimore, *Whitefield*, 1: 256; Whitefield, *Journal, London to Georgia*, 31; Gillies, *Memoirs of Whitefield*, 37; Whitefield to Daniel Abbot, Feb. 17, 1739, in Thomas, "Whitefield and Friends," 79. There is some controversy about whether Whitefield was referring to Hanham Mount or to the place he called "the mount on Rose Green." He refers to both in his journals, but does not always indicate which "mount" he means; see "John Wesley at the Brickyard," *Proceedings of the Wesley Historical Society*, 37–38, available at http://www.biblicalstudies.org.uk/pdf/whs/03-2.pdf, accessed May 5, 2013; Dallimore shows that John Cennick identified the first mount as Rose Green (*Whitefield*, 1:256n3).

42. Whitefield, *Journal, London to Georgia*, 40; Gillies, *Memoirs of Whitefield*, 38.

43. William Seward to James Hutton, Mar. 5, 1739, in Thomas, "Whitefield and Friends," 93; Lambert, *"Pedlar in Divinity,"* 62–63.

44. Gillies, *Memoirs of Whitefield*, 38; Whitefield to Daniel Abbot, Mar. 3, 1739, in Thomas, "Whitefield and Friends," 91. John Wesley used this saying at least as early as a letter tentatively dated Mar. 28, 1739, in Baker, *Works of John Wesley*, 25:616. Whitefield used the phrase again in a Nov. 1739 letter; see *Letters of Whitefield*, 105.

45. Whitefield, *Journal, London to Georgia*, 34–35.

46. Whitefield to the Bishop of Bristol, Feb. 24, 1739, in *Letters of Whitefield*, 493; Whitefield, *Journal, London to Georgia*, 39–40.

47. Richard Pearsall to Mr. Debardt, Mar. 3, 1739, in Thomas, "Whitefield and Friends," 90.

48. William Seward to Joseph Stennett, Apr. 17, 1739, William Seward to Joseph Stennett, Apr. 5, 1739, Whitefield to Samuel Mason, Apr. 7, 1739, all in ibid., 292, 197.

49. Whitefield to Mr. Debardt, Mar. 10, 1739, William Seward to Daniel Abbot, Mar. 10, 1739, in ibid., 177, 175.

50. Whitefield to Mr. Debardt, Mar. 10, 1739, in ibid., 177.

51. Whitefield to John Wesley, Mar. 3, 1739, in Baker, *Works of John Wesley*, 25:605.

52. Ibid.

53. John Wesley to Whitefield, Mar. 20, 1739, in Baker, ed., *Works of John Wesley*, 25:611.

54. Whitefield to John Wesley, Mar. 20, 23, 1739, in ibid., 25: 611–12; Ward and Heitzenrater, *Works of John Wesley*, 19:37.

55. Ward and Heitzenrater, *Works of John Wesley*, 19:37–38.

56. John Wesley to James Hutton and the Fetter Lane Society, Apr. 2, 1739, in Baker, *Works of John Wesley*, 25:620.

57. "Shoe laces" quotation in Gareth Lloyd, *Charles Wesley and the Struggle for Methodist Identity* (Oxford, 2007), 34, 52; Ward and Heitzenrater, *Works of John Wesley*, 19:46; Dallimore, *Whitefield*, 1:274–75.

58. Ward and Heitzenrater, *Works of John Wesley*, 19:46; John Wesley to James Hutton and the Fetter Lane Society, Apr. 2, 1739.

59. "Jenny a Servant Maid at Bristol" to Whitefield, May 2, 1739, in Thomas, "Whitefield and Friends," 299.

60. Ibid.

61. Ward and Heitzenrater, *Works of John Wesley*, 19:51–53 (n55), 386; "Jenny a Servant Maid at Bristol" to Whitefield, May 2, 1739, in Thomas, "Whitefield and Friends," 300.

62. Whitefield, *Journal, London to Georgia*, 79–80; William Seward to Joseph Stennett, Apr. 17, 1739, in Thomas, "Whitefield and Friends," 293.

63. "Wesley's Interview with Bishop Butler, August 16 and 18, 1739," in Ward and Heitzenrater, *Works of John Wesley*, 19:471, Dallimore, *Whitefield*, 1:342–44.

64. Isaac Watts to the Bishop of London, Aug. 15, 1739, in Thomas Milner, ed., *The Life, Times, and Correspondence of the Rev. Isaac Watts* (London, 1845), 638.

65. Thomas S. Kidd, "The Healing of Mercy Wheeler: Illness and Miracles among Early American Evangelicals," *William and Mary Quarterly*, 3rd ser., 63, no. 1 (Jan. 2006): 164–65; Gibson, *Pastoral Letter*, 20; Rack, *Reasonable Enthusiast*, 113.

66. Ward and Heitzenrater, *Works of John Wesley*, 19:54–55; Whitefield to John Wesley, June 25, 1739, in Baker, *Works of John Wesley*, 25:661–62.

67. Whitefield, *The Rev. Mr. Whitefield's Answer, to the Bishop of London's Last Pastoral Letter* (London, 1739), 11–12, 16–17; Whitefield to [the Fetter Lane Society], June 12, 1739, in *Letters of Whitefield*, 50; George Whitefield, *The Indwelling of the Spirit* (London, 1739), 7; Fogleman, *Jesus Is Female*, 158.

68. Dallimore, *Whitefield*, 1:287–88; *Country Journal or The Craftsman*, Apr. 7, 1739; Whitefield to Mr. H., Apr. 27, 1739, in Whitefield, *Letters of Whitefield*, 49; *Daily Post*, June 11, 1739.

69. Lambert, "*Pedlar in Divinity*," 47; Stout, *Divine Dramatist*, 107, 256.

70. *London Evening Post*, May 3, 1739; Anderson, *Imagining Methodism*, 94–95.

71. Peter Charles Hoffer, *When Benjamin Franklin Met the Reverend Whitefield: Enlightenment, Revival, and the Power of the Printed Word* (Baltimore, 2011), 11–12.

72. Ibid., 12, 50.

73. *London Evening Post,* May 10, 1739.

74. Whitefield, *Journal, London to Georgia,* 107, 109.

75. Ibid., 111; Braxton Boren and Agnieszka Roginska, "Benjamin Franklin and the Maximum Intelligible Range of the Human Voice," 166th Acoustical Society of America Meeting, at http://www.acoustics.org/press/166th/1aAA4_Boren.html, accessed Dec. 17, 2013.

76. Whitefield, *Journal, London to Georgia,* 96.

77. Mercy Good to Whitefield, [?], 1739, Evangelical Library (London).

78. *The Methodists, An Humorous Burlesque Poem* (London, 1739), 19–20, 22; Anderson, *Imagining Methodism,* 45.

79. *The Conduct and Doctrine of the Reverend Mr. Whitefield Vindicated* (London, 1739), 4, 6, 11.

80. Joseph Trapp, *The Nature, Folly, Sin, and Danger, of Being Righteous Over-Much* (London, 1739), 34–35; Whitefield, *Journal, London to Georgia,* 89; *London Daily Post and Daily Advertiser,* June 7, 1739.

81. Albert M. Lyles, *Methodism Mocked: The Satiric Reaction to Methodism in the Eighteenth Century* (London, 1960), 127–28.

82. Whitefield to John Miller, June 8, 1739, in Boyd Stanley Schlenther and Eryn Mant White, eds. *Calendar of the Trevecka Letters* (Aberystwyth, Wales, 2003), 24; Whitefield to Rev. James Ogilvie at Aberdeen, Aug. 3, 1739, in Thomas, "Whitefield and Friends," 433; Timothy L. Smith, "George Whitefield and Wesleyan Perfection," *Wesleyan Theological Journal* 19, no. 1 (Spring 1984): 67–70, at http://wesley.nnu.edu/fileadmin/imported_site/wesleyjournal/1984-wtj-19-1.pdf, accessed Dec. 21, 2012.

83. John Wesley to James Hutton, May 8, 1739, Whitefield to Charles Wesley, June 22, 1739, in Baker, *Works of John Wesley,* 25:644, 661n3.

84. Peter J. Theusen, *Predestination: The American Career of a Contentious Doctrine* (New York, 2009), 73, 76.

85. Whitefield to John Wesley, June 25, 1739, July 2, 1739, in Baker, *Works of John Wesley,* 25:662, 667.

86. John Wesley, *Free Grace* (Bristol, UK, 1739), 24–25. Although the original was published in Bristol in 1739, it is not clear exactly when it appeared that year—Whitefield's letter of July 2 indicated that he thought it had not appeared yet. Iain Murray says it was published soon after Whitefield left in August; see Iain Murray, "Prefatory Note," in George Whitefield, *George Whitefield's Journals* (Carlisle, Pa., 1960), 565.

87. Rack, *Reasonable Enthusiast,* 198–202; Lloyd, *Charles Wesley,* 57.

88. Whitefield, *A Continuation of the Reverend Mr. Whitefield's Journal, During the Time he was Detained in England by the Embargo* (London, 1739), 23; Whitefield to John Wesley, Mar. 26, 1740, in *Letters of Whitefield,* 156.

89. Richard Harding, *The Emergence of Britain's Global Naval Supremacy: The War of 1739–1748* (Rochester, N.Y., 2010), 21; Thomas Carlyle, *History of Friedrich II of Prussia* (London, 1897), 8:367–68. Philip Woodfine contends that Jenkins did not, in fact, appear before the Commons, with or without his preserved ear; see Woodfine, *Britannia's Glories: The Walpole Ministry and the 1739 War with Spain* (Rochester, N.Y., 1998), 2.

90. *Daily Post,* June 22, 1739; Whitefield, *Journal, Embargo,* 10; Ralph Erskine to Whitefield, July 6, 1739, in Thomas, "Whitefield and Friends," 309.

91. *London Evening Post,* June 2, 1739; *Daily Post,* June 5, 1739.

92. Whitefield, *Journal, Embargo,* 26.

93. Ibid., 27–28; Emma Griffin, *England's Revelry: A History of Popular Sports and Pastimes, 1660–1830* (Oxford, 2005), 53–54.

94. Whitefield, *Journal, Embargo,* 29–31.

95. Dallimore, *Whitefield,* 1:357–60.

96. Whitefield, *A Continuation of the Reverend Mr. Whitefield's Journal, From his Embarking after the Embargo, To his Arrival at Savannah in Georgia* (London, 1740), 5–6. See also Whitefield, *The Bishop of London's Pastoral Letter Answer'd by the Reverend Mr. George Whitefield* (London, 1739).

97. Whitefield, *Journal, Embargo,* 38–39.

98. Whitefield, *Journal, Embargo to Savannah,* 6.

CHAPTER 5. "A TOUR ROUND AMERICA"

1. Carl Bridenbaugh, ed., *Gentleman's Progress: The Itinerarium of Dr. Alexander Hamilton, 1744* (Chapel Hill, N.C., 1948), 192–93.

2. Leonard W. Labaree et al., eds., *The Autobiography of Benjamin Franklin,* 2nd ed. (New Haven, Conn., 2003), 179.

3. Ibid., 180; Hoffer, *When Benjamin Franklin,* 18, 20; *Pennsylvania Gazette,* Nov. 15, 1739.

4. James N. Green, "English Books and Printing in the Age of Franklin," in Hugh Amory and David D. Hall, eds., *A History of the Book in America,* vol. 1, *The Colonial Book in the Atlantic World* (New York, 2000), 257–61.

5. See, for example, *American Weekly Mercury,* July 5, 1739; *Boston Evening-Post,* July 30, 1739; *New-York Weekly Journal,* Sept. 3, 1739.

6. Whitefield to "my dear sister in Christ," Nov. 10, 1739, and Whitefield to "Rev. and dear sir," Nov. 10, 1739, both in *Letters of Whitefield,* 69, 77. These letters, undoubtedly written on board the *Elizabeth,* are postmarked Nov. 10, when he was able to send them.

7. Whitefield, *Journal, Embargo to Savannah,* 13, 15–16.

8. John Wesley made his own note on George Whitefield to John Wesley, Nov. 8, 1739, in Baker, *Works of John Wesley,* 25:699; Whitefield, *The Believer['']s Golden Chain* (Glasgow, 1741), 6; Whitefield to the Reverend Mr. J[ohn] W[esley], Aug. 25, 1740, Whitefield to "Dear brother H.," Nov. 10, 1739, and to "the Rev. Mr. P— —," in *Letters of Whitefield,* 87, 90, 205; Jonathan Warne, *Arminianism, the Back-Door to Popery* (London, 1738), 13; Whitefield, *Journal, Embargo to Savannah,* 19.

9. Ava Chamberlain, "The Theology of Cruelty: A New Look at the Rise of Arminianism in Eighteenth-Century New England," *Harvard Theological Review* 85, no. 3 (July 1992): 345–46; Brekus, *Sarah Osborn's World,* 83; Norman S. Fiering, "Irresistible Compassion: An Aspect of Eighteenth-Century Sympathy and Humanitarianism," *Journal of the History of Ideas* 37, no. 2 (Apr.–June 1976): 215–16.

10. Brekus, *Sarah Osborn's World,* 87–88.

11. Whitefield, *Indwelling of the Spirit*, 16; Austin quoted in Hindmarsh, *Evangelical Conversion Narrative*, 139; Claggett in Hindmarsh, *Evangelical Conversion Narrative*, 189.

12. Thomas Boston, *Human Nature in Its Four-Fold State* (Edinburgh, 1720), 193; Whitefield to [Ralph Erskine], Nov. 28, 1739, in *Letters of Whitefield*, 128–29.

13. Whitefield to "dear madam," Nov. 10, 1739, and Whitefield to "my dear friend and brother," Nov. 10, 1739, both in *Letters of Whitefield*, 71, 78.

14. Whitefield, *Journal, Embargo to Savannah*, 25.

15. Ibid., 27–29, 32–33; *Boston Gazette*, Nov. 19, 1739.

16. Whitefield, *Journal, Embargo to Savannah*, 29.

17. Ibid., 31; Kidd, *Great Awakening*, 31.

18. Whitefield, *Journal, Embargo to Savannah*, 34.

19. Ibid., 35; "extremely pleasant" and "slave city" quotations in Jill Lepore, *New York Burning: Liberty, Slavery, and Conspiracy in Eighteenth-Century Manhattan* (New York, 2005), xii.

20. Whitefield, *Journal, Embargo to Savannah*, 35.

21. Ibid., 36.

22. Ibid., 37.

23. *New England Weekly Journal*, Dec. 4, 1739.

24. Ibid.

25. *Boston News-Letter*, Nov. 22, 1739, orig. published in the *New York Gazette*, Nov. 17, 1739; "Mr. Arnold's Letter against the Reverend Mr. Whitefield, Answer'd, by Magnus Falconar, Marriner [*sic*]," *American Weekly Mercury*, Nov. 22, 1739.

26. Whitefield to "the Rev. Mr. — —," in *Letters of Whitefield*, 113.

27. Whitefield to Rev. Mr. P— —, Nov. 28, 1739, in ibid., 122–23; Ebenezer Pemberton to Whitefield, [rec'd. Nov. 28, 1739], in Whitefield, *Journal, Embargo to Savannah*, 51.

28. Kidd, *Great Awakening*, 27–30; Ward, *Protestant Evangelical Awakening*, 229, 244–46.

29. Whitefield, *Journal, Embargo to Savannah*, 41.

30. Ibid., 44.

31. Ibid., 43–45.

32. John B. Frantz, "The Awakening of Religion among the German Settlers in the Middle Colonies," *William and Mary Quarterly*, 3rd ser., 33, no. 2 (Apr. 1976): 268; Whitefield, *Journal, Embargo to Savannah*, 48.

33. Whitefield, *Journal, Embargo to Savannah*, 58, 67.

34. Lorena S. Walsh, "Feeding the Eighteenth-Century Town Folk, or, Whence the Beef?," at Colonial Williamsburg Research Division, http://research.history.org/Historical_Research/Research_Themes/ThemeRespect/Feeding.cfm, accessed May 5, 2013; Jane Wilson McWilliams, *Annapolis: City on the Severn* (Baltimore, 2011), 45–46.

35. Whitefield, *Journal, Embargo to Savannah*, 58; McWilliams, *Annapolis*, 57–58.

36. Richard J. Cox, ed., "Stephen Bordley, George Whitefield and the Great Awakening in Maryland," *Historical Magazine of the Protestant Episcopal Church* 46, no. 3 (Sept. 1977): 303–4.

37. Cox, "Stephen Bordley," 305–7.

38. Whitefield, *Journal, Embargo to Savannah*, 62–63; James Blair et al., *The Present State of Virginia, and the College* (London, 1727), 2.

39. Whitefield, *Journal, Embargo to Savannah*, 63; Linda L. Sturtz, *Within Her Power: Propertied Women in Colonial America* (London, 2002), 89–110.

40. Whitefield, *Journal, Embargo to Savannah*, 63.

41. Ibid., 64; Walsh, "Feeding the Town Folk"; *Virginia Gazette*, Dec. 14, 1739, 3; Lisa Smith, *The First Great Awakening in Colonial American Newspapers: A Shifting Story* (Lanham, Md., 2012), 75.

42. "The Charter of the College of William and Mary," in *The History of the College of William and Mary from its Foundation, 1660, to 1874* (Richmond, Va., 1874), 3; Thad W. Tate, "James Blair (ca. 1655–1743)," *Dictionary of Virginia Biography*, at http://www.EncyclopediaVirginia.org/Blair_James_ca_1655-1743, accessed Aug. 7, 2012.

43. Whitefield, *Journal, Embargo to Savannah*, 64–65; Lee Gatiss, ed., *The Sermons of George Whitefield* (Wheaton, Ill., 2012), 1:19.

44. Whitefield, *Journal, Embargo to Savannah*, 65–66; Whitefield to [Gilbert Tennent], Dec. 15, 1739, in *Letters of Whitefield*, 138.

45. Whitefield, *Journal, Embargo to Savannah*, 68–69.

46. Herbert R. Paschal, *A History of Colonial Bath* (Raleigh, N.C., 1955), 59.

47. Whitefield, *Journal, Embargo to Savannah*, 70.

48. Ibid., 71.

49. Ibid., 74; Whitefield to Samuel Mason, Dec. 29, 1739, in Schlenther and White, *Trevecka Letters*, 31; David Eltis and David Richardson, *Atlas of the Transatlantic Slave Trade* (New Haven, Conn., 2010), 51.

50. Alan Taylor, *American Colonies* (New York, 2001), 334, 336.

51. Ibid., 240.

52. Whitefield, *Journal, Embargo to Savannah*, 77–78.

53. Ibid., 78–79.

54. Emma Hart, *Building Charleston: Town and Society in the Eighteenth-Century British Atlantic World* (Charlottesville, Va., 2010), 39–40; Eliza Lucas quoted in Walter J. Fraser, Jr., *Charleston! Charleston! The History of a Southern City* (Columbia, S.C., 1989), 63.

55. Louis P. Nelson, "The Diversity of Countries: Anglican Churches in Virginia, South Carolina, and Jamaica," in David S. Shields, ed., *Material Culture in Anglo-America: Regional Identity and Urbanity in the Tidewater, Lowcountry, and Caribbean* (Columbia, S.C., 2009), 75.

56. Kidd, *Great Awakening*, 68–69; Whitefield, *Journal, Embargo to Savannah*, 80; "burnt wine" quotation in Fraser, *Charleston!*, 66.

57. Whitefield, *Journal, Embargo to Savannah*, 81; R. C. Nash, "Huguenot Merchants and the Development of South Carolina's Slave-Plantation and Atlantic Trading Economy, 1680–1775," in Bertrand Van Ruymbeke and Randy J. Sparks, eds., *Memory and Identity: The Huguenots in France and the Atlantic Diaspora* (Columbia, S.C., 2003), 208–40.

58. Whitefield, *Journal, Embargo to Savannah*, 83.

59. Ibid., 83–84.

60. Ibid., 85–86.

61. George Whitefield, *A Continuation of the Reverend Mr. Whitefield's Journal, After his Arrival at Georgia, To a Few Days after his Second Return Thither from Philadelphia* (London, 1741), 3–4.

62. *Boston Post-Boy*, Apr. 21, 1740; Lambert, *James Habersham*, 48–49.

63. Whitefield, *Journal, Georgia to Philadelphia*, 6; Cashin, *Beloved Bethesda*, 25–26.

64. "Journal of the Earl of Egmont," in *Colonial Records of Georgia* (Atlanta, 1908), 5: 333–34; Whitefield to Harman Verelst, Jan. 28, 1740, and Whitefield to the Trustees, Apr. 7, 1740, both in Mills Lane, ed., *General Oglethorpe's Georgia: Colonial Letters, 1733–1743* (Savannah, Ga., 1975), 436, 440–41; Whitefield to the Hon. J. W., Mar. 10, 1740, in *Letters of Whitefield*, 154; Harman Verelst to Whitefield, June 11, 1740, in Kenneth Coleman, ed., *Colonial Records of the State of Georgia: Trustees' Letter Book, 1738–1745* (Athens, Ga., 1985), 143.

65. Whitefield to Wm. D[elamotte], Nov. 10, 1739, in *Letters of Whitefield*, 109.

66. Whitefield, *Journal, Georgia to Philadelphia*, 10–11; Whitefield, *Journal, Embargo*, 18.

67. Whitefield, *Journal, Georgia to Philadelphia*, 11.

68. Ibid., 12–13.

69. Ibid., 14; Whitefield to John Wesley, Mar. 26, 1740, in *Letters of Whitefield*, 156.

70. Whitefield to Elizabeth D[elamotte], Feb. 1, 1740, in *Letters of Whitefield*, 148.

71. Stout, *Divine Dramatist*, 164; Dallimore, *Whitefield*, 1:469; Whitefield, *Journal, Georgia to Philadelphia*, 15.

72. Whitefield, *Journal, Georgia to Philadelphia*, 15; Whitefield to Mr. and Mrs. Delamotte, Apr. 4, 1740, in *Letters of Whitefield*, 159.

73. Whitefield to Miss E[lizabeth], Apr. 4, 1740, in *Letters of Whitefield*, 160.

74. Tyerman, *Life of Whitefield*, 1:367; Dallimore, *Whitefield*, 1:470; Whitefield to Wm. S[eward], [July] 26, 1740, in *Letters of Whitefield*, 194. (On the date of this letter, which Gillies registered as June 26, see Dallimore, *Whitefield*, 1:524n.)

75. Whitefield to Gilbert Tennent, Nov. 25, 1740, quoted in Dallimore, *Whitefield*, 1:474, and see generally Dallimore, *Whitefield*, 1:473–76; Whitefield to Daniel Rogers and Gilbert Tennent, Nov. 25, 1740, Southern Methodist University Special Collections. This letter also appears in Gillies's edition of Whitefield's letters, but does not include the reference to Elizabeth Delamotte.

76. Whitefield, *Journal, Georgia to Philadelphia*, 18.

CHAPTER 6. "TO REVIVE THE FLAME AGAIN"

1. Henry Abelove, ed., "Jonathan Edwards's Letter of Invitation to George Whitefield," *William and Mary Quarterly*, 3rd ser., 29, no. 3 (Jul., 1972): 488; Jonathan Edwards to Thomas Prince, Dec. 12, 1743, in *Christian History* 46 (Jan. 14, 1743/4): 368; Whitefield, *Journal, Georgia to Falmouth*, 47. Histories of this encounter between Whitefield and Edwards often quote Sarah Edwards describing Whitefield's voice as "perfect music," but the source used seems to have invented Sarah's words for literary effect; see "Diary and Letters of Sarah Pierpont," *Hours at Home* 5, no. 4 (Aug. 1867): 301. Thanks to George Marsden for pointing this out to me.

2. Whitefield to a friend in London, Jan. 18, 1740, in *Letters of Whitefield*, 505–6. The letters were originally published in the *Pennsylvania Gazette* in April and May 1740, then published as a pamphlet by Franklin later; see Hoffer, *When Benjamin Franklin*, 140n3.

3. Whitefield, *Three Letters from the Rev. George Whitefield* (Philadelphia, 1740), 2–3.

4. Fiering, *Jonathan Edwards's Moral Thought*, 229n80; William Williams to Benjamin Colman, July 1, 1740, in Benjamin Colman Papers, Massachusetts Historical Society; Whitefield, *Journal, Georgia to Philadelphia*, 22–23; Cummings quoted in Deborah Mathias Gough, *Christ Church, Philadelphia: The Nation's Church in a Changing City* (Philadelphia, 1995), 54.

5. Archibald Cummings, *Faith Absolutely Necessary, But Not Sufficient to Salvation Without Good Works* (Philadelphia, 1740), v–vi, xv; compare Whitefield, *A Letter from the Reverend Mr. Whitefield, to the Religious Societies* (Philadelphia, 1739), 10.

6. *American Weekly Mercury*, Dec. 11, 1740, 3.

7. Whitefield, *Journal, Georgia to Philadelphia*, 35.

8. William Seward, *Journal of a Voyage from Savannah to Philadelphia* (London, 1740), 4–5; Whitefield, *Journal, Georgia to Philadelphia*, 20; Whitefield, *First Two Parts of His Life*, 340.

9. Whitefield, *Three Letters*, 13; John R. Tyson, ed., *Charles Wesley: A Reader* (New York, 1989), 77–78.

10. Whitefield, *Three Letters*, 13–14; Alan Gallay, "The Great Sellout: George Whitefield on Slavery," in Winfred B. Moore, Jr., and Joseph F. Tripp, eds., *Looking South: Chapters in the Story of an American Region* (Westport, Conn., 1989), 21–22.

11. Whitefield, *Three Letters*, 14–15; Edward E. Andrews, *Native Apostles: Black and Indian Missionaries in the British Atlantic World* (Cambridge, Mass., 2013), 107.

12. "Black bitch" quote in Rebecca Anne Goetz, *The Baptism of Early Virginia: How Christianity Created Race* (Baltimore, 2012), 106, see also 86–111.

13. Whitefield, *Three Letters*, 13; on Whitefield and Alexander Garden's debate over slavery, see Young Hwi Yoon, "The Spread of Antislavery Sentiment through Proslavery Tracts in the Transatlantic Evangelical Community, 1740s–1770s," *Church History* 81, no. 2 (June 2012): 356–59; Travis Glasson, *Mastering Christianity: Missionary Anglicanism and Slavery in the Atlantic World* (New York, 2012), 121–23.

14. Gillies, *Memoirs of Whitefield*, 25; Seward, *Journal of a Voyage*, 2, 17.

15. Whitefield to a friend in London, Apr. 27, 1740, in *Letters of Whitefield*, 507; Whitefield to Dr. Barecroft, n.d., quoted in Dallimore, *Whitefield*, 1:497; Steven Craig Harper, *Promised Land: Penn's Holy Experiment, the Walking Purchase, and the Dispossession of the Delawares, 1600–1763* (Cranbury, N.J., 2006), 75.

16. Whitefield, *Journal, Georgia to Philadelphia*, 24; Robert W. Brockway, *A Wonderful Work of God: Puritanism and the Great Awakening* (Cranbury, N.J., 2003), 62.

17. Seward, *Journal of a Voyage*, 7; Whitefield, *Journal, Georgia to Philadelphia*, 20–21.

18. Kenneth P. Minkema, "Jonathan Edwards's Defense of Slavery," *Massachusetts Historical Review* 4 (2002): 23, 32; Richard A. Bailey, *Race and Redemption in Puritan New England* (New York, 2011), 61–62, 119–120.

19. Minkema, "Edwards's Defense of Slavery," 36, 39; Marsden, *Jonathan Edwards: A Life* (New Haven, Conn., 2003), 256–58.

20. Gillies, *Memoirs of Whitefield*, 53; Seward, *Journal of a Voyage*, 7.

21. *Autobiography of Benjamin Franklin*, 177.

22. Ibid., 177.

23. Ibid., 178; Whitefield to Mr. F[ranklin], Nov. 26, 1740, in *Letters of Whitefield*, 226; B[enjamin] Franklin to John Franklin, Aug. 6, 1747, in Leonard W. Labaree, ed., *The Papers of Benjamin Franklin: January 1, 1745, through June 30, 1750* (New Haven, Conn., 1961), 3:169.

24. Whitefield, *Journal, Georgia to Philadelphia*, 31.

25. Joseph Tracy, *The Great Awakening: A History of the Revival of Religion in the Time of Edwards and Whitefield* (Boston, 1845), 232–33.

26. Charles Chauncy, *Seasonable Thoughts on the State of Religion in New England* (Boston, 1743), 213; Kidd, *Great Awakening*, 62.

27. Tracy, *Great Awakening*, 233.

28. Andrew Croswell, *Mr. Croswell's Reply to the Declaration of a Number of the Associated Ministers in Boston and Charlestown, With Regard to the Rev. Mr. James Davenport and His Conduct* (Boston, 1742), 8–9; Tracy, *Great Awakening*, 230.

29. Seward, *Journal of a Voyage*, 38, 64.

30. Whitefield, *Journal, Georgia to Philadelphia*, 36.

31. Ibid., 36–37; Whitefield, "The Lord Our Righteousness," in Whitefield, *Nine Sermons upon the Following Subjects* (London, 1742), 33; Dallimore, *Whitefield*, 1:499.

32. Whitefield, *Journal, Georgia to Philadelphia*, 38; extract from Memoirs of Mrs. Hannah Hodge, in the *Evangelical Magazine* 17 (London, 1809), 152.

33. Whitefield, *Journal, Georgia to Philadelphia*, 38–39.

34. Ibid., 40.

35. Ibid., 35–36.

36. Whitefield to Mr. M— —, an Indian Trader, May 19, 1740, in *Letters of Whitefield*, 171.

37. Whitefield, *Journal, Georgia to Philadelphia*, 48; Whitefield to the Allegany Indians, May 21, 1740, in *Letters of Whitefield*, 173; Linford D. Fisher, *The Indian Great Awakening: Religion and the Shaping of Native Cultures in Early America* (New York, 2012), 70–75.

38. Whitefield, *Journal, Georgia to Philadelphia*, 43.

39. Ibid., 44.

40. Ibid., 44–45.

41. Ibid., 45; Kidd, *Great Awakening*, 64–65.

42. Whitefield to a friend in London, Apr. 27, 1740, and Whitefield to Mr. G— — L— —, in London, May 22, 1740, in *Letters of Whitefield*, 179, 508; Frank Lambert, *Inventing the "Great Awakening"* (Princeton, N.J., 1999), 112.

43. Whitefield to J[ohn] W[esley], May 24, 1740, in *Letters of Whitefield*, 182–183.

44. Whitefield to J[ohn] W[esley], May 24, 1740, and Whitefield to J[ames] H[utton], June 7, 1740, in *Letters of Whitefield*, 182–83, 185; see also Whitefield to J[ohn] W[esley], June 25, 1740, in *Letters of Whitefield*, 189–90.

45. Whitefield to J[ames] H[utton], June 7, 1740, and Whitefield to J[ohn] W[esley], June 25, 1740 in *Letters of Whitefield*, 185, 190; Whitefield, *Journal, Georgia to Philadelphia*, 53–54.

46. Whitefield, *Journal, Georgia to Falmouth*, 4–7.

47. Andrew Croswell, *An Answer to the Rev. Mr. Garden's Three First Letters to the Rev. Mr. Whitefield* (Boston, 1741), 56–58; David Ramsay, *The History of South Carolina, from Its First Settlement in 1670 to the Year 1808* (Charleston, 1809), 14–15n; Tyerman, *Life of Whitefield*, 1:398–400; Dallimore, *Whitefield*, 1:517–19.

48. Hugh Bryan to his sister, [Nov. 13, 1740], in Hugh Bryan, *Living Christianity Delineated* (London, 1760), 7, 9, 14 [date per the *Weekly History*, June 6, 1741]; Alan Gallay, *The Formation of a Planter Elite: Jonathan Bryan and the Southern Colonial Frontier* (Athens, Ga., 1989), 33–34.

49. Whitefield, *Journal, Georgia to Falmouth*, 9–11.

50. Ibid., 12–13, 16; Gallay, *Formation of a Planter Elite*, 34.

51. *Boston News-Letter*, Apr. 12, 1739; *New England Weekly Journal*, Nov. 20, 1739.

52. Whitefield to Jonathan Edwards, Nov. 16, 1739, Whitefield to Benjamin Colman, Nov. 16, 1739, and Whitefield to [Gilbert Tennent], Jan. 22, 1740, in *Letters of Whitefield*, 120–21, 141; Kidd, *Great Awakening*, 83–84.

53. Benjamin Colman to Whitefield, Dec. 3, 1739, in *Three Letters to the Reverend Mr. George Whitefield* (Philadelphia, [1739]), 2–3, 5.

54. "Paragraph of a Letter from Philadelphia, June 5, 1740," in *Boston Weekly Post-Boy*, June 23, 1740.

55. *New England Weekly Journal*, Sept. 23, 1740.

56. Bridenbaugh, *Gentlemen's Progress*, 101–2; Carl Bridenbaugh, "Colonial Newport as a Summer Resort," *Rhode Island Historical Collections* 26, no. 1 (Jan. 1933): 3.

57. Whitefield, *Journal, Georgia to Falmouth*, 18–19; Honeyman quoted in Dallimore, *Whitefield*, 1:527n.

58. "Joseph Bennett's History of New England," in *Proceedings of the Massachusetts Historical Society* 5 (1860–62): 110–11, 114–15, 125.

59. Douglas C. Stenerson, ed., "An Anglican Critique of the Early Phase of the Great Awakening in New England: A Letter by Timothy Cutler," *William and Mary Quarterly*, 3rd ser., 30, no. 3 (July 1973): 477.

60. Timothy Cutler to the Bishop of London, May 28, 1739, in Stenerson, "Anglican Critique," 487.

61. Whitefield, *Journal, Georgia to Falmouth*, 24–25.

62. Ibid., 25.

63. Ibid., 26.

64. Ibid.; *American Weekly Mercury*, Sept. 25, 1740.

65. *American Weekly Mercury*, Oct. 2, 1740.

66. Whitefield, *Journal, Georgia to Falmouth*, 27.

67. Ibid., 27–28; Whitefield, *An Exhortation to Come and See Jesus* (London, 1739), 9; Mark Hutchinson and John Wolffe, *A Short History of Global Evangelicalism* (New York, 2012), 47.

68. Whitefield, *Journal, Georgia to Falmouth*, 28–29; Whitefield, *First Two Parts of His Life*, 393n.

69. Samuel Eliot Morison, *Three Centuries of Harvard, 1636–1936* (Cambridge, Mass., 1936), 85; *Weekly History*, May 30, 1741.

70. Whitefield, *Journal, Georgia to Falmouth*, 29.

71. Ibid., 31. The King James Version refers to the Holy Spirit as "itself" in Romans 8:26, while modern translations often use "himself."

72. Ibid., 31–32.

73. Ibid., 31, 37.

74. Ibid., 37; Whitefield, *A Continuation of the Reverend Mr. Whitefield's Journal from Savannah, June 25. 1740. To his Arrival at Rhode-Island, his Travels in the Other Governments of New-England, to his Departure from Stanford for New-York* (Boston, 1741), 69.

75. Whitefield, *Journal, Georgia to Falmouth*, 38.

76. Gilbert Tennent, *The Danger of an Unconverted Ministry* (Philadelphia, 1740), 5; Whitefield, *Journal, Georgia to Falmouth*, 38, 48.

77. Whitefield, *Journal, Georgia to Falmouth*, 41; *New England Weekly Journal*, Oct. 14, 1740; *Boston News Letter*, Oct., 16, 1740; Whitefield, *First Two Parts of His Life*, 406.

78. Whitefield, *Journal, Georgia to Falmouth*, 42; *Weekly History*, May 30, 1741.

79. Israel Loring, diary transcript, Nov. 1, 14, 15, and 29, 1739; Oct. 13 and 14, 1740; Mar. 28, 1742, Sudbury, Massachusetts, archives; Whitefield, *Journal, Georgia to Falmouth*, 43; Kidd, *Great Awakening*, 150, 156.

80. Whitefield, *Journal, Georgia to Falmouth*, 45–46.

81. Ibid., 47; Daniel Rogers Diary, Oct. 19, 1740, New-York Historical Society; Whitefield, "The Seed of the Woman, and the Seed of the Serpent," in *Nine Sermons*, 64–65. Rogers wrote that Whitefield preached on "3. Chaptr. Genesis."

82. Whitefield, *Journal, Georgia to Falmouth*, 45; Jonathan Edwards to Thomas Prince, Dec. 12, 1743, and Edwards to Whitefield, Dec. 14, 1740, in George Claghorn, ed., *The Works of Jonathan Edwards: Letters and Personal Writings* (New Haven, Conn., 1998), 16:116, 87.

83. Jonathan Edwards, *Copies of the Two Letters Cited by the Rev. Mr. Clap, Rector of the College at New-Haven* (Boston, 1745), 7.

84. Ava Chamberlain, "The Grand Sower of the Seed: Jonathan Edwards's Critique of George Whitefield," *New England Quarterly* 70, no. 3 (Sept. 1997): 374, 379.

85. Marsden, *Jonathan Edwards*, 213.

CHAPTER 7. "HEARING HIM PREACH, GAVE ME A HEART WOUND"

1. Michael J. Crawford, ed., "The Spiritual Travels of Nathan Cole," *William and Mary Quarterly*, 3rd ser., 33, no. 1 (Jan. 1976): 92.

2. Ibid., 93.

3. Ibid., 90, 93.

4. Barbara Lacey, ed., *The World of Hannah Heaton: The Diary of an Eighteenth-Century New England Farm Woman* (DeKalb, Ill., 2003), 6, 9.

5. Thomas S. Kidd, "Daniel Rogers' Egalitarian Great Awakening," *Journal of the Historical Society* 7, no. 1 (Mar. 2007): 114.

6. Daniel Rogers Diary, Oct. 22, 23, 1740.

7. Daniel Rogers Diary, Oct. 30, 1740.

8. Whitefield, *Journal, Georgia to Falmouth*, 51, 55; "The Colleges Censure George Whitefield," in Douglas Sloan, ed., *The Great Awakening and American Education: A Documentary History* (New York, 1973), 148–49.

9. Whitefield, *Journal, Georgia to Falmouth*, 53.

10. Ibid., 53–54.

11. Ibid., 55.

12. Alexander Garden, *Six Letters to the Rev. Mr. George Whitefield*, 2nd ed. (Boston, 1740), 6, 14, 36.

13. *The Querists, Or, An Extract of Sundry Passages Taken Out of Mr. Whitefield's Printed Sermons, Journals, and Letters* (Philadelphia, 1740), iii–iv.

14. Whitefield, *Journal, Georgia to Falmouth*, 56; Whitefield, *A Letter from the Reverend Mr. Whitefield, to Some Church Members of the Presbyterian Perswasion* (Boston, 1740), 6.

15. Whitefield, *Letter to Some Church Members*, 10; *The Querists*, v; Thomas Halyburton, *An Abstract of the Life and Death of the Reverend Learned and Pious Mr. Thomas Halyburton* (London, 1739), vii.

16. Whitefield, *Journal, Georgia to Falmouth*, 57–58; Daniel Rogers Diary, Nov. 2, 1740.

17. Whitefield, *Journal, Georgia to Falmouth*, 58.

18. Ibid., 59–60.

19. Ibid., 60.

20. Ibid.; Daniel Rogers Diary, Nov. 5, 1740; Whitefield, "Blind Bartimeus," in George Whitefield, *Sermons by the Late Rev. George Whitefield* (Glasgow, 1740), 234. The title of this imprint mistakenly implied that Whitefield was deceased.

21. Daniel Rogers Diary, Nov. 5, 1740; Whitefield, *Journal, Georgia to Falmouth*, 60.

22. Daniel Rogers Diary, Nov. 5, 1740; Whitefield, *Journal, Georgia to Falmouth*, 61.

23. Kidd, *Great Awakening*, 91–92, 141, 146–147; Whitefield to Mr. G[ilbert] T[ennent], Feb. 5, 1742, in *Letters of Whitefield*, 366.

24. Whitefield, *Journal, Georgia to Falmouth*, 61–62.

25. Whitefield to Jonathan Belcher, Nov. 9, 1740, in *Letters of Whitefield*, 221; Whitefield, *Journal, Georgia to Falmouth*, 62–63.

26. Whitefield, *Journal, Georgia to Philadelphia*, 40; Whitefield, *Journal, Georgia to Falmouth*, 64.

27. Whitefield, *Journal, Georgia to Falmouth*, 64–65; John Clement, "Charles Brockden," *Pennsylvania Magazine of History and Biography* 12 (1888): 188.

28. Whitefield, *Journal, Georgia to Falmouth*, 67.

29. "From the *Pennsylvania Gazette*—on hearing Mr. George Whitefield at the New Building in Philadelphia," *Weekly History*, May 30, 1741.

30. Whitefield, *Journal, Georgia to Falmouth*, 70–71, 76; Whitefield to H[owell] H[arris], Nov. 9, 1740, in *Letters of Whitefield*, 220.

31. Whitefield to the Rev. Mr. J[ohn] W[esley], Nov. 24, 1740, and Whitefield to George C——, Dec. 11, 1740, in *Letters of Whitefield*, 225, 227; Podmore, *Moravian Church*, 60, 70.

32. Whitefield to J[ames] H[utton], Nov. 24, 1740, in *Letters of Whitefield*, 224; Podmore, *Moravian Church*, 81.

33. Whitefield to J[ames] H[utton], Nov. 24, 1740, in *Letters of Whitefield*, 224; Whitefield to Hutton, Nov. 29, [1740], quoted in Podmore, *Moravian Church*, 81.

34. Dallimore, *Whitefield*, 1:474.

35. Ibid., 1:583–85; Wilson H. Kimnach and Kenneth P. Minkema, "The Material and Social Practices of Intellectual Work: Jonathan Edwards's Study," *William and Mary Quarterly*, 3rd ser., 69, no. 4 (Oct. 2012): 700n37.

36. *Weekly Miscellany*, Nov. 1, 1740; Whitefield to the Rev. Mr. [William] C[ooper], Jan. 1, 1741, Whitefield to J[ames] H[abersham], Mar. 25, 1741, Whitefield to J[ohn] C[ennick], June 8, 1741, and Whitefield to the Rev. Mr. G[ilbert] T[ennent], Feb. 2, 1742, in *Letters of Whitefield*, 230, 271, 362. There is surprisingly little primary-source evidence about the circumstances surrounding Seward's death, leading one author to question whether Seward was actually killed in Hay or whether his death resulted from complications from the initial attack; see Geoffrey L. Fairs, "Notes on the Death of William Seward at Hay, 1740," *Journal of the Calvinistic Methodist Historical Society* 58, no. 1 (Mar. 1973): 12–17.

37. Whitefield, *Journal, Georgia to Falmouth*, 76–77; Kidd, *Great Awakening*, 76.

38. Whitefield, *Journal, Georgia to Falmouth*, 77; Lambert, *James Habersham*, 40–42; letter from "a young Gentleman of Boston," Jan. 1, 1742, in Whitefield, *Continuation of the Account of the Orphan House*, in Gillies, *Works of Whitefield*, 3:447–48.

39. E. Merton Coulter, ed., *The Journal of William Stephens, 1741–1743* (Athens, Ga., 1958), 30; Whitefield to the Georgia Trustees, Aug. 17, 1742, in *Colonial Records of the State of Georgia* (Atlanta, 1914), 23:392; Whitefield to James Oglethorpe, Aug. 18, 1742, in *Letters of Whitefield*, 423; "new birth" quotation in Julie Anne Sweet, *William Stephens: Georgia's Forgotten Founder* (Baton Rouge, La., 2010), 186. On Orton, see Sweet, *William Stephens*, 194–95; Lambert, *James Habersham*, 42–45.

40. *Weekly History*, June 13, 1741, 3–4; also June 20, 1741, 1.

41. Whitefield, *Journal, Georgia to Falmouth*, 80–81.

42. To Mr. [Jonathan] B[arber] and his wife at Bethesda, Feb. 17, 1741, in *Letters of Whitefield*, 244; Whitefield to Ralph Erskine, Feb. 16, 1741, in Tyerman, *Life of Whitefield*, 1:461.

43. Ward and Heitzenrater, *Works of John Wesley*, 19:182–84; Dallimore, *Whitefield*, 2:38–39.

44. Whitefield to John Wesley, Feb. 1, 1741, in Frank Baker, ed., *The Works of John Wesley: Letters II, 1740–1755* (Oxford, 1982), 26:48–49; Tyerman, *Life of Whitefield*, 1:464.

45. Whitefield to Mrs. A[nne] D[utton], Feb. 20, 1741, in *Letters of Whitefield*, 250–51; Karen O'Dell Bullock, "Dutton [née Williams], Anne (1691x5–1765)," *Oxford Dictionary of National Biography* (New York, 2004), at http://www.oxforddnb.com/view/article/71063, accessed Oct. 12, 2012; Stephen J. Stein, "A Note on Anne Dutton, Eighteenth-Century Evangelical," *Church History* 44, no. 4 (Dec. 1975): 485–91; Fogleman, *Jesus Is Female*, 45.

46. Mack, *Heart Religion*, 19; "disciplined moral energy" quotation in Mack, *Heart Religion*, 26; Anderson, *Imagining Methodism*, 77–78; Hempton, *Methodism*, 5, 137, 149–50; Anna M. Lawrence, *One Family under God: Love, Belonging, and Authority in Early Transatlantic Methodism* (Philadelphia, 2011), 110–11.

47. Whitefield to J[ames] H[abersham], Mar. 25, 1741, in *Letters of Whitefield*, 256–57; Gillies, *Memoirs of Whitefield*, 70.

48. Whitefield manuscript quoted in Gillies, *Memoirs of Whitefield*, 69.

49. Ibid., 72.

50. Ward and Heitzenrater, *Works of John Wesley*, 19:188–89, 456; Dallimore, *Whitefield*, 2:51–52.

51. Whitefield, *A Letter to the Reverend John Wesley* (London, 1741), 5, 7.

52. Ibid., 10–11.

53. Ibid., 19–20, 27; Timothy L. Smith, "George Whitefield and Wesleyan Perfectionism," *Wesleyan Theological Journal* 19, no. 1 (Spring 1984): 71–72, available at http://wesley.nnu.edu/fileadmin/imported_site/wesleyjournal/1984-wtj-19-1.pdf, accessed Dec. 21, 2012; Dallimore, *Whitefield*, 2:66.

54. Ward and Heitzenrater, *Works of John Wesley*, 19:189–90.

55. Whitefield to a friend in London, Apr. 25, 1741, in *Letters of Whitefield*, 510; John Wesley to Whitefield, Apr. 27, 1741, in Baker, *Works of John Wesley*, 26:59–61.

56. John Wesley to Whitefield, Apr. 27, 1741, in Baker, *Works of John Wesley*, 26:59–61; Cennick quoted in Dallimore, *Whitefield*, 2:70.

57. Howell Harris to John Cennick, Oct. 27, 1740, in the *Weekly History*, July 11, 1741, 3; Whitefield to Howell Harris, Apr. 28, 1741, and Whitefield to Mr. Wm. W——, at Edinburgh, May 16, 1741, in *Letters of Whitefield*, 259–60, 261.

58. Whitefield to Howell Harris, Apr. 28, 1741, in *Letters of Whitefield*, 259–60.

CHAPTER 8. "THY MAKER IS THY HUSBAND"

1. Account from Whitefield to Mr. L——, May 11, 1742, and Whitefield to the same, May 15, 1742, in *Letters of Whitefield*, 384–88.

2. Whitefield to Mr. L——, May 11, 1742, in *Letters of Whitefield*, 386.

3. Quoted in Hindmarsh, *Evangelical Conversion Narrative*, 77, 135.

4. Description of Leith in *A New Guide to the City of Edinburgh*, 3rd ed. (Edinburgh, 1797), 125–26.

5. Ralph Erksine to Whitefield, April 10, 1741, in H. M. Paton, ed., *Scottish Historical Review* 31, no. 111, pt. 1 (Apr. 1952): 53; Thomas Boston, *Human Nature in Its Fourfold State*, 4th ed. (Edinburgh, 1744), 159; Whitefield, *Golden Chain*, 8; Noll, *Rise of Evangelicalism*, 58–59. Whitefield's list of recommended texts is in the *Weekly History*, July 4, 1741, and the *Daily Gazetteer*, Aug. 10, 1741.

6. Tyerman, *Life of Whitefield*, 1:503; Ralph Erskine to Whitefield, April 10, 1741, in Paton, *Scottish Historical Review*, 53–54.

7. Ralph Erskine to Whitefield, April 10, 1741, 55 ; Whitefield to E[benezer] E[rskine], May 16, 1741, in *Letters of Whitefield*, 262 (a slightly different version is in Tyerman); Ebenezer Erskine to Whitefield, June 1741, in Tyerman, *Life of Whitefield*, 1:506–7.

8. Whitefield to Mrs. [Anne] D[utton], at Gransden, July 17, 1741, and Whitefield to Mr. [Jonathan] B[arber], July 24, 1741, in *Letters of Whitefield*, 277–78, 280; Susan O'Brien, "A Transatlantic Community of Saints: The Great Awakening and the First Evangelical Network, 1735–1755," *American Historical Review* 91, no. 4 (Oct. 1986): 817–19.

9. Whitefield to Rebekah B., July 25, 1741, and Whitefield to Mary A., July 25, 1741, in *Letters of Whitefield*, 288–89.

10. Gilbert Tennent to Whitefield, Apr. 25, 1741, in the *Weekly History*, June 20, 1741; Whitefield to the students, &c. under convictions at the colleges of Cambridge and New-Haven, [July 1741?], and Whitefield to Mr. D——, at Boston, July 25, 1741, in *Letters of Whitefield*, 296–97.

11. *Weekly History*, Apr. 11, 1741; Whitefield to Howell Harris, Aug. 15, 1741, in Schlenther and White, *Trevecka Letters*, 58–59; Lambert, "*Pedlar in Divinity*," 69–70; O'Brien, "Transatlantic Community," 827.

12. Whitefield to J[ohn] C[ennick], Aug. 1, 1741, in *Letters of Whitefield*, 304–5; George Whitefield, *The Prodigal Son* (Glasgow, 1741), 4; Defoe quoted in Arthur Fawcett, *The Cambuslang Revival: The Scottish Evangelical Revival of the Eighteenth Century* (London, 1971), 80–81.

13. Ralph Erskine to Whitefield, Aug. 21, 1739, in Ralph Erskine, *A Letter from the Reverend Mr. Ralph Erskine to the Reverend Mr. Geo. Whitefield* (Philadelphia, 1741), 13–14; Leigh Eric Schmidt, *Holy Fairs: Scotland and the Making of American Revivalism*, 2nd ed. (Grand Rapids, Mich., 2001), 49.

14. Whitefield to J[ohn] C[ennick], Aug. 1, 1741, and Whitefield to Thomas N[oble], Aug. 8, 1741, in *Letters of Whitefield*, 305, 307.

15. Whitefield to Thomas N[oble], Aug. 8, 1741, and Whitefield to G[ilbert] T[ennent], Feb. 2, 1742, in *Letters of Whitefield*, 307–8, 363.

16. Whitefield to Thomas N[oble], Aug. 8, 1741, and Whitefield to Mr. D——A——, July 30–31, 1742, in *Letters of Whitefield*, 307–8, 413.

17. "An Extract of a Letter from a Gentleman at Edinburgh, to His Friend in London," Aug. 8, 1741, in the *Weekly History*, Aug. 22, 1741; Whitefield to the Rev. Mr. [John] W[illison], Aug. 10, 1741, and Whitefield to H[owell] H[arris], Aug. 11, 1741, in *Letters of Whitefield*, 310, 312.

18. Whitefield, *The Method of Grace* (Glasgow, 1741), 2; Keith Edward Beebe, ed., "The McCulloch Manuscripts of the Cambuslang Revival, 1742: A Critical Edition" (PhD diss., University of Aberdeen, 2003), appendix 1a, 103.

19. Beebe, "McCulloch Manuscripts," appendix 2b, 500; Whitefield, "Christ the Believer's Husband," in *Five Sermons on the Following Subjects* (London, 1747), 30.

20. Whitefield, *The Lord Our Righteousness* (Glasgow, 1741), 12, 16, 18; Beebe, "McCulloch Manuscripts," appendix 1b, 1.7. The text of the 1741 edition of *The Lord Our Righteousness* is substantially different from that in Gillies, *Works of Whitefield*, which is also the basis of Gatiss, *Sermons of Whitefield*. Gillies's edition follows more closely the text of *The Lord Our Righteousness* in Whitefield, *Nine Sermons*. Whitefield undoubtedly delivered, and probably revised, this sermon (as with most of his published sermons) many times, so it is not surprising that different texts would appear between 1741 and 1742.

21. Stout, *Divine Dramatist*, 42; Whitefield, *Saul's Conversion* (Glasgow, 1741), 10, 12, 28–29.

22. Whitefield, *Method of Grace*, 16–17, 26.

23. Ibid., 31–32; George Whitefield, *The Duty of a Gospel Minister* (Glasgow, 1741), 30.

24. George Whitefield, *Persecution, the Christian's Lot* (Glasgow, 1741), 19–21; Gatiss, *Sermons of Whitefield*, 1:19.

25. Whitefield to the Rev. Mr. J[ohn] W[esley], Oct. 10, 1741, in *Letters of Whitefield*, 331.

26. Whitefield to Peter B[öhler], Oct. 10, 1741, in *Letters of Whitefield*, 331–32; George Whitefield, *A Letter from the Reverend Mr. George Whitefield, to the Reverend Mr. John Wesley* (Boston, 1740), 27.

27. Charles Wesley to John Wesley, [Sept. 28, 1741], in Baker, *Works of John Wesley*, 26:65–66; Whitefield to Howell Harris, Dec. 28, 1741, in Dallimore, *Whitefield*, 2:141; Charles Wesley's sermon recommended in the *Weekly History*, May 1, 1742, 4; sermon praised by "Mr. Wesley" in ibid.; Whitefield to Mr. F——, Sept. 22, 1742, in *Letters of Whitefield*, 438–39; Lloyd, *Charles Wesley*, 55–56.

28. Quoted in Dallimore, *Whitefield*, 2:101–2.

29. Whitefield to Howell Harris, Aug. 22, 1741, in Schlenther and White, *Trevecka Letters*, 60; Dallimore, *Whitefield*, 2:105–6; E. Benyon, "Mrs. James, Abergavenny: Her Courtship with Howell Harris, and Her Marriage to George Whitefield," *Journal of the Calvinistic Methodist Historical Society* 27, no. 1 (1943): 14.

30. Howell Harris to Anna Williams, Nov. 19, 1741, Howell Harris to Anna Williams, Nov. 21, 1741, Howell Harris to Elizabeth [James] Whitefield, Nov. 26, 1741, and Howell Harris to [Whitefield], [Nov. 26, 1741], in Schlenther and White, *Trevecka Letters*, 66–67; Benyon, "Mrs. James," 19.

31. Lawrence Stone, *Uncertain Unions: Marriage in England, 1660–1753* (New York, 1992), 7–8; Lawrence, *One Family under God*, 162–63.

32. Dallimore, *Whitefield*, 2:109–10; Whitefield to T——E—— in Edinburgh, Nov. 27, 1741, and Whitefield to the Rev. Mr. G[ilbert] T[ennent], Feb. 2, 1742, in *Letters of Whitefield*, 342, 362; Amanda Vickery, *Behind Closed Doors: At Home in Georgian England* (New Haven, Conn., 2009), 218.

33. Mack, *Heart Religion*, 84–91.

34. W. Hammond to Whitefield, Dec. 13, 1741, Southern Methodist University Special Collections; *A Brief and Impartial Account of the Character and Doctrines of Mr. Whitefield and Mr. Wesley* (Edinburgh, 1743), 12; *London Evening Post*, Apr. 22, 1742.

35. Whitefield to Mr. W——, Feb. 2, 1742, Whitefield to Mr. James R——, Feb. 2, 1742, and Whitefield to Mr. O——, Apr. 6, 1742, in *Letters of Whitefield*, 364–65, 381; *Weekly History*, Apr. 17, 1742, 4; Albert Outler, ed., *John Wesley* (New York, 1964), 15–16; Hindmarsh, *Evangelical Conversion Narrative*, 63.

36. Whitefield to Mr. A——, Nov. 30, 1741 [also printed, with slight variations, in the *Weekly History*, Dec. 5, 1741], in *Letters of Whitefield*, 343; John Willison to a friend in Edinburgh, Oct. 8, 1741, in Thomas Prince, *Christian History*, Nov. 5, 1743.

37. Whitefield to Mr. A——, Nov. 30, 1741, Whitefield to J[ohn] C[ennick], Dec. 22, 1741, and Whitefield to Miss——, Feb. 27, 1742, in *Letters of Whitefield*, 343, 347, 373; Whitefield to John Cennick, Dec. 22, 1741, in the *Weekly History*, Jan. 2, 1742; Craig Atwood, "Understanding Zinzendorf's Blood and Wounds Theology," *Journal of Moravian History* no. 1 (Fall 2006): 35.

38. Whitefield to [James] H[abersham], Sept. 24, 1742, in *Letters of Whitefield*, 441; Whitefield to John Wesley, Mar. 11, 1742, in Baker, *Works of John Wesley*, 26:74;

Podmore, *Moravian Church*, 80–84; Milton J. Coalter, Jr., *Gilbert Tennent, Son of Thunder: A Case Study of Continental Pietism's Impact on the First Great Awakening in the Middle Colonies* (Westport, Conn., 1986), 115.

39. Extract of a letter from Mr. T. L. and J. K. of Edinburgh to the Reverend Mr. George Whitefield, Dec. 26, 1741, in the *Weekly History*, Feb. 13, 1742; William McCulloch to Whitefield, Feb. 14, 1742, in Whitefield Papers, Library of Congress; [William McCulloch] to Whitefield, Apr. 28, 1742, in the *Weekly History*, May 29, 1742; Whitefield to [William] M[cCulloch], June 8, 1742, in *Letters of Whitefield*, 401.

40. Beebe, "McCulloch Manuscripts," appendix 1a, 229.

41. "A Letter from a Minister in Boston New-England, to his Correspondent in Gorbals," *Glasgow Weekly-History*, May 14, 1742, 6.

42. William McCulloch, *A Sermon against the Idolatrous Worship of the Church of Rome* (Glasgow, 1726), introduction, 12, 34; Fawcett, *Cambuslang Revival*, 38–41.

43. Fawcett, *Cambuslang Revival*, 97–98; Whitefield to Elizabeth Whitefield, July 7, 1742, in *Letters of Whitefield*, 405; James Robe, *A Short Narrative of the Extraordinary Work at Cambuslang, near Glasgow* (Boston, 1742), 4; Hindmarsh, *Evangelical Conversion Narrative*, 194.

44. Whitefield to J[ohn] C[ennick], July 15, 1742, in *Letters of Whitefield*, 409; Fawcett, *Cambuslang Revival*, 115; letter from William McCulloch, July 14, 1742, in *Glasgow Weekly-History* 30, 2; John Erskine to [Thomas Prince], July 17, 1742, in Jonathan Yeager, ed., "John Erskine's Letterbook, 1742–45," *Miscellany of the Scottish History Society* 14 (2013): 234.

45. Schmidt, *Holy Fairs*, 108.

46. Whitefield to J[ohn] C[ennick], July 15, 1742, in *Letters of Whitefield*, 409; Fawcett, *Cambuslang Revival*, 115; letter from William McCulloch, July 14, 1742.

47. Fawcett, *Cambuslang Revival*, 116; T. C. Smout, "Born Again at Cambuslang: New Evidence on Popular Religion and Literacy in Eighteenth-Century Scotland," *Past and Present* 97 (Nov. 1982): 115; Beebe, "McCulloch Manuscripts," appendix 1a, 229; D. MacFarlan, *The Revivals of the Eighteenth Century, Particularly at Cambuslang* (Edinburgh, 1847), 66; Hindmarsh, *Evangelical Conversion Narrative*, 183n63, 194. Whitefield kept "Thy Maker is Thy Husband" in his preaching repertoire; for example, he delivered it in Brinkworth, England, in June 1743, and wrote "it was a day of espousals I believe to many"; see Whitefield to Mr. S——, June 27, 1743, in Gillies, *Works of Whitefield*, 2:29.

48. Whitefield, *Five Sermons*, 5–6, 11.

49. Ibid., 11 (emphasis in original), 16.

50. Ibid., 22; Anderson, *Imagining Methodism*, 85–87.

51. Susan Juster, *Disorderly Women: Sexual Politics and Evangelicalism in Revolutionary New England* (Ithaca, N.Y., 1994), 52–53, 64; Philip Greven, *The Protestant Temperament: Patterns of Child-Rearing, Religious Experience, and the Self in Early America* (New York, 1977), 125–27.

52. Brekus, *Sarah Osborn's World*, 111–12, 116.

53. Ned Landsman, "Evangelists and Their Hearers: Popular Interpretation of Revivalist Preaching in Eighteenth-Century Scotland," *Journal of British Studies* 28, no. 2

(Apr. 1989): 123. The total of 109 is per Beebe, "McCulloch Manuscripts," 3n6. Hindmarsh notes that the total has been variously reported from 105 to 110 (*Evangelical Conversion Narrative*, 195n5).

54. Beebe, ed., "McCulloch Manuscripts," appendix 1a, 7.

55. Ibid., appendix 1a, 7; appendix 1b, 354.

56. Ibid., appendix 2a, 163, 325; appendix 2b, 541. Whitefield to John Cennick, July 14, 1742, in the *Weekly History*, Sept. 11, 1742. Gillies's edition of Whitefield's works contains a version of this letter as well, but the more enthusiastic or Moravian-sounding passages were removed or edited. For instance, Whitefield's original letter said that he was living "very happily in my Saviour's Wounds," a phrase that does not appear in Gillies's version.

57. Beebe, "McCulloch Manuscripts," appendix 1a, 9, 13, see also appendix 1a, 59; Landsman, "Evangelists and Their Hearers," 133.

58. Beebe, "McCulloch Manuscripts," appendix 1a, 45, 129, 288–89.

59. Ibid., appendix 2b, 450; Kidd, *Great Awakening*, 285.

60. Beebe, "McCulloch Manuscripts," appendix 1b, 309–10.

61. Ibid., 310–11.

62. *The Declaration of the True Presbyterians within the Kingdom of Scotland* (Edinburgh, 1742), 6, 16–17, 23.

63. Beebe, "McCulloch Manuscripts," appendix 1a, 167; Whitefield to H[owell] H[arris], Aug. 26, 1742, in *Letters of Whitefield*, 426; William McCulloch, "An Account of the Second Sacrament at Cambuslang," *Glasgow Weekly-History* 39, 2.

64. MacFarlan, *Revivals*, 72; Whitefield to [Jonathan] B[arber], Aug. 17, 1742, and Whitefield to Mr. A— —, Aug. 27, 1742, in *Letters of Whitefield*, 417, 429; McCulloch, "Account of the Second Sacrament," 4, 8.

65. Jonathan Edwards to William McCulloch, May 12, 1743, in Claghorn, *Works of Jonathan Edwards*, 16:105; Smith, *First Great Awakening*, 5–6.

66. Smith, *First Great Awakening*, 6.

CHAPTER 9. "CLOSE ATTACKS, BUT STRONG CONSOLATIONS"

1. Whitefield to Howell Harris, Dec. 6, 1743, in Tyerman, *Life of Whitefield*, 2:79–80.

2. Whitefield to Mrs. [Anne] D[utton], June 26, 1744, in Gillies, *Works of Whitefield*, 2:59.

3. Ibid., 2:59–60.

4. Ibid., 2:60.

5. Whitefield to Mrs. [Anne] D[utton], July 4, 1744, in Gillies, *Works of Whitefield*, 2:61.

6. Whitefield, *A Continuation of the Account of the Orphan-House in Georgia, From January 1740/1 to June 1742* (Edinburgh, 1742), 4.

7. Oglethorpe quoted in Cashin, *Beloved Bethesda*, 46–47.

8. Julie Anne Sweet, "Battle of Bloody Marsh," *New Georgia Encyclopedia*, at http://www.georgiaencyclopedia.org/nge/Article.jsp?id=h-806, accessed Dec. 13, 2012; Whitefield to [James] H[abersham], Sept. 24, 1742, and Whitefield to the Earl of — —, Nov. 23, 1742, in *Letters of Whitefield*, 439–40, 467.

9. A. M., *The State of Religion in New England, since the Reverend Mr. George Whitefield's Arrival There* (Glasgow, 1742), 3–4; Whitefield, *Some Remarks on a Late Pamphlet* (Glasgow, 1742), 20.

10. Kidd, *Great Awakening*, 141–46; Benjamin Colman to Whitefield, June 3, 1742, in *Glasgow Weekly-History* 45, 3; Whitefield to the Reverend Dr. C[olman], Nov. 18, 1742, in *Letters of Whitefield*, 459.

11. *A Letter from a Gentleman in Scotland, To his Friend in New-England* (Boston, 1743), 9, 11.

12. *Genuine and Secret Memoirs Relating to the Life and Adventures of that Arch-Methodist, Mr. G. W— —fi— —d* (Oxford, 1742), 83–84; Tyerman, *Life of Whitefield*, 2:17.

13. Whitefield, *A Farewell Sermon Preached on Thursday Morning, October 28th, 1742* (Glasgow, 1742), 4, 7–10.

14. Whitefield, *Farewell Sermon*, 13, 15.

15. Whitefield to J[ames] H[abersham], Nov. 12, 1742, in *Letters of Whitefield*, 451; Whitefield to Mr. H— —, Feb. 4, 1743, in Gillies, *Works of Whitefield*, 2:8; Tudur, *Howell Harris*, 158; Jones, Schlenther, and White, *Elect Methodists*, 57–58; Elizabeth Whitefield to Howell Harris, Aug. 31, 1742, and Howell Harris to Whitefield, Oct. 15, 1742, in Schlenther and White, *Trevecka Letters*, 93, 107.

16. Tyerman, *Life of Whitefield*, 2:37.

17. Whitefield to Howell Harris, Sept. 3, 1742, in the *Weekly History*, Oct. 16, 1742, cited in Jones, Schlenther, and White, *Elect Methodists*, 60; Whitefield to John Wesley, Dec. 21, 1742, in Baker, *Works of John Wesley*, 26:97.

18. Whitefield, *A Letter from the Rev. Mr. Whitefield to the Religious Societies Lately Set on Foot in Several Parts of England and Wales* (London, 1740), 9; Whitefield to "dear brethren in Christ," Dec. 28, 1741, British Library, which is nearly the same text as Whitefield to the brethren in Wales, Dec. 28, 1741, in *Letters of Whitefield*, 511–12; Dallimore, *Whitefield*, 2:155–58; Tudur, *Howell Harris*, 88–89; Jones, "*Glorious Work in the World*," 214–20; Jones, Schlenther, and White, *Elect Methodists*, 54, 60–62.

19. Whitefield to brother S— —, Apr. 17 and 20, 1743, in Gillies, *Works of Whitefield*, 2:16.

20. Whitefield to Mrs. D— —, Oct. 5, 1743, in ibid., 2:40.

21. Whitefield to Mr. D— — T— —, Feb. 9, 1744, in ibid., 2:50–51; Elizabeth and George Whitefield to Howell Harris, Feb. 4, 1744, in Schlenther and White, *Trevecka Letters*, 174.

22. Whitefield to Mr. H— —, Jan. 18, 1744, in Gillies, ed., *Works of Whitefield*, 2:50; Dallimore, *Whitefield*, 2:167.

23. John Grace to Howell Harris, Jan. 31, 1744, in Schlenther and White, *Trevecka Letters*, 171–72; Brekus, *Sarah Osborn's World*, 90.

24. Whitefield to Mr. D— — T— —, Feb. 9, 1744.

25. Elizabeth and George Whitefield to Howell Harris, Feb. 4, 1744, and Howell Harris to [Thomas?] Price, Feb. 10, 1744, in Schlenther and White, *Trevecka Letters*, 174; Whitefield to Mr. D— — T— —, Feb. 9, 1744; Whitefield to Benjamin Colman, Feb. 22, 1744, in "Letters of Rev. George Whitefield," *Proceedings of the Massachusetts Historical Society* 10 (Oct. 1895): 301.

26. Hugh Joshua Hughes, *The Life of Howell Harris* (London, 1892), 231; Ward and Heitzenrater, *Works of John Wesley*, 19:345.

27. Whitefield to J[ohn] W[esley], Oct. 11, 1742, in *Letters of Whitefield*, 448; Whitefield to J— — S— —, Dec. 31, 1743, and Whitefield to G. H— —, Feb. 24, 1744, in Gillies, *Works of Whitefield*, 2:47, 54; Whitefield to John Wesley, Dec. 5, 1742, in Baker, *Works of John Wesley*, 26:93; Dallimore, *Whitefield*, 2:146–47.

28. [Edmund Gibson], *Observations upon the Conduct and Behaviour of a Certain Sect, Usually Distinguished by the Name of Methodists*, 2nd ed. (London, 1744), 10.

29. Whitefield, *A Letter to the Reverend Mr. Thomas Church* (London, 1744), 5; *London Gazette*, Mar. 17, 1744; Langford, *Polite and Commercial People*, 193.

30. Whitefield, *A Letter to the Right Reverend the Bishop of London, and the Other the Right Rev. the Bishops* (London, 1744), 6, 8, 25. The four editions printed were not identical in content.

31. Whitefield to Mr. T— —, Oct. 20, 1744, in Gillies, *Works of Whitefield*, 2:66–68.

32. Whitefield to Mr. — —, Oct. 30, 1744, and Whitefield to Mr. — —, Nov. 6, 1744, in ibid., 2:68–69; Elizabeth Whitefield, letter, Nov. 14, 17, 1744, in Tyerman, *Life of Whitefield*, 2:122–23; Gillies, *Memoirs of Whitefield*, 142–43.

33. Whitefield to Mr. — —, Jan. 18, 1745, in Gillies, *Works of Whitefield*, 2:72.

34. Kidd, *Great Awakening*, 153–54, 164; *Boston Evening-Post*, Mar. 14 and Apr. 11, 1743; *Boston Post-Boy*, Mar. 28, 1743.

35. Kidd, *Great Awakening*, 217–18.

36. *American Weekly Mercury*, Nov. 22, 1744; Lepore, *New York Burning*, 188.

37. *Boston Post-Boy*, May 3, 1742, in Kidd, *Great Awakening*, 115–16; Smith, *First Great Awakening*, 113; Whitefield to Mr. — —, Jan. 18, 1745, in Gillies, *Works of Whitefield*, 2:73.

38. Daniel Rogers Diary, Oct. 27, 1744.

39. "A Letter from the Country," *Boston Evening-Post*, Nov. 19, 1744.

40. Earnest Edward Eells, ed., "An Unpublished Journal of George Whitefield," *Church History* 7, no. 4 (Dec. 1938): 316–17.

41. Eells, "Unpublished Journal," 317, 320; Kidd, *Great Awakening*, 169.

42. Harvard College, *The Testimony of the President, Professors, Tutors and Hebrew Instructor of Harvard College in Cambridge, against the Reverend Mr. George Whitefield, and his Conduct* (Boston, 1744), 3–4, 8; Kidd, *Great Awakening*, 169–70; David F. Holland, *Sacred Borders: Continuing Revelation and Canonical Restraint in Early America* (New York, 2011), 61–62.

43. Yale College, *The Declaration of the Rector and Tutors of Yale College, in New-Haven, against the Reverend Mr. George Whitefield, His Principles and Designs* (Boston, 1745), 4; Whitefield, *A Letter to the Rev. the President, and Professors, Tutors, and Hebrew Instructor, of Harvard-College in Cambridge* (Boston, 1745), 21; Jonathan Edwards to a Friend, Feb. 4, 1745, in Claghorn, *Works of Jonathan Edwards*, 16:154–55; Marsden, *Jonathan Edwards*, 307–8.

44. Edwards to a Friend, Feb. 4, 1745, in Claghorn, *Works of Jonathan Edwards*, 16:161.

45. Eells, "Unpublished Journal," 326.

46. Ibid., 337, 339.

47. Ibid., 339; Whitefield to Mrs. — —, July 29, 1745, in Gillies, *Works of Whitefield*, 2:80–81; George A. Rawlyk, *Yankees at Louisbourg: The Story of the First Siege, 1745* (Wreck Cove, Nova Scotia, 1999), 45.

48. Howard H. Peckham, *The Colonial Wars, 1689–1762* (Chicago, 1964), 101–4.

49. Whitefield to Mrs. — —, July 29, 1745, in Gillies, *Works of Whitefield*, 2:82; Jonathan Edwards to a correspondent in Scotland, Nov. 1745, in Claghorn, *Works of Jonathan Edwards*, 16:197.

50. Douglas K. Fidler, "John Odlin of Exeter and the Threat to Congregational Peace and Order in Northern New England," *Historical New Hampshire* 55 (2000): 12, 14.

51. Eells, "Unpublished Journal," 341–44; *Boston Evening-Post*, Mar. 25, 1745; Diary of Daniel Rogers, Mar. 13, 1745.

52. *Pennsylvania Gazette*, Aug. 15, 1745.

53. Jonathan Edwards to friends in Scotland, [after Sept. 16, 1745], in Claghorn, *Works of Jonathan Edwards*, 16:176.

54. Ibid., 178; Marsden, *Jonathan Edwards*, 310; Fisher, *Indian Great Awakening*, 76; Frances Manwaring Caulkins, *History of Norwich, Connecticut: From its Possession by the Indians, to the Year 1866* (Hartford, Conn., 1878), 321.

55. *Diary of Joshua Hempstead* (New London, Conn., 1901), 446–47.

56. John Graham (Woodbury, Conn.) to Whitefield, Feb. 22, 1745, in Whitefield Papers, Library of Congress; Jonathan Edwards to friends in Scotland, [after Sept. 16, 1745], in Claghorn, *Works of Jonathan Edwards*, 16:178.

57. *Mr. Whi[tefiel]d's Soliloquy* [Boston, 1745], broadside.

CHAPTER 10. "HUNTING IN THE AMERICAN WOODS"

1. John W. Christie, ed., "Newly Discovered Letters of George Whitefield, 1745–1746," *Journal of the Presbyterian Historical Society* 32, no. 2 (June 1954): 69.

2. Kidd, *Great Awakening*, 254.

3. Whitefield to a Gentleman his Friend in Boston, Jan. 2, 1746, in the *Boston Gazette*, Mar. 18, 1746.

4. Robin Blackburn, *The Overthrow of Colonial Slavery, 1776–1848* (London, 1988), 96–98; Bethany Wiggin, "'For Each and Every House to Wish for Peace': Christoph Saur's *High German American Almanac* and the French and Indian War in Pennsylvania," in Linda Gregerson and Susan Juster, eds., *Empires of God: Religious Encounters in the Early Modern Atlantic* (Philadelphia, 2011), 171.

5. Johann Martin Boltzius to Whitefield, Dec. 24, 1745, in *The Colonial Records of the State of Georgia* (Atlanta, 1915), 24:434–42 (in this letter, Boltzius summarizes Whitefield's position, so the "Providence of God" quotation is from Boltzius); Johann Martin Boltzius to Whitefield, Sept. 20, 1750, Evangelical Library (London). See also Cashin, *Beloved Bethesda*, 61–62; Christopher Leslie Brown, *Moral Capital: Foundations of British Abolitionism* (Chapel Hill, N.C., 2006), 85–87.

6. Whitefield to William Hutson, Dec. 16, 1745, in Christie, "Newly Discovered Letters," 76–77.

7. Ibid.; Kidd, *Great Awakening*, 254; Gallay, *Formation of a Planter Elite*, 49; Gallay, "Great Sellout," 25–26.

8. Stout, *Divine Dramatist*, 199.

9. Gilbert Tennent, *The Necessity of Holding Fast the Truth* (Boston, 1743), 2; Kidd, *Great Awakening*, 147; Coalter, *Gilbert Tennent*, 106.

10. Tyerman, *Life of Whitefield*, 2:153.

11. Samuel Davies, *The State of Religion among the Protestant Dissenters in Virginia* (Boston, 1751), 10–11.

12. Ibid., 10–11, 17; "News from the Country," *Virginia Gazette*, Oct. 24, 1745.

13. "Transcript of a letter wrote by one in company with the Rev. Mr. Whitefield," Oct. 14, 1745, *Boston Gazette*, May 6, 1746; John K. Thornton, "African Dimensions of the Stono Rebellion," *American Historical Review* 96, no. 4 (Oct. 1991): 1103.

14. Whitefield to Mrs. Swinton, May 31, 1746, in Christie, "Newly Discovered Letters," 181; Dallimore, *Whitefield*, 2:209.

15. Whitefield to William Strahan, Nov. 27, 1745, in Christie, "Newly Discovered Letters," 71; Lilla Mills Hawes, ed., "A Description of Whitefield's Bethesda: Samuel Fayrweather to Thomas Prince and Thomas Foxcroft," *Georgia Historical Quarterly* 45, no. 4 (Dec. 1961): 364; Tyerman, *Life of Whitefield*, 2:155; Cashin, *Beloved Bethesda*, 58–60.

16. Whitefield, *A Brief Account of the Rise, Progress, and Present Situation of the Orphan-House in Georgia* (Philadelphia, 1746), 60, 62; Cashin, *Beloved Bethesda*, 56; Hawes, "Whitefield's Bethesda," 366.

17. Whitefield to Jonathan Bryan, Dec. 16, 1745, in Christie, "Newly Discovered Letters," 75–76.

18. James Hutchinson, May 21, 1743, in *Boston Evening-Post*, May 23, 1743; Smith, *First Great Awakening*, 113–14. Papers in Philadelphia and New York reprinted Hutchinson's letter.

19. *Pennsylvania Gazette*, May 22, 1746; also published in Whitefield, *Brief Account of the Orphan-House*, 65.

20. Howell Harris to Whitefield, Jan. 11, 1745, in Schlenther and White, *Trevecka Letters*, 206; Whitefield to John Syms, Nov. 30, 1745, in Christie, "Newly Discovered Letters," 73.

21. Cennick quoted in Podmore, *Moravian Church*, 91; see also Podmore, *Moravian Church*, 93; Whitefield to John Syms, Mar. 12, 1746, in Christie, "Newly Discovered Letters," 79; Tyerman, *Life of Whitefield*, 1:397; Whitefield to John Wesley, Dec. 23, 1746, in Baker, *Works of John Wesley*, 26:222–23; Jacob M. Blosser, "Constructing Modernity: Historical Imagery and Religious Identity in Charleston's Great Awakening," *South Carolina Historical Magazine* 106, no. 4 (Oct. 2005): 229–30.

22. Whitefield to John Cennick, May 2, 1746, in Christie, "Newly Discovered Letters," 84–85.

23. Whitefield to John Cennick, May 2, 1746, Whitefield to Samuel Church, May 11, 1746, and Whitefield to Mr. Smith of Boston, May 21, 1746, in Christie, "Newly Discovered Letters," 84–85, 160, 166; Whitefield to [Philip] D[oddridge], Dec. 21, 1748, in Gillies, *Works of Whitefield*, 2:215.

24. Whitefield to Hugh Bryan, Dec. 16, 1745, and Whitefield to James Davenport, May 28, 1746, in Christie, "Newly Discovered Letters," 75, 172; James Davenport to Whitefield, Jan. 15, 1745, Dr. Williams's Library (London).

25. Whitefield, *Britain's Mercies, and Britain's Duty* (Philadelphia, 1746), 24–25; Whitefield to William Strahan, Nov. 27, 1745, in Christie, "Newly Discovered Letters," 72.

26. *Boston Evening-Post*, July 7, 1746; *Boston Gazette*, Sept. 9, 1746; Mahaffey, *Accidental Revolutionary*, 106–15.

27. Whitefield, *Britain's Mercies*, 6–8, 11.

28. Whitefield to Gilbert Tennent, Feb. 27, 1742, and Tennent to Whitefield, June 7, 1742, in Moravian Archives, quoted in Coalter, *Gilbert Tennent*, 111–12.

29. Whitefield to Mr. Smith of Boston, May 21, 1746, in Christie, "Newly Discovered Letters," 166; Elizabeth Whitefield to Benjamin Colman, June 16, 1746, in J. P. Quincy, "Letter of Mrs. George Whitefield," *Proceedings of the Massachusetts Historical Society* 19 (1881–82): 180–81.

30. Gilbert Tennent, preface to Whitefield, *Five Sermons*, iii–iv.

31. Ibid., v; Tennent, *Necessity of Holding Fast*, 73–74; Craig Atwood, *Community of the Cross: Moravian Piety in Colonial Bethlehem* (University Park, Pa., 2004), 51.

32. Tennent, preface to Whitefield, *Five Sermons*, v–vi.

33. Whitefield to the Rev. J[ohn] W[esley], Sept. 11, 1747, and Whitefield to Mr. B— —, June 29, 1750, in Gillies, *Works of Whitefield*, 2:126–27, 363.

34. Whitefield to John Wesley, Oct. 14, 1746, in Baker, *Works of John Wesley*, 26:221; Whitefield to John Syms, June 26, 1746, in Christie, "Newly Discovered Letters," 264; Timothy P. Feist, "'A Stirring among the Dry Bones': George Whitefield and the Great Awakening in Maryland," *Maryland Historical Magazine* 95, no. 4 (2000): 389–408; Whitefield to the Reverend Mr. M— —, junior, May 9, 1747, in Gillies, *Works of Whitefield*, 2: 99.

35. Whitefield to Mrs. L[ongden], Aug. 26, 1746, Whitefield to a friend in London, Dec. 24, 1746 [*Christian History* (London, 1747), 28, has the date as Dec. 14], and Whitefield to — —, June 29, 1747, in Gillies, *Works of Whitefield*, 2:83, 87, 110; John Stevens to Whitefield, Nov. 22, 1746, in Whitefield Papers, Library of Congress.

36. Whitefield to Benjamin Seward, June 12, 1746, in Christie, "Newly Discovered Letters," 251; Whitefield to Mr. Franklin, June 23, 1747, in Labaree, *Papers of Benjamin Franklin*, 3:143–44.

37. Whitefield to a generous benefactor unknown, Mar. 15, 1747, in Gillies, *Works of Whitefield*, 2:90; "Extract of another letter from S. Carolina, dated March 11, 1747," in *New-York Gazette*, Apr. 27, 1747; Gallay, *Formation of a Planter Elite*, 49.

38. Whitefield to Mr. Henry S— —, Aug. 29, 1747, in Gillies, *Works of Whitefield*, 2:119; Tyerman, *Life of Whitefield*, 2:170.

39. Elizabeth Whitefield to Howell Harris, May 30, 1747, in Tyerman, *Life of Whitefield*, 2:171–72; Whitefield to Mr. J— — S— —, June 4, 1747, Whitefield to the Reverend Mr. S— —, June 23, 1747, Whitefield to — —, June 29, 1747, and Whitefield to Mr. P— —, Oct. 6, 1747, in Gillies, *Works of Whitefield*, 2:105, 107, 110, 133; Mary E. Fissell, *Patients, Power, and the Poor in Eighteenth-Century Bristol* (New York, 1991), 28.

40. William Shippen to David Vanhorne, June 30, 1747, in Whitefield Papers, Library of Congress.

41. *Christian History* (1747), 122–23; John Smith journal, Feb. 21, 1746, quoted in John Fanning Watson, *Annals of Philadelphia* (Philadelphia, 1830), 518; John Caldwell, *An*

Impartial Trial of the Spirit Operating in this Part of the World (Williamsburg, Va., 1747).

42. Whitefield to H[owell] H[arris], Feb. 28, 1748, and Whitefield to Howell Harris, Mar. 6, 1748, in *Christian History* (1747), 208, 210; Howell Harris to Whitefield, [June] 1748, in Schlenther and White, *Trevecka Letters*, 301. On Harris's theology, see Tudur, *Howell Harris*, 170–80.

43. Whitefield to Howell Harris, Mar. 6, 1748, in *Christian History* (1747), 210.

44. Whitefield to the Rev. Mr. — — of Boston, May 17, 1748, in *Christian History* (1747), 223–25. Franklin also published a copy of this letter in Philadelphia.

45. Gillies, *Memoirs of Whitefield*, 113; Michael Jarvis, *In the Eye of All Trade: Bermuda, Bermudians, and the Maritime Atlantic World, 1680–1783* (Chapel Hill, N.C., 2010), 101, 314.

46. Gillies, *Memoirs of Whitefield*, 113–15.

47. Whitefield to Mrs. F— —, June 2, 1748, Whitefield to Mr. H— —, Sept. 21, 1748, Whitefield to Mr. S— —, Sept. 23, 1748, and Whitefield to the Reverend Mr. S— —, Nov. 12, 1748, in Gillies, *Works of Whitefield*, 2:148, 179, 180, 201; Dallimore, *Whitefield*, 2:254.

CHAPTER 11. "AS I GREW MODERATE"

1. Whitefield to the Rev. Mr. S— —, June 24, 1748, Whitefield to the Countess of H[untingdon], Nov. 14, 1748, and Whitefield to the Countess of D— —, Feb. 22, 1749, in Gillies, *Works of Whitefield*, 2:143–44, 202, 237.

2. Marsden, *Jonathan Edwards*, 285–86; Jonathan Edwards, *A Treatise Concerning Religious Affections*, in John E. Smith, Harry S. Stout, and Kenneth P. Minkema, eds., *A Jonathan Edwards Reader* (New Haven, Conn., 1995), 141, 143, 147.

3. Rack, *Reasonable Enthusiast*, 115–16; Hindmarsh, *Evangelical Conversion Narrative*, 109–10.

4. Hindmarsh, *Evangelical Conversion Narrative*, 94, 100–101.

5. *Jacobite's Journal*, Mar. 19, 1748; *General Evening Post*, May 17, 1748, and January 18, 1749.

6. James Helling to Whitefield, July 12, 1748, in Whitefield Papers, Library of Congress; From a brother at Plymouth, Oct. 16, 1747, in *Christian History* (1747), 112.

7. Tyerman, *Life of Whitefield*, 2:246.

8. Whitefield to the Rev. Mr. J[ohn] W[esley], Sept. 1, 1748, in Gillies, *Works of Whitefield*, 2:170; Howell Harris, Aug. 2, 1749, in Tom Beynon, ed., *Howell Harris's Visits to London* (Aberystwyth, Wales, 1960), 229; Jones, Schlenther, and White, *Elect Methodists*, 85.

9. Rack, *Reasonable Enthusiast*, 257–61.

10. Heitzenrater, *Elusive Mr. Wesley*, 183.

11. Ibid.; Charles Wesley to Ebenezer Blackwell, Oct. 8, 1749, quoted in Tyerman, *Life of Whitefield*, 2:236; Lloyd, *Charles Wesley*, 107–8.

12. Whitefield to the Rev. Mr. J[ohn] W[esley], Sept. 1, 1748, and Whitefield to Mr. J[ames] W[hitefield], Sept. 1, 1748, in Gillies, *Works of Whitefield*, 2:170; Tyerman, *Life of Whitefield*, 2:210; Alan Harding, *The Countess of Huntingdon's Connexion: A*

Sect in Action in Eighteenth-Century England (Oxford, 2003), 38–39; Boyd Stanley Schlenther, *Queen of the Methodists: The Countess of Huntingdon and the Eighteenth-Century Crisis of Faith and Society* (Durham, UK, 1997), 38–39.

13. B[enjamin] Franklin to Whitefield, July 6, 1749, in Labaree, *Papers of Benjamin Franklin*, 3:383.

14. Whitefield to the Countess of H[untingdon], Sept. 29, 1748, in Gillies, *Works of Whitefield*, 2:186; Tyerman, *Life of Whitefield*, 2:200.

15. Whitefield to Mrs. E——, Sept. 28, 1748, and Whitefield to Mr. H——, Oct. 9, 1748, in Gillies, *Works of Whitefield*, 2:184, 191.

16. Whitefield to the Countess of H[untingdon], Nov. 14, 1748, in ibid., 2:201.

17. Whitefield to the Reverend Mr. S——, Nov. 12, 1748, in ibid., 2:201.

18. Whitefield to the Trustees of Georgia, Dec. 6, 1748, in ibid., 2:208–9; Gallay, *Formation of a Planter Elite*, 50.

19. Georg[e] Geare to Whitefield, Oct. 20, 1749, Evangelical Library (London); Wood, *Slavery in Colonial Georgia*, 76.

20. Whitefield to the Trustees of Georgia, Dec. 6, 1748, in Gillies, *Works of Whitefield*, 2:208–9; Gilbert Tennent to Whitefield, Dec. 15, 1750, in Tyerman, *Life of Whitefield*, 2:268.

21. Benjamin Franklin, *Proposals Relating to the Education of Youth in Pennsylvania* (Philadelphia, 1749), 22; Whitefield to Benjamin Franklin, Feb. 26, 1750, in Gillies, *Works of Whitefield*, 2:335–36.

22. Whitefield to Governor B[elcher], Oct. 13, 1750, in Gillies, *Works of Whitefield*, 2:384; Edward P. Cheyney, *History of the University of Pennsylvania, 1740–1940* (Philadelphia, 1940), 32.

23. Whitefield to Mr. F[ranklin], Aug. 17, 1752, in Gillies, *Works of Whitefield*, 2:440.

24. Franklin epitaph (1728) at http://www.loc.gov/exhibits/treasures/images/bf0061s.jpg, accessed May 5, 2013; Whitefield to Benjamin Franklin, Jan. 17, 1755, in Gillies, *Works of Whitefield*, 3:115; *Autobiography of Benjamin Franklin*, 178.

25. B[enjamin] Franklin to Whitefield, July 2, 1756, in Leonard W. Labaree, ed., *The Papers of Benjamin Franklin: April 1, 1755, through September 30, 1756* (New Haven, Conn., 1963), 6:468–69.

26. Ibid., 6:469.

27. Whitefield to the Countess of H[untingdon], Dec. 10, 1748, and Whitefield to H[owell] H[arris], Dec. 18, 1748, in Gillies, *Works of Whitefield*, 2:210, 212.

28. Whitefield to Dr. S——, June 14, 1749, Whitefield to the Reverend Mr. H——, June 14 and 24, 1749, Whitefield to Mr. C——, July 21, 1750, Whitefield Mr. D——, June 1, 1751, and Whitefield to Lady H[untingdon], July 12, 1751, in Gillies, *Works of Whitefield*, 2:263, 265, 367, 410, 418; *Whitehall Evening Post or London Intelligencer*, July 25, 1751.

29. "Experience of the Rev. Mr. Grimshaw, in a letter from Mr. Josiah Williams to the Rev. Malachi Blake of Blandford," Mar. 5, 1745, in *Evangelical Magazine* (Nov. 1794): 469–70; Noll, *Rise of Evangelicalism*, 123–24; *Whitehall Evening Post or London Intelligencer*, July 10, 1750.

30. [George Lavington], *The Enthusiasm of Methodists and Papists Compar'd* (London, 1749), 81.

31. Whitefield to the Rev. Mr. G——, Mar. 17, 1749, in Gillies, *Works of Whitefield*, 2:246; Whitefield, *Some Remarks on a Pamphlet* (London, 1749), 32, 40. Editions of *Some Remarks on a Pamphlet* also appeared in Philadelphia and Boston.

32. Howell Harris, Apr. 6, 12, 1749, in Beynon, *Harris's Visits to London*, 212, 214–15; Schlenther, *Queen of the Methodists*, 42.

33. Howell Harris, Aug. 4, 6, 1749, in Beynon, *Harris's Visits to London*, 230–31.

34. Howell Harris, Aug. 6–7, 1749, in ibid., 231.

35. Howell Harris, Aug. 21, Sept. 23, Dec. 2, 1749, in ibid., 235, 246, 248; Howell Harris to Anne Harris, Aug. 19, 1749, and Anne Harris to Howell Harris, Aug. 21, 1749, in Schlenther and White, *Trevecka Letters*, 317; Jones, Schlenther, and White, *Elect Methodists*, 85–86.

36. Howell Harris, Dec. 7, 11, 20, 30, 1749, and Jan. 1, 27, 1750, in Beynon, *Harris's Visits to London*, 248, 250, 252, 255, 265.

37. W. Reginald Ward and Richard P. Heitzenrater, eds., *The Works of John Wesley: Journal and Diaries III, 1743–1754* (Nashville, 1991), 20:318–19; Whitefield to Mr. L——, Jan. 27, 1750, in Gillies, *Works of Whitefield*, 2:323.

38. Elizabeth Whitefield to the Countess of Huntingdon, July 13, 1751, in Tyerman, *Life of Whitefield*, 2:275; Whitefield to the Rev. Mr. H——, Feb. 1, 1752, in Gillies, *Works of Whitefield*, 2:427.

39. Whitefield to Mr. B——, Mar. 22, 1751, in Gillies, *Works of Whitefield*, 2:404–5.

40. Whitefield to Mr. B——, Mar. 22, 1751, Whitefield to Lady H[untingdo]n, Aug. 10, 1751, and Whitefield to the Reverend Mr. B——, Jan. 31, 1753, in ibid., 2:404–5, 421, 480; Kenneth P. Minkema, "Jonathan Edwards on Slavery and the Slave Trade," *William and Mary Quarterly*, 3rd ser., 54, no. 4 (Oct. 1997): 824; "poor barbarous" in Whitefield to the Rev. Mr. Stennet, Feb. 14, 1754, in Whitefield Papers, Southern Methodist University Special Collections. See similar sentiments on the Highlanders in W. R. to Whitefield, Oct. 27, 1753, Evangelical Library (London). The sale of Providence was arranged in February 1753; see Hugh Bryan to Whitefield, May 4, 1753, in Whitefield Papers, Library of Congress.

41. Whitefield to Mr. B——, Mar. 22, 1751, in Gillies, *Works of Whitefield*, 2:405; Jonathan Bryan to Whitefield, Apr. 2, 1753, and William Brisbane to Whitefield, Sept. 10, 1753, in Whitefield Papers, Library of Congress.

42. Whitefield to Mr. Blackwell, May 21, 1752, Evangelical Library (London).

43. Ibid.; John Wesley, *Serious Thoughts upon the Perseverance of the Saints* (London, 1751), 4; Whitefield to Mr. S—— C——, Feb. 5, 1752, in Gillies, *Works of Whitefield*, 2:428; Elizabeth Whitefield quoted in Dallimore, *Whitefield*, 2:343.

44. Whitefield to Mr. C[harles] W[esley], Dec. 22, 1752, in Gillies, *Works of Whitefield*, 2:464.

45. Whitefield to C[harles] W[esley], Mar. 3, 1753, and Whitefield to Mr. ——, June 8, 1753, in Gillies, *Works of Whitefield*, 3:6, 16; Whitefield, *The True Nature of Beholding the Lamb of God, and Peter's Denial of his Lord, Opened and Explained, in Two Sermons* (London, 1753), 6; John Wesley to Whitefield, May [28?], 1753, in Baker, *Works of John Wesley*, 26:507n15, 507–8.

46. Isabel Rivers, "Hervey, James (1714–1758)," *Oxford Dictionary of National Biography*, at http://www.oxforddnb.com/view/article/13113?docPos=1, accessed Nov. 8, 2013.

47. Whitefield to Mr. S——, Aug. 1, 1752, and Whitefield to Lady H[untingdon], Sept. 22, 1752, in Gillies, *Works of Whitefield*, 2:439, 443.

48. Whitefield to Mr. B[ennet], Aug. 30, 1752, Whitefield to Governor B[elcher], Dec. 20, 1752, and Whitefield to the Reverend Mr. B——, Jan. 31, 1753, in ibid., 2:442, 461, 480.

49. John Edgar and James Beale to Whitefield,, May 20, 1753, Evangelical Library (London); William Shrubsole to Whitefield, Aug. 28, 1752, in Whitefield Papers, Library of Congress; Gillies, *Memoirs of Whitefield*, 219.

50. Schlenther, *Queen of the Methodists*, 42; *A Collection of Hymns: Consisting Chiefly of Translations from the German, Part III*, 2nd ed. (London, 1749), 62–63; Atwood, *Community of the Cross*, 64, 106–9; Fogleman, *Jesus Is Female*, 75–82.

51. Whitefield to Mr. S——, Mar. 21, 1753, in Gillies, *Works of Whitefield*, 3:9; Whitefield, *An Expostulatory Letter, Addressed to Nicholas Lewis, Count Zinzendorf, and Lord Advocate of the Unitas Fratrum* (London, 1753), 5; Andrews, *Native Apostles*, 105.

52. Whitefield to Mr. S[yms], May 27, 1753, in Gillies, *Works of Whitefield*, 3:13–14; Tyerman, *Life of Whitefield*, 2:303–9.

53. George William Pilcher, ed., *The Reverend Samuel Davies Abroad: The Diary of a Journey to England and Scotland* (Urbana, Ill., 1967), 29, 43.

54. Ibid., 44, 47; Whitefield to the Marquis of Lothian, Dec. 27, 1753, and Whitefield to [John] G[illies], Dec. 27, 1753, in Gillies, *Works of Whitefield*, 3:54–56.

55. Henry Fielding, *The Journal of a Voyage to Lisbon* (London, 1755), 218.

56. Whitefield to the Rev. Mr. Z——, Mar. 29, 1754, and Whitefield to Mr. C——, Mar. 30, 1754, in Gillies, *Works of Whitefield*, 3:70–71; Whitefield to "My dear friend," Mar. 1754, and Apr. 13, 1754, in Whitefield, *A Brief Account of Some Lent and Other Extraordinary Processions and Ecclesiastical Entertainments Seen Last Year at Lisbon* (London, 1755), 2–4, 27. On Whitefield's observations in the context of Catholic Reformation piety, see Philip M. Soergel, "Ritual and Faith Formation in Early Modern Catholic Europe," in John Van Engen, ed., *Educating People of Faith: Exploring the History of Jewish and Christian Communities* (Grand Rapids, Mich., 2004), 314–18.

57. Nicholas Schrady, *The Last Day: Wrath, Ruin, and Reason in the Great Lisbon Earthquake of 1755* (New York, 2008), 51–52; Whitefield to Mr. S——, Nov. 30, 1755, in Gillies, *Works of Whitefield*, 3:151; Whitefield, *A Short Address to Persons of All Denominations* (London, 1756), 12. *A Letter from a Clergyman at London to the Remaining Disconsolate Inhabitants of Lisbon* (London, 1755), regarding the Lisbon earthquake, is attributed to Whitefield in Eighteenth-Century Collections Online, but his authorship has not been confirmed.

58. Whitefield to Mr. C—— W——, July 20, 1754, and Whitefield to Mr. R——, Aug. 7, 1754, in Gillies, *Works of Whitefield*, 3:94, 99; *Pennsylvania Gazette*, Sept. 26, 1754.

59. *Boston Gazette*, Sept. 10, 1754.

60. Ron Chernow, *Washington: A Life* (New York, 2010), 54–57.

61. George Stockwell to Whitefield, Jan. 5, 1760, Evangelical Library (London).

62. Whitefield to Mr. V——, Oct. 14, 1754, and Whitefield to the Reverend Mr. G[illies], Nov. 25, 1754, in Gillies, *Works of Whitefield*, 3:106, 110; James Davenport to Elizabeth Whitefield, Oct. 10, 1754, Dr. Williams's Library (London).

63. Whitefield to Mr. H— —, Oct. 13, 1754, in Gillies, *Works of Whitefield*, 3:106.

64. *A Poem, on the Joyful News of the Rev. Mr. Whitefield's Visit to Boston* (Boston, 1754).

65. Edward Wigglesworth, *Some Distinguishing Characters of the Extraordinary and Ordinary Ministers of the Church of Christ* (Boston, 1754), 9, 11, 14; Whitefield, *Letter to the President and Professors*, 16.

66. Wigglesworth, *Some Distinguishing Characters*, 30; Kidd, "Healing of Mercy Wheeler," 149. Wigglesworth's belief that the gifts such as evangelism had ceased with the apostolic period is a more rigorous form of cessationism than one would typically find today. Cessationists more typically hold that the "sign gifts," including healings and tongues, had ceased, but not others needed in the normal operations of the church.

67. Whitefield to Mrs. C— —, Dec. 27, 1754, and Whitefield to Mrs. C— —, Mar. 3, 1755, in Gillies, *Works of Whitefield*, 3:111, 116; Johann Martin Boltzius to Samuel Urlsperger, Feb. 16, 1755, in Kleckley, *Letters of Boltzius*, 2:618.

CHAPTER 12. "THIS PILGRIMAGE KIND OF LIFE"

1. Whitefield to the Countess of Huntingdon, May 27, 1755, Drew University Special Collections; also transcribed in John R. Tyson, ed., *In the Midst of Early Methodism: Lady Huntingdon and Her Correspondence* (Lanham, Md., 2006), 88. This letter is an instance in which Gillies's version of one of Whitefield's letters clearly excises a controversial section, since it includes no reference to the new rift with Wesley; see Gillies, *Works of Whitefield*, 3:120. Stirk to the Countess of Huntingdon, May 14, 1755, quoted in Tyson, *In the Midst*, 87.

2. Whitefield to John Wesley, Aug. 9, 1755, in Gillies, *Works of Whitefield*, 3:133; W. Reginald Ward and Richard P. Heitzenrater, eds., *The Works of John Wesley: Journal and Diaries IV, 1755–1765* (Nashville, 1992), 21:33.

3. Whitefield to the Countess of Huntingdon, July 11, 1755, Drew University Special Collections; also transcribed in Tyson, *In the Midst*, 92; Whitefield to Lady — —, Nov. 17, 1756, Whitefield to [John] G[illies], Aug. 10, 1758, and Whitefield to Mrs. W— —, July 18, 1759, in Gillies, *Works of Whitefield*, 3:193, 239, 254.

4. William R. Nester, *The Great Frontier War: Britain, France, and the Imperial Struggle for North America, 1607–1755* (Westport, Conn., 2000), 227; Fred Anderson, *Crucible of War: The Seven Years' War and the Fate of Empire in British North America, 1754–1766* (New York, 2000), 102.

5. Whitefield to Miss P— —, Aug. 30, 1755, and Whitefield to Mr. V— —, Aug. 30, 1755, in Gillies, *Works of Whitefield*, 3:136–39.

6. Whitefield to Mr. B— —, Nov. 1, 1755, in ibid., 3:146; Johnson quoted in James Boswell, *The Journal of a Tour to the Hebrides*, ed. Percy Fitzgerald (London, 1900), 543.

7. B[enjamin] Franklin to Whitefield, July 2, 1756, in Leonard W. Labaree, *Papers of Benjamin Franklin*, 6:468; Whitefield, *Persons of All Denominations*, 9, 11, 14, 16; Mahaffey, *Accidental Revolutionary*, 130–32; Whitefield to Lady H[untingdon], Apr. 18, 1756, in Gillies, *Works of Whitefield*, 3:173.

8. Whitefield to the Bishop of B[angor, Zachary Pearce], Feb. 2, 1756, and Whitefield to the Bishop of B[angor, Zachary Pearce], Feb. 23, 1756, in Gillies, *Works of Whitefield*, 3:158, 165; Tyerman, *Life of Whitefield*, 2:355–56.

9. Whitefield to the Bishop of B[angor, Zachary Pearce], Mar. 25, 1756, Whitefield to Mr. C——, Apr. 25, 1756, Whitefield to Lady H[untingdon], May 2, 1756, and Whitefield to Mrs. B——, Dec. 30, 1756, in Gillies, *Works of Whitefield*, 3:168, 177, 196; *London Gazette*, May 1, 1756.

10. "Discern any difference" quotation in Mack, *Heart Religion*, 65; Tate Wilkinson, *Memoirs of His Own Life* (York, UK, 1790) 3:8, 12; Stout, *Divine Dramatist*, 239.

11. Whitefield to Mr. M——, Nov. 26, 1757, and Whitefield to Professor F[rancke], Mar. 5, 1758, in Gillies, *Works of Whitefield*, 3:221, 230; letter to the editor, *Lloyd's Evening Post*, Jan. 4, 1758; *Russian Cruelty* (London, 1760), 14; *London Chronicle*, Mar. 13, 1760; G. F. Nuttall, "Continental Pietism and the Evangelical Movement in Britain," in Johannes van den Berg and Jan Pieter van Dooren, eds., *Pietismus und Reveil* (Leiden, 1978), 213.

12. Patrick Fagan, *Catholics in a Protestant Country: The Papist Constituency in Eighteenth-Century Dublin* (Portland, Ore., 1998), 44; Whitefield to Mr. ——, July 9, 1757, Whitefield to Mr. I——, July 15, 1757, and Whitefield to the Reverend Mr. G[illies], Oct. 16, 1757, in Gillies, *Works of Whitefield*, 3:207–9, 213.

13. Tyerman, *Life of Whitefield*, 2:411.

14. Ibid., 2:422; Whitefield to Eleazar Wheelock, Oct. 22, 1759, in Papers of Eleazar Wheelock (Hanover, N.H., 1971), UMI microfilm.

15. Whitefield to Mr. D——, Feb. 5, 1760, in Gillies, *Works of Whitefield*, 3:259; *London Chronicle*, Feb. 2, 1760.

16. Phyllis T. Dircks, "Foote, Samuel (*bap.* 1721, *d.* 1777)," *Oxford Dictionary of National Biography*, at http://www.oxforddnb.com/view/article/9808, accessed Mar. 12, 2013.

17. Samuel Foote, *The Minor, a Comedy* (London, 1760), 8, 46, 74–75, 90; Stout, *Divine Dramatist*, 243–44; Anderson, *Imagining Methodism*, 130, 144; Thomas V. Kenney, "Shandymania: Class, Religion, and Constupration in the Pamphlet Responses to *Tristram Shandy*" (PhD diss., Fordham University, 2008), 58–64.

18. *Friendly Advice, For Dr. Squintum* (London, 1760), 2; Anderson, *Imagining Methodism*, 144.

19. Charles Hardy to Whitefield, Oct. 7, 1760, in Whitefield Papers, Library of Congress; Anderson, *Imagining Methodism*, 149.

20. Anderson, *Imagining Methodism*, 150–53; Dennis Todd, *Imagining Monsters: Miscreations of the Self in Eighteenth-Century England* (Chicago, 1995), 295n62.

21. Charles Hardy to Whitefield, Oct. 7, 1760, in Whitefield Papers, Library of Congress; Whitefield to Mr. D——, Aug. 15, 1760, in Gillies, *Works of Whitefield*, 3:262; *London Chronicle*, Oct. 23, 1760.

22. John Grayson to Whitefield, Sept. 28, 1760, and Charles Hardy to Whitefield, Oct. 7, 1760, in Whitefield Papers, Library of Congress.

23. *An Elegy on the Much Lamented Death of the Rev. Mr. George Whitefield* ([London?], 1761), broadside; *Public Ledger*, Mar. 30, 1761; Mary Grant to Whitefield, July 16, 1761, Evangelical Library (London); Whitefield to Mrs. C——, Oct. 24, 1761, in Gillies,

Works of Whitefield, 3:271; *General Evening Post*, Jan. 14, 1762. For the death notice in America, see, for example, *New-York Mercury*, May 25, 1761.

24. Whitefield to Charles Wesley, July 29, 1762, in John Wesley Family Papers, Emory University Manuscript, Archives, and Rare Book Library.

25. Whitefield to Charles Wesley, Mar. 17, 1763, Southern Methodist University Special Collections; Ward and Heitzenrater, *Works of John Wesley*, 21:411; Whitefield to John Wesley, Sept. 25, 1764, in *Arminian Magazine* (Aug. 1782): 439–40.

26. Whitefield, *Aaron's Blessing the Children of Israel* (Edinburgh, 1762), 18–19.

27. Whitefield, *Observations on Some Fatal Mistakes* (Edinburgh, 1763), 6–8; Whitefield to W— — P— —, Esq., Dec. 30, 1766, in Gillies, *Works of Whitefield*, 3:343.

28. Whitefield to Mr. S— — S— —, July 15, 1763, in Gillies, *Works of Whitefield*, 3:293.

29. *Boston Gazette*, Oct. 3, 1763; Whitefield to the Reverend Mr. G— —, Dec. 18, 1763, in Gillies, *Works of Whitefield*, 3:304.

30. *Boston Post-Boy*, Jan. 16, 1764.

31. Whitefield to Mr. S— — S— —, Mar. 10, 1764, in Gillies, *Works of Whitefield*, 3:307; Tyerman, *Life of Whitefield*, 2:472; Whitefield to Eleazar Wheelock, Jan. 12, 1764, Papers of Wheelock.

32. *Methodism Anatomiz'd* (Philadelphia, 1763), 2, 4; "phiz," *Oxford English Dictionary* (thanks to Joseph Stubenrauch for this reference).

33. B[enjamin] Franklin to Whitefield, June 19, 1764, in Leonard W. Labaree, ed., *The Papers of Benjamin Franklin: January 1 through December 31, 1764* (New Haven, Conn., 1967), 11:231–32.

34. Whitefield to Mr. R— — K— —n, Mar. 3, 1764, in Gillies, *Works of Whitefield*, 3:305; Whitefield to Eleazar Wheelock, Apr. 19, 1764, Papers of Wheelock; Kidd, *Great Awakening*, 272, 277.

35. *New Hampshire Gazette*, Mar. 30, 1764; William Gordon, *The History of the Rise, Progress, and Establishment, of the Independence of the United States of America* (London, 1788), 1:143–44.

36. Gordon, *History of the Rise*, 1:143–144; Alexander Gordon, "Gordon, William (1727/8–1807)," rev. Troy O. Bickham, *Oxford Dictionary of National Biography*, at http://www.oxforddnb.com/view/article/11088, accessed Mar. 20, 2013.

37. Whitefield to Mr. R— —, Sept. 4, 1748, in Gillies, *Works of Whitefield*, 2:172–73; W. R. Ward, "Evangelical Awakenings in the North Atlantic World," in Stewart J. Brown and Timothy Tackett, eds., *The Cambridge History of Christianity*, vol. 7, *Enlightenment, Reawakening, and Revolution, 1660–1815* (New York, 2006), 346; *London Evening Post*, Apr. 9, 1765; *Georgia Gazette*, June 20, 1765; *Boston Evening-Post*, May 27, 1765; Thomas S. Kidd, *God of Liberty: A Religious History of the American Revolution* (New York, 2010), 59–66; *Boston Evening-Post*, June 11, 1764; Schlenther, *Queen of the Methodists*, 43.

38. Whitefield to R[obert] K[ee]n, Mar. 29, 1765, Gillies, *Works of Whitefield*, 3:325; *New-York Gazette*, June 18, 1764; *Boston News-Letter*, July 19, 1764; *Boston Evening-Post*, Oct. 22, 1764; Mr. Reed to the Secretary, Dec. 21, 1764, in *Colonial Records of North Carolina* (Raleigh, N.C., 1888), 6:1060–61; Bill Hand, "The Return of George Whitefield," *New Bern Sun Journal*, Apr. 28, 2013, at http://www.newbernsj.com/news/

local-columns/bill-hand-the-return-of-george-whitefield-1.134605, accessed Apr. 29, 2013. Thanks to Mr. Hand for e-mail correspondence about sources related to Whitefield's North Carolina visits.

39. Whitefield to C— — H— —, Nov. 22, 1764, in Gillies, *Works of Whitefield*, 3:317; *New-York Gazette*, May 13, 1765. It was about eight years before the technical introduction of Wesleyan Methodism in Virginia, but the writer was referring to other evangelicals as Methodists. Whitefield corrected North Carolina Anglicans on this point, saying, "None were properly called [Methodists], but the followers of himself and Mr. Wesley." James Reed replied that while the new evangelicals might not technically be Whitefield's followers, "they sprung from the seed which he first planted in New England"; see Mr. Reed to the Secretary, Dec. 21, 1764, in *Colonial Records of North Carolina*, 6:1060–61.

40. George Fenwick Jones, ed., "A Letter by Pastor Johann Martin Boltzius about Bethesda and Marital Irregularities in Savannah," *Georgia Historical Quarterly* 84, no. 2 (Summer 2000): 288.

41. Jones, "Letter by Boltzius," 289–90; Whitefield to Mr. S— — S— —, Jan. 14, 1765, in Gillies, *Works of Whitefield*, 3:320; "Extract of a Letter from a Young Gentleman at Georgia," *Boston Evening-Post*, May 6, 1765; *London Chronicle*, Apr. 20, 1765.

42. Whitefield to James Wright, Dec. 18, 1764, in *Georgia Gazette*, Jan. 17, 1765; Whitefield to the Archbishop, June 17 and July 4, 1767, in Gillies, *Works of Whitefield*, 3:475, 478; David Hempton, *The Church in the Long Eighteenth Century* (London, 2011), 153; "bell-weather" in George A. Stevens, *The Celebrated Lecture on Heads* (London, 1765), 20; Cashin, *Beloved Bethesda*, 85–92; Tyerman, *Life of Whitefield*, 2:482, 505.

43. Vincent Carretta, ed., *Olaudah Equiano: The Interesting Narrative and Other Writings*, rev. ed. (New York, 2003), 132; Caretta, "'I began to feel the happiness of liberty, of which I knew nothing before': Eighteenth-Century Black Accounts," in Philip Morgan, ed., *African American Life in the Georgia Lowcountry: The Atlantic World and the Gullah Geechee* (Athens, Ga., 2010), 90–91.

44. William Jay, ed., *Memoirs of the Life and Character of the Late Reverend Cornelius Winter* (Bath, UK, 1808), 23; Whitefield, preface, *The Works of that Eminent Servant of Christ Mr. John Bunyan*, 3rd ed. (London, 1767), 1:iv; Allan M. Harman, "The Impact of Matthew Henry's Exposition on Eighteenth-Century Christianity," *Evangelical Quarterly* 82, no. 1 (Jan. 2010), 9–11; David Crump, "The Preaching of George Whitefield and His Use of Matthew Henry's *Commentary*," *Crux* 25, no. 3 (Sept. 1989), 19–28.

45. Jay, *Memoirs of Winter*, 24–28.

46. Ibid., 80–82.

47. *Georgia Gazette*, May 9, 1765.

48. James Habersham to Whitefield, Jan. 27, 1766, in James Habersham, *Letters of Hon. James Habersham, 1756–1775* (Savannah, 1904), 54–55; Lambert, *James Habersham*, 156–67.

49. Leonard W. Labaree, ed., *The Papers of Benjamin Franklin: January 1 through December 31, 1766* (New Haven, Conn., 1969), 13:135–36, 255n; Gillies, *Memoirs of Whitefield*, 248.

50. Whitefield to R[obert] K[ee]n, Oct. 7, 1765, in Gillies, *Works of Whitefield*, 3:332; Schlenther, *Queen of the Methodists*, 68–69.

51. W. Reginald Ward and Richard P. Heitzenrater, eds., *The Works of John Wesley: Journal and Diaries V, 1765–1775* (Nashville, 1993), 22:24, 28–29, 99; *The Life and Times of Selina Countess of Huntingdon* (London, 1839), 1:475; Tyson, *In the Midst*, 11; Schlenther, *Queen of the Methodists*, 105–10.

52. Ward and Heitzenrater, *Works of John Wesley*, 22:99; John Wesley to Mrs. Emma Moon, Dec. 6, 1767, in John Emory, ed., *The Works of the Reverend John Wesley* (New York, 1835), 6:762; Tyerman, *Life of Whitefield*, 2:531, 534; Dallimore, *Whitefield*, 2:463–64.

53. *London Chronicle*, Feb. 28, 1765; *Boston Evening-Post*, Apr. 29, 1765; Eleazar Wheelock to Whitefield, Feb. 14, 1766, Papers of Wheelock; Kidd, *Great Awakening*, 210.

54. Whitefield to Peter [Vanbergh Livingston?], Feb. 27, 1766, Papers of Wheelock; Samson Occom, journal, in Joanna Brooks, ed., *The Collected Writings of Samson Occom: Leadership and Literature in Eighteenth-Century Native America* (New York, 2006), 266–67.

55. Occom journal, in Brooks, *Samson Occom*, 267; Whitefield to the Reverend Mr. G— —, Apr. 25, 1766, in Gillies, *Works of Whitefield*, 3:335; Whitefield to Eleazar Wheelock, Feb. 9, 1767, Papers of Wheelock.

56. Samson Occom to Eleazar Wheelock, July 24, 1771, in Brooks, *Samson Occom*, 99, see also 161; Kidd, *Great Awakening*, 210–11.

57. Boswell, *Life of Johnson*, 3:223–24; Noll, *Rise of Evangelicalism*, 158–59.

58. Whitefield, *A Letter to the Reverend Dr. Durrell* (London, 1768), 26–27; W. C., *Remarks upon the Reverend Mr. Whitefield's Letter to the Vice-Chancellor of the University of Oxford* (Oxford, 1768), 2, 5.

59. Whitefield, *Letter to Durrell*, 41; Mahaffey, *Accidental Revolutionary*, 167–68.

60. Whitefield to A[ndrew] K[insman], July 2, 1768, in Gillies, *Works of Whitefield*, 3:371; *Lloyd's Evening Post*, Aug. 8, 1768; Dallimore, *Whitefield*, 2:472.

61. Jay, *Memoirs of Winter*, 80.

62. James Davenport to Elizabeth Whitefield, Oct. 10, 1754, Dr. Williams's Library (London); Whitefield to Mr. [Torial] J[o]ss, Aug. 16, 1768, and Whitefield to Mr. A— —s, Mar. 11, 1769, in Gillies, *Works of Whitefield*, 3:373, 382; "some other person" quotation in Mack, *Heart Religion*, 109 (thanks to Joseph Stubenrauch for this reference).

63. Ward and Heitzenrater, *Works of John Wesley*, 22:168, 172; Robert Keen to Whitefield, Aug. 5, 1769, in Whitefield Papers, Library of Congress.

64. *Public Advertiser*, Aug. 28, 1769.

65. Whitefield, *A Sermon by the Reverend Mr. George Whitefield Being His Last Farewell to His Friends* (London, 1769); Gillies, *Memoirs of Whitefield*, 161.

66. Whitefield, *Last Farewell to His Friends*, iii, 11, 15.

67. Ibid., 29–31.

68. Jay, *Memoirs of Winter*, 78.

CONCLUSION. "JESUS CHRIST HAS GOT THEE AT LAST"

1. [William] Aldridge, ed., *A Narrative of the Lord's Wonderful Dealings with John Marrant, A Black*, 4th ed. (London, 1785), 10–11.

2. Ibid., 11; Vincent Carretta, "Marrant, John (1755–1791)," *Oxford Dictionary of National Biography* (New York, 2004), at http://www.oxforddnb.com/view/article/73349, accessed Apr. 8, 2013.

3. *New-Hampshire Gazette*, Jan. 26, 1770.

4. Whitefield to Mr. S— — S— —, Jan. 11, 1770, in Gillies, *Works of Whitefield*, 3:412; Paul M. Pressly, *On the Rim of the Caribbean: Colonial Georgia and the British Atlantic World* (Athens, Ga., 2013), 69–70.

5. *Boston Chronicle*, Mar. 22, 1770; Tyerman, *Life of Whitefield*, 2:575–77; Whitefield, "Sermon Preached Before the Governor," in Gillies, *Works of Whitefield*, 6:382; Cashin, *Beloved Bethesda*, 94–95.

6. Gillies, *Works of Whitefield*, 3:496–500.

7. Whitefield to R[obert] K[ee]n, July 29 and Sept. 23, 1770, in Gillies, *Works of Whitefield*, 3:425, 426.

8. Whitefield to R[obert] K[ee]n, Sept. 23, 1770, in ibid., 3:427; *Massachusetts Spy*, Sept. 22, 1770; Richard Smith, testimony, in Gillies, *Memoirs of Whitefield*, 273.

9. Richard Smith, testimony, in Gillies, *Memoirs of Whitefield*, 272–74; *Boston Evening-Post*, Oct. 8, 1770; *Boston News-Letter*, Oct. 8, 1770; Robert E. Cray, Jr., "Memorialization and Enshrinement: George Whitefield and Popular Religious Culture, 1770–1850," *Journal of the Early Republic* 10, no. 3 (Autumn 1990): 345.

10. Richard Smith, testimony, in Gillies, *Memoirs of Whitefield*, 274–75.

11. Jay, *Memoirs of Winter*, 103, Lloyd, *Charles Wesley*, 57–58; Ward and Heitzenrater, *Works of John Wesley*, 22:259.

12. John Wesley, *A Sermon on the Death of the Rev. Mr. George Whitefield* (London, 1770), 19, 23, 25; Ward and Heitzenrater, *Works of John Wesley*, 22:259–60.

13. Charles Wesley, *An Elegy on the Late Reverend George Whitefield* (Dublin, 1771), 6.

14. Phillis Wheatley, *An Elegiac Poem, on the Death of that Celebrated Divine* (Boston, 1770), 5–7; Vincent Carretta, *Phillis Wheatley: Biography of a Genius in Bondage* (Athens, Ga., 2011), 74; Patricia C. Willis, "Phillis Wheatley, George Whitefield, and the Countess of Huntingdon in the Beinecke Library," *Yale University Library Gazette* 80, no. 3/4 (Apr. 2006): 168, 172.

15. B[enjamin] Franklin to Noble Wimberly Jones, Mar. 5, 1771, in William B. Wilcox, ed., *The Papers of Benjamin Franklin: January 1 through December 31, 1771* (New Haven, Conn., 1974), 18:53; Whitefield to "My Dear Doctor [Franklin]," Jan. 21, 1768, in William B. Wilcox, ed., *The Papers of Benjamin Franklin: January 1 through December 31, 1768* (New Haven, Conn., 1972), 15:29.

16. Dallimore, *Whitefield*, 1:7–8.

17. Gillies, *Memoirs of Whitefield*, 358; *London Evening Post*, July 23, 1772; Esther Singleton, *Social New York under the Georges, 1714–1776: Houses, Streets, and Country Homes, with Chapters on Fashions, Furniture, China, Plate, and Manners* (New York,

1902), 318–19; Brendan McConville, *The King's Three Faces: The Rise and Fall of Royal America, 1688–1776* (Chapel Hill, N.C., 2006), 136.

18. *New Hampshire Gazette*, Oct. 10, 1770; *An Elegiac Poem; Sacred to the Memory of the Rev. George Whitefield* (Boston, 1770), 6.

19. Nathaniel Whitaker, *A Funeral Sermon, On the Death of the Reverend George Whitefield* (Salem, Mass., 1770), 33–34; Lambert, *"Pedlar in Divinity,"* 222–23.

20. Jane Dunlap, *Poems, Upon Several Sermons, Preached by the Rev'd, and Renowned, George Whitefield* (Boston, 1771), title page, 10, 20; James G. Basker, ed., *Amazing Grace: An Anthology of Poems about Slavery* (New Haven, Conn., 2002), 192.

21. Joel T. Headley, *The Chaplains and Clergy of the Revolution* (New York, 1864), 93; Cray, "Memorialization and Enshrinement," 349–50; James Kirby Martin, *Benedict Arnold, Revolutionary Hero: An American Warrior Reconsidered* (New York, 1997), 118–19; Charles P. Hanson, *Necessary Virtue: The Pragmatic Origins of Religious Liberty in New England* (Charlottesville, Va., 1998), 6–7; "un-Protestant" quotation in Heimert, *Religion and the American Mind*, 483.

22. Minton Thrift, *Memoir of the Rev. Jesse Lee* (New York, 1823), 155–156; Cray, "Memorialization and Enshrinement," 353–54.

23. Euphemia Vale Blake, *History of Newburyport: From the Earliest Settlement of the Country to the Present Time* (Newburyport, Mass., 1854), 374–75; Colleen McDannell, *Material Christianity: Religion and Popular Culture in America* (New Haven, Conn., 1995), 42–43; "Famous Finger Donated to Drew University," Aug. 21, 2002, AP report at Boston.com, http://www.boston.com/news/daily/21/famous_finger.htm, accessed Apr. 30, 2013; Cray, "Memorialization and Enshrinement," 357–58; G. Jeffrey MacDonald, "Evangelicals on the Newburyport Trail," *Christianity Today*, July 23, 2009, at http://www.christianitytoday.com/ct/2009/july/33.34.html?start=1, accessed Apr. 30, 2013.

24. Wesley funeral sermon coin, and cherub coin, in the catalogue of Stack's May 2006 auction, http://www.stacksarchive.com/viewcat.php?auction=ST0506&heading=23909&headinglevel=3, accessed May 5, 2013; C. Wyllys Betts, *American Colonial History Illustrated by Contemporary Medals* (New York, 1894), 232–34.

25. *London Evening Post*, Mar. 10, 1774; J. F. Blacker, *Nineteenth Century English Ceramic Art* (Boston, 1911), 168–70.

26. "George Whitefield's Success," *New York Times*, Aug. 12, 1877.

27. *Times of London*, Dec. 14, 1914, 5; *El Paso Herald*, Jan. 15, 1915.

28. "Commemoration of the Two Hundredth Anniversary of the Life of George Whitefield," *Herald of Gospel Liberty*, Aug. 20, 1914; *Washington Herald*, Dec. 12, 1914, 5; *Western Liberal* (Lordsburg, N.M.), Jan. 1, 1915, 1; *Kingston Gleaner*, Dec. 12, 1914; Kidd, *Great Awakening*, 265; "East Queen Street Baptist Church," Jamaica National Heritage Trust, at http://www.jnht.com/site_east_queen_street_baptist_church.php, accessed Apr. 30, 2013.

29. "Whitefield Statue Unveiled," *Pennsylvania Gazette*, June 27, 1919; Jeanne Long, "For the Record: George Whitefield," *Penn Current*, Mar. 21, 2013, at http://www.upenn.edu/pennnews/current/2013-03-21/record/record-george-whitefield, accessed Apr. 30, 2013.

30. "Says America Owes England Huge Debt," *New York Times*, Oct. 27, 1922; "Whitefield Is Honored," *New York Times*, May 9, 1938; Harold W. Dodds, "Education and Piety: The President Speculates on Their Relationship as Shown in the Work of George Whitefield," *Princeton Alumni Weekly* 38, no. 33 (May 27, 1938).

31. Stout, *Divine Dramatist*, xvi, 289; Jon Butler, "Whitefield in America: A Two Hundred Fiftieth Commemoration," *Pennsylvania Magazine of History and Biography* 113, no. 4 (Oct. 1989): 517; Dallimore, review of Stout, *Divine Dramatist*, at Resurgence: A Ministry of Mars Hill Church, http://theresurgence.com/files/pdf/arnold_dallimore_1992-10_the_divine_dramatist—george_whitefield_and_the_rise_of_modern_evangelicalism.pdf, accessed Apr. 30, 2013; John Piper, "'I Will Not Be a Velvet-Mouthed Preacher!': The Life and Ministry of George Whitefield; Living and Preaching as Though God Were Real (Because He Is)," Feb. 3, 2009, Desiring God, http://www.desiringgod.org/resource-library/biographies/i-will-not-be-a-velvet-mouthed-preacher, accessed Apr. 30, 2013.

32. Glenn Beck, "'Glenn Beck': Founders' Friday: George Whitefield," May 17, 2010, at http://www.foxnews.com/story/0,2933,592997,00.html, accessed Apr. 30, 2013.

33. Stout, *Divine Dramatist*, xiii.

34. J. C. Ryle, *A Sketch of the Life and Labors of George Whitefield* (New York, 1854), 28; Gatiss, *Sermons of Whitefield*, 1:19. Bruce Daniels refers to Whitefield's "shallow theology" in his review of Jerome Mahaffey's *Preaching Politics*, (*Journal of American History* 95, no. 3 [Dec. 2008]: 819). While Stout concedes that Whitefield was a thoroughgoing Calvinist, he also argues that Whitefield often "showed no interest in theology" and that he had to sell the new birth "with all the dramatic artifice of a huckster"; see Stout, *Divine Dramatist*, 39–40. Daniel Pals says that Whitefield blithely "passes over scriptural exegesis or doctrinal exposition" in favor of simplistic "evangelical moralism"; see Pals, "Several Christologies of the Great Awakening," *Anglican Theological Review* 72, no. 4 (Fall 1990): 425.

35. Whitefield's will, Mar. 22, 1770, in Tyson, *In the Midst*, 214; James Habersham to the Countess of Huntingdon, Dec. 10, 1770, in *Letters of Habersham*, 6:107; Schlenther, *Queen of the Methodists*, 91; Cashin, *Beloved Bethesda*, 140–41.

36. Brown, *Moral Capital*, 105–7, 127.

37. *Boston News-Letter*, Feb. 8, 1770; *Liberator*, June 16, Aug. 11, 1832; Daniel Walker Howe, *What Hath God Wrought: The Transformation of America, 1815–1848* (New York, 2007), 425.

38. Occom journal, Apr. 2, 1786, in Brooks, *Samson Occom*, 334.

Acknowledgments

Great appreciation goes to the Earhart Foundation and to Baylor University for grants and travel assistance for the project. Thanks to my Baylor assistant Tim Grundmeier, who did exemplary work in helping prepare the whole manuscript, as well as to Baylor assistants Eric Brandt and Lucas Miller, who helped process sources; to David Ceri Jones for help in tracking down the far-flung repositories of Whitefield's papers; to Keith Beebe for guidance on the Cambuslang revival testimonies; to Philippa Koch for assistance on Whitefield's correspondence with German Pietists; library staffs, including those at the Evangelical Library, Dr. Williams's Library, the British Library, Drew University, Duke University, Emory University, Southern Methodist University, and, especially, Baylor University, for their help in compiling sources. Thanks to my mentors and friends George Marsden and David Bebbington, who as always gave excellent advice about the project; to my friend and colleague Joe Stubenrauch for reading the manuscript, and to my friend and literary agent Giles Anderson. Anonymous readers for Yale University Press made many constructive suggestions for improving the manuscript. Thanks to my wonderful Baylor colleagues in the history department and the Institute for Studies of Religion, including Jeff Hamilton, Byron Johnson, Barry Hankins, and Philip Jenkins, for their support and encouragement. It has been a pleasure to work with the publishing team at Yale University Press, especially my editor Chris Rogers. Finally, I am so grateful for my family's love and support. Without Ruby, I could not do what I do.

INDEX